American Medical Association
Physicians dedicated to the health of America

Master the AMA
Guides *Fifth*

*A Medical and
Legal Transition to the* Guides to the
Evaluation of
Permanent
Impairment,
Fifth Edition

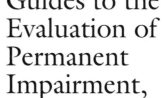

Linda Cocchiarella, MD, MSc
Stephen J. Lord, JD

Master the AMA Guides *Fifth*:
A Medical and Legal Transition to the Guides to the Evaluation of Permanent Impairment, *Fifth Edition*

© 2001 by the American Medical Association
Printed in the United States of America.
All rights reserved.

Internet address: www.ama-assn.org

Additional copies of this book may be ordered by calling 800 621-8335.
Mention product number OP721600.

ISBN 1-57947-104-8

BP55:05-P-068:4/05

To my sister Janet, for being the very best sister, for her unconditional love, support, wisdom, and integrity; for my mother, who showed me the meaning of responsibility; and for my father, who encouraged me to strive for my dreams.

My sincerest gratitude to my mentors and dear friends who helped me complete this project: M. Robling, A. Bove, D. Bennett, S. Darnell, and V. Persky. Your vision, integrity, determination, and faith have inspired me, strengthened my senses, and enriched my life.

For all injured workers; may your impairments be appropriately assessed, and may your abilities be recognized and encouraged.

—Linda Cocchiarella

To my son Max, for the countless hours he patiently waited for me to finish researching and writing so we could finish homework or go for a walk, and to my coauthor for her patience and perseverance in completing this work with me.

—Stephen Lord

What is man? the Bible asks.

A voter, the politician answers,
A machine, the engineer replies,
A worker, the economist proclaims.

To the poet, a person is neither an economic entity nor a statistical cipher. A person's a person with a mind that can perceive the truth, with a heart that understands love and beauty, with eyes that can behold the glories of the sunset, and cheeks that can feel the gentle winds of morning.

—Adapted from Henry H. Kessler,
Disability Determination and Evaluation

Preface

The American Medical Association's (AMA's) new book *Master the AMA Guides Fifth (Master)* enables the experienced *Guides* user to quickly make the transition from the Fourth Edition of the AMA *Guides* to the Fifth Edition. *Master* introduces the new *Guides* user to the fundamentals and subtleties of using the *Guides* for impairment and disability rating.

The *Guides'* recommendations for assessment of permanent impairment are sometimes complex. Since the *Guides* books are "guidelines," they have been interpreted in many different ways. The purposes of this book are to provide greater clarity on why certain recommendations were made, to show how to incorporate them into clinical practice, and to explain how to assess their impact on medical, legal, and state practices. *Master* also provides a state-by-state legal analysis for readers to understand how the *Guides* is used and interpreted in their own state.

Key features of *Master* that assist readers' understanding of the Fifth Edition of the AMA's *Guides to the Evaluation of Permanent Impairment* include:

- table-by-table comparisons of changes between the fourth and fifth edition tables

- a summary of new and key points within each chapter for easy reference and review

- detailed analysis of complicated cases not addressed in the *Guides*

- clarification of complex chapters, such as The Spine and Pain

- medical and legal tips for applying the *Guides* within your practice

- greater guidance regarding the assessment of pain

- analysis of different assessment methods for complex conditions, such as carpal tunnel syndrome and reflex sympathetic dystrophy

- information on how to assess causation from a medical and legal perspective

- state-by-state analysis of different applications and uses of the *Guides*.

Acknowledgments

The authors wish to thank the editorial, production, and marketing staff members at the AMA—Anthony Frankos, Mary Lou White, Barry Bowlus, Jean Roberts, Rosalyn Carlton, Ronnie Summers, and Reg Schmidt, as well as freelance developmental editor Jeannie Allison and designer Steve Straus, for their confidence and the vision to develop this book, for their input on design, and for shepherding the book through development, production, and marketing.

The authors would like to give special thanks to the coauthors and reviewers, listed below, whose significant and valued insights from a medical, legal, practice, and scientific perspective improved this book.

Gunnar Andersson, MD, PhD

William Beckett, MD, MPH

August Colenbrander, MD

Alan Colledge, MD

Marjorie Eskay-Auerbach, MD, JD

John J. Gerhardt, MD, PhD

LuAnn Haley, JD

Randall D. Lea, MD

John D. Loeser, MD

Alan Novick, MD

Victoria Persky, MD, MPH

James P. Robinson, MD, PhD

Dennis C. Turk, PhD

"The strongest bond of human sympathy outside the family relation should be one uniting all working people of all nations and tongues and kindreds."

—Abraham Lincoln, 1864

Table of Contents

ix

Philosophy, Purpose, and Appropriate Use of the *Guides*

Introduction

This chapter provides an overview of key points and changes (identified with an icon **G**) made in Chapter 1 of the AMA *Guides to the Evaluation of Permanent Impairment, Fifth Edition* (*Guides 5th*), illustrates these changes in a table comparison, and discusses the purpose and implications of the major changes, with illustrative examples. The numbered section titles within this chapter correspond to sections within Chapter 1 of *Guides 5th*. Only key principles or important changes are included in this chapter.

Chapters 1 and 2 of the *Guides 5th* present the philosophy and key principles that are applied throughout the book. It is essential that users of the *Guides 5th* read the first two chapters before using the *Guides*. Concepts that were previously discussed in the Fourth Edition Appendix have been revised and incorporated into the first two chapters.

Key Points and Changes

History

G The AMA *Guides* incorporates scientific evidence from the major medical specialties and consensus opinions, where evidence was lacking.

The objective of the *Guides* is to provide a standardized method to assess permanent impairment and the impact of the permanent impairment on the ability to perform activities of daily living (ADL). It is strongly recommended that physicians and other users refer to this latest *Guides* Fifth Edition, since the Fifth Edition encompasses the most current criteria and procedures for impairment assessment.

Impairment, Disability, and Handicap
Impairment
Impairment is a loss of use or derangement of any body part, organ system, or organ function (*Guides 5th*, p 2).

Permanent impairment is assessed by a physician; each state will determine, on the basis of its statutes, what constitutes a physician.

G Impairment is no longer defined as a condition that interferes with an individual's ability to perform activities of daily living (ADL).

G Under the Fifth Edition, impairments can be classified as nonratable or ratable.

G Medical impairment can develop from an injury or illness.

G Not all impairments interfere with ADL. These are not ratable impairments.

G Only impairments that interfere with ADL qualify for an impairment rating based on the *Guides*. Such impairments are ratable in terms of a percentage of the whole person.

Impairment assessment includes both anatomic and functional loss, with some body systems emphasizing one type (ie, either functional or anatomic loss).

Functional loss means a reduction in the ability of a body part or system to perform a task in its normal or usual way, compared with either known populations or the individual's prior known history.

Anatomic loss means any measurable diminution of "normal" anatomic integrity, compared with either known populations or the individual's prior known history.

G ADL include self-care, communication, physical activity, sensory function, nonspecialized hand activity, travel, sexual function, and sleep.

G ADL no longer include social activities, recreational activities, and work. The ability to perform social and recreational activities or work is important in the assessment of disability and is not considered when determining an impairment rating.

G Under the Americans With Disabilities Act, federal law treats an impairment as protected from a variety of defined forms of discrimination if the impairment "substantially interferes with a major life activity."

Physicians need to consider the impact of the condition on individuals' ability to perform ADL.

G Maximal (or maximum) medical improvement (MMI) refers to a condition or state that is well stabilized and unlikely to change substantially in the next year with or without medical treatment.[1]

An impairment is permanent when it has reached MMI.

G *Permanent* no longer refers to a change by more than 3%, since it is not possible to accurately assess a 3% change in an impairment.

Normal refers to a range or zone that represents healthy functioning and varies with age, gender, and other factors, such as environmental conditions (*Guides 5th*, p 2).

G *Normal* is defined from either an individual or a population perspective, depending on the preinjury information that is available and the physician's clinical judgment concerning the best estimate of normal.

G *Normal* may be determined by means other than studies of representative populations carried out with valid measures. *Normal* may also be determined by a comparison with a preinjury or preillness state or a complementary body part (eg, right and left legs).

Impairment ratings or percentages are consensus-derived estimates that reflect both the severity of the condition and the degree to which the impairment decreases an individual's ability to perform ADL (work is excluded) (*Guides 5th*, p 4).

Whole person impairment percentages estimate the impact of the impairment on the individual's overall ability to perform ADL.

G A 0% impairment rating indicates that an impairment may be present, but that impairment does not impact the ability to perform ADL. This situation is considered to be a "nonratable impairment."

G Updated statistics regarding the growing use of the *Guides*: 40 of 51 jurisdictions use the *Guides* in workers' compensation cases by statute, by regulations, or by administrative/legal practice.[2]

Disability

Disability is an alteration of an individual's capacity to meet personal, social, or occupational demands or statutory or regulatory requirements because of an impairment (*Guides 5th*, p 8).

G Impairments can but do not necessarily lead to functional limitations or disability.

G Functional limitations or disability can both lead to further impairment.

The Organ System and Whole Body Approach to Impairment

Individuals with impairments in organs or body systems are given regional impairments.

All regional impairment ratings are converted to a whole person impairment rating.

Philosophy and Use of the Combined Values Chart

The Combined Values Chart combines multiple impairments into a summary value, so that the whole person impairment is equal to or less than the sum of all the individual impairments.

Combine multiple regional body impairments by means of the Combined Values Chart.

Incorporating Science With Clinical Judgment

G Subjective concerns, such as fatigue, pain, and difficulty in concentrating, when not accompanied by measurable abnormalities, are not given separate impairment ratings.

Where impairment ratings are not provided for a particular impairment, the *Guides* suggests that physicians use clinical judgment to discuss impairment and its impact on ADL.

Causation, Apportionment Analysis, and Aggravation

G Causation, for application of the *Guides* (by physicians), refers to an identifiable factor (eg, accident or exposure) that results in a medically identifiable condition.

G Determining medical causation requires a detailed analysis of whether the factor could cause the permanent impairment and whether circumstances in the individual case support causation.

G Legal standards for causation vary from state to state.

Use of the Guides

The most recent edition of the *Guides* is recommended as the latest blend of science and medical consensus.

Impairment Evaluations in Workers' Compensation

G Physicians need to identify the state workers' compensation law that applies to the situation they are asked to evaluate.

Determine which edition of the *Guides* or other state guidelines are required for the assessment.

Impairment ratings or percentages should not be used as direct estimates of disability (*Guides 5th*, p 13).

Impairment assessment is a necessary first step for determining disability.

Employability Determinations

The physician needs to establish whether the individual can perform essential job functions, without endangering himself or herself, others, or the environment.

The Physician's Role Based on the Americans With Disabilities Act (ADA)

Definition of disability under the ADA differs with the application in the *Guides*.

It is the physician's responsibility to determine if the impairment results in functional limitations.

Comparison of Tables Between the Fifth and Fourth *Guides* Editions

The following table summarizes the key points and changes in tables between the fourth and fifth editions of the *Guides*.

Comparison of Tables Between the Fifth and Fourth *Guides* Editions

Table Topic	5th Edition Table Number	4th Edition Table Number	Summary of Changes in 5th Edition
Definitions and inter-pretations of impair-ment and disability	1-1		New; compares definitions from lead-ing or typical groups.
ADL	1-2	Revised from Glossary, 4th p 317	Omits social and recreational activities as a component of ADL
Scales for measure-ment of IADL and ADL	1-3		New; commonly used scales to measure ability to perform ADL and instrumen-tal activities of daily living (IADL)

1.1 History

This new section discusses the development process for the Fifth Edition. The Fifth Edition is similar to the Fourth, since many of the original chapter chairs from the Fourth Edition were retained to oversee the same chapters for the Fifth Edition. For the Fifth Edition, however, new contributors were added, as major specialty societies (listed in the preface) provided nominees for reviewers, chapter chairs, and contributors. All contributors and specialty societies were encouraged to obtain and incorporate the latest scientific recommendations from their field. In some cases, chapters were circulated among committees and members holding leadership positions within the specialty society. Although a true Delphi method was not followed, each chapter had at least three scientific reviewers, and major chapters were reviewed by more than 10 people. The Fifth Edition revision focused on updating diagnostic or examination criteria, incorporating medical consensus statements when available, and correcting inconsistencies.[3] The numbers assigned to impairment ratings were not significantly changed. However, changes in the diagnostic criteria resulted in changes in the impairment ratings for some major conditions, including low back pain. The *Guides* still recommends that permanent impairment be assessed by a physician. Each state determines what constitutes a physician, based on its statute.

1.2 Impairment, Disability, and Handicap

1.2a Impairment

Impairment is a loss, loss of use, or derangement of any body part, organ system, or organ function (*Guides 5th,* p 2). Impairment is no longer defined as a condition that interferes with an individual's ability to perform activities of daily living (ADL); this concept reflects an impairment rating. Not all impairments interfere with ADL. However, an impairment that interferes with an individual's ability to perform the ADL listed in *Guides* Table 1-2, reprinted here, generally is of sufficient severity to meet the criteria for an impairment rating. Only impairments that interfere with ADL qualify for an impairment rating based on the *Guides*.

Table 1-2 Activities of Daily Living Commonly Measured in Activities of Daily Living (ADL) and Instrumental Activities of Daily Living (IADL) Scales

Activity	Example
Self-care, personal hygiene	Urinating, defecating, brushing teeth, combing hair, bathing, dressing oneself, eating
Communication	Writing, typing, seeing, hearing, speaking
Physical activity	Standing, sitting, reclining, walking, climbing stairs
Sensory function	Hearing, seeing, tactile feeling, tasting, smelling
Nonspecialized hand activities	Grasping, lifting, tactile discrimination
Travel	Riding, driving, flying
Sexual function	Orgasm, ejaculation, lubrication, erection
Sleep	Restful, nocturnal sleep pattern

EXAMPLE

Bob sustains a scalp laceration at work with scarring of approximately 3 cm, which is covered by his hair and does not affect any of his ADL. He would have an impairment (eg, scalp scar) but would not be given an impairment rating since the scar does not affect his ability to perform ADL.

EXAMPLE

Susan acquires a carpal tunnel syndrome arising out of and in the course of her work as a carpenter. Two years after surgery, she has scarring, residual pain, and some permanent loss of strength in her right (dominant) hand. She has difficulty grasping objects that require fine motor activity, such as buttoning her sleeves, and her sensation in three fingers has not returned. On the basis of her impairment, median neuropathy, and its impact on the ability to perform ADL because of loss of dexterity, she would qualify for an impairment rating.

In Bob's case, the Fourth Edition could assign a rating between 0% and 9%, although examples in the text assign a 0% impairment rating for similar impairments that don't impact ADL. Under the Fifth Edition, Bob unequivocally has no ratable impairment. In Susan's case, the impairment is ratable under both the fourth and fifth editions, because she has residual sensory and motor changes after her surgery that impact her ability to perform ADL.

Impairment assessment includes both anatomic and functional loss, with some body systems emphasizing one area. When anatomic changes are present, a range of functional consequences can occur, some of which may lead to ratable impairment. Impairments do not necessarily lead to functional limitations or disability; the relationships between these terms are not linear but bidirectional. Thus, functional limitations can lead to further impairment, as indicated in Figure 1-1 (*Guides 5th*) and reprinted here.

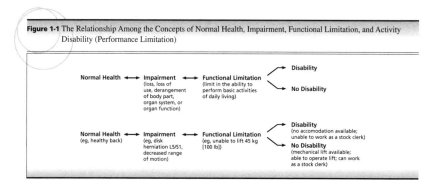

Figure 1-1 The Relationship Among the Concepts of Normal Health, Impairment, Functional Limitation, and Activity Disability (Performance Limitation)

Activities of daily living, historically and in the Fifth Edition, are listed in Table 1-2. For the Fifth Edition, ADL include self-care, communication, physical activity, sensory function, nonspecialized hand activity, travel, sexual function, and sleep. ADL no longer include social and recreational activities or work. The ability to perform social and recreational activities or work is important in the assessment of disability and is not considered when an impairment rating is determined.

The concept of excluding work or complex social or recreational activities was developed during the initial creation of the *Guides* and its impairment ratings in 1958. "Evaluation (rating) of permanent impairment is an appraisal of the nature and extent of the patient's illness or injury as it affects his personal efficiency in the activities of daily living. These activities are self-care, normal living postures, ambulation, elevation, traveling and nonspecialized hand activities. It is not and never can be the duty of physicians to evaluate the social and economic effects of permanent impairment."[4]

The following table lists the differences in all the editions of the *Guides* pertaining to the impact of ADL.

ADL Category	AMA Guides First Edition (1958)	Second Edition Revised (1971)	Third Edition Revised (1990)	Fourth Edition Revised (1993)	Fifth Edition Revised (2000)
Self-care	Self-care	Self-care and personal hygiene: urinating, defecating, brushing teeth, combing hair, bathing, dressing oneself, eating	Self-care and personal hygiene: urinating, defecating, brushing teeth, combing hair, bathing, dressing oneself, eating	Self-care and personal hygiene: eliminating, grooming, bathing, dressing, eating	Self-care and personal hygiene: urinating, defecating, brushing teeth, combing hair, bathing, dressing oneself, eating
Normal living postures	Normal living postures	Normal living postures: sitting, lying down, standing	Normal living postures: sitting, lying down, standing	Physical activity, intrinsic: standing, sitting, reclining, walking, stooping, squatting, kneeling, reaching, bending, twisting, leaning Physical activity, functional: carrying, lifting, pushing, pulling, climbing, exercising	Physical activity: standing, sitting, reclining, walking, climbing stairs
Ambulation	Ambulation	Ambulation: walking, climbing stairs	Ambulation: walking, climbing stairs		
Elevation	Elevation				
Traveling	Traveling	Travel: driving, riding, flying	Travel: driving, riding, flying	Travel: driving, riding, traveling by airplane, train, or car	Travel: driving, riding, flying
Nonspecialized hand activities	Nonspecialized hand activities	Nonspecialized hand activities: grasping, lifting, tactile discrimination	Nonspecialized hand activities: grasping, lifting, tactile discrimination	Hand functions: grasping, holding, pinching, percussive movements, sensory discrimination	Nonspecialized hand activities: grasping, lifting, tactile discrimination

Note: In the Fifth Edition column, the "Ambulation" category content appears under the "Sensory function: hearing, seeing, tactile feeling, tasting, smelling" row alignment. The Sensory function entries:

| | | | | Sensory function: hearing, seeing, tactile feeling, tasting, smelling | Sensory function: hearing, seeing, tactile feeling, tasting, smelling |

continued on page 10

ADL Category	AMA Guides First Edition (1958)	Second Edition Revised (1971)	Third Edition Revised (1990)	Fourth Edition Revised (1993)	Fifth Edition Revised (2000)
Sexual function		Having normal sexual function and participating in usual sexual activity	Having normal sexual function and participating in usual sexual activity	Participating in desired sexual activity	Orgasm, ejaculation, lubrication, erection
Sleep		Restful nocturnal sleep pattern	Restful nocturnal sleep pattern	Restful sleep pattern	Restful nocturnal sleep pattern
Social and recreational activities		Ability to participate in group activities	Ability to participate in group activities	Participating in individual or group activities, hobbies, or sports	
Communication		Writing, typing, seeing, hearing, speaking	Writing, typing, seeing, hearing, speaking	Writing, using keyboard, reading, hearing, speaking	Writing, typing, seeing, hearing, speaking

The concept of ADL is important, since the ability to perform ADL is historically and currently a major determinant of the numeric percentage impairment rating. An impairment that has a minimal effect on ADL will have a lower impairment rating than one that affects many ADL. Different researchers and users identify different key activities as ADL; hence, there is no one standardized list.[5] During the 1970s, the category of ADL use in non-*Guides* applications was expanded to account for activities performed by those living in the community, such as mobility, cooking, etc, and is referred to as IADL (instrumental activities of daily living).[6]

The Fifth Edition chose to use the original ADL concept, which reflects the initial *Guides* interpretation of ADL and was the basis for the development of the impairment ratings. It seemed inappropriate to significantly alter the ADL without making comparable changes in the numeric ratings.

Assess the individual's ability to perform ADL in the most appropriate way for each individual and the impairment. First, consider the condition and identify what ADL it impacts. This determination is based on clinical judgment and knowledge of the medical literature concerning the condition. Then, on the basis of the complexity of the condition and the number and severity of ADL impacted, the physician may choose one of the following options to obtain a more objective assessment than self-reporting:

1. For some sensory impairments (eg, hearing loss), the impairment is the ADL (eg, hearing is an ADL). The impairment rating then accounts for ADL.

2. Use clinical judgment to determine the extent and number of ADL affected. For some limited conditions, such as a nasal fracture, a clinical assessment is likely to be reproducible and accurate. For more complex conditions with many functions affected, such as a major stroke, a more comprehensive assessment with greater reproducibility and accuracy is warranted.

3. Use a scale to assess ADL that has been developed specifically for the condition and, for some conditions, is referenced in the *Guides* (eg, assessment of hip replacement results, p 548, Table 17-34).

4. Use a functional capacity evaluation or similar tool to assess the impact of the condition on ADL.

5. Use one of the questionnaires referenced in Chapter 1 used to assess ADL. These questionnaires have been validated and use a combination of observed and self-reported abilities to perform ADL.

EXAMPLE

Jeff sustains a documented herniated disk at L4-5 with bilateral radiculopathy and loss of reflexes. After therapy, he has some improvement in pain. He refuses surgery, since his father died shortly after an elective surgery, and they had similar health histories. Jeff at MMI would meet criteria for diagnosis-related estimate (DRE) category lumbar III (10%-13%). Because of the severity of his condition and symptoms, he has difficulty performing most physical activity ADL (eg, walking and climbing stairs), and his sleep is disturbed. He is unable to ride in a car for more than 30 minutes without considerable exacerbation of his symptoms. The difficulty in performing basic ADL has been observed and documented in his physical therapy notes. Jeff would qualify for a 13% whole person impairment based on the severity of his condition and its impact on ADL. Given his condition, the pain is expected and already accounted for within the current rating. An additional rating for pain, based on the Pain chapter (Chapter 18), is not warranted.

MEDICAL TIP

Physicians need to consider the impact of the condition on an individual's ability to perform ADL before assigning an impairment rating. For many impairments, a range of ratings can be assigned, on the basis of the extent of limitations of ADL.

LEGAL TIP

Administrators and adjudicators should ascertain that the physician evaluator has adequately accounted for the impact of the condition on the ability to perform ADL. Absence of an account for impact on ADL may make the rating (or lack of one) questionable.

However, in some states' benefit systems, any anatomic or functional loss constitutes a ratable impairment, regardless of its impact on ADL.

Impairment Ratings or Percentages

Impairment ratings or percentages are consensus-derived estimates that reflect both the severity of the condition and the degree to which the impairment decreases an individual's ability to perform ADL (work is excluded). Impairment ratings for the *Guides* were first developed for sequential body systems, beginning with the extremities and back. Numeric ratings were assigned on the basis of a relative value weighting, using values from published disability tables, and perceived value, depending on the severity of the condition and its impact on ADL. Numeric ratings also provide a quantitative, standardized interpretation to qualitative terms such as *slight*, *marked*, and *moderate*, which vary in interpretation. It was a simpler task to achieve greater consistency when impairment ratings were developed with a body system, among a group of related specialists, eg, orthopedists. However, when impairment ratings were developed for all the body systems, without a uniform set of criteria for comparison being regularly used, differences in weighting systems arose for different organ systems, based on specialty opinions. Using a common reference system, such as ADL, can decrease variability among specialties in assigning impairment ratings.

Total body functioning and the ability of the body to perform the ADL were the uniform criteria to which the impairment ratings referred, but these activities were never weighted or compared with each other. Thus, when the eight categories of ADL as listed in Table 1-2, Fifth Edition, are examined, are they weighted equally? Would the ability to see be given a higher weight, since it can significantly impact all the other categories? Would it be given less weight, since in highly adapted individuals, almost all the other ADL can be performed (except for driving or flying)? These are complex questions and decisions, requiring the study and incorporation of many perspectives. Answers to these questions were not developed during the revision of the Fifth Edition or any previous editions, but they may be addressed in a subsequent edition. Moreover, answers to questions like these may be as much about social, economic, and political values of certain human activities and body functions as about anything uniquely medical. Nonetheless, an evaluating physician may consider and discuss these factors in detail in the report.

Since impairment ratings in the *Guides* have been changed in earlier editions, without regard to the above considerations, it was decided that this edition would not significantly alter the impairment ratings, unless it was necessary to rectify inconsistencies or errors. Numeric ratings that have been changed in the *Guides 5th* will be discussed within each chapter, along with the rationale for each change.

Impairment ratings based on primarily anatomic criteria have incorporated the functional consequences of that condition. Therefore, when an individual is given an impairment rating of 5% for loss of the little finger (eg, amputation), it is assumed that hand function will be limited in terms of some non-specialized hand activities. Individuals may experience some differences in terms of function without their little finger, based on their individual abilities to adapt. Unless other impairments are present, the impairment rating for this condition is fixed at 5%. In contrast, in the neurology chapter, an individual with a mononeuropathy, affecting mainly the fifth finger, may have a nerve impairment ranging from 1% to 5% depending on the severity of the condition and its impact on that individual's ability to perform ADL. The physician evaluating an impairment needs to be conversant in criteria for rating impairments for each body system and incorporate the extent of individual assessment of anatomic or functional losses within the impairment ratings. In cases where the impairment rating is fixed (usually on the basis of anatomic loss), the physician can comment on the extent of functional adaptation, in comparison with what is normally seen for that condition or with what may have been considered normal for that individual before the injury. When impairments affect multiple body systems, the physician may need to combine multiple approaches. Chapters with the greatest emphasis on the anatomic approach are the upper extremity, lower extremity, and spine, in descending order. Both the lower extremity and spine chapters take function and ability to perform ADL into greater consideration.

Impairment ratings are not rounded to the nearest 5% as indicated in earlier editions of the *Guides*, since this would artificially inflate or lower the impairment rating, possibly with significant consequences to an individual who could be denied any disability coverage, even if errors are balanced out on a population basis. Impairment ratings for individual body parts or organs are combined by means of the Combined Values Chart. The Combined Values Chart combines multiple impairments into a summary value, so that the whole person impairment is equal to or less than the sum of all the individual impairments.

EXAMPLE

John falls while skiing and sustains a compound and displaced nasal fracture with noticeable and permanent disfigurement. One of John's major hobbies is cooking. Since his sense of smell has markedly diminished, he has decreased his cooking and experienced a permanent change in his eating habits, and has lost 15 lb in the 4 months following the skiing accident. On the basis of Table 11-5, page 256, John has two of three criteria within class 1, placing him at 3%, and considering the impact of his impairment on his sense of smell and eating with documented, consistent weight loss, his impairment could be increased up to 5%, the maximum level in this category.

MEDICAL TIP

Despite limitations, whole person impairment (WPI) percentages estimate the impact of the impairment on the individual's overall ability to perform ADL.

Combine multiple regional body impairments by means of the Combined Values Chart.

All regional impairment ratings are converted to a WPI rating.

A 0% impairment rating indicates that an impairment may be present, but that impairment does not impact the ability to perform ADL.

A 90% to 100% WPI rating indicates "a very severe organ or body system impairment requiring the individual to be fully dependent on others for self-care, approaching death" (*Guides 5th*, p 5).

> **LEGAL TIP**
>
> Impairment ratings, although used more or less directly to determine disability awards in some states, have a different use in the *Guides*. The *Guides* warns that impairment ratings should not be the sole basis for a disability award, because the *Guides'* WPI ratings do not account for social, recreational, or occupational impact. Not accounting for social, recreational, or occupational impact constitutes grounds for this warning.

1.2b Disability

Disability is an alteration of an individual's capacity to meet personal, social, or occupational demands or statutory or regulatory requirements because of an impairment. Impairment ratings should not be used as direct estimates of disability unless the impairment results in no more interference with personal, social, or occupational demands than is already considered in the anatomic or functional loss implicit in the impairment rating. Impairment assessment is a necessary first step for determining disability.

In workers' compensation, disability traditionally refers to the loss of income-earning capacity caused by an impairment. If an impairment is not ratable, it usually means that no disability exists, since a ratable impairment is usually a legal requirement for calculating further disability.

> **MEDICAL TIP**
>
> Physicians who assess disability need to understand the impairment, its impact on ADL, and the interaction of the impairment with the environment (work, social) for which a disability determination is requested.

> **LEGAL TIP**
>
> Under the Fifth Edition guidelines, some disability claims will be defeated because of the Fifth Edition's nonratable impairments (those that are recognizable anatomic losses that do not interfere with any ADL). A disability award also accounts for the anatomic or functional loss measured by the impairment. Common phrases used in workers' compensation are "disability in excess of impairment" and "disability inclusive of impairment."

Normality

The definition of *normal* in the Fifth Edition has been expanded from the Fourth Edition. Both editions acknowledge that normal represents a range or zone and can vary with age, sex, and other factors. However, the Fourth Edition definition indicates that "normal is determined by sufficient, valid studies of representative populations" (*Guides 5th*, p 2). Although the Fourth Edition approach is appropriate for population comparisons, it is not the most accurate comparison on an individual basis because of individual variability. Both population and individual normal values need to be integrated by the physician who evaluates an individual under the Fifth Edition guidelines. The Fifth Edition's approach to "normal" may be considered in assessing both anatomic and functional loss.

For example, when an individual has a chest radiograph or electrocardiogram performed, those individual measures of chest and cardiac function are compared both with population known normal values and, ideally, with the individual's previous radiograph or electrocardiogram. Therefore, what was "normal or customary" for the individual serves also as the baseline for comparison with the individual's current condition.

EXAMPLE

John, a former college track champion, is drawn to work as a wilderness area park ranger partly because of his interest in continuing to work outdoors with vigorous physical activity. As part of his yearly checkup, John has pulmonary function studies, which show his pulmonary function to be within the top 5% of the population in terms of physical fitness. John is the lead player on his league's basketball team and helps his team win local championships. While fighting a forest fire, John's self-contained breathing apparatus fails, and John develops a significant inhalation injury. Resultant physical changes are most evident on his pulmonary function studies, which now show his respiratory function to be within normal for his age and height, but at a 20% decline from their value 6 months earlier. John can no longer compete athletically at the level he was accustomed to. John would not qualify for an impairment rating by means of the population pulmonary function criteria, but his impairment evaluation assessment needs to indicate this change, as well as its impact on his career and social activities.

Another question that frequently arises with normality is the question of "normal aging." Certain chapters, such as the respiratory and musculoskeletal chapters, base some normal values on age-adjusted population values. Although many functions decline over time, such as hearing and vision, many scientists assert that these changes are partly caused by continued environmental exposures (eg, ambient, urban noise exposure, or unprotected sun exposure).[7] Aging changes are believed to be caused by a mixture of environmental, genetic, and personal behaviors (eg, nutrition, exercise). The question of major interest for many readers of this book is whether the observed change is really the result of "normal aging" (eg, the compilation of genetic, lifestyle, and nonwork, environmental exposures) or whether it is caused by work or a specific event.

EXAMPLE

Jim, aged 43, has been a carpet installer for 20 years and, on a daily basis, uses knee flexion and extension movements as a "carpet kicker" for several hours a day to ensure that carpet edges are installed flat along the wall and corners. Although he played some basketball and football informally during high school, he never had any knee injuries. Both knees show arthritic changes, without arthritis elsewhere, and it is becoming more difficult to do his job. Are his knee changes caused by many years of knee stress on his job or the other "environmental" mixture?

Although the *Guides* does not specifically address this challenging question, it does provide a framework, indicating that normal values for the population, individual norms, scientific precedence (eg, epidemiologic studies on carpet installers), and clinical judgment (knowledge of preexisting conditions, family history) are all needed to assess the "normal pattern" for an individual and what contribution, if any, is work related. A discussion of causation is presented in Appendix A.

MEDICAL TIP

Normal is defined from either an individual or a population perspective, depending on the preinjury and health history information available, as well as the physician's clinical judgment concerning the best estimate of normal.

Normal may be determined by means other than studies of representative populations carried out with valid measures. *Normal* may also be determined by a comparison with a preinjury or preillness state, or a complementary body part (eg, right and left legs).

LEGAL TIP

The Fifth Edition recognizes that smaller losses may have greater limitations in individuals who are aged or may have other preexisting impairments. The Fifth Edition, because of the ability to determine a rating within a range, allows for an increased impairment rating for the same injury in an individual for whom it has a greater impact on the ability to perform ADL, as may be the case with older or more infirm individuals, compared with an individual who is at or near the center of the "normal" curve of the population.

1.3 The Organ System and Whole Body Approach to Impairment

The concepts in this section are unchanged from the Fourth Edition. The Fifth Edition continues to use the same relative weights for body parts as in the Fourth Edition, except for the upper extremity chapter, which changed the weighting system or relative importance of the fingers. All other weights were retained, since they have been widely used and there is not a scientific consensus as to how the weights should be changed.

1.4 Philosophy and Use of the Combined Values Chart

The Combined Values Chart was unchanged from the Fourth Edition. This chart, listed on pages 604 to 606 of the Fifth Edition, enables the user to combine multiple body part impairments into a single, whole person impairment rating, which reflects the impact of the condition on the whole person. The formula and chart were designed to be nonadditive and to ensure that multiple impairments would not exceed 100% WPI.

In general, combine all impairment ratings from one body part or system with another. The few exceptions, when impairment ratings are added, are when a single joint involves complex motions, for example, at the thumb or elbow. Impairment ratings around these joints would be added as detailed in the respective chapter.

Note that the Combined Values Chart, in using a single combination method for all impairments, does not account for combinations of multiple impairments that can have a greater than additive effect on function. In such circumstances, the Combined Values Chart could provide a lower WPI rating than is functionally indicated. For example, loss of both legs is not equivalent functionally to loss of a leg and a nondominant hand. The physician can explain the functional implications of multiple, combined impairments when the WPI rating does not fully portray whole person function.

1.5 Incorporating Science With Clinical Judgment

This new section indicates that the physician needs to acknowledge the presence of subjective complaints and findings, such as fatigue and pain, but unless these are accompanied by objective or measurable abnormalities, subjective complaints cannot independently receive an impairment rating. Also new and noteworthy is the acknowledgment that the *Guides* cannot provide an impairment rating for all impairments, and if a condition is unlisted, the physician is to use his or her best judgment and compare the unrated condition to a similar rated condition as a guide. Impairment rating requires both the art and science of medicine, which practically refers to the need to incorporate clinical judgment, anecdotal experience, and scientific findings or plausibility into a supported medical opinion.

1.6 Causation, Apportionment Analysis, and Aggravation

1.6a Causation

Determining *causation* is discussed in greater detail in the Fifth Edition than in the Fourth Edition. Causation, for purposes of the *Guides*, refers to an identifiable factor (eg, accident or exposure) that results in a medically identifiable condition, usually injury or disease. Determining medical causation requires a detailed analysis of whether the factor could cause the permanent impairment and whether circumstances in the individual case support causation. Legal standards for causation vary from state to state.

Definitions of causation differ in the medical and legal arena. Indeed, even medically, *cause* may have multiple definitions.[8] A popular set of standards to distinguish causal from noncausal associations was proposed by Hill,[9] which, from an epidemiologic perspective, has some significant limitations.[10] Readers interested in causation are referred to Appendix A of this book, where these issues are discussed in greater detail.

On the basis of statistical analysis, a factor is considered causative if the probability of achieving an association by chance is less than 5%. In other words, a factor is causative of the observed condition if the probability of achieving an association *other than* by chance is 95% or greater. For legal applications, however, *causation* often refers to a state of probability of more likely than not, or greater than 51%, or through the use of the "but for" test, all of which may be lower levels of association than is typically used in scientific assessment. The *Guides* recommends a synthesis of medical, clinical, and scientific judgment in determining causation.

MEDICAL TIP

Physicians should determine the definition of causation in the state where they practice and make a decision based on their clinical and scientific knowledge.

LEGAL TIP

Simple statistical references to "causation" frequently beg the question of how to determine a cause for a condition when multiple causes are or may be present. Multiple causes of a condition lead to our later discussion of "apportionment." For most legal purposes, a cause-and-effect relationship is established if the effect (usually a disease or injury) would not have occurred "but for" the purported cause (usually an accident or exposure). Medical evidence in such instances usually requires a physician's testimony or report that, on a medically more probable than not basis, the identified "cause" resulted in the observed medical condition.

All users of the *Guides* should be aware that the definitions of causation are many. A practical tip for eliminating confusion in this area is to supply a definition of causation when asking questions about the causes of a condition or when rendering an opinion about a condition's cause.

1.6b Apportionment Analysis

Apportionment refers to a distribution or allocation of causation among multiple factors that caused or significantly contributed to the injury or disease and resulting impairment.

EXAMPLE

Ted is involved in a motor vehicle accident arising out of and in the course of his employment and suffers a concussion, torn rotator cuff, and multiple fractured ribs. The rib fractures heal uneventfully; he has occasional headaches, which are new. The rotator cuff surgery creates a mixed result with permanent residual loss of range of motion. Ted had also been a major league pitcher, and previously had had several elbow surgeries and one prior rotator cuff surgery that led to his retirement. The upper extremity had been rated at a 7% loss of the whole person as a result of the prior surgeries, but after the industrial accident, the rating increased to 13% whole person impairment. Only 6% of the impairment is "apportionable" to the industrially related motor vehicle accident.

Aggravation refers to a factor(s) that alters the course or progression of the medical impairment. Aggravation is a legal concept as well as a medical one. Aggravation may be a form of subsequent causation that also requires apportionment.

EXAMPLE

Ted, from the previous example, slips and falls at home after recovering from the motor vehicle accident. He suffers another concussion, his headaches increase in severity and frequency, and his mentation is less clear. He claims that the concussion, headaches, and difficulties with mentation from the motor vehicle accident became more symptomatic as a consequence of the slip and fall. His employer claims that the slip and fall is a separate, unrelated event and that there is no "causal" connection between the two events. Physicians' opinions are likely necessary regarding the role of the concussion in the now chronic headaches and mentation changes that followed the slip and fall. The slip and fall injury "aggravated" the preexisting headaches.

1.7 Use of the Guides

The most recent edition is recommended as the latest and most accurate blend of science and medical consensus. This revised section discusses the increasing use of the *Guides* in the United States and abroad, either used as the standard or adapted, as in Florida or Oregon, for their state use.

The table on page 22, Using *Guides* to Evaluate the Degree of Medical Impairment, based on surveys collected in 1999, shows which states use the *Guides*, the edition in use at the time of the survey, and which states automatically shift to the most recent, ie, Fifth Edition.[11] Note also that states listed as using the Fourth Edition but not required to use a guide should use the Fifth Edition. Appendix B provides an updated list of states that use the Fifth Edition.

Using *Guides* to Evaluate the Degree of Medical Impairment

Jurisdiction	Guide Used	Guide Required	Guide in Use
Alabama	X		AMA *Guides*, 4th edition
Alaska	X	X	AMA *Guides*, 4th edition
Arizona	X	X	AMA *Guides*
Arkansas	X	X	AMA *Guides*, 4th edition
California	X	X	State's own guide
Colorado	X	X	AMA *Guides*, 3rd edition revised
Connecticut	X		AMA *Guides*
Delaware	X		AMA *Guides*, 4th edition
District of Columbia	X		AMA *Guides*, current edition
Florida	X		AMA *Guides* and state's own guide
Georgia	X	X	AMA *Guides*, 4th edition
Hawaii	X	X	AMA *Guides*, 4th edition
Idaho	X		AMA *Guides*, 4th edition and *Manual for Orthopedic Surgeons*
Illinois	—	—	—
Indiana	X		AMA *Guides*, latest edition
Iowa	X		AMA *Guides*, 4th edition
Kansas	X	X	AMA *Guides*, 4th edition
Kentucky	X	X	AMA *Guides*, latest edition
Louisiana	X	X	AMA *Guides*, latest edition
Maine	X	X	AMA *Guides*, 4th edition
Maryland	X	X	AMA *Guides*, 3rd or 4th edition
Massachusetts	X	X	AMA *Guides*
Michigan	—	—	—
Minnesota	X		State's own guide
Mississippi	X	X	AMA *Guides*, 4th edition
Missouri	—	—	—
Montana	X	X	AMA *Guides*, 4th edition
Nebraska	X		AMA *Guides* and *Manual for Orthopedic Surgeons*
Nevada	X	X	AMA *Guides*, 4th edition
New Hampshire	X	X	AMA *Guides*, latest edition
New Jersey	—	—	—
New Mexico	X	X	AMA *Guides*, latest edition
New York	X		State's own guide, not formally adopted by statute
North Carolina	X	X	State's own guide
North Dakota	X	X	AMA *Guides*, 4th edition
Ohio	X	X	AMA *Guides*, 4th edition
Oklahoma	X	X	AMA *Guides*, 4th edition
Oregon	X	X	State's own guide, based largely on AMA *Guides*, 3rd edition revised
Pennsylvania	X	X	AMA *Guides*, 4th edition
Rhode Island	X	X	AMA *Guides*, 4th edition
South Carolina	X		AMA *Guides*
South Dakota	X	X	AMA *Guides*, 4th edition
Tennessee	X	X	AMA *Guides*, 4th edition, and *Manual for Orthopedic Surgeons*
Texas	X	X	AMA *Guides*, 3rd edition, 2nd printing (dated February 1989)
Utah	X	X	AMA *Guides*, 4th edition, and state's own guide
Vermont	X	X	AMA *Guides*, latest edition
Virginia	X		AMA *Guides*, 4th edition, is most commonly used
Washington	X	X	AMA *Guides*, 4th edition, and state's own guide
West Virginia	X	X	AMA *Guides*, 4th edition
Wisconsin	X	X	State's own guide
Wyoming	X	X	AMA *Guides*, 4th edition

Barth PS, Niss M. *Permanent Partial Disability Benefits: Interstate Differences.* Cambridge, Mass: Workers' Compensation Research Institute; 1999: Table 3–17.

1.8 Impairment Evaluations in Workers' Compensation

This revised section outlines the general principles pertaining to workers' compensation in the United States, acknowledging that despite similar features, no two states are exactly alike. This section emphasizes, as in the Fourth Edition, that "impairment percentages derived from the *Guides* criteria should not be used as direct estimates of disability. Impairment percentages estimate the extent of the impairment on whole person functioning and account for basic activities of daily living, not including work" (*Guides 5th*, p 13).

1.9 Employability Determinations

Employability assessment determines an individual's ability to perform the essential requirements of the job without endangering himself or herself, others, or the work environment. Several jurisdictions use vocational experts to assess disability as a function of employability. Impairment is, again, a necessary predicate for the rating. The following tables identify how some states determine vocational restrictions.[11]

Jurisdictions That Use Vocational Experts to Rate Disability		
Alabama	Massachusetts	Ohio
Arizona	Nebraska	Rhode Island
Idaho	New York	Tennessee
Iowa	North Dakota	Wisconsin
Kentucky		

Barth PS, Niss M. *Permanent Partial Disability Benefits: Interstate Differences.* Cambridge, Mass: Workers' Compensation Research Institute; 1999.

Jurisdictions Where the State Agency Performs the Rating Function

Jurisdiction	Basis of Agency Rating
Arizona	Evaluation of medical, vocational, and labor-market reports.
California	The permanent-disability schedule and a review of medical reports.
Oregon	The statute and administrative rules, including the state's disability rating standards.
Washington	Although the state encourages ratings by medical examiners, the agency often is required to provide the numerical rating.
Wisconsin	Agency staff members review the doctor's rating to be sure it meets the minimums established by administrative code. They also calculate loss in the use of fingers and losses in hearing and vision.

Barth PS, Niss M. *Permanent Partial Disability Benefits: Interstate Differences.* Cambridge, Mass: Workers' Compensation Research Institute; 1999.

1.10 Railroad and Maritime Workers

This section was unchanged from the Fourth Edition and pertains only to the use of the *Guides* for railroad and maritime workers.

1.11 The Physician's Role Based on the Americans With Disabilities Act (ADA)

This section was included to provide physicians with some understanding of the ADA and to indicate its differences from the AMA *Guides.* The purpose of the ADA was to end discrimination against individuals with disability. Hence, the terms and application would understandably differ from those of workers' compensation statutes, which were designed to compensate for workplace injury and illness and their wage-earning consequences.

Under the ADA, *disability* is a physical or mental impairment that substantially limits a major life activity. Interference with a major life activity requires much more proof than interference with an activity of daily living. Moreover, disability under the ADA is intended to be measured with corrective or ameliorative aids such as eyeglasses or contact lenses. Impairments that may constitute significant disabilities under other social benefit systems may constitute no disability at all under the ADA. Complete loss of vision in one eye, an impairment under the Fifth Edition and previous editions and a presumptive disability under many workers' compensation laws, may not even be a disability under the ADA, where the other eye retains normal or exceptional vision.

Although definitions of disability differ between the ADA and workers' compensation, both systems require a medical basis, ie, impairment, for the finding that a disability exists. Under the ADA, the impairment usually must have more severe consequences for ADL than in workers' compensation, and the ADA consequence may or may not be related to ability to work.

MEDICAL TIP

The physician is responsible for assessing impairment and its corresponding functional limitations and, if requested, to notify the employer about an individual's abilities and limitations.

LEGAL TIP

Attorneys, employers, and benefit administrators should be aware that medically identified limitations do not necessarily indicate a substantial limitation on a major life activity.

1.12 Summary

This new section indicates that the role of the physician is to evaluate all the medical information and provide as comprehensive a medical picture of the individual as possible, beyond an impairment rating, including a discussion of the person's abilities and limitations. Combining the medical and nonmedical information discussed in Chapter 1 will provide an improved understanding regarding how the impairment may affect the individual's work ability.

References

1. American Medical Association. *Guides to the Evaluation of Permanent Impairment, 5th Edition.* Chicago, Ill: American Medical Association; 2000:2.

2. Barth PS, Niss M. *Permanent Partial Disability Benefits: Interstate Differences.* Cambridge, Mass: Workers Compensation Research Institute; 1999.

3. Cocchiarella L, Turk MA, Andersson G. Improving the evaluation of permanent impairment. *JAMA.* 2000;283:532-533.

4. *A Guide to the Evaluation of Permanent Impairment of the Extremities and Back, by the Committee on Medical Rating of Physical Impairment. Special Edition The Journal of the American Medical Association, February 15, 1958.*

5. McDowell I, Newell C. Physical disability and handicap. In: *Measuring Health: A Guide to Rating Scales and Questionnaires.* 2nd ed. New York, NY: Oxford University Press; 1996:48.

6. McDowell I, Newell C. Physical disability and handicap. In: *Measuring Health: A Guide to Rating Scales and Questionnaires.* 2nd ed. New York, NY: Oxford University Press; 1996:48-49.

7. Roizen M, Stephenson A. *Real Age: Are You as Young as You Can Be?* New York, NY: Cliff Street Books; 1999.

8. *Dorland's Illustrated Medical Dictionary, 28th ed.* Philadelphia, Pa: WB Saunders; 1994.

9. Hill AB. The environment and disease: association or causation? *Proc R Soc Med.* 1965;58:295-300.

10. Rothman KJ. *Modern Epidemiology.* Boston, Mass: Little, Brown; 1986.

11. Barth PS, Niss M. *Permanent Partial Disability Benefits: Interstate Differences.* Cambridge, Mass: Workers Compensation Research Institute; 1999.

Practical Application of the *Guides*

Introduction

This chapter provides an overview of key points and changes (identified with an icon **G**) made in Chapter 2 of the AMA *Guides to the Evaluation of Permanent Impairment, Fifth Edition* (*Guides 5th*), illustrates these changes in a table comparison, and discusses the purpose and implications of the major changes, with illustrative examples. The numbered section titles within this chapter correspond to sections within Chapter 2 of the *Guides 5th*. Only key principles or important changes are included in this chapter.

Chapters 1 and 2 of the *Guides 5th* present the philosophy and key principles that are applied throughout the book. It is essential that users of the *Guide 5th* read the first two chapters before using the *Guides*. Concepts that were previously discussed in the Fourth Edition Appendix have been revised and incorporated into the first two chapters.

The focus and title of Chapter 2 of the *Guides* have changed from records and reports in the Fourth Edition to practical application of the *Guides* in the Fifth Edition to reflect a broader purpose. The new chapter is divided into six sections:

2.1. Defining Impairment Evaluations

2.2. Who Performs Impairment Evaluations?

2.3. Examiners' Roles and Responsibilities

2.4. When Are Impairment Ratings Performed?

2.5. Rules for Evaluation

2.6. Preparing Reports

Key Points and Changes

Key points and new additions within each section are summarized below and discussed in detail within this chapter.

Introduction

G Impairment ratings performed by the *Guides* are reproducible. Two physicians, following the methods of the *Guides* to evaluate the same individual, should reach similar conclusions and report similar results.

Defining Impairment Evaluations

G An impairment evaluation is a medical evaluation performed by a physician, using a standard method as outlined in the *Guides* to determine permanent impairment.

G An impairment evaluation may or may not contain an impairment rating that is a quantitative assessment of the ability to perform activities of daily living (ADL) as defined by the *Guides*.

G An independent medical evaluation (IME) is a subset of impairment ratings.

G An IME is performed by an independent medical examiner who evaluates but does not provide care for the individual.

Who Performs Impairment Evaluations?

G Impairment evaluations may be performed by a treating physician or a nontreating physician, depending on the state's requirements and the preferences of the individual, physician, and requesting party.

Examiners' Roles and Responsibilities

G The physician's role in performing an impairment evaluation is to provide an independent, unbiased assessment of the individual's medical condition, including its effect on function, and identify abilities and limitations to performing activities of daily living as listed in Table 1-2.

The physician is responsible for performing a medical evaluation that addresses medical impairment in the body or organ system and related systems.

The physician needs to ensure that the examinee understands that the evaluation's purpose is medical assessment, not medical treatment.

G If new diagnoses are discovered, the physician has a medical obligation to inform the requesting party and individual about the condition and recommend further medical assessment.

When Are Impairment Ratings Performed?

Permanent impairment ratings are provided when the medical condition is static and well stabilized, at maximal medical improvement (MMI).

Rules for Evaluation

The physician needs to obtain the individual's consent to share the medical information with other parties who will be reviewing the evaluation, unless otherwise provided by law.

Convert organ system to whole person impairments, then combine multiple whole person impairments by using the Combined Values Chart.

Improve consistency by replicating measurements, especially when measuring range of motion. Generally, these measurements should fall within 10% of each other and are rounded to the nearest whole number.

Pain, consistent with a particular condition, is already accounted for in each body system rating.

G Additional assessment of pain is performed when the pain is excessive for the medical condition or may meet criteria for a chronic pain syndrome.

When feasible, remove or eliminate an individual's prosthesis or assistive device before the impairment assessment. An exception is vision assessment, which should be done with corrective lenses on.

The physician may choose to report measurements without and with the assistive device in place.

Adjustments for Effects of Treatment or Lack of Treatment

The physician may increase the impairment estimate by a small percentage (eg, 1% to 3%) to adjust for treatment or lack of treatment effects.

If a patient declines therapy for a permanent impairment, that decision neither decreases nor increases the estimated percentage of the individual's impairment.

Preparing Reports
Key Features of the Clinical Evaluation (See Section 2.6, p 21)

a. Obtain a detailed history of the medical condition(s), onset, course, symptoms, findings on previous examination(s), treatments, and responses to treatment, including adverse effects.

b. Obtain a detailed occupational history; description of work activities, specific type and duration of work performed, materials used in the workplace, any temporal associations with the medical condition and work, frequency, intensity, and duration of exposure and activity, and any protective measures.

c. Report and discuss current clinical status, current symptoms, review of symptoms, physical examination, and a list of contemplated treatment, rehabilitation, and any anticipated reevaluation.

d. Obtain diagnostic study results and summarize outstanding pertinent diagnostic studies. These may include laboratory tests, electrocardiograms, exercise stress studies, radiographic and other imaging studies, rehabilitation evaluations, mental status examinations, and other tests or diagnostic procedures.

e. Explain the medical basis for determining whether the person is at MMI. If not, estimate and discuss the expected date of full or partial recovery (MMI).

f. Identify diagnoses, impairments, functional limitations, and the impact of the medical impairment(s) on the ability to perform activities of daily living and, if requested, complex activities such as work.

g. Calculate an impairment rating and discuss rating criteria.

h. Identify any medical consequence of performing a complex activity such as work.

i. Identify any restrictions or accommodations for standard activities of daily living or complex activities such as work.

j. Calculate and discuss the impairment rating indicating the criteria evaluated and met, and reference the appropriate tables and pages.

k. Convert from body system impairments to whole person impairments.

l. Combine whole person impairments using the Combined Values Chart.

m. Include a summary list of impairments and impairment ratings by percentage, including calculation of the whole person impairment.

Comparison of Figures Between the Fifth and Fourth *Guides* Editions

The following table summarizes the key points and changes in Figure 1 (Fourth Edition) and Figure 2-1 (Fifth Edition) of the *Guides*.

Comparison of Figures Between the Fifth and Fourth *Guides* Editions

Figure Title	5th Edition Figure Number	4th Edition Figure Number	Summary of Changes in 5th Edition
Sample Report for Permanent Medical Impairment	2-1	1	Includes sections to list discussion of rating criteria and rationale

Introduction

The purpose of the *Guides 5th* Chapter 2 is to provide a reproducible method for physicians to use to conduct and report an impairment evaluation. Impairment ratings performed by the *Guides* are reproducible. Two physicians, following the methods of the *Guides* to evaluate the same individual, should achieve and report similar results.

2.1 Defining Impairment Evaluations

This new section seeks to clarify misunderstandings regarding the use of common terms in impairment evaluation. An impairment evaluation is a medical evaluation performed by a physician, using a standard method as outlined in the *Guides,* to determine permanent impairment. An impairment evaluation may or may not contain an impairment rating, which is a quantitative assessment of the ability to perform activities of daily living (ADL) as defined by the *Guides.* An independent medical evaluation (IME) is a subset of impairment evaluations. An IME is performed by an independent medical examiner who evaluates, but does not provide care for, the individual. An IME may be used to determine whether an examinee has reached maximal medical improvement (MMI), to provide alternative treatment options, and to render impairment ratings. Local laws may also define "evaluation of impairment."

MEDICAL TIP

Determine, for your state, the current practice for both workers' compensation and injury claims, whether an impairment evaluation is done by a treating physician, an independent evaluator, or both.

> **LEGAL TIP**
>
> Evaluations performed by evaluators out of state in jurisdictions that have special credentialing are sometimes treated under separate rules or exceptions. Failure to have a rating provided by the correct type of evaluator may defeat a significant claim for impairment or disability benefits, and may also prevent reimbursement for the evaluation encounter.

2.2 Who Performs Impairment Evaluations?

This new section discusses who is able to perform impairment ratings. The Fifth Edition of the *Guides* recognizes the distinction between impairment ratings, which may be performed by the treating physician, and an independent medical evaluation, performed by a nontreating physician. However, the *Guides* does not specify a preference. Some states enable the treating physician to perform the evaluation but generally do not have the physician provide a numeric rating. Depending on the expertise of the examiner and the information available, both impairment assessments and IMEs can meet the need of a third party for an unbiased evaluation. The key difference is that the treating physician has an ongoing relationship with the individual and may act as his or her advocate. Therefore, there may be some motivation to portray the impairment as more disabling to secure greater benefits. The independent evaluator has no ongoing relationship with the examinee and will not be influenced by that relationship. Both examiners have a relationship with the third party who has requested the evaluation and are subject to similar pressures to minimize or maximize reporting of impairment.

Each state or system, not the *Guides*, determines which physician can perform impairment ratings. Some states and systems require physicians to be in practice a certain number of hours per week and to take a training program or receive registration or certification. Some jurisdictions enable impairment ratings to be done by physicians who have not seen the individual, but have reviewed the medical data. This often is problematic, as the physician cannot comment on whether the person is at MMI at the time the records are being reviewed; he or she may have improved or deteriorated. If such an evaluation is done in limited cases, the evaluation is only as valid and accurate as the medical reports on which the nonexamining physician makes a determination. The preference is to have the evaluating physician perform the physical examination.

Nearly all states and the District of Columbia allow medical impairment ratings to be performed by medical doctors, osteopathic physicians, chiropractic physicians, dentists, psychologists, and podiatrists.[1] As identified in the table on page 34, in 25 states and the District of Columbia, the opinion of the treating physician is given special weight by statute, administrative regulation, custom, or case law.[2] Only in Colorado, Connecticut, Massachusetts, North Dakota, Pennsylvania, Texas, West Virginia, and Wyoming must a neutral medical panel be used. In most states, the use of medical panels or independent evaluators is optional. In Arizona, Iowa, Michigan, Nevada, Tennessee, Utah, and Vermont, medical panels and neutral physicians apparently are not used, although in Utah the Industrial Commission's medical officer appears to perform an oversight function to advise the Commission when ratings are in dispute.[3]

MEDICAL TIP

Check with your state workers' compensation board to see the requirements for performing impairment evaluations. Determine if your state requires or offers training in impairment evaluation. Obtain additional training on impairment evaluation if needed, through the AMA.

LEGAL TIP

In states that require additional qualification, certification, or registration for evaluators, a physician's failure to obtain the appropriate credential may generate more paperwork and conflict for all parties involved, including the physician. Also, a rating given by a nonqualified physician may delay the processing of a claim for benefits.

2.3 Examiners' Roles and Responsibilities

This section is new to the Fifth Edition and emphasizes the physician's role in providing an independent, unbiased assessment of the individual's medical condition, including its effect on function, and in identifying abilities and limitations to performing ADL as listed in Table 1-2. A physician performing an evaluation on behalf of a third party is responsible for performing a medical evaluation that evaluates medical impairment in the injured body or organ system and related systems. The physician needs to ensure the examinee understands that the evaluation's purpose is medical assessment, not medical treatment.

Chapter 1

"Is the Opinion of the Treating Physician Given Special Weight" in Impairment-Rating Disputes?

Jurisdiction	Yes	By Statute	By Case Law	By Custom
Alabama	X	X		
Alaska				
Arizona				
Arkansas	X		X	X
California	X	X		
Colorado	X			X
Connecticut				
Delaware				
District of Columbia	X		X	X
Florida				
Georgia	X			X
Hawaii				
Idaho	X		X	X
Illinois	X		X	X
Indiana				
Iowa	X		X	X
Kansas				
Kentucky				
Louisiana	X		X	
Maine	X		X	
Maryland	X			X
Massachusetts				
Michigan				
Minnesota				
Mississippi	X		X	X
Missouri	X			X
Montana	X		X	
Nebraska				
Nevada				
New Hampshire				
New Jersey	X			X
New Mexico				
New York				
North Carolina	X		X	X
North Dakota				
Ohio				
Oklahoma				
Oregon[a]	X	X	X	
Pennsylvania	X		X	
Rhode Island				
South Carolina	X			X
South Dakota	X			X
Tennessee	X		X	
Texas[b]				
Utah				
Vermont	X			X
Virginia	X		X	
Washington	X		X	
West Virginia				
Wisconsin	X			X
Wyoming				

[a] Oregon reports that weight is given to the treating physician's opinion by administrative rule also.

[b] By statute in Texas, the treating physician's opinion is not given any special weight.

Barth PS, Niss M. *Permanent Partial Disability Benefits: Interstate Differences*. Cambridge, Mass: Workers' Compensation Research Institute; 1999:51-52.

If new diagnoses are discovered, the physician has a medical obligation to inform both the requesting party and the individual about the condition and recommend further medical assessment. When relevant, the evaluator may also suggest treatments that have been overlooked or may have been outside the expertise of others who have provided medical care.

The skills required for impairment evaluation are usually not a part of traditional medical training. Impairment evaluation also requires skills in occupational, functional, as well as more traditional anatomic assessment.

Physicians performing these evaluations also have a responsibility to understand the regulations of practice for IMEs in their state of practice. In many systems, an examinee's failure to attend an IME scheduled by a third party (employer or insurer) may result in the denial of some or all benefits.

Unlike the Fourth Edition, which indicates that the physician focuses on the primary impairment or impairing condition of most concern to the individual, the Fifth Edition indicates that the physician needs to identify all relevant impairments that affect function.

EXAMPLE

Susan has carpal tunnel syndrome (CTS) associated with her repetitive activities at work. She also has poorly controlled diabetes, which may have caused her CTS. Although her workplace would not contribute to the diabetic impairment, any previous documentation of peripheral neuropathy could be cause for apportionment and raise questions of causation of the CTS.

MEDICAL TIP

Evaluate the individual completely, addressing any impairments that may relate to the impairment of major interest.

LEGAL TIP

The impairment evaluation either causes or eliminates many disputes in workers' compensation cases. Evaluators' reports that lack basic information suggested by the *Guides* (or local rules) may raise suspicions on the part of either a benefit payer or the examinee, setting the stage for additional conflict.

2.4 When Are Impairment Ratings Performed?

This new section details that permanent impairment ratings are performed only when the medical condition is static and well stabilized at MMI. The condition is not necessarily rated after the injury, as was recommended in the spine section of the musculoskeletal chapter in the Fourth Edition, but when the impairment is stable and permanent.

Impairment evaluations may also be conducted in circumstances where an individual complains of deterioration or a third party alleges improvement, after some lapse of time from a previous rating of a condition or impairment.

In workers' compensation, impairment evaluations are usually performed within a certain time period after the occupational accident or exposure that leads to the condition(s) being evaluated. Since permanent impairment and disability benefits are usually considered indemnity or income benefits, they are usually governed by legally defined periods of limitation. That is, the benefit must be claimed within a set time period (often 1 year) after the causative event. The causative event is often the date of the accident or exposure, the date when temporary income benefits are stopped, or the date of MMI. Evaluations performed more than a year after that event (the end of that period) might come too late for the award of a benefit. The period of limitations is "tolled" in most states by the filing of a petition, complaint, application, or other process that initiates a contested case in front of a workers' compensation judge, board, commission, mediator, referee, or other hearing officer. When a period is tolled, evaluations and reports may be requested or become available during the litigation of the claim. Periods of limitation vary widely from jurisdiction to jurisdiction.

Since disability has been shown to be less severe with cases handled proactively, with aggressive case management and early therapy, it behooves the physician to ensure that the injured worker receives prompt and coordinated care. This approach is also consistent with an underlying premise of workers' compensation, namely, to return the injured worker to preinjury status and gainful employment as quickly as possible, consistent with prudent medical practices.

EXAMPLE

A broken wrist is at MMI 3 months after the incident with a 0% whole person impairment (WPI). More than 3 years later, osteoarthritis develops with no apparent intervening cause. A new impairment evaluation indicates that wrist motion is reduced, resulting in a 20% upper extremity WPI.

MEDICAL TIP
Treating physicians may have cases open for much longer, waiting until a state of MMI has been reached. Evaluating physicians need to ensure that providers consider the individual to have reached a plateau in terms of improvement. Designating an individual as being at MMI indicates that the condition is unlikely to change substantially only in the next year.

LEGAL TIP
Even in contested cases, early medical management can reduce recovery time. Reduced recovery time reduces direct expenses and returns the worker to gainful employment more expeditiously.

Many plaintiffs' and claimants' attorneys advise their clients that no award will ever replace a good-paying job, and when one considers the benefit to both employees and employers, attentive and thorough medical care after an accident may demonstrate a commitment to the employee that fosters a feeling of well-being and loyalty.

Positive encounters in the recovery process enhance both medical and vocational outcomes and reduce overall medical and disability expenses.

2.5 Rules for Evaluation

Section 2.5 of the Fifth Edition discusses many new and important concepts critical to impairment rating.

2.5a Confidentiality

The physician needs to obtain the individual's consent to share medical information with other parties who will be reviewing the evaluation. Most workers' compensation laws provide for sharing without obtaining additional consent. However, an independent evaluator should routinely disclose his or her role as that of someone who will be providing an evaluation to parties other than the examinee.

2.5b Combining Impairment Ratings

An evaluator should typically report findings on the basis of an organ system and whole person impairment. Convert organ system impairments to whole person impairments, then combine multiple whole person impairments by using the Combined Values Chart. Chapter 1 in this book discusses the philosophy of the Combined Values Chart in greater detail.

EXAMPLE

Jake is in a motor vehicle accident and sustains a cervical neck sprain, disk herniation at C6-7 with radiculopathy, and a tear of the anterior cruciate ligament in the left knee. His cervical radiculopathy, present after MMI, warrants a 15% whole person impairment (WPI), and his anterior cruciate ligament function, with moderate laxity after surgical repair, is given a 7% WPI rating. Combining 15% and 7% by means of the Combined Value Chart gives a 21% WPI rating.

2.5c Consistency

The Fifth Edition expressly encourages improved consistency by replicating measurements, especially when measuring range of motion. These measurements generally should fall within 10% of the mean and are rounded to the nearest whole number.

Impairment ratings in the Fifth Edition are rounded to the next nearest whole integer for greater accuracy, not to the nearest 0% or 5% as indicated in the Fourth Edition. The Fourth Edition suggested that impairments be rounded to the nearer of the two values, ending in 0 or 5. Not rounding will allow for some differences as to whether a physician decides on an impairment rating of 3% or 5%, or 31% or 33%. However, individuals with a small impairment, who may have been given an impairment rating of 2%, when rounded down would get a rating of 0%, which in many states would preclude them from any permanent impairment or disability benefit. The Fifth Edition eliminates this arbitrary half-decile statistical preference, consistent with other changes that encourage greater accuracy and recognize variation in individuals.

M E D I C A L   T I P

The physician's report should justify why a particular rating was chosen, recognizing that small differences may arise on the basis of examination and individual variability.

L E G A L   T I P

Some tables in the *Guides* treat any measurable impairment less than a fixed whole-number percentage (eg, Table 5-12, where [WPI <10%] = 0%; Table 15-3, where [WPI <5%] = 0%) as a 0% whole person impairment. Query whether medical justification may exist for allowing impairment in these just noticeable ranges, assuming that some ADL impact may be present.

2.5e Pain

Pain, consistent with a particular condition, is already accounted for in each body system rating. Additional assessment of pain is performed when the pain is excessive for the medical condition and is not accounted for by the conventional impairment rating.

If an individual has chronic, severe pain (eg, low back pain) that might be controlled by a surgical procedure that is refused, then the current, untreated condition forms the clinical basis for that individual's evaluation. Hence, if surgery is recommended for a herniated disk with intractable pain, the individual would not receive an additional pain rating under Chapter 18, since the pain is expected for someone with that condition who refuses surgery.

In the following states, objective medical evidence (eg, radiologic studies, blood tests, measurable loss of range of motion) must be present as a condition for rating medical impairment: Arizona, Arkansas, California, Colorado, Idaho, Iowa, Kansas, Kentucky, Minnesota, Montana, New Hampshire, New Jersey, New Mexico, Oklahoma, Oregon, Texas, Utah, Washington, and West Virginia.[4] That is, purely subjective patient complaints alone are insufficient for an award of impairment. Given the Fifth Edition's reliance on reduced performance of ADL as a determinant for an impairment rating, one may argue that these states' approach is now to be followed by any state or system that automatically refers to the most recent edition of the *Guides*.

MEDICAL TIP
An additional assessment for pain, with the use of the pain chapter, is provided only when pain is plausible and greater than expected for a particular impairment.

LEGAL TIP
Note that many states discount purely subjective complaints of pain as a basis for impairment rating. Any pain rating needs to be documented on the basis of the criteria in Chapter 18, Pain.

2.5f Using Assistive Devices in Evaluations

When feasible, remove or eliminate an individual's prosthesis or assistive device before the impairment assessment. As in the Fourth Edition, an exception is vision assessment, which should be performed with corrective lenses on. The physician may choose to report measurements with and without the assistive device in place.

2.5g Adjustments for Effects of Treatment or Lack of Treatment

The physician may increase the impairment estimate by a small percentage (eg, 1% to 3%) to adjust for treatment or lack of treatment effects. Before awarding an additional 1% to 3% for treatment effects, recognize that this option has some similarities to expected pain accompanying a medical condition. The use of medications for some conditions is also expected. For example, an individual who received a heart valve transplant and is taking anticoagulants, as expected, would not receive an additional 1% to 3% impairment rating. However, if while taking the anticoagulants the person has episodic gastrointestinal tract bleeding, with difficulty controlling the international normalized ratio, that individual could be given an additional impairment rating because of the unexpected difficulty with the medication, which impacts ADL.

A person may decline surgical, pharmacologic, or therapeutic treatment of an impairment without a change in impairment rating. This poses a challenge to the physician in determining the level of stability, given the refusal of treatment. Once that untreated state is recognized, then the physician can provide a rating, acknowledging that it measures only MMI without treatment.

MEDICAL TIP
Carefully record response to treatment, whether beneficial or adverse effects.

LEGAL TIP
Some states may reduce an impairment or disability award because of an individual's unsafe or unsanitary practices after the individual suffers an occupational injury or disease. In some extreme cases, refusal to undergo treatment may constitute such a practice, eg, an individual with poorly controlled diabetes who refuses antibiotics for a severe extremity infection that resulted from a work-related laceration requires amputation of the extremity.

2.5h Changes in Impairment From Prior Ratings

This section expands on information regarding apportionment in Chapter 1. In addition, in states that use different editions of the *Guides* and wish to apportion ratings, the physician needs to assess the similarity of the editions' approaches. Apportionment is appropriate only if the methods were similar and yielded similar results. State regulations take precedence.

MEDICAL TIP
If apportionment is requested on impairment ratings performed under two different *Guides* editions, the physician will need to compare approaches between both editions. Use the summary outlines in each chapter of this book to quickly identify key changes that may assist in apportionment .

LEGAL TIP
A preexisting condition may be ratable at greater than 0% WPI under a previous edition but is ratable at 0% under the Fifth Edition. If impairment is evaluated and rated under the Fifth Edition, because a prior impairment rating was not assigned or an earlier edition does not apply, then the preexisting condition should also be evaluated and rated by means of the Fifth Edition. Thus, in cases where the Fifth Edition results in 0% WPI for a preexisting condition, some opportunities for apportionment may be lost.

2.6 Preparing Reports

This section of the Fifth Edition of the *Guides* provides a "how-to" checklist for evaluators for performing a **basic** or more detailed impairment evaluation. For a work-related assessment, include a detailed occupational history in addition to the essential components. The summary list below outlines critical elements of the impairment evaluation from Section 2.6 of the Fifth Edition and encompasses this need for objective evidence in Section 2.6a.4.

Key Features of the Clinical Evaluation (See Section 2.6, p 21)
2.6a.1, Detailed History of the Medical Condition(s)

Onset: _____

Course: _____

Symptoms:_____

Findings on previous examination(s): _____

_____

Treatments: _____

Responses to treatment, including adverse effects:_____

_____

2.6a.2, Detailed Occupational History

Activity	Materials Used	Temporal Association to Condition	Frequency of Use	Intensity of Use	Duration of Exposure	Protective Measures

2.6a.3, Current Clinical Status

Current symptoms: _____

Review of symptoms: _____

Physical examination: _____

Treatment

   Actual: _____

   Planned: _____

Anticipated reevaluation:_____

2.6a.4, Diagnostic Study Results

Laboratory tests: _____

Electrocardiograms: _____

Exercise stress studies: _____

Radiographic and other imaging studies: _____

_____

Other tests or diagnostic procedures: _____

_____

2.6a.5, Date of MMI
If MMI not reached, estimate and discuss the expected date of full or partial recovery with no further expected changes.

2.6a.6, Diagnoses, Impairments, Functional Limitations

Diagnosis	Impairment	Functional Limitations	ADL impact

2.6a.7, Causation and Apportionment

Discuss causation as outlined in Appendix A.

2.6a.8-2.6c Calculate and Discuss the Impairment Rating Indicating the Criteria Met, and Reference the Appropriate Tables and Pages

Impairment	Method of Assessment	Chapter/ Tables	Body Part Rating	Organ System Rating	Whole Person Rating	Total Rating

2.6a.9, Restrictions or Accommodations for Standard Activities of Daily Living or Complex Activities Such as Work

Discuss medical consequence of performing a complex activity, such as work.

M E D I C A L   T I P
Ensure that impairment evaluation reports contain the key information listed above.

L E G A L   T I P
Reports provided to administrators, attorneys, and adjudicators should follow either the protocols provided by the *Guides* or reporting formats established by law or rule in a state or other jurisdiction. In particular, a report that omits or inadequately discusses material in bold print, or required in the jurisdiction, may be subject to challenge.

References

1.   Barth PS, Niss M. *Permanent Partial Disability Benefits: Interstate Differences.* Cambridge, Mass: Workers' Compensation Research Institute; 1999:Table 18.

2.   Barth PS, Niss M. *Permanent Partial Disability Benefits: Interstate Differences.* Cambridge, Mass: Workers' Compensation Research Institute; 1999:Table 19.

3.   Barth PS, Niss M. *Permanent Partial Disability Benefits: Interstate Differences.* Cambridge, Mass: Workers' Compensation Research Institute; 1999:Table 20.

4.   Barth PS, Niss M. *Permanent Partial Disability Benefits: Interstate Differences.* Cambridge, Mass: Workers' Compensation Research Institute; 1999:Table 3-21.

Chapter 3

The Cardiovascular System: Heart and Aorta

Introduction

This chapter provides an overview of key points and changes (identified with an icon **G**) made in Chapter 3 of the AMA *Guides to the Evaluation of Permanent Impairment, Fifth Edition (Guides 5th),* illustrates these changes in a table comparison, and discusses the purpose and implications of the major changes, with illustrative examples. The numbered section titles within this chapter correspond to sections within Chapter 3 of *Guides 5th.* Only key principles or important changes are included in this chapter.

The cardiovascular system chapter has been revised to incorporate major changes in the field of cardiology. It has been separated into two chapters to account for the different approaches between heart and aorta impairments, now covered in Chapter Three 3, and systemic and pulmonary arteries, now covered in Chapter 4 of the *Guides 5th.*

This chapter will address only major changes in the assessment of heart and aortic impairments, and will indicate some case examples of interest in workers' compensation and personal injury settings. The impairment ratings in the *Guides 5th* Cardiovascular System have not changed, although the criteria within an impairment class have been altered in a few cases. This chapter outlines the changes between the fifth and fourth editions for sections of particular interest in the workers' compensation and personal injury settings.

Key Points and Changes

G   Normal cardiac function pertains to an individual who performs all activities
of daily living without cardiovascular symptoms, has some reserve capacity
that allows comfortable exercise without the development of major cardiovascular symptoms, has a left ventricular ejection fraction that falls within
normal limits, and completes at least 80% of age-and gender-predicted
functional aerobic capacity during exercise stress testing (*Guides 5th*, p 28).

G   If assessing causation for coronary heart disease (CHD), determine from the
medical literature whether the associated risk factors or occupational groups
are at increased risk for CHD.

Comparisons of Tables Between the Fifth and Fourth *Guides* Editions

The following table summarizes the key points and changes in tables
between the fourth and fifth editions of the *Guides*.

Comparison of Tables Between the Fifth and Fourth *Guides* Editions

Table Topic	5th Edition Table Number	4th Edition Table Number	Summary of Changes in 5th Edition
NYHA cardiac disease functional classification	3-1	1	Stylistic
Five treadmill protocol METS/functional class relationships	3-2	2	None
METS during bicycle ergometry	3-3	3	None
Severity of valve stenosis	3-4	4	Aortic valve areas have increased
Impairment due to valvular heart disease	3-5	5	Stylistic
Impairment due to coronary heart disease	3-6a	6	Stylistic
Maximal and 90% of maximal achievable heart rate	3-6b, 3-7	7	None
Congenital heart disease	3-8	8	Stylistic
Cardiovascular hypertension		9	Now in Chapter 4 at 4-1 and 4-2; see next chapter
Cardiomyopathy	3-9	10	Stylistic
Pericardial heart disease	3-10	11	Stylistic
Arrhythmias	3-11	12	Stylistic
Summary	3-12		New

Introduction

The Fifth Edition has revised the impairment criteria for valvular disease, on the basis of guidelines from the American Heart Association and American College of Cardiology. Other revisions include updates to diagnosis and prognosis for coronary artery disease and cardiomyopathy. A case example and an excellent summary of cardiac impairment assessment are included at the end of the chapter to facilitate use.

3.1 Principles of Assessment

The assessment of cardiac impairment depends on the integration of subjective factors, such as symptoms, with objective factors, including clinical signs and functional tests. The New York Heart Association (NYHA) functional class of cardiac disease listed in Table 3-1 is a widely used functional scale that incorporates subjective symptoms with clinical signs to rate the extent of cardiac function. This scale establishes the major criteria for assigning individuals to a class of cardiac impairment. It also enables the physician to compare individuals with different cardiac impairments, using a common scale for cardiac function.

The other commonly used tests and measures of cardiac function include exercise testing, functional capacity, left ventricle function, cardiac ejection fraction, and diastolic determination.

Of note in the Fifth Edition is a new definition of normal cardiac function, being that of "an individual who performs all activities of daily living without cardiovascular symptoms, has some reserve capacity that allows comfortable exercise without the development of major cardiovascular symptoms, has an LV ejection fraction that falls within normal limits, and completes at least 80% of age- and gender-predicted functional aerobic capacity during exercise stress testing" (*Guides 5th*, p 28).

3.2 Valvular Heart Disease

The criteria in Table 3-4, for valve areas and corresponding areas of stenosis, have been changed. Although the criteria for severity (mild, moderate, and severe) of stenosis were changed, the criteria and impairment ratings in Table 3-5 to rate valvular heart disease are unchanged. New cases have been added.

Chapter 3

3.3 Coronary Heart Disease

Criteria for rating coronary heart disease (CHD) have not changed. As in the Fourth Edition, the physician must ascertain that the individual has reached MMI before an impairment rating is performed. Of major interest in workers' compensation cases is whether work-related stress, either physical or mental, precipitated a CHD event such as a myocardial infarction. Both editions indicate that although CHD is most commonly caused by atherosclerosis of the coronary arteries, leading to reduced blood flow, other causes of reduced blood flow, such as spasm, can lead to CHD.

EXAMPLE

Jack, a 57-year-old senior manager, is told for the third time in 5 years that his company is being bought. He is required to fire most of his division—10 employees—with poor settlement packages, and he will either need to relocate his family again, after two previous major moves, or lose his job with a minimal settlement package. There is a good possibility that, even with relocation, his remaining division and his position will be terminated within a year. His wife has been ill during the last year with an immune disorder, and Jack has been her major caregiver. He plays golf almost weekly as his major form of exercise. He is about 10% overweight and is not hypertensive, although his last cholesterol determination was elevated at 230 mg/dL; low-density lipoprotein cholesterol level was 135 mg/dL, and high-density lipoprotein cholesterol level, 45 mg/dL. His father died at age 79 of prostate cancer. His mother is still living.

That evening, Jack goes to bed early, and the following morning, he has a limited myocardial infarction that the cardiologists attribute to spasm, since his coronary arteries have insignificant obstruction. Subsequent treadmill testing indicates that he is able to obtain 90% of his predicted heart rate without developing signs of ischemia or hypotension.

His impairment rating, based on the AMA *Guides*, would be class 2, 10% to 29% whole person impairment. The physician is also asked to determine whether this myocardial infarction is stress- and work-related. Given this history, stress is found to be the major precipitant. However, the physician needs to perform an assessment of the work-related vs non–work-related stress to determine the work-relatedness of this event.

MEDICAL TIP

Assess the degree of cardiac permanent impairment.

If requested to assess causation, review the medical literature for associations between CHD and workplace exposures. Evaluate these documented associations in the context of the individual's complete medical and social history to determine whether factors such as family history, smoking, cholesterol level, and atherosclerosis were present and key determinants.

LEGAL TIP

Many states have presumptive heart-lung laws for police and firefighters. These presumptions mean that any heart or lung disorder that becomes symptomatic during the course of employment is presumed to arise out of employment. Physicians are frequently asked either to buttress a workplace event as the "cause" of an infarct or to refute the workplace cause by assessing risk factors that would have led to an infarct regardless of time, place, or environment.

3.4 Congenital Heart Disease

3.5 Cardiomyopathies

3.6 Pericardial Heart Disease

Sections 3.4, 3.5, and 3.6 and their impairment rating criteria are unchanged. Slight changes were made in terminology in the criteria for assessing pericardial heart disease.

3.8 Cardiovascular Impairment Evaluation Summary

Table 3-12 provides an excellent overview of the clinical evaluation findings and impairment criteria for impairments of the cardiovascular system (heart and aorta), cross-referenced to appropriate impairment rating tables in the *Guides 5th* cardiovascular system chapter.

Table 3-12 Cardiac Impairment Evaluation Summary

Disorder	History, Including Selected Relevant Symptoms	Examination Record	Assessment of Cardiac Function
General	Cardiovascular symptoms (eg, fatigue, palpitations, dyspnea, chest pain) and general symptoms; impact of symptoms on function and ability to do daily activities Prognosis if change anticipated Review medical history	Comprehensive physical examination; detailed cardiovascular system assessment	Data derived from relevant studies (eg, ECG, echocardiography, stress tests, cardiac catheterization)
Valvular Heart Disease	Discuss symptoms and any resulting limitation of physical activity (eg, angina) Address cardiac output, pulmonary and systemic congestion	Note rate, rhythm, heart sounds, and other organ function	Doppler echocardiography or cardiac catheterization
Coronary Heart Disease (CHD)	Angina pectoris; reduced ventricular function; limitation of physical activity due to fatigue; palpitations; dyspnea; anginal pain	Detailed history Note rate, rhythm, heart sounds, and other organ function	Coronary angiography; chest x-ray; ECG; EF; studies may be obtained at rest and during and after exercise
Congenital Heart Disease	Dyspnea; fatigue; palpitations; symptoms of end-organ dysfunction	Note rate, rhythm, heart sounds, and other organ function	ECG; chest roentgenogram; radioisotope studies; echocardiography; hemodynamic measurements; angiography
Cardiomyopathies	Exertional dyspnea; angina; syncope; pulmonary or systemic organ congestion	Note rate, rhythm, heart sounds, and other organ function	Echocardiography; ECG; chest roentgenogram; abnormal ventricular function; dynamic outflow tract obstruction
Pericardial Heart Disease	Chest pain Note active inflammation, increase in ESR	Note rate, rhythm, heart sounds (pericardial rub, early diastolic pericardial knock), and other organ function	ECHO-pericardial effusion, thickening, or calcification; thickened pericardium on CT scan or MRI; cardiac catheterization
Arrhythmias	Syncope; weakness and fatigue; palpitations; dizziness; chest heaviness; shortness of breath	Note rate, rhythm, heart sounds; document arrhythmia and estimate its frequency	ECG: frequent premature complexes, tachycardia Echocardiogram: atrial enlargement

End-Organ Damage	Diagnosis(es)	Degree of Impairment
Include assessment of sequelae, including end-organ damage and impairment	Record all pertinent diagnosis(es); note if they are at maximal medical improvement; if not, discuss under what conditions and when stability is expected	Criteria outlined in this chapter
Assess relevant organs (eg, lungs, kidneys) for congestion or dysfunction	Aortic or mitral valve stenosis; mitral valve prolapse; aortic or mitral valve regurgitation; aortic and/or mitral valve disease; ventricular dysfunction	See Table 3-5
Assess relevant organs (eg, brain, lungs, kidneys, eyes, peripheral vascular system)	MI; angina pectoris; coronary artery vasospasm; ventricular failure	See Table 3-6
Assess relevant organs (eg, brain, lungs, kidneys, peripheral vascular system)	Valve stenosis, septal defects; valve anomalies; tetralogy of Fallot; Ebstein's anomaly; vessel transposition; Eisenmenger's complex	See Table 3-8
Assess relevant organs (eg, brain, lungs, kidneys, peripheral vascular system)	Dilated or congested; hypertrophic; restrictive	See Table 3-9
Assess relevant organs (eg, brain, lungs, kidneys, peripheral vascular system)	Constrictive or idiopathic pericarditis; tamponade; tumor; pericardial effusion; pericardial damage	See Table 3-10
Assess relevant organs (eg, brain, lungs, kidneys, peripheral vascular system)	Syncope; VT; atrial fibrillation; complete heart block; premature complexes	See Table 3-11

Chapter 3

The Cardiovascular System: Systemic and Pulmonary Arteries

Introduction

This chapter provides an overview of key points and changes (identified with an icon **G**) made in Chapter 4 of the AMA *Guides to the Evaluation of Permanent Impairment, Fifth Edition (Guides 5th)*, illustrates these changes in a table comparison, and discusses the purpose and implications of the major changes, with illustrative examples. The numbered section titles within this chapter correspond to sections within Chapter 4 of *Guides 5th*. Only key principles or important changes are included in this chapter.

This chapter presents part 2 of the cardiovascular system and discusses the systemic and pulmonary arteries, also known as the arterial peripheral vascular system. This *Master the Guides Fifth* chapter addresses *only* major changes and important content in the assessment of vascular impairments, with a case example of interest in workers' compensation.

Key Points and Changes

G Normal cardiac function pertains to an individual who performs all activities of daily living without cardiovascular symptoms, has some reserve capacity that allows comfortable exercise without the development of major cardiovascular symptoms, has a left ventricular ejection fraction that falls within normal limits, and completes at least 80% of age- and gender-predicted functional aerobic capacity during exercise stress testing (*Guides 5th*, p 28).

G If assessing causation for coronary heart disease (CHD), determine from the medical literature whether the associated risk factors or occupational groups are at increased risk for CHD.

G Hypertension (HTN) is an elevation of the systolic blood pressure to greater than or equal to140 mm Hg, or diastolic blood pressure to greater than 89 mm Hg on two or more separate readings (*Guides 5th*, p 66).

G Any impairment due to pulmonary hypertension would be combined with any accompanying respiratory impairment.

Comparison of Tables Between the Fifth and Fourth *Guides* Editions

The following table summarizes the key points and changes in tables between the fourth and fifth editions of the *Guides*.

Comparison of Tables Between the Fifth and Fourth *Guides* Editions

Table Topic	5th Edition Table Number	4th Edition Table Number	Summary of Changes in 5th Edition
Classification of HTN	4-1		New
Impairment due to hypertensive cardio-vascular disease	4-2	9	Impairment rating unchanged; criteria within classes changed to reflect new criteria for HTN
Diseases of the aorta	4-3		New
Impairment of the upper extremity due to peripheral vascular disease	4-4	13	Criteria here are con-sistent with Table 16-17 in the upper extremities chapter
Impairment of the lower extremity due to peripheral vascular disease	4-5	14	Insignificant
Pulmonary HTN rating criteria	4-6		New
Cardiovascular impairment evaluation summary	4-7		New

Chapter 4

Introduction

The *Guides 5th* chapter integrates new findings and expands the discussion regarding impairment assessment for hypertension in the peripheral and pulmonary arteries. More case examples are added to facilitate application. The *Guides 5th* cardiovascular chapter may overlap with vascular conditions covered in the extremity chapters. For conditions such as Raynaud's phenomenon, which affects the peripheral arterial circulation, both this chapter and the upper extremity chapter use the same criteria to assess permanent impairment.

The impairment ratings have not changed within the systemic arteries, although the criteria in the impairment classes have been altered to reflect the latest medical knowledge. New impairment ratings and new criteria were introduced into the assessment of pulmonary hypertension. New impairment ratings for pulmonary hypertension follow the classification system used to assess aorta impairments.

4.1 Hypertensive Cardiovascular Disease

The chapter incorporates the new criteria for diagnosis of hypertension (HTN) recommended by the US Joint National Committee on Prevention, Detection, Evaluation, and Treatment of High Blood Pressure (JNC-6). HTN is an elevation of the systolic blood pressure (BP) to greater than or equal to 140 mm Hg or diastolic BP greater than 89 mm Hg on two or more separate readings (*Guides 5th*, p 66). In the Fourth Edition, the authors considered HTN a permanent impairment only when the diastolic BP was greater than 90 mm Hg. Since HTN is asymptomatic until late stages, and does not initially impact activities of daily living (ADL), impairment rating is based on the degree of hypertension and clinical or subclinical end-organ damage, as seen in the eyes, heart, brain, or kidney.

The criteria for being classified into classes 1 to 4 have been changed to reflect more recent knowledge concerning the implications of elevated BP and end-organ damage. End-organ damage is rated only once; for example, class 4 in Table 4-2 requires HTN and heart failure. An individual rated as class 4 would not receive an additional rating for heart failure, which is accounted for in this class.

Elevated BP would rarely be considered work-related, although individuals can develop increases in BP under stress. If requested, it may be possible to apportion the impairment rating due to HTN from that due to a cardiovascular end event.

EXAMPLE

Suppose Jack, the 59-year-old individual discussed in Chapter 3, has a slightly different medical history. In addition to his experience of marked stress when told his company is being bought out for the third time and he needs to relocate again to keep his job, he has a history of HTN. His long-standing history of HTN was not optimally controlled, with mild proteinuria. After hearing the news at work, he has chest pain and suffers an acute myocardial infarction (MI). On the basis of his cardiac catheterization and angioplasty, his MI is found to be caused by both atherosclerosis and spasm. After his condition is stable and he undergoes cardiac rehabilitation, he is rated as a class 3, 35% whole person impairment (WPI) (Table 3-6a). His medical records indicate that his BP meets criteria for a class 2, 15% WPI, on the basis of Table 4-2. If one were asked to apportion the causes, one could subtract the HTN rating from the sequelae of MI.

Impairment Rating = 35% WPI due to MI – 15% WPI due to HTN = 20% WPI rating due to the nonhypertensive factors leading to an MI.

M E D I C A L   T I P
Ensure that BP is recorded on two different readings and use the highest BP value for rating purposes, after maximum medical improvement (MMI) with appropriate medication.

L E G A L   T I P
Some states require a physical incident, like lifting or straining, not merely a perceived or cognizant event, such as hearing bad news or witnessing an unpleasant but distant event, to support a conclusion that the MI results from the employment activity. Where Jack has a history of HTN and other significant predisposing disease processes, proving the workplace cause of the MI becomes more difficult.

4.2 Diseases of the Aorta

This is a new section; aortic impairments other than valvular disorders were not covered in the *Guides* Fourth Edition. The impairment rating classes are similar to those used for valvular heart disease in the Fourth Edition (Table 5). Aortic disorders are evaluated on the basis of symptoms, objective findings of an aortic abnormality, and symptoms after surgery.

4.3 Vascular Diseases Affecting the Extremities

This section is similar to its counterpart in the Fourth Edition. The major change is new diagnostic criteria added for the diagnosis of Raynaud's phenomenon, which is consistent with criteria in the upper extremity. Differentiate Raynaud's symptoms due to vasoreactivity from obstructive physiology, which is more severe. Use objective testing (laser Doppler flowmetry or arterial pressure ratio) to document obstructive physiology.

MEDICAL TIP

To use Raynaud's phenomenon as the basis for an upper extremity rating, ensure that diagnostic criteria are met. Objective, destructive changes when present, such as finger-brachial indices of <0.8, or low digital temperatures with decreased laser Doppler signals, warrant a higher impairment rating.

LEGAL TIP

Compare evaluation in this chapter with evaluation in Chapters 16 (Table 16-17) and 17 (Table 17-38). Any variation should be noted, and in the unlikely event of difference, the higher rating should be given.

Chapter 4

4.4 Diseases of the Pulmonary Arteries

This section is new in the Fifth Edition, using criteria for pulmonary hypertension developed by the World Health Organization, with class impairment ratings based on criteria for aortic disorders. In an occupational setting, pulmonary hypertension would most likely develop as a sequela of severe respiratory disease. In that case, the individual would receive ratings based on the respiratory disorder, which would be combined with a rating from pulmonary hypertension.

4.5 Cardiovascular Impairment Evaluation Summary

Table 4-7 provides an excellent overview of the clinical evaluation findings and impairment criteria for impairments of the cardiovascular system (systemic and pulmonary arteries) cross-referenced to appropriate impairment rating tables in the chapter.

Table 4-7 Cardiac Impairment Evaluation Summary

Disorder	History, Including Major Relevant Symptoms	Examination Record	Assessment of Cardiac Function
General	Determine degree of functional impairment with regard to activities of daily living	Jugular venous pressure; comment on carotid and peripheral vascular pulses; heart and lung exam; abdominal exam; fundoscopic exam; blood pressure taken in supine, sitting, and standing positions	Data derived from relevant studies (eg, ECG, echocardiogram, stress tests, cardiac catheterization)
Hypertensive Cardiovascular Disease	Determine symptoms that document cardiac, renal, and cerebrovascular limitation	Comprehensive; note end-organ conditions	ECG, echocardiogram, stress testing, catheterization; serum BUN and creatinine, urinalysis and urinary protein excretion, creatinine clearance or GFR assessment; renal ultrasound; head CT or MRI scan; angiography
Aortic Disease	Determine impairment of daily activities and of cardiac and peripheral vascular function	Comprehensive examination	Transthoracic and transesophageal echocardiography; CT and/or MRI imaging; aortic angiography
Peripheral Vascular Disease	Full history, including degree of limitation of activities of daily living	Comprehensive examination	Stress testing; ankle-brachial pressure indices and transcutaneous oximetry; peripheral angiography; venous imaging with dye or ultrasound/Doppler Lymphatic assessment with contrast or tagged markers
Pulmonary Circulation Disease	Detailed history with regard to functional impairment and prior medical issues, medication usage, and occupational exposure	Comprehensive examination	Echocardiography; pulmonary angiography; CT or MRI imaging

Chapter 4

	End-Organ Damage	Diagnosis(es)	Degree of Impairment
	Include assessment of sequelae, including end-organ damage and impairment	Record all pertinent diagnosis(es); note if they are at maximal medical improvement; if not, discuss under what conditions and when stability is expected	Criteria outlined in this chapter
	Heart; eyes; kidney; brain; monitor for proteinuria, elevated creatinine, reduced creatinine clearance, and abnormal urinary sediment; funduscopic changes including silver-wiring and arterio-venous crossing changes	Hypertension; left ventricular hypertrophy; hypertensive hypertrophic cardiomyopathy; hypertension-related systolic heart failure; hypertension-related diastolic heart failure; hypertensive nephrosclerosis; hypertensive encephalopathy; stroke; TIA	See Table 4-2
	Heart; aorta	Aortic aneurysm—thoracic or abdominal; aortic dissection; aortic coarctation; aortic atherosclerosis See also aortic valvular regurgitation	See Table 4-3
	Upper and lower extremities	Raynaud's phenomenon; arterial and venous ulceration; claudication; arterial aneurysms excluding the aorta; ischemic digital amputation, gangrene, and thromboangiitis obliterans Venous disorders, including edema, induration, stasis dermatitis, cellulitis, ulceration, and thrombosis Lymphatic disorders, including lymphedema, lymphangitis, and cellulitis	See Tables 4-4 and 4-5
	Assess cardiac and pulmonary damage	Primary and secondary pulmonary hypertension; pulmonary embolism; pulmonary veno-occlusive disease; pulmonary vein stenosis	See Table 4-6

Chapter 4

Chapter 5

The Respiratory System

Introduction

This chapter provides an overview of key points and changes (identified with an icon **G**) made in Chapter 5 of the AMA *Guides to the Evaluation of Permanent Impairment, Fifth Edition* (*Guides 5th*), illustrates these changes in a table comparison, and discusses the purpose and implications of the major changes, with illustrative examples. The numbered section titles within this chapter correspond to sections within Chapter 5 of the *Guides 5th*. Only key principles or important changes are included in this chapter.

Key Points and Changes

Principles of Assessment

G Respiratory impairments that decrease lung function and affect the ability to perform activities of daily living (ADL) are given an impairment rating.

G Respiratory impairments (eg, a limited pleural plaque) that do not affect lung function or ADL, although considered an impairment, would not be given an impairment rating.

G The section on occupational history emphasizes the key components: a chronologic history of work activities, the type of work, materials used, the frequency and intensity of exposure or activity, and any personal protective equipment available.

Symptoms Associated With Respiratory Disease

Integrate respiratory symptoms with the physical examination and clinical studies for accurate interpretation.

Tobacco Use and Environmental Exposure Associated With Respiratory Disease

Take a thorough history of environmental exposures, including smoking history.

G Chronic cigarette smoking can cause chronic bronchitis, emphysema, and lung cancer, and may exacerbate asthma.

G Cough and mucous expectoration from tobacco smoking can sometimes be reversed, and the risk of bronchogenic cancer decreases significantly with discontinuation of smoking.

Examinations, Clinical Studies, and Other Tests for Evaluating Respiratory Disease

The physician needs to perform a detailed respiratory examination and may need chest radiographs, computed tomography (CT) or high-resolution computed tomography (HRCT), and pulmonary function tests.

Chest radiographs correlate poorly with respiratory impairments caused by airflow limitation, such as asthma and emphysema. They are more helpful with respiratory impairments with fibrotic changes.

G CT and HRCT are more sensitive (ie, more likely to detect early respiratory changes in certain pulmonary diseases, such as asbestosis).

G Discontinue respiratory medications for at least 24 hours before spirometry when feasible.

The highest scores on pulmonary function tests (spirometry) are the primary determinants for ascertaining whether respiratory impairment is present.

Use the spirogram values indicating the best effort.

Apply a correction of 0.88 to spirometric values from African Americans, since, as a population, they have lower spirometric values.

G For individuals of other ethnic groups, use the spirometric values for North American whites or other population norms as referenced in the *Guides*.

G Normal lung function is now based on the "lower limit of normal" or the 95% confidence interval for forced vital capacity (FVC), forced expiratory volume in 1 second (FEV_1), and diffusing capacity for carbon monoxide (DCO).

Respiratory Impairments

Impairment ratings are given only for a respiratory impairment that meets the criteria for a respiratory disorder as indicated in Table 5-12 and that impacts ADL. All respiratory impairments that meet spirometry criteria are rated by means of Table 5-12.

G Occupational asthma is rated on the basis of severity of the condition, medication use, and impact on ADL incorporating recommendations from the American Thoracic Society.

G Occupational asthma requires the assessment and scoring of three criteria: postbronchodilator FEV_1; percent change in FEV_1 or the provocative concentration of methacholine or histamine that causes a 20% fall in FEV_1 (PC_{20}) or equivalent to indicate airway hyperresponsiveness; and medication use.

Comparison of Tables Between the Fifth and Fourth *Guides* Editions

The following table summarizes the key points and changes between the fourth and fifth editions of the *Guides*.

Comparison of Tables Between the Fifth and Fourth *Guides* Editions			
Table Topic	**5th Edition Table Number**	**4th Edition Table Number**	**Summary of Changes in 5th Edition**
Dyspnea	5-1	1	None
Normal FVC for men	5-2a	2	Comment regarding subtraction for confidence interval (CI) deleted
Lower limit of FVC for men	5-2b		New; subtracted 95% CI from values in 5-2a
Normal FVC for women	5-3a	3	Comment regarding subtraction for CI deleted
Lower limit of FVC for women	5-3b		New; subtracted 95% CI from values in 5-3a
Normal FEV_1 for men	5-4a	4	None
Lower limit of FEV_1 for men	5-4b		New; subtracted 95% CI from values in 5-4a
Normal FEV_1 for women	5-5a	5	None
Lower limit of FEV_1 for women	5-5b		New; subtracted 95% CI from values in 5-5a
Normal DCO for men	5-6a	6	None
Lower limit of DCO for men	5-6b		New; subtracted 95% CI from values in 5-6a
Normal DCO for women	5-7a	7	None
Lower limit of DCO for women	5-7b		New; subtracted 95% CI from values in 5-2a; provides subtractions of CI from 5-7a
Physical work intensity classification	5-8	9	None
Asthma	5-9		New; provides numeric classification for asthma severity

Chapter 5

Table Topic	5th Edition Table Number	4th Edition Table Number	Summary of Changes in 5th Edition
Asthma	5-10		New; provides WPI % ratings for asthma
Karnofsky scale	5-11	11	None
Impairment classification for respiratory disorders	5-12	8	Higher threshold for class 2 impairment
Respiratory impairment evaluation summary	5-13		New; summarizes clinical evaluation of permanent respiratory impairments, cross-referenced to *Guides* tables

Comparison of Tables Between the Fifth and Fourth *Guides* Editions, *continued*

Introduction

The *Guides 5th* respiratory chapter now includes expanded discussion of conditions such as asthma, hypersensitivity pneumonitis, and pneumoconiosis. A new system for rating impairment caused by asthma has been added. Use of 80% predicted for the lower limit of normal FEV_1 and FVC and 70% predicted for the lower limit of normal for DCO has been replaced with use of the lower 95% confidence interval. A new section has also been added on rating occupational asthma, based on severity of the condition, medication use, and impact on ADL, incorporating recommendations from the American Thoracic Society. Sleep apnea information has been updated, although ratings are not provided. However, individuals with pulmonary hypertension from sleep apnea can be rated under the *Guides* section on vascular disease. If necessary, the physician can use the ratings for sleep disturbances provided in the nervous system chapter, especially if the sleep disturbance has a central nervous system component.

5.1 Principles of Assessment

This new section emphasizes the difference between a pulmonary impairment and impairment rating. Respiratory impairments that decrease lung function and affect the ability to perform ADL are given an impairment rating. Some respiratory impairments (eg, a limited pleural plaque) may not affect function or ADL but would be noted as impairments. The physician determines whether a respiratory impairment is present and, if so, whether the impairment meets the criteria for a respiratory disorder that impacts ADL, qualifying for an impairment rating as listed in Table 5-12.

The medical history that includes information on symptoms, tobacco use, and environmental and occupational exposures has been expanded. The section on occupational history emphasizes the key components: a chronologic history of work activities, the type of work, materials used, the frequency and intensity of exposure or activity, and any personal protective equipment available. Symptoms, although diagnostically useful and necessary, are not the sole criteria for impairment ratings. Symptoms that indicate respiratory impairment require confirmation with clinical findings, such as pulmonary function tests.

5.2 Symptoms Associated With Respiratory Disease

The major symptoms of respiratory disease, including dyspnea, cough, sputum production, hemoptysis, wheezing, and chest pain or tightness, were slightly revised in the *Guides 5th*. Classifying the severity of symptoms, such as dyspnea, will assist in determining the impact of the impairment on ADL. Respiratory symptoms need to be integrated with the physical examination and clinical studies for accurate interpretation.

5.3 Tobacco Use and Environmental Exposure Associated With Respiratory Disease

The *Guides 5th* emphasizes the need to take a thorough history of environmental exposures, including cigarette smoking. Chronic smoking can cause chronic bronchitis, emphysema, and lung cancer, and may exacerbate asthma. Respiratory impairment is also more common among smokers. Physicians may be asked to separate out the effects of tobacco smoke from environmental exposure.

For individuals who had pre–work placement pulmonary function testing or a documented history of respiratory impairment caused by smoking, the respiratory impairment from smoking may be apportioned if data indicated that a ratable impairment resulted from tobacco use.

EXAMPLE

John, a 50-year-old welder, has welded intermittently over 10 years but has worked for the last 5 years in a plant where he is exposed to significant welding fumes. John is 188 cm in height and weighs 86.4 kg, with a 35-pack-year (1-pack/day) smoking history. Prior to starting this latest welding job, he had preplacement pulmonary function tests, which showed an observed FVC of 5.28 L, predicted of 5.56, and ratio of observed to predicted of 95%; observed FEV_1 of 3.85 L, predicted of 4.37, and ratio of observed to predicted of 88%; observed FEV_1/FVC of 73%; DCO of 91%; and oxygen consumption (VO_2) of 18 mL/kg. On the basis of these values, John had a 0% respiratory whole person impairment (WPI) prior to his current employment.

Eighteen months ago while employed at this facility, John develops a chronic, productive cough and is diagnosed with chronic bronchitis. John continues to smoke one pack of cigarettes per day, smoking during breaks at work. His repeat pulmonary function test results now meet criteria for a 10% respiratory WPI. His initial pulmonary function testing did not meet criteria for a ratable impairment; therefore, his prior tobacco use and welding exposure do not constitute an apportionable, preexisting condition.

M E D I C A L   T I P
Obtain detailed information on smoking and occupational exposures when relevant.

L E G A L   T I P
Enhanced susceptibility resulting from tobacco smoke is not by itself a preexisting, apportionable condition or impairment. In the occupational setting, the employer in most states is obligated to "take the workers as he finds them."

5.4 Examinations, Clinical Studies, and Other Tests for Evaluating Respiratory Disease

This section in *Guides 5th* expands on concepts discussed in the Fourth Edition. The physician needs to perform a detailed respiratory examination and may need chest radiographs, CT or HRCT, and pulmonary function tests. Chest radiographs correlate poorly with respiratory impairments caused by airflow limitation, such as asthma and emphysema. They are more closely correlated with respiratory impairments with fibrotic changes, as seen with some interstitial disorders such as silicosis or pneumoconiosis.

CT and HRCT are more sensitive and more likely to detect early or milder interstitial abnormalities in certain pulmonary diseases, such as asbestosis. These tests are discussed in greater detail in the Fifth Edition.

Pulmonary function tests play a central role in determining whether a respiratory impairment qualifies for an impairment rating. Pulmonary function tests assess mechanical properties of the lung, are quantifiable and reproducible, and can provide a historical assessment. However, an individual can have normal pulmonary functions and still have lung disease. Normal pulmonary function tests indicate that the respiratory system has normal gas volume capacity, normal resistance to airflow, and normal gas diffusion. Individuals with normal pulmonary function test results can still have cancer, a localized infection, or even asthma if there was no obstruction at the time the test was performed.[1]

The scores on pulmonary function tests, DCO, and, in select individuals, VO_2 max, are the primary determinants for establishing the class of respiratory impairment. Pulmonary function tests include spirometry that measures FVC, FEV_1, and the ratio of these measurements (FEV_1/FVC). The physician should use the highest FVC and FEV_1 values to calculate the ratio, even if these measurements occur on different respiratory efforts, even if they are after bronchodilator use. Bronchodilators are administered if the FEV_1/FVC is below 0.70 or if there is wheezing on physical examination. The physician should note that any values obtained were after bronchodilator use. Use the spirogram indicating the best effort. It is essential that the pulmonary function tests be performed on standardized equipment with validated administrative techniques. When tolerated, respiratory medications should be removed for at least 24 hours before spirometry.

Both the Fourth and Fifth Editions use the normal values for pulmonary function determined by Crapo et al.[2] A correction of 0.88 is applied to spirometric values from African Americans, since, as a population, they have lower spirometric values. Although these values are commonly used and were used in the Fourth Edition, these are not the only normal values, especially for individuals of other ethnic groups. For other ethnic or mixed groups, the physician may use the values for North American whites, or other population norms as referenced in the *Guides*.[3-5]

A new set of "lower limit of normal values" for FVC, FEV_1, and DCO was introduced into the Fifth Edition. These numbers, based on recommendations from the American Thoracic Society, indicate that the lower limit of normal lies at the fifth percentile of the population.[6] In the Fifth Edition, the lower limits of normal are used to distinguish between class 1 and class 2 of respiratory impairment in Table 5-12.

Use of the lower limit of normal for determining class 1 and class 2 status will result in some changes compared with the Fourth Edition. By using the lower limit of normal, some men who qualified for class 1 and 2 impairment will be pushed back into a lower class. It will especially affect men who are shorter and older. Women will be less severely affected, but, again, it will most affect women who are shorter and older. This change was instituted based on the widely held assumption that respiratory function can be considered within normal functional levels for all individuals who *are* above the 95% confidence interval for height, age, and sex.

Cardiopulmonary exercise testing is used judiciously when an individual's symptoms do not correlate with pulmonary function tests, to differentiate cardiac from respiratory impairment, and to provide further information on the nature and severity of an impairment.

5.4g Criteria for Rating Impairment Due to Respiratory Disease

The physician performs spirometry and DCO on all individuals who have a respiratory impairment. VO_2 max may also be indicated in some individuals.

To not receive an impairment rating or to be placed in class 1 for a 0% impairment, the individual must have met the lower limit of normal for FVC, FEV_1, FEV_1/FVC, and DCO or VO_2 max. If any of these criteria are not met, the individual is placed in a higher impairment rating class.

The only significant change in Table 5-12 in the Fifth Edition is that the lower limit of normal is used for classes 1 and 2.

Table 5-12 Impairment Classification for Respiratory Disorders, Using Pulmonary Function and Exercise Test Results*

Pulmonary Function Test	Class 1 0% Impairment of the Whole Person	Class 2 10%-25% Impairment of the Whole Person	Class 3 26%-50% Impairment of the Whole Person	Class 4 51%-100% Impairment of the Whole Person
FVC	Measured FVC ≥ lower limit of normal (see Tables 5-2b and 5-3b) *and*	≥ 60% of predicted and < lower limit of normal *or*	≥ 51% and ≤ 59% of predicted *or*	≤ 50% of predicted *or*
FEV_1	Measured FEV_1 ≥ lower limit of normal (see Tables 5-4b and 5-5b) *and*	≥ 60% of predicted and < lower limit of normal *or*	≥ 41% and ≤ 59% of predicted *or*	≤ 40% of predicted *or*
FEV_1/FVC	FEV_1/FVC ≥ lower limit of normal† *and*			
Dco	Dco ≥ lower limit of normal (see Tables 5-6b and 5-7b) *or*	≥ 60% of predicted and < lower limit of normal *or*	≥ 41% and ≤ 59% of predicted *or*	≤ 40% of predicted *or*
Vo_2max	Vo_2max ≥ 25 mL/(kg•min) *or* > 7.1 METS	≥ 20 and < 25 mL/(kg•min) *or* 5.7-7.1 METS	≥ 15 and < 20 mL/(kg•min) *or* 4.3 to < 5.7 METS	< 15 mL/(kg•min) *or* < 1.05 L/min *or* < 4.3 METS

*FVC indicates forced vital capacity; FEV_1, forced expiratory volume in the first second; DCO, diffusing capacity for carbon monoxide; Vo_2max, maximum oxygen consumption; and METS, metabolic equivalents (multiples of resting oxygen uptake). DCO is primarily of value for persons with restrictive lung disease. In classes 2 and 3, if FVC, FEV_1, and FEV_1/FVC are normal and DCO is between 41% and 79%, then an exercise test is required to determine level of impairment.

†Refer to Crapo RO, Morris AH, Gardner RM for the lower limit of normal for FEV_1/FVC.[2]

> ### MEDICAL TIP
>
> If the physician is asked to apportion respiratory impairment between two causative factors (eg, cigarette smoking and chronic obstructive pulmonary disease) and subsequent exposure to coal dust and coal worker's pneumoconiosis, use the same criteria for rating both impairments. It would not be appropriate to rate the earlier impairment on the basis of the Fourth Edition and the subsequent impairment with *Guides 5th*, unless both impairments qualify for class 3 rating or higher. Since impairment rating criteria within classes 1 and 2 respiratory impairment are significantly different, use the same table and method for evaluating different impairments.

> ### LEGAL TIP
>
> The *Guides* (in both fourth and fifth editions) does not account for early stages of respiratory impairment; that is, there is no allowance for an impairment between 0% and 10%. Again, note that a preexisting condition is not the same as a preexisting impairment. The preexisting condition must meet the minimum criteria in class 2 of Table 5-12 to be considered a preexisting impairment. Tables in the Fifth Edition treat any measurable impairment less than a fixed whole-number percentage (Table 5-12, where [WPI <10%] = 0%; Table 15-3, where [WPI <5%] = 0%).

5.5 Asthma

The Fifth Edition discusses asthma in greater detail, especially the classification for occupational asthma. Occupational asthma can be caused by sensitizers or irritants. Sensitizers are classified as either high molecular weight or low molecular weight. Individuals with sensitizer-induced asthma, on the basis of an allergic response to the allergen, need to discontinue further exposure.

Before determining an impairment rating for asthma, the physician needs to ensure that the asthma is stable, at MMI, and well managed. An evaluation to determine whether a permanent impairment rating is assigned for asthma requires the assessment and scoring of three criteria: postbronchodilator FEV_1; percent change of FEV_1 or PC_{20} or equivalent to indicate airway hyperresponsiveness; and medication use. Medication use can be determined on the basis of the history presented in medical records. Add the scores from these criteria to obtain a summary score for respiratory impairment. If the individual meets the threshold in any one of these categories, as indicated in Table 5-9, he or she would receive a score between 1 and 11, which would meet the criteria for a permanent impairment rating. The total score is translated into a WPI rating, as indicated in Table 5-10. These impairment percentages were chosen because they correspond to the same rating classes as used for all respiratory impairments.

Chapter 5

Table 5-10 Impairment Rating for Asthma*		
Total Asthma Score	% Impairment Class	Impairment of the Whole Person
0	1	0%
1-5	2	10%-25%
6-9	3	26%-50%
10-11 or asthma not controlled despite maximal treatment, ie, FEV_1 remaining <50% despite use of > 20 mg/day of prednisone	4	51%-100%

*The impairment rating is calculated as the sum of the individual's scores from Table 5-9. FEV_1 indicates forced expiratory volume in the first second.

EXAMPLE

Joan develops asthma while working as a laboratory animal handler. Subsequent testing indicates that she has an allergy to guinea pig proteins. Although she does not work with animals in her new job, she has mild to moderate asthma attacks on a monthly basis. During testing when she is asymptomatic, her FEV_1 is 85% of predicted, which is greater than the lower limit of normal (score 0) postbronchodilator FEV_1. A methacholine challenge test indicates airway hyperresponsiveness at 4 mg/mL (score = 1). She uses bronchodilators several times per month (score = 1), before strenuous activity, such as housecleaning, and when exposed to dust, colds, or cold, dry air. She avoids homes with furbearing pets whenever possible. Her findings are consistent with an asthma score of 2, indicating a class 1 impairment. Since she has minimal impairment of her ADL, she would be given a rating of 15%.

MEDICAL TIP
Review prior records to determine the minimum medication needed to control exacerbations and assess how ADL are impacted.

5.6 Obstructive Sleep Apnea

5.7 Hypersensitivity Pneumonitis

5.8 Pneumoconiosis

Sections 5.6, 5.7, and 5.8 and their impairment rating criteria are unchanged.

5.9 Lung Cancer

The *Guides 5th* provides discussions of several respiratory conditions, including obstructive sleep apnea, hypersensitivity pneumonitis, pneumoconiosis, and lung cancer. Sleep apnea is not given an impairment rating in this chapter. However, some individuals with sleep apnea and centrally mediated dysfunction can be rated in the nervous system chapter.

The other respiratory conditions, including others not in the above list, can be rated by means of Table 5-12. Lung cancer, with tumor present, is still rated as class 4, with a Karnofsy scale used to assess the impact of the condition on ADL.

5.10 Permanent Impairment Due to Respiratory Disorders

This section lists the pulmonary function and exercise test criteria for determining permanent impairment, followed by case examples. To choose an exact impairment rating percentage, determine the impact on ADL, and select an impairment rating within the range that reflects that impact.

5.11 Respiratory Impairment Evaluation Summary

Table 5-13 provides an excellent overview of the clinical evaluation findings and impairment criteria for impairments of the respiratory tract, cross-referenced to appropriate impairment rating tables in the chapter.

Chapter 5

Table 5-13 Repiratory Impairment Evaluation Summary

Disorder	History, Including Selected Relevant Symptoms	Examination Record	Assessment of Respiratory Function
General	Respiratory symptoms (eg, cough); general symptoms Impact of symptoms on function and ability to do daily activities; prognosis if change anticipated Review medical history	Comprehensive physical examination; detailed respiratory system assessment	Data derived from relevant studies (eg, pulmonary function tests)
Obstructive Disorders	Dyspnea; cough; sputum production; infections; medication use; exercise tolerance	Note breath sounds, wheeze, loud P$_2$, jugular vein distention, right heart prominence	Pulmonary function: spirometry, lung volumes, diffusing capacity, methacholine challenge, radiographs
Restrictive Disorders	Dyspnea; cough; fatigue; sputum; exercise tolerance	Chest wall excursion; crackles; clubbing	Pulmonary function: spirometry, lung volumes, diffusing capacity, imaging studies
Cancer	Exercise tolerance; dyspnea; chest pain; fatigue; weight loss; tobacco use; environmental exposures	Chest wall excursion; crackles; clubbing; adenopathy	Bronchoscopy; pulmonary function tests; biopsy

References

1. Functional Assessment of the Lung and Diagnostic Techniques. In: Dale D, Federman D, eds. *Scientific American Medicine.* New York, NY: Scientific American Medicine; 1997.

2. Crapo RO, Morris AH, Gardner RM. Reference spirometric values using techniques and equipment that meet ATS recommendations. *Am Rev Respir Dis.* 1981;123:659-664.

3. Hankiinson JL, Bang KM. Acceptability and reproducibility criteria of the American Thoracic Society as observed in a sample of the general population. *Am Rev Respir Dis.* 1991;143:516-521.

4. Hankiinson JL, Odencrantz JR, Fedan KB. Spirometric reference values from a sample of the US general population. *Am J Respir Crit Care Med.* 1999;159:179-187.

5. American Thoracic Society. Standardization of spirometry, 1994 update. *Am J Respir Crit Care Med.* 1995;152:1107-1136.

6. American Thoracic Society. Lung function testing: selection of reference values and interpretational strategies. *Am Rev Respir Dis.* 1991;144:1202-1218.

End-Organ Damage	Diagnosis	Degree of Impairment
Include assessment of sequelae, including end-organ damage and impairment	Record all pertinent diagnosis(es); note if they are at maximal medical improvement; if not, discuss under what conditions and when stability is expected	Criteria outlined in this chapter See Table 5-12
Assess relevant organs (eg, cardiac function, cor pulmonale)	Asthma; chronic bronchitis and emphysema; other obstructive diseases	See Table 5-12 for asthma See Tables 5-9 and 5-10
Assess cardiac function	Idiopathic pulmonary fibrosis; asbestosis; pneumoconiosis; chest wall disorders; others	See Table 5-12
Assess other organ function; signs of metastases	Squamous, adeno, small cell, etc	See Table 5-11

Chapter 6

The Digestive System

Introduction

This chapter provides an overview of key points and changes (identified with an icon **G**) made in Chapter 6 of the AMA *Guides to the Evaluation of Permanent Impairment, Fifth Edition* (*Guides 5th*), illustrates these changes in a table comparison, and discusses the purpose and implications of the major changes, with illustrative examples. The numbered section titles within this chapter correspond to sections within Chapter 6 of *Guides 5th*. Only key principles or important changes are included in this chapter.

This chapter addresses only major changes in the assessment of digestive impairments and indicates some areas of interest in workers' compensation. The impairment ratings have changed only in the colon disorders, for greater consistency with the upper intestine rating scale.

Key Points and Changes

G For digestive disorders, integrate subjective and objective data to determine the extent of the impairment on activities of daily living (ADL).

Weight loss is an essential criterion for evaluating severity and consequences of gastrointestinal disorders.

Digestive impairment ratings reflect anatomic, physiologic, and functional abnormalities.

G Colon and rectal disorders are given the same weighting as upper digestive tract disorders.

Hernia impairments and even repairs, which are uncomplicated and do not impact the ability to perform ADL, are not given an impairment rating.

Comparison of Tables Between the Fifth and Fourth *Guides* Editions

The following table summarizes the key points and changes in tables between the fourth and fifth editions of the *Guides*.

Comparison of Tables Between the Fifth and Fourth *Guides* Editions

Table Topic	5th Edition Table Number	4th Edition Table Number	Summary of Changes in 5th Edition
Desirable weights for men by height and body build	6-1	1	Single table divided into separate tables for men and women; no content changes
Desirable weights for women by height and body build	6-2	1	Single table divided into separate tables for men and women; no content changes
Permanent impairment due to upper digestive tract disorders	6-3	2	None
Permanent impairment due to colonic and rectal disorders	6-4	3	Class 3 increased to 25%-49% (previously 25%-39%), and class 4 increased to 50%-75% (previously 40%-60%)
Permanent impairment due to anal disorders	6-5	4	None
Permanent impairment due to surgically created stomas	6-6	5	None
Permanent impairment due to liver disease	6-7	6	Ratings and criteria unchanged; table split into two different tables
Permanent impairment due to biliary tract disease	6-8	6	None
Permanent impairment due to herniation	6-9	7	None
Digestive system impairment evaluation summary	6-10		New

Introduction

The digestive system chapter incorporates major changes in the gastroen-
terology field. Treatment for peptic ulcer disease can now eradicate this
formerly permanent impairment. Liver transplantation, parenteral nutrition,
and advancement in intestinal anastomosis and stomas have led to decreased
permanent impairment ratings. The digestive system, which includes the
alimentary canal, liver, biliary tract, and pancreas, is organized according to
the major organs.

6.1 Principles of Assessment

The assessment of digestive impairment depends on the integration of subjective factors, such as symptoms, with objective factors, including clinical
signs and functional tests. Major objective clinical studies include imaging
procedures, endoscopy, biopsy, and functional tests. This section of the
Guides outlines clinical investigations for each area of the digestive tract.

Weight loss is an essential criterion for evaluating severity and consequences
of gastrointestinal disorders. When preinjury or preillness weight is not the
most desirable weight, the physician needs to use clinical judgment regarding
the most suitable weight.

Symptoms and signs that were previously discussed separately in each
organ or body area are now discussed as a group in this section.

A gastrointestinal system has no impairment rating when "an individual…
performs all activities of daily living with only normal, occasional
gastrointestinal symptoms; no limitation of activities; no special diet;
and no required medications, with adequate reserve capacity that allows
the body to obtain the required nutrition and maintain normal weight."

6.2 Upper Digestive Tract (Esophagus, Stomach and Duodenum, Small Intestine, and Pancreas)

The criteria in Table 6-3 for rating impairment of the upper digestive tract are unchanged. The case examples indicate some revisions, namely that gastric ulcers that are healed through recent antibiotic protocols would not meet criteria for a permanent impairment rating. In the Fourth Edition, before curative therapy was available, ulcers were not cured and were therefore given a permanent impairment rating.

6.3 Colon, Rectum, and Anus

The impairment ratings (IRs) for colon, rectal, and anal impairments are changed and are now consistent with the upper digestive tract IRs. Lower alimentary tract disorders warrant the same weights as upper alimentary tract disorders; hence, the impairment ratings for classes 3 and 4 were increased in the Fifth Edition. A condition such as chronic, recurrent Crohn's disease, Example 6-20, now has a 45% whole person impairment (WPI) rating compared with the previous 35% WPI rating. The classes and ratings for anal disease are unchanged.

MEDICAL TIP

Assess the degree of digestive system permanent impairment. To determine whether work factors were a cause of the condition, review the medical history, workplace environment, and medical literature to see if such a relationship is reported and whether certain occupational cohorts are at increased risk for gastrointestinal events.

LEGAL TIP

Herniations constitute the most common impairment in workers' compensation cases reported from this chapter. Other digestive system impairments can arise from multiple trauma (eg, from motor vehicle accidents, impalement, crush accidents, falls) but can also arise from environmental exposures, resulting in occupational disease. Note also that legal cause may be different than medical cause. Digestive system impairment may also combine with or arise from human immunodeficiency virus or acquired immunodeficiency syndrome impairments (see Chapter 9).

6.4 Enterocutaneous Fistulas

6.5 Liver and Biliary Tract

6.6 Hernias

Sections 6.4, 6.5, and 6.6 impairment rating criteria are largely unchanged. As indicated in Example 6-29, an uncomplicated hernia that does not limit the ability to perform ADL is given a 0% WPI rating.

6.7 Digestive System Impairment Evaluation Summary

Table 6-10 provides an excellent overview of the clinical evaluation findings and impairment criteria for impairments of the digestive tract, cross-referenced to appropriate impairment rating tables in the chapter.

Table 6-10 Digestive System Impairment Evaluation Summary

Disorder	History, Including Selected Relevant Symptoms	Examination Record	Assessment of Dysfunction
General	Gastrointestinal symptoms (eg, change in appetite, pain, diarrhea) and general symptoms; impact of symptoms on function and ability to do daily activities Prognosis if change anticipated Review medical history	Comprehensive physical examination; detailed GI system assessment	Data derived from relevant studies (eg, barium swallow, upper and lower endoscopy)
Esophageal Disease	Dysphagia for solids and/or liquids G-E reflux Previous proximal gastrectomy or interposition surgery Need for dilations and/or medications History of aspiration Limitation of physical activity	Evidence of weight loss Duration of symptoms Evidence of scleroderma or other mesenchymal disease Previous motility studies for achalasia or diffuse spasm	Location and degree of stricture Is proximal esophagus dilated? Endoscopic appearance and biopsy results
Stomach Diseases	Vomiting, weight loss, past gastrectomy dumping symptoms; family history of ulcer or endocrinopathy Persistent ulcer diathesis despite treatment Any history of use of ulcerogenic drugs (NSAIDS, ASA) Limited physical activity	Weight loss; diabetes with neuropathy	Size of gastric pouch Location and function of gastro-jejunal amastomosis Endoscopic evaluation of structures Motility studies
Small Intestine Disease	Diarrhea (frequency, nocturnal); abdominal colic and distention History of volvulus Hemorrhage Family history of celiac sprue, motility disorder Weight loss Previous surgery Limited activity	Note weight loss Abdominal distention, masses Perianal disease Arthropathy Presence of dermatitis herpetiformis	Barium studies Possibly enteroclysis study, jejunal cultures, and mucosal biopsy Antigliadin antibody Motility studies Amount of intact small intestine (estimate whether more or less than 200 cm)
Pancreatic Disease	History of acute pancreatitis (documented) Frequency; duration; associated jaundice, nausea, anorexia; alcohol intake; adequacy of pain control GI bleeding (consider splenic vein thrombosis) Associated chronic lung disease (think of cystic fibrosis)	Abdominal masses; fistulae; previous gallstones; evidence of weight loss; jaundice	Ultrasound pancreas and biliary tract Consider transduodenal ultrasonography, CT scan, ERCP, measure of steatorrhea, plain film of abdomen for calcification Sweat Na+ to exclude cystic fibrosis

	Assessment of End-Organ Damage	Diagnosis(es)	Degree of Impairment
	Include assessment of sequelae, including end-organ damage and impairment	Record all pertinent diagnosis(es); note if they are at maximal medical improvement; if not, discuss under what conditions and when stability is expected	Criteria outlined in this chapter
	Motility studies if indicated Response to therapy Need for esophageal stent or interposition surgery Frequency of dilations	GERD with inflammatory stricture Barrett's esophagus with or without malignant change Stricture secondary to scleroderma Achalasia, diffuse spasm, Zenker's diverticulum	See Table 6-3
	Response to dietary management Trial of antisecretory drugs, prokinetic agents	Postgastrectomy state Diabetic gastroparesis Possible Zollinger-Ellison syndrome Paraesophageal hernia with gastric volvulus	See Table 6-3
	Effects of malabsorption of iron, B_{12}, folate tetany Failure to grow Response to gluten restriction, steroids Parenteral nutrition	Celiac sprue possible lymphoma complication Regional enteritis; Crohn's; ischemic bowel disease Radiation enteritis Chronic pseudo-obstruction; mechanical obstruction (adhesions)	See Table 6-3
	Degree of fat maldigestion and malabsorption Presence of diabetes mellitus Need for pain control, including celiac plexus and/or splanchnic block	Alcoholic pancreatitis Chronic relapsing pancreatitis Pancreatitis secondary to biliary tract disease Cystic fibrosis	See Table 6-3

Table 6-10 Digestive System Impairment Evaluation Summary (continued)

Disorder	History, Including Selected Relevant Symptoms	Examination Record	Assessment of Dysfunction
Large Intestine Disease	History of previous colon surgery (length remaining, nature of anastomoses) Bleeding; need for transfusions Stool frequency, pattern (nocturnal incontinence) Abdominal pain Weight loss Limited activity	Abdominal masses Perianal disease Fistulae arthropathy	Sigmoidoscopy; colonoscopy Possible barium studies; mucosal biopsies Defecation studies; motility; possible EMG of sphincter activity
Liver disease	Alcohol intake (past, present) Previous use of hepatotoxic drugs Presence of ascites, edema, jaundice, iron overload (multiple transfusions) History of GI hemorrhage Pruritus; primary biliary cirrhosis Limited physical activity	Cutaneous and ocular signs of chronic liver disease Ascites; edema; skin pigmentation (hemochromatosis) Evidence of previous surgery in region of liver Keyser-Fleischer rings in eyes Evidence of ulcerative colitis Xanthomata	Nutritional status, including hemoglobin, protein, prothrombin time Platelets Etiologic studies, including complete hepatitis serology markers Renal function HIV studies Diabetes if hemochromatosis (serum iron and ferritin saturation antitrypsin Antimitochondrial antibody; exclude genetic and infiltrative diseases (eg, amyloidosis, sarcoidosis, polycystic disease) Copper studies
Biliary Tract Disease	Previous biliary tract surgery Episodes of cholecystitis, biliary colic, jaundice Family history of bilirubin metabolism disorder Bleeding; pruritus	Previous attempts at dissolution therapy and or lithotripsy Jaundice Presence of scratch marks Splenomegaly Abdominal fistula	Ultrasound studies ERCP Transhepatic cholangiography if needed Prothrombin time
Hernia	Discomfort, pain associated with postural changes Limited physical activity	Abdominal protrusion or swelling	Roentgenography; CT scan

Assessment of End-Organ Damage	Diagnosis(es)	Degree of Impairment
Uncontrollable diarrhea; intractible constipation Megacolon	Inflammatory bowel disease; ulcerative colitis; Crohn's disease; colectomy with ileostomy or ileoanal pouch anastomosis	See Table 6-4
CNS tolerance to hemorrhage Fluid and salt overload Possible pancreatic insufficiency Secondary development of hepatoma Intractable prothrombin time prolongation; platelet deficiency; leukopenia	Alcoholic liver disease; cirrhosis; hepatoma; posthepatitic cirrhosis (previous HBV, HCV); hemochromatosis; Wilson's disease Primary biliary cirrhosis Sclerosing cholangitis	See Table 6-7
Persistent hyperbilirubinemia after obstruction relieved Findings at surgery	Biliary tract stricture; impacted stones; sclerosing cholangitis Primary biliary cirrhosis	See Table 6-8
Possible incarceration or strangulation of bowel or omentum	Abdominal wall hernia; umbilical hernia; incisional hernia; inguinal hernia; femoral hernia	See Table 6-9

The Urinary and Reproductive Systems

Introduction

This chapter provides an overview of key points and changes (identified with an icon **G**) made in Chapter 7 of the AMA *Guides to the Evaluation of Permanent Impairment, Fifth Edition* (*Guides 5th*), illustrates these changes in a table comparison, and discusses the purpose and implications of the major changes, with illustrative examples. The numbered section titles within this chapter correspond to sections within Chapter 7 of the *Guides 5th*. Only key principles or important changes are included in this chapter.

Key Points and Changes

G For urinary and reproductive impairments, integrate subjective and objective data to determine the extent of the impairment on activities of daily living (ADL).

G *Combine* an additional *1% to 3%* with the renal impairment rating because of treatment effects, medication effects, or pain not customary for a particular condition.

G Rate primary bladder impairments in this chapter. Use the nervous or musculoskeletal system approach to bladder problems caused by nerve or musculoskeletal problems.

G All tables are revised to eliminate overlap in ratings at 10%, 15%, 20%, 25%, 35%, 40%, and 60%.

Comparison of Tables Between the Fifth and Fourth *Guides* Editions

The following table summarizes the key points and changes in tables between the fourth and fifth editions of the *Guides*.

Comparison of Tables Between the Fifth and Fourth *Guides* Editions

Table Topic	5th Edition Table Number	4th Edition Table Number	Summary of Changes in 5th Edition
Permanent impairment due to upper urinary tract disease	7-1	1	Lost use of single kidney included in class 1; kidney transplant in class 2; peritoneal dialysis and hemodialysis in class 4
Permanent impairment due to urinary diversion disorders	7-2	2	Stylistic
Permanent impairment due to bladder disease	7-3		New; class 2 increased to 16%-40% (previously 15%-34%), and class 3 increased to 41%-70% (previously 35%-59%) and class 4, 60%-95%; see *Guides 4th*, section 11.3
Permanent impairment due to urethral disease	7-4		New; class 2 changed to 11%-20% (previously 10%-20%), and class 3, 21%-40%; see *Guides 4th*, section 11.4
Permanent impairment due to penile disease	7-5		New; classes unchanged from *Guides 4th*, section 11.5a; overlap eliminated
Permanent impairment due to scrotal disease	7-6		New; classes unchanged from *Guides 4th*, section 11.5b; overlap eliminated

Comparison of Tables Between the Fifth and Fourth *Guides* Editions, *continued*

Table Topic	5th Edition Table Number	4th Edition Table Number	Summary of Changes in 5th Edition
Permanent impairment due to testicular, epididymal disease	7-7		New; classes unchanged from *Guides 4th*, section 11.5c; overlap eliminated
Permanent impairment due to prostate and seminal vesicle disease	7-8		New; classes unchanged from *Guides 4th*, section 11.5d; overlap eliminated
Permanent Impairment due to vulval and vaginal disease	7-9		New; classes unchanged from *Guides 4th*, section 11.6a; overlap eliminated
Permanent impairment due to cervical and uterine disease	7-10		New; classes unchanged from *Guides 4th*, section 11.6b; overlap eliminated
Permanent impairment due to fallopian tube and ovarian disease	7-11		New; classes unchanged from *Guides 4th*, section 11.6c; overlap eliminated
Urinary and reproductive systems impairment evaluation summary	7-12		New

Introduction

The urinary and reproductive systems chapter has been revised to incorporate advances in urology, especially changes in the understanding of bladder impairment, and in the reproductive system. The urinary system consists of the upper urinary tract (kidneys and ureters), the bladder, and the urethra. The impairment ratings and criteria have changed in bladder disorders. The male and female reproductive organs are discussed in separate sections within this chapter and are unchanged from the Fourth Edition.

7.1 Principles of Assessment

The assessment of urologic and reproductive impairment depends on the integration of subjective factors, such as symptoms, with objective factors, including clinical signs and functional tests. If urinary impairment accompanies other impairments, such as musculoskeletal impairment, determine each impairment separately and combine these into a whole person impairment (WPI) rating.

7.2 The Urinary System

This section discusses common clinical symptoms, signs, and studies to assess urinary impairment. There is additional discussion about the use of specific tests to distinguish pathology in specific areas of the urinary tract.

7.3 Upper Urinary Tract

The upper urinary tract disorders include the kidneys and ureters. As in the Fourth Edition, this section discusses impairment ratings for loss of one kidney (10% WPI rating), even with normal kidney function, since the normal organ and safety factor is lost. Successful renal transplantation remains at a class 2, or 15% to 34% WPI, the exact number dependent on the impact on ADL.

This section also mistakenly indicates that the physician may "add 0% to 5% to the final renal function impairment estimate, as discussed in Chapter 1 [p 145]." The correct interpretation is that the physician can *combine* an additional *1% to 3%* with the renal impairment rating because of treatment effects, medication effects, or pain not customary for a particular condition. The remainder of this section is nearly identical to the Fourth Edition.

7.4 Urinary Diversion

This section is unchanged from the Fourth Edition.

7.5 Bladder

The impairment criteria and ratings in this section were changed to create broad, nonoverlapping impairment ranges, and include results from urodynamic studies. The ratings for bladder disease, in Table 7-3, differ from the other tables in the *Guides* for bladder impairment, namely Table 15-6 in the spine chapter for neurologic bladder impairment and Table 13-9 in the nervous system chapter. The ratings in Table 7-3 pertain mainly to primary bladder disorders, conditions in which the main problem originates in the bladder. When bladder impairment is the result of dysfunction of the nervous system, as with spinal or neurologic disorders, the bladder impairment is assessed on the basis of tables in the spine or nervous system chapters.

The following table outlines the differences between bladder impairment as discussed in the urology and nervous system chapters. There is considerable similarity between the approaches. The slightly lower bladder ratings within the spine and nervous system chapters are partly due to the recognition that neurologic bladder dysfunction would be combined with other neurologic or musculoskeletal deficits.

Differences in Bladder Impairment in Chapters 7 ((The Urinary and Reproductive Systems) and 13 (The Central and Peripheral Nervous System)

Impairment Class	Urinary Table 7-3, Rating Impairment Due to Bladder Disease	Spine Table 15-6d and Nervous System Table 13-19
1	0%-15%	1%-9%
	Signs and symptoms, intermittent treatment, normal functioning between malfunctioning	Some degree of voluntary control, impaired by urgency or intermittent incontinence
2	16%-40%	10%-24%
	Signs and symptoms, severe nocturia, continuous treatment	Good bladder reflex activity, limited capacity, intermittent emptying without voluntary control
3	41%-70%	25%-39%
	Poor reflex activity (intermittent urine dribbling, loss of control) and/or no voluntary control on micturition; reflex or areflexic bladder on urodynamics	Poor reflex activity, intermittent dribbling, no voluntary control
4		40%-60%
		No reflex or voluntary control of bladder

The spine and nervous system maximum bladder impairments are limited at 60% WPI. If other nonbladder symptoms are present (eg, radiculopathy, back pain), use the bladder ratings under Chapter 13 or 15.

The bladder impairment in this chapter reaches a maximum of 70%. Use the ratings in this chapter and especially those between 61% and 70% for a primary condition of the bladder. Bladder conditions rated in the urinary chapter are not combined with other impairments affecting the bladder and are therefore given a higher impairment rating.

Note that case studies 17-18, 17-19, and 17-20, with marked neurologic dysfunction, listed in the *Guides 5th*, use the bladder disease criteria to rate bladder impairment. It is more appropriate to use the criteria listed in the spine or nervous system chapter, which could provide the same rating as listed in these cases.

The *Guides 5th* section on bladder impairment also differs from the Fourth Edition interpretation. The following examples indicate how the Fifth Edition bladder ratings are adjusted to account for the impairment's impact on ADL.

EXAMPLE 7-16

Chronic cystitis; minimal impact on ADL

Fifth Edition rating: 10% WPI

Fourth Edition rating: 20% WPI

EXAMPLE 7-20

Neurogenic bladder impairment; marked impact on ADL

Fifth Edition rating: 60% WPI

Fourth Edition rating: 50% WPI

7.6 Urethra

This section was revised, with a new class (class 3) created to account for ureteral dysfunction that results in urinary incontinence. The impairment ratings in classes 1 and 2 were modified to prevent overlapping impairment ratings. New case examples were added to the retained Fourth Edition examples.

7.7 Male Reproductive Organs

This section in the Fifth Edition is the same as in the Fourth Edition. In both editions, the degree of reproductive impairment for men is weighted on the basis of age. Increase the impairment rating by 50% for men younger than 40 years, and decrease the impairment by 50% for those older than 65 years. For the remaining ages, the impairment rating remains as listed. This weighting is applied to all male reproductive impairments.

7.8 Female Reproductive Organs

This section has been revised to provide case studies of greater relevance; however, the impairment criteria and ratings are unchanged in the Fifth Edition.

Table 7-12 Urinary and Reproductive Systems Impairment Evaluation Summary

Disorder	History, Including Selected Relevant Symptoms	Examination Record	Assessment of Function
General Urinary	Urology symptoms (eg, change in frequency of micturition, dysuria, chills, fever, hematuria, infection, loin or abdominal or costovertebral pain, loss of appetite, weight loss, impaired stamina, edema, dry, dusky skin)	Comprehensive physical examination; abdominal palpation for tenderness; scrotal exam; testes and epididymis exam; rectal exam; prostate exam; vaginal and rectal exam; urine: gross for sugar and albumin; microscopic; culture and cell cytology; ultrasound kidney; cystograde exam with retrograde exam if needed	Blood BUN; creatinine; electrolytes; 24-hr creatinine clearance; fasting blood sugar; renal isotope studies for kidney function; intravenous pyelogram (urogram) for tumors or stone disease or spiral CT; voiding and retrograde cystourethrogram to rule out a stricture; urodynamics; bladder pressure studies for neurogenic bladder dysfunction
Male Reproductive	Sexual history of erections, ejaculation, discharge, scrotal pain, tenderness, reproduction, dysuria, hematuria, nocturia	Genital and rectal examination; prostatic exam	Evaluation of penile blood flow; urinalysis; semen analysis; ultrasound; vasography, hormone levels
Female Reproductive	Abnormalities of menstruation, pain, discharge, change in sensation, altered lubrication	Pelvic examination	Cervical and vaginal smears; ultrasound; hormonal assays; hysterosalpingography; laparoscopy; CT; MRI

MEDICAL TIP
For individuals who have a reproductive impairment and are no longer interested in reproduction, their impairment, which affects ADL less, would be at the lower range of the scale. For someone desiring children, the impairment rating would be higher.

LEGAL TIP
Male and female reproductive and sexual disorders are not commonly considered in workers' compensation disability (employability) determinations. However, sexual function and reproduction may be major life activities in Americans With Disabilities Act analyses. In either system, mental and behavioral consequences (loss of concentration, depression) of lost or reduced sexual function may also impact a disability determination.

7.9 Urinary and Reproductive Systems Impairment Evaluation Summary

Table 7-12 provides an overview of the clinical evaluation findings and impairment criteria for impairments of the urinary and reproductive systems, cross-referenced to appropriate impairment rating tables in the chapter.

	End-Organ Damage	Diagnosis(es)	Degree of Impairment
	Renal failure leading to uremia; congestive heart failure; hepatorenal failure; damage due to metastatic disease—spine, prostate, lungs	Cystitis; bladder tumor; testicular tumor; traumatic loss of testes; urethral damage and stricture; enlarged prostate	Criteria outlined in this chapter; Tables 7-1, 7-2, 7-3, and 7-4
		Absent kidney; polycystic kidney disease; malpositioned kidneys; renal stone disease; renal tumors; neurogenic bladder	
		Erection disorders; fertility disorders	
	Penile or prostatic; if cancer, distant metastatic sites	Impotence; ejaculatory dysfunction; infertility; prostatitis; benign prostatic hypertrophy; cancer of reproductive organs (penile, testicular, prostatic)	Tables 7-5, 7-6, 7-7, and 7-8
	Pelvic area; abdomen	Vaginitis; infection; ulceration; atrophy or hypertrophy; dysplasia; infertility; endometriosis; cancer; strictures; stenosis	Tables 7-9, 7-10, and 7-11

Chapter 8

The Skin

Introduction

This chapter provides an overview of key points and changes (identified with an icon **G**) made in Chapter 8 of the AMA *Guides to the Evaluation of Permanent Impairment, Fifth Edition* (*Guides 5th*), illustrates these changes in a table comparison, and discusses the purpose and implications of the major changes, with illustrative examples. The numbered section titles within this chapter correspond to sections within Chapter 7 of the *Guides 5th*. Only key principles or important changes are included in this chapter.

Key Points and Changes

G Additional skin impairments are discussed in this edition: contact dermatitis, natural rubber latex allergy, and skin cancer.

Determine that the skin impairment has reached maximal medical improvement (MMI).

G Assign impairment ratings based on three criteria: the frequency with which skin disorder signs and symptoms are present, the performance of activities of daily living (ADL), and whether or not treatment is needed.

Integrate findings from the clinical examination, diagnostic procedures, medication history, and impact on ADL to determine the severity of the condition and, hence, which rating should be selected within a class.

When other impairments coexist with skin impairments, combine the skin with the other whole person impairment rating.

Comparison of Tables Between the Fifth and Fourth *Guides* Editions

The following table summarizes the key points and changes in tables between the fourth and fifth editions of the *Guides*.

Comparison of Tables Between the Fifth and Fourth *Guides* Editions

Table Topic	5th Edition Table Number	4th Edition Table Number	Summary of Changes in 5th Edition
Structure, functions, and disorders	8-1	1	Perturbations now described as disorders
Criteria for rating permanent impairment	8-2	2	Minor stylistic change in criteria descriptions
Skin impairment evaluation summary	8-3		New; summarizes clinical evaluation of permanent skin impairments, cross-referenced to *Guides* tables

Introduction

The skin chapter in the Fifth Edition is very similar to the Fourth Edition in content, although it has been considerably reorganized. The introduction in the *Guides 5th* contains introductory comments on use of the chapter and background on the function of skin, which was previously discussed in the *Guides* Fourth Edition, Section 13.1, Structure and Function. Of note are new sections on the rating of contact dermatitis, natural rubber latex allergy, and cancer. The rating system for assessment of skin impairments is essentially the same as in the Fourth Edition.

8.1 Principles of Assessment

This new section reorganizes information from the Fourth Edition into a section that addresses signs and symptoms and clinical procedures. Assessment of skin disorders requires an integration of clinical findings from the physical evaluation with appropriate use of diagnostic procedures.

Clinical findings include symptoms and signs, which are documented when feasible. Among the clinical symptoms encountered, such as redness, burning, and pruritus, only pruritus is discussed in detail. It is recommended that the physician monitor for objective signs of pruritus. Common clinical investigations include patch testing, biopsy, and relevant laboratory studies. The reader is referred to text references for further discussion. Patch tests require expert application and interpretation to differentiate allergic from irritant contact dermatitis.

This section of *Guides 5th* also states that all skin disorders discussed in this chapter are evaluated on the basis of the same criteria outlined in Table 8-2, Criteria for Rating Permanent Impairment Due to Skin Disorders. To decide on the specific impairment class, determine three criteria: the frequency and intensity of signs and symptoms, the impact of the impairment on ADL, and the frequency and complexity of medical treatment. Although all three criteria are required for placement in a particular class, the impact on ADL is the most discriminating feature among classes. Once a class is determined, decide the specific impairment rating based on the severity of the condition and required treatment.

8.2 Disfigurement

Assess the impact of skin disfigurement on ADL. Although the physician is encouraged to discuss the improvement of the condition with cosmetic improvements, the impairment rating is determined without use of cosmetic improvements, since prosthetic or other supplements to improve function are removed for assessment of impairment, as indicated in Chapter 1. If the skin disfigurement involves the face, consult the ear, nose, and throat chapter, Section 11.3. Either section can be used for facial disfigurement. If an inconsistency exists between these sections, use the section that provides the higher impairment rating to the individual.

8.3 Scars and Skin Grafts

Assess scars and skin grafts on the basis of their impact on skin function and ADL. A minimal scar that does not require treatment and does not disturb function or ADL would not receive an impairment rating. If the scar or skin graft resulted from injury to another body part, as with an extremity or nerve, the individual would receive separate impairment ratings for both the extremity or nerve condition and the scar or skin graft, assuming it was significant.

EXAMPLE

A 45-year-old chef's assistant sustains a deep laceration to the ventral surface of his left hand. Although it heals with a slightly visible 2-cm scar, there is no change in function of his hand. Despite numerous hand washings, daily use of gloves, and contact with potential irritants, he is asymptomatic. Given that his right hand is dominant, it does not affect any of his ADL or work activities.

Impairment Rating

Since the patient has a skin disorder without impact on function or ADL and requires no treatment, he would not receive an impairment rating.

EXAMPLE

A 45-year-old gardener living in Florida sustains a left-hand laceration and residual 2-cm scar on the ventral surface of his dominant right hand. When performing ADL and anything requiring a full palmar grip, he experiences some discomfort. He also needs to use sunscreen, since the scar seems to become more sensitive with sun exposure.

Impairment Rating

Since this scar impacts ADL and exposure to some conditions, such as increased sun discomfort, he would qualify for an impairment rating of 2% to 3%.

8.4 Contact Dermatitis

Contact dermatitis is an inflammatory disease caused by skin contact with a material that causes damage through an allergic or irritant reaction. The two types of contact dermatitis, allergic and irritant, are defined on the basis of the underlying cause: whether the material produces an immunologic or an irritant-based reaction in the skin. The list of allergens and irritants is long.

The evaluation is made once the individual has reached MMI. For some individuals, despite the discontinuation of exposure, a chronic dermatitis may persist that requires ongoing medical and lifestyle management. The interruption to ADL, medication needs, and severity of the condition should be considered when assigning an impairment rating.

> ### MEDICAL TIP
>
> Evaluate medical records to determine a state of stability or a regular pattern of exacerbations. Weekly or monthly exacerbations may be consistent with MMI of the condition.

> ### LEGAL TIP
>
> Dermatitis may be recognized by state statute as an occupational disease in many jurisdictions. Statutory recognition usually reduces the complexity of proving workplace causation.

8.5 Natural Rubber Latex Allergy

Natural rubber latex allergy (NRLA) is discussed in the Fifth Edition as a cause of several manifestations, including contact urticaria, angioedema, allergic rhinitis, conjunctivitis, asthma, and anaphylaxis. There is some debate regarding its role in the causation of contact dermatitis, although the association between NRLA and contact dermatitis is clearly established in the medical literature.

For skin impairment caused by NRLA, use Table 8-2. Combine skin impairment with any additional permanent impairment associated with NRLA, such as asthma (Chapter 5, The Respiratory System), sinusitis (Chapter 11, Ear, Nose, Throat, and Related Structures), or depression (Chapter 14, Mental and Behavioral Disorders) by means of the Combined Values Chart.

EXAMPLE

A 38-year-old health care worker with only a childhood history of eczema develops severe dermatitis, angioedema of the face during acute attacks, and asthma after working with natural rubber latex gloves. Positive patch test and radioallergosorbent testing confirm the diagnosis. After cessation of exposure, she continues to have contact dermatitis, requiring weekly use of topical cortico-steroids and daily use of hand creams. She has difficulty with fine manipulation, including buttoning her child's clothes, and must significantly limit contact with water. Tactile sensation is markedly reduced. Grasping small objects is problematic. Her hands hurt most days of the week. The quality of sexual relations with her husband has diminished. Physical exam indicates multiple fissures, crusting, and edema throughout the palms and fingers. Swelling and pain cause decreased range of motion. Her asthma flares up several times per month, requiring use of bronchodilators.

Impairment Rating

Contact dermatitis: Her limited performance of some ADL, continued skin disorder even when not exposed to natural rubber latex, and requirement of nearly constant treatment would place her in class 2 WPI. Since her limitation of ADL affects many ADL, she would qualify for the upper range of WPI rating of class 2, 24%.

Asthma: A positive methacholine challenge and a minimum score of 2 for class 2 placement are assumed, with a WPI rating of 10% for sporadic flare-ups.

Combined WPI rating: Combining 24% (skin) with 10% (asthma), by means of the Combined Values Chart, gives 32% WPI. Additional evaluation for mental and behavioral symptoms may be warranted.

8.6 Skin Cancer

This is a new section for the *Guides 5th.* For cases of melanoma with evidence of metastases, a class 5, or 85% to 95% WPI rating, is usually warranted. For individuals with basal cell or squamous cell carcinoma, the impairment rating will depend on the tumor burden after treatment, when MMI is reached, and the impact of the condition on ADL as listed in Table 8-2.

M E D I C A L   T I P
Ensure that the individual has reached MMI before assigning an impairment rating.

L E G A L   T I P
Alleged occupationally caused cancers should be documented with a thorough report of exposure. When available, provide industrial hygiene reports of the workplace(s) where alleged exposure has occurred.

8.7 Criteria for Rating Permanent Impairment Due to Skin Disorders

This section provides the criteria for rating dermatologic disorders and many new and revised case examples.

8.8 Skin Impairment Evaluation Summary

Table 8-3 provides an excellent overview of the clinical evaluation findings and impairment criteria for impairments of the skin, cross-referenced to appropriate sections in the skin chapter and Table 8-2.

Table 8-3 Skin Impairment Evaluation Summary

Disorder	History, Including Selected Relevant Symptoms	Examination Record	Assessment of Skin Function
General	Duration, location of rash; itch, redness, welts, eczema, blisters, pimples; nail or pigment change; hair loss; ulcers, scars, growth, grafts Progression, remission, exacerbants Work history, hobbies, etc Associated conditions: atopy, eczema, asthma, rhinitis Impact on activities of daily living	Detailed skin exam: location, symmetry, demarcation Extent, pattern of involvement Sun-exposed or covered area involvement, infection, cellulitis, acute/chronic dermatitis, welts; pigment, hair, or nail changes; scar, grafts, growths Comprehensive physical exam as appropriate	Biopsy Cultures; microscopic scrapings (KOH, etc) Allergy tests (patch, prick, RAST, etc) Specialty; consult as appropriate
Urticaria	Acute; chronic Duration; frequency; location; progression Identify cause: food, infection, allergy, medication, systemic disease, physical agent, familial, etc	Extent; duration (>48-72 hours?) Location, distribution	As appropriate; complete blood count, differential, TSH Complement profile; biopsy if fixed Allergy tests (RAST, open prick, etc)
Dermatitis	Duration, location, itch, redness, nail or pigment change Progression and remission factors Atopy; childhood eczema Work, hobbies, etc	Papules; papulovesicles; erythema; serous discharge; crusting; edema; scale; lichenified or thickened plaques	Clinical presentation and history Biopsy; cultures; allergy tests (see general skin disorders)
Pigmentary Changes	Increased, decreased pigment Congenital; acquired; dermatomal Duration; location; progression Preceding dermatosis Causes: inflammation, chemical contact, occupation, infection, physical, metabolic, endocrine, drugs, neoplasm, etc	Local, disseminated; extent, pattern; Wood's light exam See general skin disorders	Labs as appropriate; biopsy; scrapings (KOH) See general skin disorders
Scars	Burns; trauma; disease grafts; family history (Ehlers-Danlos); other causes Neoplasm; ulcer; dermatitis (x-ray or stats)	Evaluate skin graft function; detail scar dimensions, shape, location, nature; any ulceration, depression, or evaluation	Atrophic or hypertrophic; pliability; changes in underlying structure
Psoriasis	Family history; age at onset; infection; medication Localized; disseminated; pustular Extent of involvement	Extent and location of involvement; type of lesion (plaque, pustular, etc)	Biopsy; lab: streptococcal antibody titers
Bullous Disorders	Congenital; acquired Duration; extent; location; mucosal Family history Pruritus; hand changes; neoplasm	Localized; generalized Vesicles; bullae; hand changes; neoplasm	Biopsy (routine, immunofluorescence); serologic studies (immunofluorescent antibodies), culture; nutritional assessment

End-Organ or System Damage	Diagnosis(es)	Degree of Impairment
Includes assessment of other organs: sinuses, respiratory, systemic components to skin disease Includes assessment of skin damage or sequelae (scars, pigmentation, alopecia, etc)	Record all pertinent diagnoses, medical status, and further treatment plans Prognosis Impact on activities of daily living Date of MMI; list accommodations	Criteria outlined in chapter Description of clinical findings and how these relate to *Guides* criteria Explanation of each estimated impairment List all impairment percentages; estimate whole person impairment percentage (see Table 8-2)
Mucosal angioedema; rhinitis; asthma; anaphylaxis	Acute or chronic urticaria; recurring urticaria; angioedema	See Table 8-2
Exfoliate erythroderma; atopy; rhinitis; asthma	Atopic Contact (allergic irritation) Acute; subacute; chronic Urticaria, photosensitivity, seborrheic; exfoliative, stasis; hand and foot, nummular dermatitis	See general skin disorders, Table 8-2
Systemic changes; deafness; neurologic disorders	Vitiligo, postinflammatory, hyper-hypopigmentation; chemical; scars	See Section 8.2, Disfigurement, and Table 8-2
None for skin unless other organs exposed	Scar; hypertrophic scar; keloid graft	See Table 8-2
If urethritis, conjunctivitis, diarrhea, arthritis, consider Reiter's, psoriatic arthritis	Psoriasis vulgaris; pustular; exfoliative (see general skin exam; see table)	See general skin exam and Table 8-2
Psoriatic arthritis Neoplasm; esophageal; neurologic; mental, behavioral; ophthalmologic (conjunctival, symblepharon)	Impetigo; contact dermatitis; insect bites; pemphigoid; pemphigus; dermatitis herpetiformis; epidermolysis; bullosa (congenital, acquired); linear IgA disease	See general skin exam and Table 8-2

Chapter 9

The Hematopoietic System

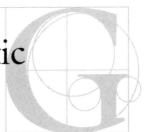

Introduction

This chapter provides an overview of key points and changes (identified with an icon **G**) made in Chapter 9 of the AMA *Guides to the Evaluation of Permanent Impairment, Fifth Edition* (*Guides 5th*), illustrates these changes in a table comparison, and discusses the purpose and implications of the major changes, with illustrative examples. The numbered section titles within this chapter correspond to sections within Chapter 9 of the *Guides 5th*. Only key principles or important changes are included in this chapter.

The hematopoietic system chapter has been revised to incorporate major changes in the field of hematology. In the Fourth Edition, impairment rating was more dependent on the effects of hematologic disorders on other body systems. In the *Guides 5th,* end-organ effects are recognized as the major underlying criterion, but an impairment rating (IR) is now given for individuals who have hematologic disorders without symptomatic manifestations in other organ systems, if there is an impact on activities of daily living (ADL). Treatment for human immuno-deficiency virus (HIV) has changed the course of HIV permanent impairment. This chapter will address only major changes to the assessment of hematopoietic impairments and illustrate some case examples of interest in workers' compensation.

Key Points and Changes

G For hematopoietic disorders, integrate subjective and objective data to determine the extent of the impairment on ADL.

G The degree of impairment for anemia is related to the anemia's severity, need for transfusion, and impact on the ability to perform ADL.

Hematopoietic impairment ratings consider altered function of other end organs.

Determine permanent impairment from HIV infection only after a complete assessment of each of the potentially affected organ systems.

IRs for white blood cell disorders are based on symptoms, clinical signs, the severity of the condition, and the impact on the ability to perform ADL.

G Determine IR for hemorrhagic, platelet, and thrombotic disorders on the basis of Table 9-4.

G Thrombotic disorders requiring long-term anticoagulation increase bleeding risk and constitute whole person impairment (WPI) in the range of 10%.

Comparison of Tables Between the Fifth and Fourth *Guides* Editions

The following table summarizes the key points and changes in tables between the fourth and fifth editions of the *Guides*.

Comparison of Tables Between the Fifth and Fourth *Guides* Editions

Table Topic	5th Edition Table Number	4th Edition Table Number	Summary of Changes in 5th Edition
Functional classification of hematologic system disease	9-1		New; provides a description of symptoms and their impact on ADL
Permanent impairment due to anemia	9-2	1	Slight change in IRs; 5th Edition ratings continuous from 0%
Permanent impairment due to white blood cell disease	9-3	Section 7.5	New; 5th Edition IR classes are exclusive; class 4 increased to 100% from 95%
Permanent impairment due to hemorrhagic and platelet disorders	9-4	Section 7.6	New; new IRs, with four classes as in Table 9-3
Hematologic impairment evaluation summary	9-5		New

9.1 Principles of Assessment

The assessment of hematopoietic impairment depends on the integration of subjective factors, such as symptoms, with objective factors. A new classification (Table 9-1) describes the severity of the condition (none, minimal, moderate, and marked) and its correlation with ADL. Since most of the hematologic impairments are organized into four classes, the physician can use this description as an aid to determine the appropriate class for each condition, based on severity and ADL.

9.2 Anemia

The criteria for rating impairment due to anemia listed in Table 9-2 are slightly changed from the Fourth Edition.

Guides users should note that anemia may sometimes be caused by occupational disease (Example 9-3) or injury (Example 9-7). The degree of impairment for anemia is related to the anemia's severity, need for transfusion, and impact on the ability to perform ADL. Criteria for rating impairment are unchanged, although the ratings have been slightly changed to create continuous categories. Thus, an individual with a mild anemia who is asymptomatic but has an anemia that impacts ADL could obtain an IR of 0% to 10%. This range would be most likely for an individual asymptomatic at rest but symptomatic during ADL (eg, standing for a prolonged period, walking, cooking).

9.3 Polycythemia and Myelofibrosis

This section, as in the Fourth Edition, discusses diagnostic criteria for polycythemia and myelofibrosis. Impairment is rated based on end-organ damage, such as liver damage, which can accompany these conditions.

9.4 White Blood Cell Diseases or Abnormalities

This section expands the discussion on white blood cell disorders. White blood cells (leukocytes) include granulocytes, lymphocytes, and monocytes-macrophages. White blood cells can be impaired in number and function. IRs are based on symptoms and clinical signs, indicating the severity of the condition and the impact on the ability to perform ADL. The most significant addition to this chapter has been an expanded discussion of HIV infection. HIV infection destroys a type of lymphocyte (CD4T), resulting in impairment of the normal immune response, increasing the risk of infection and cancer. Both the fourth and fifth editions consider HIV a primary hematologic disorder, with accompanying permanent impairments in other organ systems.

This section discusses the stages of HIV infection, based on symptoms, signs, and CD4 counts. Some of the examples (9-10, 9-12, 9-15, 9-17) also refer to an HIV RNA measure, which reflects the amount of HIV present in the blood. The physician should determine permanent impairment from HIV infection only after a complete assessment of each potentially affected organ system (renal, respiratory, dermatologic, etc), and any accompanying infection and cancer. Combine the IRs from different organ systems using the Combined Values Chart.

The presence of HIV and similar blood-borne pathogens in workers' compensation brings new relevance to this chapter. The progressive nature and the as yet experimental treatment of HIV and its later stage, AIDS, raise new legal complications for a legal system that presumes definitive diagnoses and a predictable course of treatment. Although the *Guides* Fifth Edition appears to treat HIV and AIDS as conditions that reach MMI, their very definitions presume that HIV and AIDS are progressive and fatal.

The IRs (Tables 9-3 and 9-4) were slightly changed to ensure that class IRs do not overlap, and class 4 was increased to 100% WPI primarily to account for individuals with advanced HIV or cancer.

Some examples (9-10, 9-12) discuss assessment of asymptomatic individuals with HIV infection. Depending on their cell counts, viral load, and impact on ADL, they can receive IRs ranging up to 15%.

EXAMPLE

While working as a nurse, Susan sustains a needlestick injury from a known HIV-infected patient. She undergoes antiviral therapy while awaiting the results of her blood test, which turn out to be negative for HIV infection. Susan does not have a permanent impairment from the needlestick injury because she was not infected.

MEDICAL TIP
Antiretroviral therapy can have significant toxicity. The physician, as noted in Chapter 1, can increase the IR by combining an additional 1% to 3% for treatment effects with a nonzero impairment rating. For individuals who may have contracted HIV infection after exposure, and who begin prophylactic therapy, the physician should wait until it becomes evident whether the individual is truly infected with HIV before providing an IR. Since HIV is generally progressive, IRs may need to be revised periodically on the basis of the individual's condition.

LEGAL TIP
Physicians, attorneys, and administrators should consider whether a period of time after HIV infection without symptoms constitutes MMI, given the known, irreversible course after the intermediate stage. The text suggests that after CD4 levels are less than 0.50×10^9/L (intermediate stage), antiretroviral therapy is recommended. Because known treatment is not successful at a high rate either for cure or remission, a strong argument is present that after the CD4 level is less than 0.50×10^9/L, the individual is not at MMI. As noted in the Medical Tip, the treatment itself may impair ADL.

9.5 Hemorrhagic and Platelet Disorders

This section was revised in the Fifth Edition, with a new set of criteria developed (Table 9-4) based on the functional classification of hematologic system disease listed in Table 9-1, using the rating system for white blood cell disorders. For bleeding disorders, the physician needs to consider symptoms, signs, need for treatment, and interference with ADL.

9.6 Thrombotic Disorders

This section now includes a discussion of acquired thrombotic disorders (Section 9.6b), which can occur after multiple trauma, immobility, and surgery. Although a specific impairment rating table is not listed in this section, the physician should use Table 9-4 pertaining to hemorrhagic and platelet disorders. Long-term anticoagulation constitutes an impairment in the 10% range, because of increased bleeding risk (p 207).

9.7 Hematologic Impairment Evaluation Summary

Table 9-5 provides an excellent overview of the clinical evaluation and impairment rating criteria for hematologic disorders, cross-referenced to appropriate impairment rating tables in the chapter.

Table 9-5 Hematologic Impairment Evaluation Summary

Disorder	History, Including Selected Relevant Symptoms	Examination Record	Assessment of Hematologic Function
General	Symptoms of end-organ impairment, eg, cardiovascular (eg, fatigue, palpitations, chest pain); respiratory (eg, shortness of breath); infections; general symptoms Impact of symptoms on function and ability to do daily activities Prognosis if change anticipated Review medical history	Comprehensive physical examination with focus on affected end-organ systems assessment	Data derived from relevant studies: complete blood counts, serology testing, biopsies of bone, lymph nodes
Red Blood Cell	Symptoms (eg, shortness of breath on exertion, dizziness, throbbing headaches, fatigue) Resulting limitation of physical activity or complications (eg, angina)	Other organ dysfunction (eg, brain, heart, kidneys)	Complete blood count, hemoglobin electrophoresis, etc
White Blood Cell	Fatigue, frequent infections, etc	Detailed history (ie, infections)	Complete blood count, etc
Platelet	Abnormal bleeding from gums, mouth, GI tract, urinary tract Poor hemostasis with trauma Family history of abnormal clotting	Epistaxis; petechiae; purpura; occult fecal blood; splenomegaly; evidence of thrombosis	Complete blood count with platelet count; bleeding time; relevant platelet aggregation studies (prothrombin and partial thromboplastin time to rule out other coagulation disorders)
Bleeding	Excessive bruising Prolonged spontaneous, traumatic bleeding From birth or acquired disorder Family history of bleeding disorder Muscle or joint pain or swelling	Hematoma; joint or muscle swelling; easy bruisability	Complete blood count with platelet count; bleeding time; prothrombin and partial thromboplastin time; fibrinogen factor levels

End-Organ Damage	Diagnosis(es)	Degree of Impairment
Include assessment of sequelae, including end-organ damage and impairment	Record all pertinent diagnosis(es); note if they are at maximal medical improvement; if not, discuss under what conditions and when stability is expected	Criteria outlined in this chapter
Assess relevant organs (eg, heart, lungs, kidneys) for congestion or dysfunction	Anemias; sickle cell; hemolysis; chronic disease; polycythemias	See Table 9-2
Assess relevant organs (eg, heart, lungs, kidneys, lymph nodes)	Leukemia; lymphoma	See Table 9-3
Due to hemorrhage	Immune thrombocytopenic purpura (ITP); HIV or drug-associated thrombocytopenia; thrombotic thrombocytopenia (TTP); myelodysplasia; leukemia; platelet functional disorder; essential thrombocythemia	See Table 9-4
Due to hemorrhage, hemarthrosis, or nerve impingement	Hemophilia; factor deficiency; Von Willebrand's disease; dysfibinogenimia; disseminated intravascular coagulation	See Table 9-4

Chapter 10

The Endocrine System

Introduction

This chapter provides an overview of key points and changes (identified with an icon **G**) made in Chapter 10 of the AMA *Guides to the Evaluation of Permanent Impairment, Fifth Edition* (*Guides 5th*), illustrates these changes in a table comparison, and discusses the purpose and implications of the major changes, with illustrative examples. The numbered section titles within this chapter correspond to sections within Chapter 10 of the *Guides 5th*.

This *Master the Guides Fifth* chapter will address *only* major changes to the assessment of endocrine impairments.

Key Points and Changes

G For endocrine disorders, integrate subjective and objective data to determine the extent of the impairment on activities of daily living (ADL).

G An impairment rating (IR) for an endocrine condition reflects the severity of the condition, the need for medication, and the impact of the impairment on ADL.

G The IR can be increased between 1% and 3% because of incomplete return to normal health or adverse consequences of medication.

An individual with diabetes controlled by diet, who is asymptomatic, does not meet criteria for an IR.

The Fifth Edition also provides a rating between 5% and 15% for individuals with severe osteoporosis and pain that impacts ADL.

Comparison of Tables Between the Fifth and Fourth *Guides* Editions

The following table summarizes the key points and changes in tables between the fourth and fifth editions of the *Guides*.

Comparison of Tables Between the Fifth and Fourth *Guides* Editions

Table Topic	5th Edition Table Number	4th Edition Table Number	Summary of Changes in 5th Edition
Permanent impairment due to hypothalamic-pituitary axis disorders	10-1		New; nonoverlapping classes and considers ADL in IR; replaces Section 12-1
Permanent impairment due to thyroid disease	10-2		New; ratings now in tabular form; replaces Section 12-2
Permanent impairment due to hyperparathyroid disease	10-3	1	None
Permanent impairment due to hypoparathyroidism	10-4	2	None
Permanent impairment due to hypoadrenalism	10-5	3	None
Permanent impairment due to hyperadrenocorticism	10-6	4	None
Permanent impairment due to pheochromocytoma	10-7	5	None
Permanent impairment due to diabetes mellitus	10-8		New; replaces text in Section 12.6
Permanent impairment due to hypoglycemia	10-9		New; replaces text in Section 12.6
Endocrine system impairment evaluation summary	10-10		New

Introduction

The *Guides 5th* endocrine chapter incorporates major changes in the field of endocrinology. The Fifth Edition discusses each component of the endocrine system separately. Therefore, the hypothalamic-pituitary complex, thyroid, parathyroids, adrenals, islet cell tissue of the pancreas, and gonads all have their own sections. The impairment ratings have not changed; the Fifth Edition contains updates of investigative and diagnostic criteria for endocrine disorders, with most of the changes pertaining to the diagnosis of diabetes.

10.1 Principles of Assessment

The assessment of endocrine impairment depends on the integration of subjective factors, such as symptoms, with objective factors, including clinical signs and functional tests. Major objective clinical studies are discussed in the section pertaining to each organ system.

Endocrine impairment develops from altered endocrine gland hormone secretion and the consequent effects on nonendocrine tissues. Unlike most other disorders, since the endocrine system produces hormones that affect other target tissues, an impairment in the endocrine system usually requires medication to replace the lacking hormone, suppress overproduction, or counteract the target tissue effects. Thus, an IR for an endocrine condition reflects the severity of the condition, the need for medication, and the impact of the impairment on ADL. Inclusion of ADL in this chapter is new in the Fifth Edition. When the medication does not totally compensate for the abnormal functioning, the IR can reflect the endocrine or hormonal change in terms of normal activity or ability to respond to stress. As indicated in Chapter 2, the IR can be increased by between 1% and 3% because of incomplete return to normal health or adverse consequences of the medication.

Combine any endocrine IR with an IR from damage to target tissues. Thus, a whole person impairment (WPI) rating from a prolactin-secreting pituitary adenoma and the WPI rating for resulting vision loss would be combined for a total WPI rating.

10.2 Hypothalamic-Pituitary Axis

The criteria listed in Table 10-1 for rating impairment of the hypothalamic-pituitary axis disorders are basically unchanged; the categories are now mutually exclusive instead of overlapping, as in the Fourth Edition. The major change is that the physician needs to consider the impact on ADL, in addition to the symptoms and signs of the condition, before determining the IR.

10.3 Thyroid

10.4 Parathyroids

10.5 Adrenal Cortex

10.6 Adrenal Medulla

10.7 Pancreas (Islets of Langerhans)

There are no significant changes in the IRs and criteria for the disorders discussed in Sections 10.3, 10.4, 10.5, and 10.6 in the Fifth Edition, compared with the Fourth. Disorders of the pancreas, including diabetes, are discussed in greater detail. Although they are not published in the *Guides*, the physician should use the latest criteria for the diagnosis of diabetes, based on the American Diabetes Association revised criteria. Diagnose diabetes with:

1. Symptoms of diabetes and a glucose level of 200 mg/dL (11.1 mmol/L) or more, without regard to the time since the last meal, or

2. Fasting plasma glucose level of 126 mg/dL (7.0 mmol/L) or more, with *fasting* indicating no caloric intake for at least 8 hours, or

3. Two-hour plasma glucose level of 200 mg/dL (11.1 mmol/L) or more
   during an oral glucose tolerance test.[1]

In evaluating whether diabetes is well controlled, the American Diabetes
Association recommends fasting plasma glucose level less than 120 mg/dL
(6.7 mmol/L) and glycosylated hemoglobin less than 7% as treatment goals.[2]

Note that on the basis of Table 10-8, for an asymptomatic individual with
diabetes controlled by diet, no IR is warranted. Note also that some of the
conditions described in the examples in the Fifth Edition's Chapter 10
are consequences of pharmaceutical treatment (eg, glucocorticoids) for other
injury or disease.

MEDICAL TIP

Pancreatitis and pancreatic cancer can manifest as low back pain, which may be mistakenly
attributed to a workplace cause.

Evaluate the adequacy of treatment on the basis of American Diabetes Association criteria.

Although the impact on ADL is not always explicitly listed in the table criteria, consider the
impact on ADL before determining a specific IR.

LEGAL TIP

Laws in a few state jurisdictions may also play a part in determining the value of complete
or partial loss or loss of use of a body part, organ, or body system, even without reference
to ADL.

Diabetes, and any separate impairment caused by it, may constitute a preexisting
impairment for apportionment purposes, particularly if the diabetic condition is
uncontrolled at the time of an occupational accident or exposure and contributes to the
work-related injury or illness.

10.8 Gonads

10.9 Mammary Glands

Sections 10.8 and 10.9 have no significant changes.

Chapter 10

10.10 Metabolic Bone Disease

The Fifth Edition also provides a rating between 5% and 15% for individuals with severe osteoporosis and pain that impact ADL. Pain is accounted for in this setting. It would be highly unusual for an individual to have excess pain beyond the expected that would necessitate an additional rating within the pain chapter.

Table 10-10 Endocrine System Impairment Evaluation Summary

Disorder	History, Including Selected Relevant Symptoms	Examination Record	Assessment of Endocrine Function
General	Change in growth; fatigue; weakness; nausea; irritability; etc	Height; weight; blood pressure; pulse rate; skin temperature, texture, and moisture; general muscle strength and mass	As indicated below
Hypothalamic-Pituitary Axis	Discuss symptoms such as menstrual cyclicity, galactorrhea, polyuria, fatigue, weakness, and headache	Note breast discharge Visual field examination and assessment of target organs as described below	Measure prolactin, growth hormone, IGF-1, urine specific gravity, serum osmolality, CT or MRI of pituitary, and function of target organs
Thyroid	Fatigue; weakness; slowing of mental process; cold or heat intolerance; nervousness; weight loss; palpitations; eye changes, such as exophthalmos and diplopia; goiter; change in bowel habits	Achilles' deep tendon reflexes; thyroid size and nodularity; presence of tremor; anxiety or generalized slowness; proptosis of eyes and their movement	Serum free thyroxine, total triiodothyronine, and TSH Radioiodine uptake and scan of thyroid; ultrasound of thyroid; fine needle aspiration of thyroid nodule
Parathyroids	Fatigue; weakness; nausea, polyuria; renal calculi; muscular irritability; paresthesias; tetany; seizures	Chvostek's and Trousseau's signs	Serum calcium; phosphorus; parathyroid hormone Urinary calcium excretion; renal ultrasound; bone densitometry; ultrasound; MRI; sestamibi scan of parathyroid gland
Adrenal Cortex	Weakness; easy bruisability; hirsutism; acne; weight gain; depression; menstrual irregularities; fungal infections	Blood pressure; weight and its body distribution; skin; muscle strength; edema	Plasma cortisol and aldosterone; urinary cortisol excretion; suppression and stimulation tests of cortisol; plasma ACTH; measurement of other steroid metabolites; serum electrolytes; urinary 17-KS excretion; bone densitometry; CT or MRI examination of abdomen
Adrenal Medulla	Episodes of headache, palpitations, diaphoresis, apprehension, and weakness	Blood pressure; pulse rate	Urinary measurement of catecholamines and their metabolites; plasma catecholamines and suppressive response to clonidine; CT or MRI exam of the adrenals
Pancreas (Islets of Langerhans)	Polyuria; polydipsia; weight loss; weakness; diaphoresis; tachycardia; blurred vision; confusion; loss of consciousness; convulsions; symptoms relevant to dysfunction of end organs of diabetes mellitus (eg, eyes, kidneys, nervous system, heart, and vascular system)	Blood pressure; pulse rate; weight; skin; eyes; neurologic; heart; presence of pulses	Plasma glucose; insulin or C-peptide; HbA_{1c}; lipids; urinalysis; CT or MRI exam of pancreas
Gonads	Lack of secondary sexual development; irregular menstrual cycles or amenorrhea; infertility; precocious development of secondary sexual characteristics; hirsutism and virilization; lack of endurance and strength	Gonads; secondary sexual characteristics; height	Plasma gonadotropins; testosterone; estradiol; progesterone; semen analysis; pelvic ultrasound; x-ray for determination of skeletal age
Mammary Glands	Inappropriate milk production; growth in the male; lack of development in the female; medication history	Breast	Estradiol; testosterone; free thyroxine; liver function tests
Metabolic Bone Disease	Fractures; medications; malignancies; renal disease	Skeletal abnormalities	Bone densitometry, such as DEXA; urinary calcium excretion; skeletal metabolic markers

10.11 Endocrine System Impairment Evaluation Summary

Table 10-10 provides an excellent overview of the clinical evaluation findings and impairment criteria for impairments of the endocrine tract, cross-referenced to appropriate impairment tables in the chapter; Sections 10.8, 10.9, and 10.10; and Chapter 7.

End-Organ Damage	Diagnosis(es)	Degree of Impairment
Include assessment of sequelae, including end-organ damage and impairment	Record all pertinent diagnosis(es); note if they are at maximal medical improvement; if not, discuss under what conditions and when stability is expected	Criteria outlined in this chapter
Dysfunction of relevant organs, such as ovaries, testes, thyroid, adrenal, skeleton, and heart Is often reversible to varying degrees with treatment	Diabetes insipidus, prolactinoma, acromegaly, Cushing's disease, panhypopituitarism, or deficiency of any one or more pituitary hormones	See Table 10-1
Eye muscles and other retro-orbital tissue Other end-organ dysfunction usually reversible with treatment	Hyperthyroidism; hypothyroidism; thyroid nodule; goiter; carcinoma	See Table 10-2
Renal; skeletal	Hypoparathyroidism; hyperparathyroidism	See Tables 10-3 and 10-4
Skeletal; possible fracture Other end-organ dysfunction usually reversible with treatment	Addison's disease; Cushing's syndrome; adult-onset adrenal hyperplasia	See Tables 10-5 and 10-6
Possible cerebrovascular accident from severely elevated blood pressure	Pheochromocytoma	See Table 10-7
Eyes; kidneys; nervous system; cardiovascular; skin	Diabetes mellitus; insulinoma; reactive hypoglycemia	See Tables 10-8 and 10-9
Gonads; skin; skeletal	Gonadal dysgenesis; premature ovarian failure; precocious puberty; polycystic ovarian syndrome; seminiferous tubule dysgenesis; orchitis	See Section 10.8 and Chapter 7, The Urinary and Reproductive Systems
Breast	Galactorrhea; hypoplasia; gynecomastia	See Section 10.9
Skeleton	Osteoporosis; osteomalacia	See Section 10.10

References

1. American Diabetes Association. Report of the Expert Committee on the Diagnosis and Classification of Diabetes Mellitus. *Diabetes Care.* 1999; 24(suppl 1). Available at: http://journal.diabetes.org/FullText/Supplements/DiabetesCare/Supplement101/S5.htm

2. American Diabetes Association. Standards of medical care for patients with diabetes mellitus (position statement). *Diabetes Care.* 2001;24(suppl 1):S33-S43.

Chapter 11

Ear, Nose, Throat, and Related Structures

Introduction

This chapter provides an overview of key points and changes (identified with an icon **G**) made in Chapter 11 of the AMA *Guides to the Evaluation of Permanent Impairment, Fifth Edition* (*Guides 5th*), illustrates these changes in a table comparison, and discusses the purpose and implications of the major changes, with illustrative examples. The numbered section titles within this chapter correspond to sections within Chapter 11 of the *Guides 5th*. Only key principles or important changes are included in this chapter.

Key Points and Changes

G For ear, nose, and throat (ENT) disorders, integrate subjective and objective data to determine the extent of the impairment on activities of daily living (ADL).

Do not use assistive devices when determining hearing impairment rating (HIR).

ENT impairment ratings reflect anatomic, physiologic, and functional abnormalities.

Tinnitus (ringing in the ears) continues to receive up to an additional 5% in the impairment rating (IR), which is combined with the binaural HIR before conversion to the whole person impairment (WPI) rating.

G The effects of facial disfigurement can vary tremendously, as can remaining function; IRs range from 0% to 50% WPI.

G A case of temporomandibular joint (TMJ) disorder, with radiologic changes and pain, but without any impact on ADL, would not meet criteria for an IR, even with consideration under Chapter 18, Pain.

G The IR for partial or complete bilateral loss of olfaction or taste is 1% to 5%, compared with a single value of 3% as listed in the Fourth Edition.

G Speech and voice disorders are now rated on the basis of the same characteristics: audibility, intelligibility, and functional efficiency, as indicated in Table 11-8.

Comparison of Tables Between the Fifth and Fourth *Guides* Editions

The following table summarizes the key points and changes in tables between the fourth and fifth editions of the *Guides*.

Comparison of Tables Between the Fifth and Fourth *Guides* Editions

Table Topic	5th Edition Table Number	4th Edition Table Number	Summary of Changes in 5th Edition
Monaural hearing loss and impairment	11-1	1	Error corrected at DSHL 345
Computation of binaural hearing impairment	11-2	2	Errors corrected at the upper range of hearing loss
Relationship of binaural hearing to WPI	11-3	3	None
Impairment due to vestibular disorders	11-4		New; incorporates Section 9.1c; categories made nonoverlapping
Permanent impairment due to facial disorders and/or disfigurement	11-5	4	Combines facial disorders and disfigurement; incorporates Section 9.2
Permanent impairment due to air passage defects	11-6	5	Stylistic
Relationship of dietary restrictions to impairment	11-7	6	Stylistic
Voice/speech impairment	11-8	7	Stylistic
Oral reading paragraph—Smith house		8	Placed in text in 5th Edition in Section 11.4d
Voice/speech impairment related to WPI	11-9	9	Stylistic
ENT impairment evaluation summary	11-10		New

Introduction

The ENT chapter has been revised to incorporate major changes in the field of ENT and related structures. A new section was added for the assessment of voice impairment. Facial disorders and disfigurements have been combined in a single table for more consistency. The IRs have changed only in the sections on facial disorder and disfigurement, olfaction, and taste.

11.1 Principles of Assessment

The assessment of ENT impairment depends on the integration of subjective factors, such as symptoms, with objective factors, including clinical signs and functional tests. Do not use assistive devices when determining hearing impairment rating. Hearing can be reported with and without the use of assistive devices, but only uncorrected hearing is used for determining an IR.

11.2 The Ear

The assessment and rating of hearing impairment remains unchanged. Determine the hearing impairment for each ear (monaural hearing impairment) at levels of 500, 1000, 2000, and 3000 Hz. Add the four hearing levels (dB) for each ear separately (see p 247). Use Table 11-1 to convert this value to a monaural hearing impairment for each ear and Table 11-2 to convert the monaural level to a binaural HIR. The binaural HIR is then converted to a WPI rating. With this method, the better ear continues to be weighted more heavily, since its function would more significantly determine the impact on ADL. A few errors in Table 1 of the Fourth Edition were corrected. Tinnitus (ringing in the ears) continues to receive up to an additional 5% in the IR, which is combined with the binaural HIR before conversion to the WPI rating. Tinnitus is rated only when hearing loss is present, either unilateral or bilateral. Although some evaluators have expressed concern that tinnitus, which is subjective and not objectively measured, should not be given an additional IR, the *Guides* recognizes that individuals with this troublesome condition, which impacts ADL, merits additional rating.

Chapter 11

M E D I C A L   T I P
When tinnitus is present, it is usually described as high-pitched hissing or ringing.[1] Audiometry responses are usually sharp without uncertainty.

L E G A L   T I P
If a nervous system disorder produces hearing or vestibular impairment, the condition may warrant rating from the nervous system chapter (Chapter 13) as well as this chapter. In workers' compensation, hearing loss is often a scheduled disability.

11.3 The Face

This section now combines Fourth Edition Section 9.2, pertaining to the face, with Fourth Edition Table 4, pertaining to facial disfigurement, and lists the new IRs in Table 11-5. Facial disfigurement is a subcategory of facial disorders, and there was considerable overlap in these categories in the Fourth Edition. Facial disorders now incorporate nasal loss, using the 50% IR for nasal loss as the upper limit of facial disorder or disfigurement. These broad classes can now account for the considerable variation that can occur with facial disorders and disfigurement and their impact on ADL. Some of the limits on IRs in the Fourth Edition were retained. Severe disfigurement above the brow line warrants a 1% WPI, while below the upper lip it may be 8% WPI. The physician may adjust these IRs on the basis of individual circumstances. As noted, "Effects on individuals can vary tremendously, as can remaining function" (*Guides 5th*, p 255). Impairment from accompanying nervous system damage would be combined with an IR from facial disorders or disfigurement

---

MEDICAL TIP

Consider the effect of the facial disorder on the ability to perform ADL, which may involve a psychological assessment.

Any additional mental impairment resulting from the condition would be assessed and described qualitatively in the IR report, since no percentages are assigned to mental IRs.

LEGAL TIP

Disfigurement may be a condition ratable as a scheduled benefit in some states, regardless of whether it interferes with ADL or the degree of its interference with ADL. Because of its variability, some states simply establish a politically acceptable or compromised disability for this condition.

11.4 The Nose, Throat, and Related Structures

The ratings in the following sections may also overlap or describe conditions that may arise from nervous system disorders. In the event that the condition in this section overlaps or is the same as that described in the central nervous system chapter, use the higher rating for the same condition. However, if the IR measurements measure different aspects of function or anatomy, the ratings from both chapters may be combined.

11.4b Mastication and Deglutition

Although this section's IR remains unchanged, it provides an example of TMJ dysfunction assessment, including its effect on eating. In Example 11-18, the individual receives a rating for TMJ changes, documented by surgery and radiographs and resulting in changes in diet and pain. The rating listed here includes pain, which can occur in some cases of mastication and deglutition. If the physician believes the pain is more than expected, an additional IR can be given for pain, based on the pain chapter (Chapter 18), but only when ADL impact is present. A case of TMJ disorder, with radiologic changes and pain, but without any impact on ADL, would not meet criteria for an IR.

MEDICAL TIP

This section was designed to be used for individuals with objective findings and functional changes involving mastication and deglutition. The physician should document the extent of jaw dysfunction necessitating a dietary change.

LEGAL TIP

Causation of TMJ disorders remains controversial, especially when the disorder is asserted as a consequence of an accident that does not initially appear to affect the jaw or its related structures. Note also that some states award impairment benefits for the loss of a tooth, even though the loss may have no ADL consequences.

11.4c Olfaction and Taste

The IR for partial or complete bilateral loss of olfaction or taste is 1% to 5%, compared with a single value of 3% as listed in the Fourth Edition. Again, consider the impact of the condition on the ability to perform ADL. If both senses are impaired, assign separate IRs and combine these by means of the Combined Values Chart.

11.4e Voice

The section on speech is unchanged in the Fifth Edition; however, a new discussion of voice impairment was added. Speech and voice disorders are now rated on the basis of the same characteristics: audibility, intelligibility, and functional efficiency as indicated in Table 11-8. Voice and speech impairments are converted to WPI on the basis of the same criteria as in the Fourth Edition.

11.5 Ear, Nose, Throat, and Related Structures Impairment Evaluation Summary

Table 11-10 provides an excellent overview of the clinical evaluation findings and impairment criteria for impairments of the ENT tract, cross-referenced to appropriate impairment rating tables in the chapter and Section 11.4c.

Reference

1. Sataloff RT, Sataloff J. *Occupational Hearing Loss, Second Edition, Revised and Expanded*. New York, NY: Marcel Dekker; 1993:193.

Table 11-10 Ear, Nose, Throat, and Related Structures Impairment Evaluation Summary

Disorder	History, Including Selected Relevant Symptoms	Examination Record	Assessment of Physical Function
General	Ear, nose, and throat symptoms (eg, hearing loss, dizziness, or vertigo) and general symptoms; impact of symptoms on function and ability to do daily activities; prognosis if change anticipated; review medical history and any resulting limitation of physical function	Comprehensive physical examination; detailed relevant system assessment	Data derived from relevant studies (eg, audiometry)
Hearing Impairment	Comprehensive history including family history, developmental history of trauma, noise, and drug exposure; surgical procedures; symptoms of imbalance (eg, unsteadiness or vertigo); ear-popping; history of tinnitus; age; associated metabolic and/or endocrine disorders	General physical examination; ear, nose, and throat examination; findings from pneumonotoscopy, tuning-fork tests, hearing tests, balance function tests, and radiographic tests; metabolic evaluation	Otologic examination on tuning-fork tests; tympanometry; behavioral, audiometry, and auditory brain (evoked) response tests; electrocochleography tests; electronystagmography; metabolic and endocrine studies as necessary
Vestibular Impairment	Discuss symptoms and antecedent events; determine associated symptoms (eg, nausea, vomiting, or tinnitus); review medications; trauma; disorders associated with dizziness	Complete physical examination findings; audiologic evaluation; balance tests; electronystagmogram; blood pressure; radiologic studies	Blood pressure tests; provocative maneuvers; audiometry; electronystagmogram tests; x-rays as appropriate
Structural Facial Impairment	Case history (including symptoms) relative to facial structure and integrity; relate to other organ systems (eg, skin, eye, alimentary tract, and upper airway); social acceptability	Description of comprehensive examination of head and neck, especially the face; cutaneous abnormalities; description of supporting structures of the face such as lips; record of eye examination; photographic records; radiologic records; records of psychosocial behavior	Consider data from relevant physical findings; assess cutaneous findings, structural abnormalities, and neurologic impairments
Facial Disfigurement	History of burns, trauma, or infection; dysplasia; social factors	Records of physical findings of face, head, and neck; neurologic studies; photographic records	Consider data from clinical examination of face and facial nerve studies; photographic studies
Impairment of Respiration (Air Passage Defects)	Medical history (especially respiratory function) related to upper airway, lower airway, and lungs; consider signs and symptoms of breathlessness and dyspnea; limitations of exercise; sleep disorders; consider related systems (eg, pulmonary, cardiac, allergy, metabolic, neurologic, or psychological systems)	Data from examination of head and neck, especially nasal, oropharyngeal, and tracheobronchial airways; rhinometric studies; endoscopic findings; pulmonary function tests; radiologic findings; ultrasound studies	Examination of airway; rhinometry; endoscopy; pulmonary function tests; radiologic studies; ultrasound studies of airway
Impairment of Mastication and Deglutition	History and symptoms of mastication and/or deglutition difficulty; history of dietary habits and restrictions; history of burns or trauma; records of related systems (eg, gastrointestinal, neurologic, endocrine, or dental systems)	Comprehensive examination of nose and throat; records of temporomandibular joint function; results of speech articulation tests; esophageal function tests; endocrine studies; neurologic reports; assessment of pain if present; dental reports	Examination of nose, throat, and oropharynx; examination of temporomandibular joint function; x-rays of head and neck; swallowing studies; esophageal examination; esophageal studies; dental findings
Impairment of Olfaction and/or Taste	Ear, nose, and throat infections; head trauma; structural or foreign body nasal obstruction; nasal allergy; infections of nose and sinuses; history of head and neck tumors; drug use	Tests for odor identification; tests for taste identification; results of x-rays of head and neck; results of MRI and CT studies of head and neck; allergy tests	Subjective tests for odor identification; subjective tests for taste identification; electrical taste tests; x-rays of head and neck; MRI and CT studies of head; cranial nerve function tests; test for nasal allergens
Voice and Speech Impairment	History of general health and development; history of speech development and dysfluency; history of onset of speech and/or voice symptoms; history of surgery, trauma, infections, tumors, and treatment	Records of general medical examination; ear, nose, and throat examination; reports of hearing tests, neurologic evaluations, and pulmonary function studies; reports of laryngeal surgery and endocrine and metabolic evaluations	Records of general medical examination; examination of ears, nose, throat, and larynx; laryngoscopy; voice analysis; strobovideolaryngoscopy; speech analysis; pulmonary function tests; laryngeal electromyography

Physical Findings	Diagnosis	Degree of Impairment
Assessment of sequelae including end-organ damage and impairment	Record all pertinent diagnoses; note if they are at maximal medical improvement; if not, discuss under what conditions and when stability is expected	Criteria outlined in this chapter
Assess relevant organs; external ear and middle ear functions; eustachian tube function; status of hearing by audiometry; status of electrophysiologic tests as applicable	Conductive, sensorineural, mixed, and functional hearing loss; tinnitus; Meniere's disease	See Table 11-5
Signs of otitis media and head trauma; audiogram; auditory brain (evoked) response findings; electronystagmogram findings; evidence of cardiovascular, endocrine, metabolic, and/or ocular disorders	Otitis media; head trauma; drug side effects; vestibular neuronitis; seizure disorder; syncope; hyperventilation; benign positional vertigo; endolymphatic hydrops; CPA tumor Cardiovascular, endocrine, metabolic, functional, and/or ocular disorders	See Table 11-4
Examine cutaneous aspects of face; examine supporting (structural) aspects of face, head, and neck; consider integrity and appearance of lips, nose, eyebrows, and eyelids; radiologic studies of head and neck; CT scans; MRI scans; assess related systems (eg, visual, cutaneous, respiratory, neurologic, and psychosocial)	Visible scars; abnormal pigmentation; depressed fracture of facial bones and/or nasal cartilage; mutilation of nose or ear; distortion of anatomic facial structure; notable facial distortion; loss of social acceptance	See Table 11-5
Examine face; assess physical findings; perform facial nerve function tests; make photographic records	Facial nerve paresis or paralysis; deformity or loss of external ear or nose	See Table 11-5
Partial obstruction of nose and/or oropharynx, larynx, trachea, or bronchi; complete obstruction of nose and/or nasopharynx; tracheotomy or tracheostomy	Air passage defect with no, mild, moderate, severe, or profound dyspnea; permanent tracheotomy or tracheostomy	See Table 11-6
Abnormal temporomandibular joint function; pain (see Chapter 18); contributory dental conditions; gastroenterologic findings (see Chapter 6)	Temporomandibular joint disorder; pain (see Chapter 18); neurologic diagnoses (see Chapter 13); gastroenterologic diagnoses (see Chapter 6)	See Table 11-7
Nasal obstruction due to mucosal edema, nasal polyps, septal or turbinate occlusion of airway, or nasal tumor; physical findings may be normal except for presenting symptom; surgery sequela	Nasal septal deviation; nasal airway occlusion by turbinate bone; allergic rhinitis; nasal polyps; sinusitis; foreign body in nose; traumatic anosmia; drug toxicity; dermoid encephalocele; meningocele; intracranial or other tumor	See Olfaction and Taste (Section 11.4c)
Assess laryngeal structures; assess vocal cord function and articulators of oropharynx; assess palatal function; assess phonation, articulation, and speech intelligibility; consider esophageal speech; include assessment of respiratory, neurologic, and psychiatric findings when applicable	Pulmonary function disorder; phonatory disorder (eg, voice fatigue, weak voice, abnormal pitch, melodic variation, hoarseness, harshness, or breathiness); articulatory disorder; larynx or airway tumor; myasthenia gravis; esophageal speech	See Table 11-8

Chapter 11

Chapter 12

The Visual System

Introduction

This chapter provides an overview of key points and changes (identified with an icon **G**) made in Chapter 12 of the AMA *Guides to the Evaluation of Permanent Impairment, Fifth Edition* (*Guides 5th*) and discusses the purpose and implications of the major changes, with illustrative examples. The numbered section titles within this chapter correspond to sections within Chapter 12 of the *Guides 5th*.

The vision chapter has been totally revised from the Fourth Edition. The purpose of this chapter is to explain the rationale for these changes and to outline key concepts of importance to non-ophthalmologists. As with the Fourth Edition, the *Guides 5th* vision chapter is best used by an ophthalmologist. Ophthalmologists can find additional detail in the references.[1-3] Since the vision chapter has many terms that are not understood by non-ophthalmologists, and that are new, these terms are defined in the following box. Because the *Guides 5th* vision chapter is completely revised, this chapter will not have a table-by-table comparison with the Fourth Edition.

CALCULATED VALUES

VAS **Visual Acuity Score:** Used to convert the nonlinear Snellen acuity values for each eye to a linear scale, suitable for calculations. When an ETDRS-type letter chart (see below) is used, the score increases with 1 point for each letter read correctly.

VFS **Visual Field Score:** Used to convert the visual field data for each eye to a linear scale, suitable for calculations. The score increases by 1 point for each point seen on the field grid. The reference to tunnel vision (ie, concentric field loss) is inappropriate. One of the objectives of the new grid is to give a fairer rating to nonconcentric losses such as hemianopias.

FAS Functional Acuity Score: Used to combine the VAS values for each eye to a single value estimating the acuity-related ADL abilities of the person. The formula used is: FAS = (3 ¥ VAS_{OU} + VAS_{OS})/5.

FFS Functional Field Score: Used to combine the VFS values for each eye to a single value estimating the field-related ADL abilities of the person. The formula used is: FFS = (3 × VFS_{OU} + VFS_{OD} + VFS_{OS})/5.

FVS Functional Vision Score: Combines the FAS and FFS values to obtain an overall estimate of the vision-related ADL abilities of the person. The formula used is: FVS = (FAS × FFS)/100. The value may be adjusted for visual impairments not reflected in visual acuity or visual field loss. See also Table 12-1.

VES Visual Efficiency Scale: A scale devised by Snell in 1925 to estimate the employability of individuals with vision loss. The scale was used through the Fourth Edition and has now been replaced by the Functional Vision Score.

IR   Impairment Rating: Any of the above scores, subtracted from 100.

VSI Visual System Impairment: VSI = 100 − FVS.

WPI Whole Person Impairment: 50% VSI is considered 50% WPI, but 100% VSI (total blindness) is considered 85% WPI because of the assumed use of compensating skills.

COMMON ABBREVIATIONS

OD   Oculus Dexter: Refers to the right eye.

OS   Oculus Sinister: Refers to the left eye.

OU   Oculi Unitas (the eyes as one unit): Refers to the use of both eyes (binocular vision).

M   M-unit: Unit to measure letter size for visual acuity measurement. 1 M-unit = 1.45 mm or about 1/16". A standard eye can recognize 1 M-unit at 1 meter, 2M at 2 meters, etc.

D   Diopter: The reciprocal of a distance in meters (1/2 m = 2 D, 1/3 m = 3 D, etc). Useful for recording the focal distance of lenses and the viewing distance in near vision tests.

ETDRS: A standard method for visual acuity measurement promoted by the National Eye Institute and others for use in clinical studies. The acronym refers to the Early Treatment Diabetic Retinopathy Study in which it was first used.

ICD-9-CM: The official US Health Care Classification. It is a Clinical Modification and extension for use in the United States of the ICD-9, the 9th revision of the International Classification of Diseases of the World Health Organization (WHO).

CF   **Count Fingers:** An outdated way of measuring reduced vision. The use of an actual letter chart at 1 meter (as explained in Section 12.2 b) is preferred.

HM   **Hand Motions:** An outdated way of measuring reduced vision. The use of an actual letter chart at 1 meter (as explained in Section 12.2 b) is preferred.

NLP   **No Light Perception:** Indicates total blindness.

Key Points and Changes

Vision is quantitatively assessed and an impairment rating is determined on the basis of the best-corrected visual acuity (eg, using glasses, contact lenses, and/or implanted lenses).

Vision loss, without correction (eg, without the use of glasses), can be reported; however, it is not the basis for the impairment rating.

Vision terminology in the Fifth Edition follows medical reporting: right eye = OD, left eye = OS, and vision from both eyes = OU.

G Table 6 in the Fourth Edition, which converts visual system impairment to whole person impairment, has been removed and replaced with a scale to allow for adjustment for limitations in activities of daily living (ADL) and individual adjustments for specific conditions, including glare sensitivity, contrast, color, photophobia, reduced or delayed light and dark adaptation, color vision defects, binocularity, stereopsis, suppression, and diplopia.

G The impairment ratings (IRs) in the Fifth Edition are generally lower than in the Fourth Edition, because their basis has been changed from an employability estimate to an estimate of limitations in ADL (see below).

G The Fifth Edition introduces the option to adjust the VSI for factors other than visual acuity and visual field, if the effect of these factors is well documented and exceeds the effect of the visual acuity and visual field loss.

Chapter 12

G If the visual system impairment (VSI) is 50% or less, then the whole person impairment (WPI) rating = VSI. For VSI greater than 50%, the WPI = 50 × 0.7 × (VSI − 50).

G Detailed formulas are required for calculating visual and whole person impairment when both visual field and visual acuity losses are present; see *Guides* section 12.4d, examples 12-12 to 12-14.

Introduction

Retained from the Fourth Edition is the relationship of the vision system to the individual as a whole: a 90% to 100% visual system impairment rating corresponds to a 74% to 85% whole person impairment.

The most significant changes to the Fifth Edition are summarized in this section. These include the following:

1. The most prominent change in the Fifth Edition is the introduction of a new "functional vision score" (FVS) to replace the previous "visual efficiency scale." The FVS defines a 20/200 visual acuity to be equal to a 50% visual impairment, or 50% WPI.

   The Visual Efficiency Scale, which persisted through the Fourth Edition, was conceived by Snell in 1925. It reflected the thinking of that era that vision rated at 20/200 or less was hardly worth having. The outdated term *legal blindness* is a remnant of this thinking. The term is a misnomer, since (*a*) there are no illegal levels of vision loss, and (*b*) 90% of those labeled "legally blind" are not blind but have remaining vision.

   Snell based his scale on the observation that persons with 20/200 visual acuity had lost 80% of their employability in 1925. Accordingly, he rated that visual acuity level as "20" out of 100. That rating was never meant to imply that those persons had lost 80% of their vision. The vision chapter was revised to shift the emphasis from a one-step process that estimated employability to a two-step process: (*a*) an estimate of the ability to perform ADL (a medical and *Guides* assessment) and (*b*) an estimate of a reasonable compensation (an administrative and/or legal decision—beyond the scope of the *Guides*). The new FVS is aimed at providing the first step.

   The FVS reflects the classification of vision loss in ICD-9-CM (1978). On the FVS scale, 20/200 scores a more realistic 50 points, with as much room for differentiation above as below this level. This scale is consistent with a general classification of functional losses for any organ system and with the *Guides* concepts that assess impairment based on the ability to perform ADL. An FVS rating of 50 points does not imply 50% employability. Some totally blind people are gainfully employed; some normally sighted people are not. This is why the *Guides* requires a second step to judge employability and related factors. The new vision chapter is more consistent with the philosophy of the *Guides* as it reflects ADL and not employability, as did the Snell scale. Like the Visual Efficiency Scale, the FVS is a measure of vision retained. The IR as used in the Guides is obtained by subtracting its value from 100.

2. The new chapter gives more explicit guidelines for visual acuity measurement. Where possible, ETDRS–type charts (first developed for the Early Treatment Diabetic Retinopathy Study) should be used. This is especially important around the 20/200 level. The US statutory definition ("20/200 or less") is ambiguous because it depends on the chart used. On traditional charts that have no lines between 20/100 and 20/200, the definition effectively becomes "less than 20/100." On an ETDRS-type chart (with lines at 20/100, 20/125, 20/160, and 20/200) the definition becomes more appropriately "less than 20/160." If a newer chart is not available, the individual should be brought to 10 ft, so that "less than 20/160" can be measured as "less than 10/80."

3. Additional ratings given for diplopia and aphakia have been removed, noting that the physician can assess their impact on ADL and discuss these in the report in a qualitative manner. In the Fourth Edition, only a few factors other than visual acuity and visual field were mentioned explicitly. The new chapter has a provision that the final FVS can be adjusted for any other visual conditions, if necessary. Such adjustments must be well documented and justified by the examiner.

4. Near vision measurements are now optional. If near vision, after appropriate correction, is impaired beyond the limitations reflected in the distance acuity value and impacts ADL, this can be accounted for by averaging the visual acuity score (VAS) for distance and the VAS for near (note that visual acuity values cannot be averaged directly). Table 12-11 and Sections 12.5d and 12.5e contain instructions for proper near vision measurement and for using a modified Snellen formula.

5. The Fourth Edition allowed for several, mutually incompatible, visual field scoring methods. The new visual field score (VFS) is based on a single grid pattern. It provides a higher rating for visual field losses in the two lower quadrants because of the functional significance of visual field loss in these quadrants. It provides a fairer rating for hemianopia.

6. The prior formula for visual impairment (3 × better eye + 1 × lesser eye)/4 has been replaced by the following formula: (3 × OU + OD + OS)/5. This provides a fairer weighting of binocular vision, to account for circumstances in which the binocular function is not identical to that of the better eye. This is especially important for visual field loss where retained field areas in one eye can compensate in part for corresponding areas that are lost in the other eye.

7. The IR for the visual system = 100 – FVS.

The old chapter contained extensive tables to calculate combined values. These tables were needed because pocket calculators did not exist in 1925 and because the underlying formula was hidden. The calculations were based on vision retained, while the rows and columns were labeled for vision lost. In the new chapter, the calculations are made explicit and the availability of a pocket calculator is assumed.

In summary, the new chapter has eliminated many internal inconsistencies from prior revisions. The vision chapter has been made consistent with the definitions of statutory vision loss and with ICD-9-CM, the official US health care classification. The medical impairment ratings in many cases are lower than in the Fourth Edition, since the estimates pertain now to ADL and not employability or disability. Directly comparing the old scores to the new ones would be a mistake because they represent different estimates (an estimate of employability in 1925 in the Fourth Edition vs an estimate of ADL ability in 2000 in the Fifth Edition).

12.1 Principles of Assessment

Assessment of vision impairment in the Fifth Edition is based on a combination of visual acuity and visual field assessment, as it was in the Fourth Edition; however, the detailed calculations differ. Visual acuity describes the ability of the eye to perceive details. Visual field is the ability of the eye to detect objects in the periphery of the visual environment. However, the detailed rules for combining these assessments have been changed.

The new system in the Fifth Edition combines the visual acuity scores (VAS) for OD, OS, and OU into a functional acuity score (FAS) and then combines that score with a similarly determined functional vision score (FVS). The Fourth Edition instead first combined acuity and field values for the better eye and then combined them with a similar value for the lesser eye, as if the two eyes were independent organs. The Fifth Edition method accounts better for the fact that good visual acuity in one eye can compensate for poor acuity in the other eye. A good field in one eye can compensate for field loss in the other eye. However, visual acuity cannot compensate for field loss or vice versa.

12.2 Impairment of Visual Acuity

In the Fourth Edition, visual acuity was measured for near and far distances and a single percentage loss of central vision was developed, using the combination of these numbers, as listed in the Fourth Edition, Table 3 (p 8/212). If either monocular aphakia or monocular pseudophakia were present, this would have been considered to be an additional acuity impairment and the acuity impairment value was increased, also represented in the same Table 3.

The additional impairment rating in the Fourth Edition for *monocular aphakia* was removed. The extra rating was based on the fact that monocular aphakia with spectacle lens correction used to cause disturbing differences in image size between the eyes. This problem was eliminated by the introduction of implant lenses, which are now the standard treatment. The extension to monocular pseudophakia (the presence of an implant lens) was a mistake, introduced when lens implantation was still considered an experimental procedure. Therefore, the Fifth Edition has no numerical correction for monocular aphakia or monocular pseudophakia.

In the rare cases where there are aphakia-related problems, they can be handled under the general adjustment rule.

The Fifth Edition provides more detailed instruction to the physician as to how to determine visual acuity, especially for individuals with low vision. In the old chapter it was assumed that binocular acuity equaled the acuity of the better eye. This is usually true, but there are exceptions. In the new chapter, binocular visual acuity is mentioned explicitly, since most ophthalmologists measure it routinely.

It is also recommended that the older term *legal blindness*, representing individuals with an acuity of 20/200 or less, be replaced by the term *severe vision loss*, since these individuals are not medically or functionally blind. *Blind* refers to individuals with no light perception.

In the Fifth Edition, the IR is primarily determined by the distance visual acuity. The physician can account for near distance (reading acuity) if the near distance acuity is significantly worse than the distance acuity. The physician would average both acuity scores and use the average score for determining the impairment acuity. In both editions, the visual acuity impairment rating takes the vision of both eyes into account, even if only one eye is affected.

The new chapter makes near vision assessment optional and provides guidelines for measuring it accurately. The objective of using near vision tests in most offices is more to assess reading comfort than to measure visual acuity. The near vision scales in the old chapter were incompatible with the scales for distance vision. For a one-line difference in visual acuity, from reading of newsprint (1M) at 50 cm (20 in) to reading of newsprint at 40 cm (16 in), the near vision IR increased inexplicably from 10% to 50%, while the same visual acuity drop on a distance chart resulted in only a 10% higher impairment rating from 15% to 25%. Letter sizes should be reported in M-units, since this is the only objectively defined unit for letter size. It applies to letter charts as well as to reading samples. Printers' points are dependent on the type style used (eg, 8-point Arial = 9-point Times Roman), and the widely used Jaeger numbers have no numerical value at all. Jaeger's original numbers refer to item numbers in the catalogue from which he selected his reading samples in 1854. Today's Jaeger ratings vary widely, depending on the card used.

After determining the VAS for each eye separately, these values are combined to a single functional acuity score (FAS) for the person, as indicated in Table 12-3, page 284. The formula FAS = $(3 \times OU + OD + OS)/5$ ensures that proper weight is given to binocular vision, while not ignoring the function of each eye separately. The visual acuity impairment rating is $100 - FAS$. The FAS provides an estimate of visual acuity–related ADL skills, the most important of which is reading.

Contrast sensitivity loss was not mentioned in the old chapter. Today it is recognized as a potential source of visual complaints. *Note:* Visual acuity refers to the ability to recognize small letters of high contrast. Contrast sensitivity refers to the ability to recognize larger objects with poor contrast. Since contrast sensitivity measurement has not yet been standardized, and since it often coexists with visual acuity loss, a formal scale was not included in the new chapter. Where appropriate, contrast sensitivity loss that is not reflected in accompanying visual acuity loss can be handled under the general adjustment rule (see *Guides* Section 12.4b, p 297).

The visual acuity impairment ratings listed in the Fifth Edition do not directly correspond to those in the Fourth Edition because of the changes in assessment, with an emphasis on function and a new weighting system. Many of the impairment ratings are lower in the Fifth Edition than in the Fourth Edition to reflect the fact that employability and disability effects are not included in the impairment ratings.

The following examples taken from the Fifth Edition will illustrate the changes between the two editions (only visual acuity is considered here):

EXAMPLES

Example 12-1

Visual acuity loss only

VOU 20/40, VOD 20/40, VOS 20/40

Fifth Edition IR: FAS = 85, 15% visual IR, 10% to 29% WPI, class 2

Fourth Edition IR: VES = 85, 15% visual IR, 14% WPI

Example 12-2

VOU 20/15, VOD 20/15, VOS not present because of work-related accident, prosthesis

Fifth Edition IR: FAS = 84, 16% visual acuity IR, 10% to 29% WPI, class 2

Fourth Edition IR: VES = 75, 25% visual system IR, 24%+ WPI

Note: Most monocular persons experience very little handicap in ADL. The Fourth Edition overestimated monocular losses.

Example 12-3

VOU 20/40, VOD 20/40, VOS 20/400, assume no difference in near vision

Fifth Edition IR: FAS = 75, 25% visual acuity IR, combine with visual field loss in VOS

Fourth Edition IR: VES = 66, 4% visual acuity IR, combine with visual field loss in VOS

MEDICAL TIP
Absence of depth perception is present in many people. Many are unaware of it and are not handicapped. Loss of depth perception usually results from loss of visual acuity in one eye and is then rated according to the visual acuity loss.

LEGAL TIP
It may become even more important under the Fifth Edition to examine the effects of vision loss on specific work activities. In the Fourth Edition, the effects on generic employability were assumed to be included in the Snellen tables, but they have been excluded in the Fifth Edition because disability assessment is a multistep process beyond the *Guides*. If an eye is lost because of an industrial accident, the loss of that eye is not specifically accounted for in a separate table, as it was in the Fourth Edition (Table 6).

Chapter 12

12.3 Impairment of the Visual Field

The guidelines for measuring the visual field of each eye have not changed. New are the instructions on how to convert the visual field measurements to a visual field score (VFS) and on how to determine the binocular field of vision. Since there is no equipment that can accurately measure the binocular field, it is recommended that the fields be measured monocularly and that the binocular field be determined from an overlay of the two fields. The definition of statutory vision loss is a field of 10° radius. The old *Guides* formula made this a 12.5° radius. The alternative method using the Easterman monocular grid made it a 15° radius. Furthermore, the *Guides* formula gave equal weights to the upper and lower half fields, while the Easterman grids doubled the weight for the lower field.

The new system has only one grid that can be implemented with pencil and paper (like the old *Guides* formula) or with an overlay grid (like the Easterman grids). The new grid is compatible with the statutory definition and with the ICD-9-CM scoring system. The new grid gives the lower field 50% extra weight.

The new grid gives 50 points to the central 10° and 50 points to the field outside 10°. Thus, the equivalence of a field loss to 10° and a visual acuity loss to 20/200 is maintained. The extra weight for the central field is appropriate because this area corresponds to 50% of the primary visual cortex; it is clinically justified since even small blind spots near the center of fixation can interfere significantly with reading and similar activities. Loss of peripheral vision is significant for mobility, which is less sensitive to small blind spots.

Since the old formula required an 80-point loss to qualify for statutory vision loss, nonconcentric losses were not treated fairly. One would have to lose more than three quarters of the field to qualify. Under the new rules, a 50-point loss suffices. Thus, a *hemianopia* (a condition where either the left or the right half of the field is lost in both eyes because of a stroke or injury of the right or left half of the visual cortex of the brain) is now classified more fairly as equivalent to a concentric loss (tunnel vision) to 10°.

The visual field loss assessment now more heavily weighs the lower quadrants of the visual field, which plays a more important role in visual function. The Fourth Edition added 5% to the visual field loss, if an inferior quadrant was impaired, and 10% for the inferior half of a visual field. The Fifth Edition adds two additional meridians for analysis to the lower quadrants, for a total of 10 meridians, six of these in the lower field. The Fourth Edition considered eight meridians, four of these in the lower field.

12.4 Impairment of the Visual System

Both the fourth and fifth editions include visual acuity and visual field loss in their determination of visual impairment. The Fourth Edition combined these parameters, using the Combined Values Chart, while the Fifth Edition multiplies functional scores and converts the total functional score into a visual impairment rating that is 100% or less. The visual impairment rating is converted into a WPI rating, with the VSI equal to WPI for values less than or equal to 50% VSI, or for VSI greater than or equal to 50%, the WPI = $50 \times 0.7 \times (VSI - 50)$. In cases where additional visual impairments exist that are not reflected in visual acuity or visual field changes, individual adjustments of up to 15 points can be made to the VSI rating. Such adjustments will then also affect the WPI. The need for such adjustments must be well documented and discussed in the report. Visual changes that require individual assessment are discussed in detail in Section 12.4b of the *Guides* and include, but are not limited to, the following impairments: contrast sensitivity, glare sensitivity, color vision defects, binocularity, stereopsis, suppression, and diplopia.

Diplopia had a separate scale, but no instructions were provided for the conditions under which it should be measured. Since those conditions can have a major effect on the presence or absence of bothersome diplopia, the diplopia scale was omitted. If diplopia is disturbing and interferes with daily living skills, the FVS and the VSI rating may be adjusted, as it can be for other factors, indicated in Section 12.4b.

12.5 Visual Acuity Measurement at Near (Reading Acuity)

The Fifth Edition of the *Guides* contains a detailed discussion of the assessment of near vision. As mentioned, this was automatically included in the Fourth Edition and has been made optional in the Fifth Edition. In most cases, it needs to be included in the vision assessment.

In most cases, visual acuity and reading acuity will be similar, obviating the need for a separate measurement. In cases where they differ, the physician needs to understand why the difference exists and can account for this additional impairment by means of Tables 12-10 and 12-11.

Chapter 12

Summary

This chapter does not contain a sample template or summary; however, use of Table 12-10, reprinted below, will ensure that the physician assesses the key components of vision and determines their impact on ADL. The table lists examples of conditions that fall into various ranges. Their precise position within each range should be determined by following the detailed calculation rules.

Table 12-10 Classification of Impairment of the Visual System and of the Whole Person*

Class 1 0%-9% Impairment of the Whole Person	Class 2 10%-29% Impairment of the Whole Person	Class 3 30%-49% Impairment of the Whole Person	Class 4 50%-61% Impairment of the Whole Person	Class 5 62%-73% Impairment of the Whole Person	Class 6 74%-85% Impairment of the Whole Person
Visual System Impairment Rating (estimate of visual ability loss)					
0%-9%	10%-29%	30%-49%	50%-69%	70%-89%	90%-100%
Functional Vision Score (estimate of visual abilities)					
FFS: ≥ 91 points	FFS: 90-71 points	FFS: 70-51 points	FFS: 50-31 points	FFS: 30–11 points	FFS: ≤ 10 points
Range of normal vision	Near-normal vision (mild vision loss)	Moderate vision loss	Severe vision loss	Profound vision loss	(Near-) Total vision loss
Both eyes have normal visual fields and					
visual acuity of 20/25 or better	visual acuity of 20/60 or better	visual acuity of 20/160 or better	visual acuity of 20/400 or better	visual acuity of 20/1000 or better	visual acuity worse than 20/1000
Both eyes have normal visual acuity and					
visual fields better than 50°	visual fields better than 30°	visual fields better than 10°	visual fields of 10° or less	visual fields of 6° or less	visual fields of 2° or less
	One eye has 20/200 or less; the other eye is normal	One eye has 20/200 or less; the other eye has 20/80	One eye has 20/200 or less; the other eye has 20/200		
	One eye lost (other eye normal)	Both eyes lost the upper half-field	Both eyes lost the lower half-field		
			Homonymous hemianopia		
Estimated ability to perform activities of daily living					
Normal (or near-normal) performance			Restricted (or failing) performance		
Has reserve capacity	Lost reserve capacity	Need for vision enhancement aids	Slower than normal, even with enhancement aids	Marginal visual performance, even with aids	Cannot perform visually; needs substitution aids

* The examples in this table refer to visual acuity loss alone or to visual field loss alone. Use Tables 12-2, 12-3, 12-5, and 12-6 and the rules in this section to calculate an impairment value when there is both visual acuity loss and visual field loss. If VSI ≤50%, WPI = VSI. If VSI >50%, WPI is adjusted based on the formula WPI = 50 + 0.7 × (VSI – 50).

References

For additional background information on visual assessment, consult:

1. Workgroup for the International Society for Low Vision Research and Rehabilitation. *Guide for the Evaluation of Visual Impairment.* Available from Pacific Vision Foundation, San Francisco, Calif; 1999 ($5; fax: 415 346-6562).

2. Colenbrander A. *Measuring Vision and Vision Loss.* Vol IV. *Clinical Opthalmology.* Philadelphia, Penn: Lippincott Williams & Wilkins; 2001; chap 51.

3. Colenbrander A. Vision. In: Demeter SL, Anderson GBJ, Smith GM, eds. *Disability Evaluation.* 2nd ed. American Medical Association; in press.

Chapter 13

The Central and Peripheral Nervous System

Introduction

This chapter provides an overview of key points and changes (identified with an icon **G**) made in Chapter 13 of the AMA *Guides to the Evaluation of Permanent Impairment, Fifth Edition* (*Guides 5th*), illustrates these changes in a table comparison, and discusses the purpose and implications of the major changes, with illustrative examples. The numbered section titles within this chapter correspond to sections within Chapter 13 of the *Guides 5th*. Only key principles or important changes are included in this chapter.

Key Points and Changes

G Impairment rating criteria for neurologic impairments include an assessment of the ability to perform activities of daily living (ADL).

Evaluate cerebral function first when assessing neurologic disorders.

G There are four categories of cerebral function to assess: consciousness and awareness, whether permanent or intermittent (seizures, syncope); mental status and integrative functioning; use of language (aphasia or dysphasia); and emotional or behavioral disorders.

Identify and select the cerebral area of greatest impairment as the cerebral impairment; combine this with other nervous or body system impairments.

G The criteria for episodic loss of consciousness and awareness have been expanded to include criteria for syncope, which was treated as a separate entity in the Fourth Edition.

G Additional methods to assess traumatic brain injury, dementia, and cognitive deficits are discussed.

G The upper classes of impairment ratings have been reduced for both sleep and arousal disorders, and emotional and behavioral disorders for greater consistency throughout the chapter.

G All cranial nerve impairments are rated and evaluated the same as in the Fourth Edition except for vision loss (optic nerve CN II).

G If optic nerve or visual cortex damage results in loss of acuity (vision) or peripheral field, evaluate vision loss in the neurology chapter; if both acuity and peripheral fields are affected, evaluate vision loss in the vision chapter.

Gait and movement disorders can be used to evaluate individuals with neurologically based impairment of the lower extremities.

For upper extremity disorders that are neurologically based, impairment ratings are higher for the dominant extremity.

G Spinal cord disorders are no longer evaluated by the spine chapter.

G Spinal cord disorders are rated on the basis of the combination of any loss of extremity use, bowel, bladder, sexual, or respiratory impairment.

G Chronic pain impairments caused only by causalgia, posttraumatic neuralgia, and reflex sympathetic dystrophy are evaluated by means of the functional assessment tables for either upper or lower extremity–gait impairments (Tables 13-16, 13-17, and 13-15).

G Peripheral nerve injuries are assessed in a similar manner in the nervous system and upper extremity chapters; however, the impairment ratings and criteria differ slightly.

Comparison of Tables Between the Fifth and Fourth *Guides* Editions

The following table summarizes the key points and changes in tables between the fourth and fifth editions of the *Guides*.

Comparison of Tables Between the Fifth and Fourth *Guides* Editions

Table Topic	5th Edition Table Number	4th Edition Table Number	Summary of Changes in 5th Edition
Neurologic impairments that are combined with most severe cerebral impairment	13-1		New; lists other neurologic impairments to combine with one cerebral impairment (the most severe)
Consciousness and awareness	13-2	4	Upper limit ratings of classes 2 and 3 increased; class 3 no longer includes life support; ADL impacts explicitly referenced
Episodic loss of consciousness or awareness	13-3	5, 22	Increase in upper limits of class 1 range to incorporate syncope from former Table 22
Sleep and arousal	13-4	6	Ranges and upper limits of classes 2, 3, and 4 increased; supervision eliminated from class 2 criteria
Clinical dementia	13-5		New; provides rating basis for dementia; used with Table 13-6
Mental status	13-6	2	Based on clinical dementia table and ADL; definitional changes, class percentages same
Aphasia and dysphasia	13-7	1	Change in terminology in class 3
Emotional or behavioral disorders	13-8	3	ADL consideration added to each class; ratings increased in classes 3 and 4
Optic nerve and visual cortex–related visual acuity loss	13-9	7	Expanded from 5 to 6 classes of severity
Optic nerve and visual cortex–related visual field loss	13-10	8	Expanded from 3 to 6 classes; impairment stated only in terms of whole person impairment (WPI); binocular effects included; consistent with new approach in vision chapter

Chapter 13

Comparison of Tables Between the Fifth and Fourth *Guides* Editions, *continued*

Table Topic	5th Edition Table Number	4th Edition Table Number	Summary of Changes in 5th Edition
Cranial nerve V	13-11	9	ADL included
Cranial nerve VII	13-12	10	Class 2 now mild to moderate bilateral facial weakness
Cranial nerve VIII	13-13	11	Class 2 now moderate (formerly minimal); class 3 now moderately severe (formerly moderate)
Cranial nerves IX, X, and XII	13-14	12	Cranial nerve X explicitly included; uncontrolled spasmodic torticollis dropped from class 1
Station and gait	13-15	13	Stylistic only
One upper extremity, central nervous system (CNS)–related impairment	13-16	14	Stylistic only
Nervous system–related impairment of both upper extremities	13-17	15	Stylistic only
Respiratory impairment	13-18	16	Stylistic only
Urinary impairment	13-19	17	Stylistic only
Anorectal impairment	13-20	18	Stylistic only
Sexual impairment	13-21	19	Stylistic only
Upper extremity chronic pain	13-22		New; similar to Table 14 in Fourth Edition; application differs
Peripheral nerve pain or sensory deficit	13-23	20	Classes increase from 5 to 6; new class 3 includes pain with activity
Peripheral nerve loss of muscle power and motor function	13-24	21	Classes are ranked 1-6, lowest to greatest deficit, instead of grades 5-0, lowest to greatest deficit
Summary of nervous system impairment evaluation	13-25		New; summarizes steps to assess nervous system impairment

Introduction

The nervous system chapter has been renamed to reflect the separate sections of the chapter, addressing both the central (brain and spinal cord) and peripheral nervous systems. Several important changes are reflected in this chapter. A more detailed discussion of neurologic assessment is provided, including descriptions of clinical studies. Function and ADL are emphasized, along with measurement scales for cognitive dysfunction. Some rating scales have been altered for better consistency.

13.1 Principles of Assessment

This section has been expanded to emphasize that a permanent neurologic impairment is any anatomic, physiologic, or functional abnormality or loss that remains after maximal medical improvement, and that the rating criteria also reflect the impairment's impact on the ability to perform ADL. Brain impairment is assessed initially and separately. Any subsequent (additional) impairment, not directly caused by brain impairment, is combined with brain impairment.

Some impairment ratings were changed in the *Guides 5th* to develop consistency among the conditions, categories, and impact on ADL.

The sections on clinical symptoms and signs and a description of commonly used clinical studies were extensively rewritten and expanded.

Neurologic signs or symptoms, constituting an impairment, do not warrant an impairment rating if there is no impact on the ability to perform ADL. The nervous system is able to compensate for many physiologic changes, because of its flexibility and redundancy, so that anatomic changes to it do not necessarily interfere with ADL.

M E D I C A L   T I P
Impact on ADL is the key determinant for where within a range an individual is placed.

L E G A L   T I P
The use of the terms *anatomic, physiologic,* and *functional* in defining losses and abnormalities that may produce permanent neurologic impairment should be compared with statutory terms used to define impairment. The use of these terms in the Fifth Edition is not meant to broaden or contradict the fundamental definition of impairment stated in Chapter 1 or in the Glossary.

Chapter 13

Also, consider that each class of impairment identified contains a range of 5% to 30%. Care should be used in determining whether an individual is closer to the top or bottom of the range.

13.3 Criteria for Rating Cerebral Impairments

Cerebral impairments are evaluated by defining whether there has been a change in the level of consciousness or awareness. This is necessary to ensure that subsequent evaluation of the brain is possible. If an individual has decreased consciousness, other brain functions such as cognition will be significantly impaired. Severe dysfunction in cognition or awareness may make it impossible to reliably assess the other areas of brain function.

Several changes have been implemented in the section on cerebral impairments. First, some criteria within classes have been changed, with conditions such as syncope now incorporated within the general category of episodic disorders. Second, some impairment ratings have been changed as indicated below for greater consistency throughout the *Guides* and to narrow the range of impairment rating with a class to account for smaller differences in function. Third, there are changes in the Fifth Edition as to which categories could be combined with cerebral impairments. In the *Guides 5th*, both episodic loss of consciousness and sleep and arousal disorders, which are mediated through the brain, are considered within the group of cerebral disorders and now only combined with non–cerebrally mediated disorders listed in Table 13-1 (p 308).

In the *Guides 5th*, disorders of consciousness or awareness currently include episodic losses of consciousness caused by seizures or syncope or sleep disturbances. Thus, these disturbances are treated as cerebral dysfunction, with only the highest impairment used. Previously, in the Fourth Edition, a seizure disorder could be combined with other cerebral disorders, such as aphasia or dysphasia.

The following table lists the categories of cerebral dysfunction for both editions, the main differences being that the prior reference to special types of preoccupation is now included either in emotional or behavioral disorders or in the mental and behavioral disorder chapter.

Categories of Cerebral Dysfunction

5th Edition	4th Edition
Consciousness and awareness	Consciousness and awareness
Aphasia or dysphasia	Aphasia or communication disturbance
Mental status and highest integrative functioning	Mental status and integrative functioning
Emotional or behavioral disorders	Emotional or behavioral disorders
Not defined in this edition	Special types of preoccupation or obsession

After noting any deficits in consciousness and awareness, if further areas of brain function can be assessed, the physician then evaluates dysfunction in three other domains: mental status, understanding and use of language, and emotional or behavioral disturbances.

After determining the extent of dysfunction and impairment ratings in these four areas, the physician selects the highest level of impairment as the cerebral impairment. A single area of cerebral impairment is combined with other, noncerebral neurologic impairments, as indicated in the table on page 152.

Some ratings were changed in categories of cerebral impairment as listed in the table on page 153. These rating changes were made to provide greater consistency throughout the *Guides*. Classes of severe impairment, with almost complete dependence on another, are rated in multiple chapters as having up to a 70% to 90% impairment. Thus, the upper classes were adjusted to reflect this degree of incapacitation in the areas of consciousness and awareness; communication impairment (dysphasia and aphasia); mental status, cognition, and highest integrative function; and emotional or behavioral impairments, as indicated below.

Chapter 13

Combining Neurologic Impairments (X indicates impairments that cannot be combined)

	Consciousness or Awareness	Sleep and Arousal	Mental Status, Cognition, and Integrative Function	Language, Dysphasia, Aphasia	Behavioral/Emotional	Cranial Nerve	Station, Gait, and Movement	Extremity Disorders	Spinal Cord	Chronic Pain	Peripheral Nervous System
Consciousness or Awareness		X	X	X	X						
Sleep and Arousal	X		X	X	X						
Mental Status, Cognition, and Intergative Function	X	X		X	X						
Language, Dysphasia, Aphasia	X	X	X		X						
Behavioral/Emotional	X	X	X	X							
Cranial Nerve											
Station, Gait, and Movement											
Extremity Disorders											
Spinal Cord											
Chronic Pain											
Peripheral Nervous System											

Changes in Cerebral Impairment Rating Between the Fifth and Fourth Editions

	Consciousness and Awareness		Dysphagia and Aphasia		Emotional Mental Status	or Behavioral						
	5th Edition	4th Edition	5th Edition	4th Edition	5th Edition	4th Edition	5th Edition	4th Edition	5th Edition	4th Edition	5th Edition	4th Edition
Class 1	0-14	0-14	0-14	0- 9	0- 9	0-14	0-14	0-14	0-14
Class 2	15-39	15-29	10-24	10-24	15-29	15-29	15-29	15-29
Class 3	40-69	30-49	25-39	25-39	30-49	30-49	30-69	30-49
Class 4	79-90 State of semicoma or coma requiring complete dependence	50-90	40-60	40-60	50-70	50-70	70-90 Severe limitation in ADL; total dependence	50-70

Since these categories overlap, the physician can award the same impairment rating as had been specified in the Fourth Edition. The broader ranges enable greater consideration for the impact on the full spectrum of ADL.

The criteria for episodic loss of consciousness and awareness have been expanded to include criteria for syncope, which was treated as a separate entity in the Fourth Edition. The criteria for episodic seizure disorders and impairment ratings remain unchanged. However, by placement of syncope criteria in Table 13-3 (p 312), the impairment ratings for syncope have increased in class 1 from 1% to 9% WPI to 0% to 14%, and in class 2 from 10% to 29% to 15% to 29%. This change was made because of the similar nature of the impact of episodic impairments on ADL; thus, it was considered appropriate to group these related syndromes, which are centrally mediated and have similar potential of impact on ADL.

EXAMPLE

Diagnosis: Dementia, seizure disorder, and hemiplegia of the nondominant side

Fifth Edition Impairment Rating: 49% impairment due to dementia; combine with appropriate ratings due to hemiplegia; dementia rating higher rating than for seizure disorder; choose the highest cerebral impairment

Fourth Edition Impairment Rating: 49% due to dementia; combine with 10% due to seizures and impairment due to hemiplegia

13.3b Episodic Neurologic Impairments

Episodic neurologic impairment has been expanded to include not only seizure disorders but episodic conditions with a neurologic basis, such as syncope, or loss of awareness, convulsive disorders, and arousal and sleep disorders. *Episodic* is defined as more than one occurrence. For some conditions (eg, syncope) that are not rated in another chapter, the physician can use the guidelines in this chapter, recognizing that the origin of the problem may not be neurologic. As previously discussed, the rating for seizure episodic disorders remains the same as in the Fourth Edition. The rating for other episodic disorders, such as syncope, is changed.

EXAMPLE

A 57-year-old woman with a history of hypertension and a stroke began having syncopal episodes, with abrupt positional changes. A tilt table test indicated a drop in blood pressure of 15/10 mm Hg, without an increase in pulse rate, with some loss in recollection of events.

Fifth Edition: Her impairment rating for the syncopal episodes would range from 1% to 14%, depending on the impact on ADL.

Fourth Edition: Impairment rating would have been 1% to 9%, depending on the impact on ADL.

13.3c Arousal and Sleep Disorders

The section on arousal and sleep disorders has been revised. As previously noted, the impairment ratings were altered to achieve greater consistency with the other cerebral criteria with similar severity and impairment in ADL. In addition, physicians are encouraged to evaluate sleepiness with the Epworth Sleepiness Scale, which assists placement within a particular class.

This section can be used to assess documented sleep disorders of multiple origins, either nervous system, mental and behavioral, cardiovascular, or respiratory. The respiratory chapter discusses obstructive sleep apnea but does not provide a rating system. The clinician can use Table 13-4 from this chapter to provide an impairment rating for sleep disorders.

EXAMPLE

John is a bystander and witness to extreme violence in the convenience store where he works. On a windy but sunny day, a gunman enters and shoots several customers, while John hides under the counter, where the wastebasket is kept. As the gunman is leaving, he notices John, fires a shot that misses, and flees to escape the authorities. Two of the customers die. John becomes depressed; is treated for depression for 9 months, including 6 months with antidepressants, with resolution of his depression; and continues in counseling for more than a year. However, he continues to have nightmares and sleep disturbances on a monthly basis, sometimes as often as every other week. Polysomnography indicates abnormal sleep patterns, with poor and interrupted rapid-eye-movement–stage sleep.

John is reminded of the events on a monthly basis, when he sees something familiar, such as clothes someone wears like one of the victims or the gunman, someone helping someone else, or weather similar to the day of the event. He previously traveled but now has difficulty flying or being in confined spaces, without control, for long periods of time. John could receive between a 1% and a 9% permanent impairment, based on his sleep disturbance and the determined impact on his ADL.

Notwithstanding his recovery from depression, John's sleep is severely disturbed when he attempts employment in a service environment that requires contact with the public. His disability is substantially greater than his impairment.

MEDICAL TIP

p disorder criteria were designed primarily for individuals with primary
they can also be used for individuals with documented secondary sleep
psychiatric disorders, which are not easily rated.

LEGAL TIP

Significant disorders, often from high class 2 through class 4, throughout this chapter will frequently lead to substantial, if not total, disability from work.

Note also that exhaustion due to a chronic sleep disorder may preclude successful reintegration into the workforce.

13.3d Mental Status, Cognition, and Highest Integrative Function

This expanded section now provides specific tools for the clinician to assess impairment caused by mental status changes. Ratings for mental status impairment have not changed; however, the physician has additional instructions on how to evaluate altered mental status and cognition. Neuropsychologic testing is discussed and may be useful for more subtle changes. For more overt changes, physicians can use scales such as the clinical dementia rating.

Note that Example 13-22 combines a 40% WPI rating due to a mentation impairment with other neurologic impairments. The comment concludes with, "If there are other impairments, the combined rating of those impairments should be added" (appropriate wording should indicate "the combined rating of those impairments should be included") (*Guides 5th*, p 322).

EXAMPLE

John, an insurance adjuster, falls down while skiing a steep slope. He is not wearing a helmet and becomes unconscious for at least 10 minutes. Investigations at the hospital indicate a subdural hematoma, and he is diagnosed with traumatic brain injury. One year later, John still has some episodes of disorientation, with learning difficulties and an inability to pursue his previous hobbies, including model building and home repairs. His appearance, previously very neat, now tends toward slovenly, and he needs prompting regarding his personal care. Neuropsychological testing indicates multiple deficits in orientation, judgment, home and hobbies, and personal care. On the basis of those findings and a score of 1.0 on the clinical dementia rating, John is rated at a 29% WPI.

He is precluded from employment that requires the use of discretion and professional judgment and is restricted to employment where he can be closely supervised at all times. His work disability is nearly total.

MEDICAL TIP

Use a clinical evaluation tool, either established cognitive or neuropsychological testing scales, to assess impairment caused by changes in mental status, cognition, and integrative function. For subtle cognitive changes, use neuropsychological testing.

LEGAL TIP

Even though the examples here and in Chapter 13 result in lower than 50% WPI, their impact on employability is substantial, such that disability may be a far greater, or total, percentage of the whole person.

13.3e Communication Impairments: Dysphasia and Aphasia

This section rates spoken and written language problems that originate from neurologic dysfunction, as from a stroke, seizure disorder, encephalopathy, or traumatic brain injury. Speech disorders resulting from ear, nose, or throat dysfunction are addressed in Chapter 11. Ratings for these disorders were unchanged between the fourth and fifth editions.

13.3f Emotional or Behavioral Impairments

Neurologically mediated emotional or behavioral disorders are evaluated in this section. For example, changes in emotion and personality may be seen in individuals with injury to specific areas of the brain. Changes such as the following can be seen:

Area of Brain	Emotional/Behavioral Change
Right hemisphere	Inappropriate jocularity
Left hemisphere	Dysphasia; depression
Left temporolimbic	Ideational
Right temporolimbic	Mood disturbance
Diffuse-dementia	Mood liability; aberrant motor changes

Chapter 13

Although it is increasingly recognized that many psychiatric disorders have concurrent central nervous system (CNS) changes, which may precede the psychiatric symptoms, this section was not designed to rate primary psychological/behavioral conditions. If concrete, neurologic syndrome disorders are absent, use the mental and behavioral chapter. This section also refers to a widely used tool, the Neuropsychiatric Inventory (NPI), which can be used by physicians to assess diffuse neurologically based dysfunction that manifests as behavioral disorders.

13.4 Criteria for Rating Impairments of the Cranial Nerves

This section addresses specific impairments of cranial nerve dysfunction. The assessment and rating of cranial nerve II–optic nerve impairment have been significantly changed to account for changes in vision and the impact on performance of ADL. Vision changes caused by optic nerve or neurologic dysfunction can be rated in the neurology chapter if the visual loss involves either visual acuity or visual field loss. In the case of loss of acuity and visual field, consult the vision chapter (Chapter 12). The changes between the fourth and fifth editions that pertain to vision are discussed in detail in Chapter 12.

All other ratings and criteria for cranial nerve dysfunction have been essentially unchanged in the Fifth Edition compared with the Fourth Edition. The criteria for cranial nerve V (trigeminal nerve) dysfunction now emphasize the importance of determining the impact on ADL before assigning an impairment rating. Note that when a condition such as postherpetic neuralgia affects cranial nerve V, pain becomes the central criterion on which the impairment rating is determined, and an additional rating is not provided for pain. It may be appropriate to use the pain chapter to evaluate postherpetic neuralgia affecting other body regions that are not addressed in the other chapters.

13.5 Criteria for Rating Impairments of Station, Gait, and Movement Disorders

The *Guides 5th* section on station, gait, and movement disorders provides a few examples of neurologic disorders (eg, both motor neuron disease and a stroke) producing changes in movement and gait. The section on station, movement, and gait disorders was designed primarily for movement disorders of a primary neurologic nature and is not to be used for other, non–primary neurologic disorders, unless no other rating method is available to describe the impairment. For example, an individual with low back pain caused by a herniated disk may have a gait disorder but would be rated instead in the spine chapter, since that is the site of the major disorder and it is more specific. Individuals with spinal cord injury, however, are rated on the basis of dysfunction of multiple systems, such as station and gait (Table 13-15) and upper extremity impairment (Table 13-17), as detailed in Section 13.7.

13.6 Criteria for Rating Impairments of Upper Extremities Related to Central Impairment

This section is used instead of the upper extremity chapter (Chapter 16) for evaluating upper extremity disorders caused by brain dysfunction, as in the case of a stroke, Parkinson's disease, multiple sclerosis, etc. Section 13.8 uses the same table for the rating of causalgia and reflex sympathetic dystrophy (RSD). The upper extremity chapter is used for most non-CNS origins of upper extremity impairments. Any use of Tables 13-16 and 13-17 (reprinted below) for non-CNS disorders should be explained in writing. This section is unchanged from the Fourth Edition. It continues to provide higher ratings for the dominant rather than nondominant hand, unlike the upper extremity chapter, which does not differentiate for handedness.

Table 13-16 Criteria for Rating Impairment of One Upper Extremity

Class 1		Class 2		Class 3		Class 4	
Dominant Extremity 1%-9% Impairment of the Whole Person	Nondominant Extremity 1%-4% Impairment of the Whole Person	Dominant Extremity 10%-24% Impairment of the Whole Person	Nondominant Extremity 5%-14% Impairment of the Whole Person	Dominant Extremity 25%-39% Impairment of the Whole Person	Nondominant Extremity 15%-29% Impairment of the Whole Person	Dominant Extremity 40%-60% Impairment of the Whole Person	Nondominant Extremity 30%-45% Impairment of the Whole Person
Individual can use the involved extremity for self-care, daily activities, and holding, but has difficulty with digital dexterity		Individual can use the involved extremity for self-care, can grasp and hold objects with difficulty, but has no digital dexterity		Individual can use the involved extremity but has difficulty with self-care activities		Individual cannot use the involved extremity for self-care or daily activities	

Table 13-17 Criteria for Rating Impairments of Two Upper Extremities

Class 1 1%-19% Impairment of the Whole Person	Class 2 20%-39% Impairment of the Whole Person	Class 3 40%-79% Impairment of the Whole Person	Class 4 80%+ Impairment of the Whole Person
Individual can use both upper extremities for self-care, grasping, and holding, but has difficulty with digital dexterity	Individual can use both upper extremities for self-care, can grasp and hold objects with difficulty, but has no digital dexterity	Individual can use both upper extremities but has difficulty with self-care activities	Individual cannot use upper extremities

Chapter 13

The consensus among writers of this chapter was that, when brain dysfunction results in loss of use of the dominant vs the nondominant extremity, there will be a permanent and differential change in function. Therefore, this is reflected in the impairment ratings. The consensus with contributors to the upper extremity chapter was that a differential rating should not be applied, since the non-preferred extremity may become as capable of functioning as the preferred extremity. "If hand dominance has a significant impact on the ability to perform ADL, this can be discussed in the impairment evaluation report" (*Guides*, p 435).

M E D I C A L   T I P

If the dominant upper extremity is impaired, discuss the functional implications for performing ADL, after maximum medical improvement is reached.

L E G A L   T I P

For workers' compensation purposes, most states that use a statutory schedule for amputations also do not differentiate between dominant and nondominant upper extremities.

13.7 Criteria for Rating Spinal Cord and Related Impairments

In the *Guides 5th*, spinal cord disorders were removed from the orthopedic spine chapter, and the evaluation is now based on a neurologic approach, because the disorder is mainly neurologically based. In the Fourth Edition, spinal cord disorders including cauda equina syndrome and paraplegia were evaluated by means of a combination of DRE categories.

The neurologic approach to an individual with cauda equina or spinal cord injury, resulting in paraplegia, quadriplegia, or other CNS disorders, is to assess the condition, body parts, or functions that are impaired and combine all appropriate whole person ratings.

Criteria and ratings for losses in respiration, bladder function, anorectal function, and sexual function have remained unchanged and are reprinted in the *Guides* section from their respective chapters for convenience.

Tables 13-16 and 13-17 may be used for spinal cord disorders as well as brain lesions. Table 13-17 marks one of the few places where the *Guides* acknowledges a cumulative, rather than an incremental, effect of multiple extremity impairments. According to Table 13-16, if the same impairment affected both arms, the *Guides* would require combination of the ratings. For example, an individual with no bilateral upper extremity use in self-care could be rated as low as 58% WPI by combining 40% and 30% from Table 13-16. However, Table 13-17 rates this bilateral condition at no less than 80% WPI.

EXAMPLE

After diving into a shallow body of water while on vacation, John sustains a head and spinal cord injury with bilateral facet dislocation at the C4 and C5 levels, and loss of function of both upper extremities (C5 and C6). He has no bowel or bladder dysfunction but is unable to walk, although he has some motor function of his lower extremity.

Fifth Edition: Table 13-17 gives 80% impairment for loss of use of both upper extremities, combined with 39% WPI for inability to walk. The total WPI is 88%.

Fourth Edition: The 35% DRE (diagnosis-related estimate) cervicothoracic category V, combined with 75% inability to walk, gives a total combined impairment of 84%.

13.8 Criteria for Rating Impairments Related to Chronic Pain

This new section discusses the assessment of chronic pain for neurologically based disorders. Neurologic conditions covered in this section include the diagnoses of causalgia, posttraumatic neuralgia, and reflex sympathetic dystrophy (RSD). The neurologists have specifically chosen not to use the terminology of complex regional pain syndrome I and II, which is used in the upper extremity chapter, because they believe these conditions do not reflect two diagnostic criteria that can be grouped.

Since these painful neurologic conditions have uncertain etiologies and pathologies, yet marked objective changes in function, it was felt to be appropriate and consistent with the philosophy of the impairment ratings to rate these conditions solely on the basis of functional use of the upper or lower extremities.

Chapter 13

The following table indicates the differences in approach for these disorders in the neurology and upper extremity chapters. The upper extremity chapter provides a system for trying to define the specific nerves and dermatomes affected and assigning greater weight to particular nerves or regions that are affected. The upper extremity system of assessment is complex and does not differ significantly for most impairments in this chapter. The physician is free to use either chapter's method in evaluating causalgia, posttraumatic neuralgia, or RSD. As stated in the *Guides*, when both methods equally apply, the physician should use the method that provides the higher rating.

Comparison of the Rating Methods for RSD and Causalgia Between Chapter 13 (The Central and Peripheral Nervous System) and Chapter 16 (The Upper Extremities)

Chapter for Rating Causalgia/RSD	Ease of Use	Emphasis	Method	Maximum Impairment Rating
Chapter 13, Neurology	Simpler	Function, extremity dominance accounted for	Assess ADL; assess gait	60% upper extremity; 60% lower extremity
Chapter 16, Upper Extremity	Complex	Anatomy, individual nerves, sensory, motor assessment	Sensory, motor function	100% upper extremity for severe complex regional pain syndrome II

EXAMPLE

Fifth edition, Chapter 13 (The Central and Peripheral Nervous System): An individual with postsurgical RSD holds her right arm close to her body; the hand is dusky, with fingers tightly adducted and not separable, and she is unable to move the wrist without severe pain. Proximal muscles have disuse atrophy. Radiographs indicate diffuse demineralization, supporting the diagnosis. She has total disuse of the dominant extremity for self-care activities. On the basis of Table 13-22, she could be given a WPI rating of 40% to 60%.

Fifth Edition, Chapter 16 (The Upper Extremities): Severe RSD, extending to the elbow, without more proximal changes, can result in a 95% upper extremity impairment or 57% WPI. Extension of the RSD beyond the elbow would constitute a 60% WPI. Less severe changes, where motor or sensory function is present, would require individual nerve analysis and a rating of less than 57%.

13.9 Criteria for Rating Impairments of the Peripheral Nervous System, Neuromuscular Junction, and Muscular System

The procedures in this section, as well as the upper and lower extremity chapters, are the same as for assessment of peripheral nerve injuries. However, categories of sensory deficit caused by peripheral nerve disorders differ in the nervous system chapter from categories for sensory deficit in the upper extremity categories. The approach in the nervous system chapter is simpler, allows for a better determination of disorders with less impairment (< 25%), and also accounts differentially for pain that is forgotten and that is present during activity. The nervous system approach is especially good for polyneuropathies. This system can also be used for rating carpal tunnel syndrome. Both rating systems differ slightly from that in the Fourth Edition. The following table outlines the differences in approach and ratings of sensory loss in the nervous system and upper extremity chapters.

Approaches to Sensory Loss Caused by Peripheral Neuropathy

Nervous System Chapter	Upper Extremity Chapter
0%: No loss of sensation, abnormal sensation, or pain	0%: No loss of sensibility, abnormal sensation, or pain
1%-10%: Normal sensation except for pain, or decreased sensation with or without pain, forgotten during activity	1%-25%: Distorted superficial tactile sensibility (diminished light touch), with or without minimal abnormal sensations or pain, that is forgotten during activity
11%-25%: Normal sensation except for pain, or decreased sensation with or without pain, present during activity	
26%-60%: Decreased sensation with or without pain, interfering with activity	26%-60%: Distorted superficial tactile sensibility (diminished light touch and two-point discrimination), with some abnormal sensations or slight pain, that interferes with some activities
61%-80%: Decreased sensation with or without pain or minor causalgia that may prevent activity	61%-80%: Decreased superficial cutaneous pain and tactile sensibility (decreased protective sensibility) with abnormal sensations or moderate pain, that may prevent some activities
81%-95%: Decreased sensation with severe pain or major causalgia that prevents activity	81%-99%: Deep cutaneous pain sensibility present; absent superficial pain and tactile sensibility (absent protective sensibility), with abnormal sensations or severe pain, that prevents most activity
	100%: Absent sensibility, abnormal sensations, or severe pain that prevents all activity

Motor deficits and loss of power are evaluated with the same procedure and ratings in the nervous system, upper extremity, and lower extremity chapters. Multiple nerve disorders are combined in all these chapters.

13.10 Nervous System Impairment Evaluation Summary

Table 13-25 provides an overview of the clinical evaluation findings and impairment criteria for impairments of the nervous system, cross-referenced to appropriate tables in the chapter.

Table 13-25 Nervous System Impairment Evaluation Summary

Disorder	History, Including Selected Relevant Symptoms	Examination Record	Assessment of Neurologic Function
General	Neurologic symptoms may include: alterations in level of consciousness, confusion, memory loss, difficulties with language, headache, visual blurring, double vision, fatigue, facial pain and weakness, ringing in the ears, dizziness, vertigo, difficulty swallowing or speaking, weakness of one or multiple limbs, difficulty walking or climbing stairs, shooting pain, numbness and tingling in the extremities, tremor, loss of coordination, loss of bladder or rectal control, and sexual dysfunction Impact of symptoms on function and ability to do daily activities Review medical history	Constitutional; measure vital signs: blood pressure sitting or standing, supine blood pressure, pulse rate and regularity, respiration, temperature, height; examine visual, cardiovascular, musculoskeletal systems; assess gait and station, motor function, including muscle strength and tone in upper and lower extremities Evaluate higher integrative functions, orientation, recent and remote memory, attention span and concentration, language, fund of knowledge, cranial nerves II-XII Examine sensation (eg, touch, pinprick, vibration, proprioception), deep tendon reflexes, note pathologic reflexes Test coordination	Data derived from relevant studies (eg, EEG, lumbar puncture, neuropsychological assessment, evoked potentials, cartoid duplex examination, CT scan, MRI, MRA, PET, SPECT, NCV, EMG, quantitative sensory tests, automatic function assessment
Central Nervous System: 1. Consciousness Disorders 2. Arousal Disorders 3. Cognitive Impairments 4. Language Disorders 5. Behavioral or Emotional Disorders 6. Cranial Nerve Disorders 7. Station, Gait, and Movement Disorders 8. Disorders of the Extremities 9. Spinal Cord Disorders	Discuss relevant symptoms and any resulting limitation of daily activities	See above physical exam Expand upon relevant areas	CT scan, MRI, EEG, etc
Neurologic Impairment With Chronic Pain	Discuss relevant symptoms and any resulting limitation of daily activities	See above physical exam See Chapter 18, Pain	Expand upon relevant areas Radiographs; bone scan; Doppler
Peripheral Nervous System: 1. Neuromuscular Junction Disorders 2. Muscular System Disorders	Discuss relevant symptoms and any resulting limitation of daily activities	See above physical exam Expand upon relevant areas	EMG; NCV

	End-Organ Damage	Diagnosis	Degree of Impairment
	Include assessment of sequelae, including end-organ damage and impairment	Record all pertinent diagnosis(es); note if they are at MMI; if not, discuss under what conditions and when stability is expected	Criteria outlined in this chapter
	Assess relevant systems (eg, mental and behavioral, upper and lower extremities)	Epilepsy; seizures; syncope/dizziness; loss of awareness, sleep apnea; narcolepsy: periodic limb movements; dementia; traumatic brain injury; aphasia; dysphasia; cranial nerve disorders II-XII	See Tables 13-2 through 13-9, 13-14 through 13-18, and 13-21 through 13-24
	Assess relevant systems (eg, mental and behavioral, pain)	Reflex sympathetic dystrophy; causalgia; posttraumatic neuralgia	See Table 13-22
	Assess relevant systems (eg, upper and lower extremities)	Spinal root; brachial plexus; peripheral nerve; autonomic nervous system disorders	See Tables 13-23 and 13-24

Chapter 14

Mental and Behavioral Disorders

Introduction

This chapter provides an overview of key points and changes (identified with an icon **G**) made in Chapter 14 of the AMA *Guides to the Evaluation of Permanent Impairment, Fifth Edition* (*Guides 5th*), illustrates these changes in a table comparison, and discusses the purpose and implications of the major changes, with illustrative examples. The numbered section titles within this chapter correspond to sections within Chapter 14 of the *Guides 5th*. Only key principles or important changes are included in this chapter.

Key Points and Changes

Establish and document any mental and behavioral diagnosis by means of *DSM-IV* criteria.

Use established psychological tests when needed to increase diagnostic acumen.

This edition provides only qualitative or ordinal ratings for mental and behavioral disorders, including none, mild, moderate, marked, and extreme impairment.

Numerical impairment ratings are not assigned, since these spheres of functioning are most indicative of disability rather than impairment.

Qualitative assessment of mental and behavioral impairments depends on assessing the degree of functioning in four spheres: activities of daily living (ADL), social functioning, concentration, and adaptation.

The degree of functioning is described ordinarily in terms of none, mild, moderate, marked, and extreme impairment.

G Extreme impairment in one or more spheres, or marked impairment in two or more spheres, probably precludes the performance of most complex tasks, such as work, without considerable support or accommodation.

G Effects of medication, as indicated in Chapter 2 of the *Guides*, may warrant an increase in the impairment rating, by up to 3%, if they are necessary and impact ADL.

G The chronic nature of some mental and behavioral impairments indicates there may be remissions, rather than a cure. Thus, individuals can still have a permanent impairment, even if their condition is in remission.

G An individual with a somatoform pain disorder does not receive an additional rating in the pain chapter.

G Somatoform pain disorder is diagnosed only for individuals who meet *DSM-IV* criteria.

A new Table 14-2 lists some commonly diagnosed impairments, their signs and symptoms, and the areas of function commonly affected by each diagnosis.

Comparison of Tables Between the Fifth and Fourth *Guides* Editions

The following table summarizes the key points and changes in tables between the fourth and fifth editions of the *Guides*.

Comparison of Tables Between the Fifth and Fourth *Guides* Editions

Table Topic	5th Edition Table Number	4th Edition Table Number	Summary of Changes in 5th Edition
Impairment due to mental and behavioral disorders	14-1	1	None
Selected impairments and common limitations in ability	14-2		New; provides examples of limitations in ability associated with several mental impairments

Introduction

The Fifth Edition mental and behavioral disorder chapter was slightly revised, and additional case studies were included. A qualitative assessment, without numerical impairment ratings, was retained. There was not sufficient scientific evidence, nor was a consensus developed, as to what numerical ratings could be assigned. The *Guides* approach does not recommend use of numerical ratings as was used in the Third Edition. The Fifth Edition removed much of the Fourth Edition discussion of Social Security criteria, which pertained to disability assessment.

Unlike the other chapters in the *Guides*, the mental and behavioral chapter provides several unique challenges for its application. First, mental and behavioral disorders frequently accompany other medical impairments. The physician who is evaluating low back pain or carpal tunnel syndrome may not have the expertise necessary to identify concomitant psychological disorders. Second, in many cases where a concomitant mental or behavioral disorder was suspected, the condition may not have been thoroughly evaluated because of the stigma still assigned to mental and behavioral disorders, or because, in the case of workers' compensation, an additional impairment rating and award was not provided. Third, assessing and separating medical impairment from the disability of mental and behavioral disorders is very problematic and has not been successfully achieved. Because of its very nature, the brain and its behavioral function encompass complex activities, such as behavior in work or social settings, which apply primarily to disability assessment. The functions of the brain, such as cognition, which do not involve complex interactions with the environment, can be assessed within the neurology chapter. However, it is the complex functions of the brain, the individual, the emotional totality, and his or her interactions with the environment, either in social or work settings, that is commonly assessed by psychiatry. These complex interactions and adaptations refer more to disability assessment than to medical impairment. Hence, in the mental and behavioral chapter, the distinctions between impairment (eg, brain function) and disability (eg, interaction of one's mental functions with the environment) become blurred, and an assessment of solely permanent impairment is difficult and probably not very meaningful.

Since the changes to the Fifth Edition are limited, the purpose of this chapter is to illustrate ways in which the mental and behavioral chapter can be used.

Chapter 14

> ## MEDICAL TIP
>
> If the physician suspects a concomitant psychological disorder, consider performing a screening test, which will assist in the determination of whether psychiatric referral is needed.
>
> Ensure that the test screens for conditions commonly seen within a workers' compensation or personal injury setting, such as depression, mood disorder, substance abuse, and somatoform disorder.
>
> If individuals are reluctant to see a psychiatrist for evaluation, indicate that it is important to obtain a full assessment of how their condition impacts their ADL and work.

> ## LEGAL TIP
>
> States can use the qualitative ratings if desired and assign a numerical rating based on loss of use or function, if state law allows for such nonscheduled impairment ratings.

14.1 Principles of Assessment

As outlined in the Fourth Edition, the Fifth Edition recommends that the physician evaluate the condition on the basis of *DSM-IV* criteria. The evaluator performs a comprehensive review of the condition and assesses the individual's ability to function over time and the response to treatment and rehabilitation. In assessing mental and behavioral impairment, the physician must obtain information from both medical and nonmedical sources that indicate the individual's ability to perform daily activities, including the ability to concentrate, be persistent, pace oneself, and tolerate mental demands, including stress. Assess behaviors over time, so that any patterns are identified, since functioning can vary considerably when evaluated in a single moment.

Well-established psychological tests, such as the Wechsler Adult Intelligence Scale (WAIS) and the Minnesota Multiphasic Personality Inventory-2 (MMPI-2), may improve diagnostic acumen.

> ### M E D I C A L   T I P
>
> When assessing permanence, indicate whether the condition has been observed over a sufficient time frame to identify a pattern. Variations in behavior can then be seen as anticipated changes within an overall pattern of a permanent impairment.
>
> When necessary, use well-established psychological tests to establish the diagnosis and monitor the clinical course.

> ### L E G A L   T I P
>
> WAIS or MMPI-2 or other testing may be considered necessary to establish "objectivity" in the evaluation. Testing to confirm the permanency and nontransitory nature of a mental or behavioral impairment may also reduce challenges to a rating for mental or behavioral impairment.

14.2 Psychiatric Diagnosis and Impairment

This section of the *Guides 5th* incorporates and reorganizes information in sections 14.1 and 14.4 of the Fourth Edition. The *DSM-IV* criteria have replaced the *DSM-III-R* criteria cited in the Fourth Edition for assessing permanent impairment. The *DSM-IV* criteria are not a detailed description of psychiatric disorders. *DSM-IV* includes symptoms necessary to make a *DSM-IV* diagnosis but does not enumerate all symptoms and signs seen with a diagnosis.[1] Axis IV, which assesses psychosocial and environmental problems, and Axis V, which provides a global assessment of functioning, including an assessment of some disabilities, are important to incorporate into the impairment assessment.

In evaluating psychiatric impairments, consider the effects of medication, which can lead to an increase in the impairment when side effects are present that impact the ADL. Also consider the effects of motivation, which often link impairment and disability. Thus, an individual with a psychiatric condition such as a personality disorder may be more motivated to adapt with increased functioning in a supportive environment, compared with a more stressful, demanding environment.

Rehabilitation may be able to improve function, lessening the impairment and certainly the disability. The discussion on rehabilitation is slightly increased in the Fifth Edition, indicating again that a psychiatric impairment, like a physical one, may never regain full function, but it may attain sufficient function to minimally impact ADL.

Chapter 14

14.3 A Method of Evaluating Psychiatric Impairment

The *Guides 5th* retains some concepts developed by the Social Security Administration (SSA) to assess impairment severity; however, the report now needs to include detailed information on the ability to perform ADL. To assess psychiatric impairment, determine function in four major spheres: (1) ability to perform ADL; (2) social functioning; (3) concentration, persistence, and pace; and (4) deterioration or decompensation in work or worklike settings.

Note that the mental and behavioral impairment assessment encompasses disability-related aspects, such as adaptability to work, critical to mental and behavioral health. Recall also that some functions, though not narrowly defined within ADL, can impact ADL in significant ways. For example, social functioning and concentration, persistence, and pace may also have significant ramifications for ADL. For example, limited social functioning can prevent shopping for groceries. Problems with concentration, persistence, and pace may limit preparation of meals or simple household cleanliness.

Assess the degree of impairment—either none, mild, moderate, marked, or extreme in each sphere—as indicated in Table 14-1 of the Guides. The *Guides* notes that the qualitative or ordinal scales are not equally distributed, meaning that a moderate impairment does not imply a 50% reduction in functioning. The degree of impairment is defined in the *Guides* as follows: none: no impairment in function; mild: the impairment is compatible with most useful functioning; moderate: the impairment is compatible with some, but not all, useful functioning; marked: the impairment significantly impedes useful functioning; and extreme: the impairment is not compatible with useful functioning. Extreme signifies complete dependency on another person for care.

How can the physician apply the following information to assessment of work ability? As listed in the *Guides,* if an individual has either an extreme impairment in one or more areas or a marked limitation in two or more spheres, it is unlikely that the individual will be able to perform complex activities, such as work, without considerable support and accommodation. The need, degree, and reasonableness of accommodation need to be assessed on an individual basis.

The aspects of functioning noted in Table 14-1 and as indicated above are unchanged from the table in the Fourth Edition, except that ADL no longer include social and recreational activities. This set of activities was also removed from the ADL list in Chapter 1, as previously noted. Since social and recreational activities are complex, they pertain more to disability than impairment assessment.

14.4 Assessing Impairment Severity

This section has been expanded in the *Guides 5th*. When determining the severity of an individual's mental and behavioral impairment, consider the effects of treatment, structured settings, variability of mental disorders, effects of common mental and behavioral conditions, and the assessment of workplace function.

Determination of the ability to function within the workplace requires the assessment of general and specific workplace skills. General skills or capacities, as defined by the SSA and adapted by the *Guides,* include (1) understanding and memory, (2) sustained concentration and persistence, (3) social interaction, and (4) adaptation.

MEDICAL TIP
Before assessing the specifics of the workplace, identify the individual's abilities in the above capacities. If insufficient ability is present within these capacities, the individual is unlikely to be able to work in a traditional work setting.

LEGAL TIP
These four severity criteria may in many jurisdictions be more appropriately focused on the lack of wage-earning capacity, rather than a medically determined impairment. The reader should note that these criteria were not simply adapted from the SSA's regulations, but were created by SSA to determine the individual's ability to work. In most workers' compensation systems, this determination is not part of the impairment evaluation, although it may be in those state systems that apply a mathematical or algebraic multiplier to the *Guides'* percentages of whole person impairment to determine a disability rating.

Section 14.4 also includes a discussion of the effects of common mental and behavioral conditions such as substance abuse, personality disorders, and somatoform pain disorders, which often accompany other medical impairments. For an individual to be classified with any of these conditions, he or she needs to meet the criteria for the condition as identified by the *DSM-IV* guidelines.

EXAMPLE

John is a bystander and witness to extreme violence in the convenience store where he works. On a windy but sunny day, a gunman enters and shoots several customers while John hides under the counter, where the wastebasket is kept. As the gunman is leaving, he notices John, fires a shot that misses, and flees to escape the authorities. Two of the customers die. John becomes depressed; is treated for depression for 9 months, including 6 months with antidepressants, with resolution of his depression; and continues in counseling at the time of the evaluation. He continues to have nightmares and sleep disturbances on a monthly basis, sometimes as often as nightly. Sleep studies, including polysomnography, indicate abnormalities, including an intermittent loss of rapid-eye-movement sleep and abnormal alpha waves. He is reminded of the events on a monthly basis when he sees something familiar, such as clothes someone wears like one of the victims or the gunman, or weather similar to the day of the event. He previously traveled but now has difficulty flying or being in confined spaces, without control, for long periods of time. John could receive between a 1% and a 9% permanent impairment from Chapter 13 (central and peripheral nervous system) on the basis of his sleep disturbance and the determined impact on his ADL.

Depending on the degree to which these disturbances affect the four areas noted above (ADL; social; pace, persistence and concentration; and adaptation), a qualitative psychiatric impairment may also be combined with the sleep disturbance impairment.

14.4e.1 Substance Abuse and Personality Disorders

This area poses significant problems in workers' compensation because the substance abuse is usually not associated with a workplace accident or exposure. Apportionment of cause to the preexisting dependency that prolongs or enhances a disability is commonly found in cases where substance abuse is present. That is, if a workplace accident or exposure leads to a disability that is prolonged or heightened by a substance abuse problem, the disability caused by the substance abuse is apportioned to non–work-related cause or causes.

14.4e.2 Somatoform Pain Disorders

Somatoform pain disorder is defined in the *Guides 5th* as a preoccupation with pain in the absence of physical findings that adequately account for the pain and its intensity, as well as the presence of psychological factors that are judged to have a major role in the onset, severity, exacerbation, and maintenance of pain (*Guides 5th*, p 366).

If an individual has a somatoform pain disorder, he or she is not rated in addition by the pain chapter. An individual with another impairment, such as low back pain, may also be classified as having a somatoform pain disorder if he or she meets the criteria. In that case, the individual would be given a qualitative assessment, based on the four spheres of functioning, but would not be assigned an additional, numerical impairment rating.

14.4e.3 Malingering

Malingering refers to a simulation or exaggeration of physical illness for an external gain, such as disability payments, obtaining controlled substances, or another perceived benefit. With malingering, the individual intentionally produces symptoms or physical signs and is aware of his or her motivation for doing so. Malingering is not considered a mental disorder according to *DSM-IV* because, under some circumstances, malingering may be beneficial and adaptive, for instance, feigning illness in a prisoner-of-war camp. Consider malingering when there is a discrepancy between objective findings and subjective complaints, or when symptoms are ill defined or overly dramatized.[2]

MEDICAL TIP

If a physician suspects malingering, indicate the areas of discrepancy, preferably multiple, between observed or expected findings and symptoms. Also identify where the discrepancy appears.

LEGAL TIP

Tests or documentation to identify malingering may significantly assist in the diagnosis and constitute legal evidence for proof of malingering. Malingering as used in the *Guides* and *DSM-IV* may be defined differently under state law.

14.5 Examples of Impairment Due to Mental and Behavioral Disorders

14.6 Format of the Impairment Report

Sections 14.5 and 14.6 of the *Guides 5th* are new. The case examples, in particular, illustrate the importance of identifying the areas of function, where emotional difficulties arise, and how their behaviors alter function and can lead to significant disability.

The examples in the Fifth Edition do not differentiate between those elements of assessment that should be called "impairment" as distinguished from "disability." These aspects can be distinguished to a limited degree in the report. Section 14.6 details the essential components of the impairment report.

M E D I C A L   T I P

For examples such as 14-1, 14-2, and 14-3 with class 2 or greater limits in social functioning, concentration, or adaptation, identify the impact of these limitations on the ability to perform ADL.

L E G A L   T I P

As with the section on pain, the format of the report should closely follow both the *Guides* and any *DSM-IV* requirements. In the Fifth Edition, the outline format of the report makes its use easier for both the physician and nonphysician user.

Notwithstanding the lack of percentages in the fifth and fourth editions, the evaluator may assign a percentage of the whole person rating to a mental or behavioral disorder. In most cases, this rating will be based on the evaluator's clinical experience, with appropriate references to the classes of impairment stated in Table 14-1 and, if the disorder is listed, from Table 14-2. The lack of percentages may be troubling in states that award disability as a mathematical or algebraic coefficient of impairment.

As will be noted in the chapter that discusses the Fifth Edition's treatment of pain, anything less than a meticulous report, in the format stated in Chapter 14, may be subject to attack on the grounds that it fails to comply with generally and currently accepted medical standards.

References

1. Goldman LS, Wise TN, Brody DS. Psychiatric diagnosis. In: *Psychiatry for Primary Care Physicians*. Chicago, Ill: American Medical Association; 1998:31.

2. Goldman LS, Wise TN, Brody DS. Somatoform and related disorders. In: *Psychiatry for Primary Care Physicians*. Chicago, Ill: American Medical Association; 1998:286.

Chapter 15

The Spine

Introduction

This chapter provides an overview of key points and changes (identified with an icon **G**) made in Chapter 15 of the AMA *Guides to the Evaluation of Permanent Impairment, Fifth Edition* (*Guides 5th*), illustrates these changes in a table comparison, provides a brief overview of spine anatomy, and discusses the purpose and implications of the major changes, with illustrative examples. The numbered section titles within this chapter correspond to sections within Chapter 15 of the *Guides 5th*. Only key principles or important changes are included in this chapter.

Key Points and Changes

Principles of Assessment

G Impairment is rated only when the individual has reached maximal medical improvement (MMI).

The spine consists of five regions: cervical, thoracic, lumbar, sacral, and coccygeal. The first three regions are of main clinical importance and are discussed in detail in the *Guides 5th*.

Base the spine history primarily on the individual's own statements rather than secondhand information.

It is not appropriate to question the individual's integrity.

Describe in detail the chief complaint and the quality, severity, anatomic location, frequency, and duration of symptoms; initiating, exacerbating, and alleviating factors; and the way in which the condition interferes with daily activities.

Document the relationship of clinical findings to any previous spine problems.

Judiciously use information from medical records.

Report and discuss inconsistencies within the clinical evaluation and medical record review.

G The spine physical examination should focus on objective findings such as range of motion (ROM), reflexes, muscle strength, atrophy, sensory deficits, root tension signs, gait, and the need for assistive devices.

To be of diagnostic value, clinical symptoms and signs must be consistent with the imaging findings.

Pain commonly seen with the condition is already included in the impairment ratings.

G If pain is disproportionate for the condition, use the pain chapter for determining whether a qualitative and additional quantitative amount (1%-3%) should be combined with the diagnosis-related estimate (DRE) or ROM rating.

Determining the Appropriate Method for Assessment

G The term *method* has replaced the Fourth Edition term *models* when referring to DRE or ROM.

G When to use the DRE or ROM method is now clearly explained in the spine chapter.

The DRE method is still the primary method of choice for evaluating spine injury or illness.

G Spinal cord injury is evaluated according to the functional approach described in the nervous system chapter.

G The word *differentiators* in the Fourth Edition has been replaced by the term *objective findings*, which has been defined and explained.

G Criteria for alterations of motion segment integrity have been revised to reflect current scientific knowledge.

In the few instances in which the ROM and DRE methods can both be used, evaluate the individual with both methods and award the higher rating.

For reevaluation, the following applies: if the ROM method is used initially, it must be used again. If the DRE method is used initially, the DRE or ROM method may be used subsequently, if a different spine region is involved.

DRE Method

G Use the DRE method as the principal method to evaluate impairment from a distinct injury, if the impairment can be well characterized by the DRE method or if the cause of the impairment is not easily determined and the DRE method describes the impairment.

Also use the DRE method for individuals with corticospinal involvement with decompression and multilevel fusions within the same region.

G Individuals with corticospinal tract involvement treated with decompression and multilevel fusions within the same region should be rated by the DRE method because assessing ROM in paralyzed individuals is difficult.

G The diagnosis of herniated disk must be documented by an appropriate imaging study.

G Impairments within a DRE category encompass a range, with adjustments of up to 3% to account for treatment effects and changes in the ability to perform activities of daily living (ADL).

ROM Method

G The ROM method is used for recurrent conditions, when conditions occur within a single spine region.

G Use the ROM method if, *within a single spine region* (eg, lumbar, thoracic, or cervical), there are multiple events or pathologies:

- Multilevel involvement (eg, L3-L4 and L4-L5 or radiculopathy at multiple levels (L3-L4, L4-L5, and L5-S1)

- Multiple recurrences/episodes—or radiculopathy at multiple levels (eg, L4-L5 and L5-S1)

- Multilevel motion segment alteration

- Multiple fractures

Also use the ROM method for:

- Spinal stenosis with radiculopath, except following trauma

- Conditions not well represented by the DRE method

Comparison of Tables Between the Fifth and Fourth Guides Editions

The following table summarizes the key points and changes in tables between the fourth and fifth editions of the *Guides*.

Comparison of Tables Between the Fifth and Fourth *Guides* Editions

Table Topic	5th Edition Table Number	4th Edition Table Number	Summary of Changes in 5th Edition
Physical examination	15-1		New; identifies key components of physical examination
Common radicular syndromes	15-2		New; provides common lumbar and cervical nerve root-based motor and sensory deficits and reflex changes
DRE category differentiators		71	Deleted; revised version in Box 15-1
Lumbar spine DRE impairment	15-3	70, 72	Ranges allow 3% adjustment; categories VI through VIII deleted from this chapter; more thorough diagnostic descriptions; *lumbosacral* term eliminated
Thoracic spine DRE impairment	15-4	74	Ranges allow 3% adjustment; categories VI through VIII deleted from this chapter; more thorough diagnostic descriptions; *thoracolumbar* term eliminated
Cervical spine DRE impairment	15-5	73	Ranges allow 3% adjustment; categories VI through VIII deleted from this chapter; more thorough diagnostic descriptions; *cervicothoracic* term eliminated
Corticospinal tract impairment	15-6		New; replicates terminology and ratings from nervous system chapter

Table Topic	5th Edition Table Number	4th Edition Table Number	Summary of Changes in 5th Edition
Specific spine disorders used as part of ROM method	15-7	75	No significant changes
Lumbar flexion and extension (ROM)	15-8	81	No significant changes
Lumbar lateral bending and ankylosis (ROM)	15-9	82	Bending supplants the term *flexion*; stylistic changes—left-sided measurements listed first
Thoracic flexion and ankylosis (ROM)	15-10	79	No significant changes
Rotational measure of abnormal thoracic motion and ankylosis (ROM)	15-11	80	"Rotation" replaces "flexion and extension" in average range 60° description; otherwise, stylistic changes only
Cervical extension or flexion or ankylosis impairment (ROM)	15-12	76	Midrange increase in lost degrees of cervical motion
Cervical lateral bending motion and ankylosis impairment (ROM)	15-13	77	*Bending* supplants the term *flexion*; otherwise, no significant changes
Rotational measure of abnormal cervical motion and ankylosis (ROM)	15-14	78	No significant changes
Sensory loss impairment	15-15	11	Revised descriptors; grades reversed; new grade of sensory deficit added (grade 0 = 100%); see Table 16-10
Determining impairment caused by loss of power and motor deficits	15-16	12	Stylistic changes from the previous edition; also at Table 16-11
Unilateral spinal nerve root impairment affecting the upper extremity	15-17	13	Column for combined motor and sensory deficit not included; also at Table 16-13
Unilateral spinal nerve root impairment affecting the lower extremity	15-18	83	Eliminates range of lower extremity impairment (now produced by calculation on p 423)
Selected pelvic disorder impairments	15-19		Replicates 4th Edition text
Spine evaluation summary	15-20		Replaces 4th Edition Figure 80

Introduction

This section summarizes changes to the *Guides 5th*: clear instructions are given for use of the DRE and ROM methods; permanent impairment is evaluated only at MMI; the DRE method now includes a range, with adjustments up to 3%; spinal cord injury is evaluated according to the functional approach; DRE "differentiators" have been replaced by more "objective findings"; and threshold values to define alteration of motion segment integrity (AOMSI) have been increased.

The musculoskeletal chapter was divided into three separate chapters for the Fifth Edition: spine, upper extremities, and lower extremities. Having separate chapters facilitates use and acknowledges the differences in approach to evaluating these musculoskeletal impairments. The Fourth Edition included all of these topics in a single chapter.

Basic Anatomy

Both editions of the *Guides* assume the reader understands basic spine anatomy. The spinal nerves exit the spinal cord as nerve roots. The nerve roots may combine and intermingle to form the cervical plexus and brachial plexus in the upper extremity, and the lumbosacral plexus in the lower extremity. Peripheral nerves then exit from the plexus.

Thus, the femoral nerve is derived from nerve roots L2, L3, and L4. When pressure is applied to a nerve root, motor or sensory changes can be felt in the multiple peripheral nerves, to which those roots contribute. The physician assesses both motor and sensory function of peripheral nerves to determine whether a single or multiple nerve roots are affected. There is often some degree of overlap in innervation, and clinical determinations must be confirmed by electrical or imaging studies. This has practical application in the *Guides*, since discerning whether a single nerve root is involved would entail use of the DRE method, while multiple root involvement at multiple levels within the same spinal region (eg, multivertebral involvement in the lumbar region, spinal stenosis) would indicate use of the ROM method of assessment.

Nerve function can be affected by changes in anatomy or physiology at three regions: where the nerve originates in the spinal column, upon exit through the neural foramen or bony spinal canal, or at a peripheral site. Regardless of the diagnosis, if an individual has definitive clinical signs indicating nerve root impairment and objective studies such as imaging consistent with the clinical signs, then the physician needs to integrate this information to determine whether nerves at one or more levels within the same region of the spine are affected. If one level is affected, use the DRE method when possible. If nerves or vertebrae at more than one level within the same spinal region are involved, then use the ROM method.

Physicians assess nerve function through sensory discrimination, reflexes, and motor strength. Common tests for sensory function are pinprick and light touch, done over a specific dermatome to attribute loss of sensory function to a specific nerve. The dermatomes depicted in Figures 15-1 and 15-2 (*Guides 5th*) are accurate for most individuals, but variations exist.[1] Motor function is assessed through strength and reflex testing. Other specialized maneuvers in the physical exam, such as the straight leg raising (SLR) test, also help determine if a nerve root is involved.

15.1 Principles of Assessment

This section in the Fifth Edition emphasizes the importance of understanding Chapters 1 and 2, which define the philosophy and application of *Guides* principles. A detailed history is essential in spine evaluation and needs to integrate the individual's description of the illness with findings from medical and work reports when available.

In the spine chapter, a *region* refers to either the cervical, thoracic, lumbar, or sacral spine. Prior terminology, eg, cervicothoracic, has been replaced by a single spine region, eg, cervical or thoracic, to more accurately reflect accepted anatomic and clinical terminology. Impairments that span two regions, eg, cervical-thoracic, are evaluated on the basis of the more proximal region. Thus, evaluate thoracolumbar on the basis of thoracic criteria and lumbosacral on the basis of lumbar criteria. A spinal level refers to an area bounded by two vertebrae, a single spinal disk, and associated nerve roots and nerves.

As indicated in Chapters 1 and 2, the ratings noted in the spine, as well as other chapters in the *Guides,* account for pain that is customary for a given condition. Thus, the ratings for low back pain with radiculopathy, as well as other painful spine conditions, already account for the expected pattern of pain that accompanies these conditions, recognizing that variability is present among individuals. The pain chapter was designed for use only in cases in which pain is biologically and behaviorally credible and is in excess of what is expected for a particular impairment. It was not intended for use in all patients with low back pain. Incorporating the pain chapter in spine assessments is discussed in the pain chapter and in examples in this chapter.

15.1a Interpretation of Symptoms and Signs

The spine examination section has been revised and expanded. Identification of key findings, such as single-level radiculopathy, will enable the examiner to choose the DRE evaluation method quickly. Other findings, such as multiple-level involvement, will quickly alert the examiner to use the ROM method. The purpose of the exam is to identify the degree of impairment and the impairment's impact on ADL (if any) and to enable the physician to determine which evaluation strategy is most accurate: the DRE or the ROM method. The Fourth Edition contained an assessment of sciatic nerve tension signs, loss of motion segment integrity, special studies, differentiators, and structural inclusions. In the Fifth Edition, the term *differentiators* has been abandoned, and instead, Box 15-1 lists clinical findings and their definitions now used to place an individual in a particular DRE category. The definitions of these clinical terms, some of which were called *differentiators,* are discussed in the DRE section and below.

The examination section expands on nerve tension signs, including appropriate testing methods. The physician needs to integrate the clinical assessment of sensory, motor, and reflex findings, identify any nerve tension signs, and synthesize these findings with the relevant imaging studies to determine whether radiculopathy is present. *Radiculopathy* in the *Guides* is defined as significant alteration in the function of a nerve root or nerve roots and is usually caused by pressure on one or several nerve roots (*Guides 5th,* p 382).

Neurologic Tests

In the neurologic exam, document associated motor and sensory changes, with any reflex changes noted for the expected level of neurologic involvement. Table 15-2 (p 376) and Figures 15-1 and 15-2 illustrate autonomous zones. Several different systems exist for defining sensory and motor deficits for particular nerve roots. The *Guides* has attempted to incorporate the most widely recognized deficits for nerve root involvement. These tables are designed to serve as a reference and to determine whether symptoms correspond to objective pathologic changes.

It is important to note sciatic nerve tension signs, since these are clinical findings suggestive of radiculopathy, primarily for nerve roots L4, L5, and S1. Radiculopathy would quickly enable placement within DRE category II (if resolved) or III or higher (if still present) when MMI is reached. Sciatic nerve tension tests, such as the SLR maneuver, can be used to clinically support a diagnosis of radiculopathy but are not synonymous with radiculopathy. The SLR maneuver must be performed properly to differentiate between hamstring tightness and sciatic nerve stretch. If feasible, test the individual in both the supine and sitting positions, and compare the results.

When the individual is supine, lift the leg by the ankle to flex the hip with the knee extended. With the individual sitting, the hip is flexed 90° and the knee is extended. The test is positive only when thigh and/or leg pain is reported along the appropriate dermatomal distribution. Record the degree of elevation at which pain occurs. A positive test, producing leg pain below the knee, is not specific for radiculopathy at a particular level; it is suggestive of lumbosacral radiculopathy.

Femoral nerve tension sign (reverse SLR) assesses the femoral nerve, which is composed of L2, L3, and L4 roots. Again, this test is not specific for a level of radiculopathy, but can be suggestive of root involvement at L2, L3, or L4. An imaging study is needed and is used in conjunction with the clinical findings to more accurately define the level of involvement and nerve root pathology.

The SLR test in disk herniation has acceptable sensitivity (72% to 97%) but is nonspecific (11% to 45%). Straight leg raising of the asymptomatic limb (eg, crossed SLR) that produces sciatica in the limb with symptoms (crossed positive) increases specificity (85% to 100%) but is less sensitive (23% to 42%) in detecting disk herniation. With time, spine-related symptoms usually improve, and a positive root tension (SLR) test is elicited only at the extremes of hip flexion (leg raising). Reverse SLR or femoral stretch test causes root tension of L2, L3, and L4 and may be a sign of disk herniations at the higher levels. This test has low sensitivity and specificity (*Guides 5th*, p 376). Note that in spinal stenosis, sciatic nerve tension signs are often absent, even when compression of the sciatic nerve is present.

Imaging studies are of greatest value for rating purposes when they are consistent with the clinical symptoms and signs. Therefore, when feasible, radiologic and magnetic resonance imaging studies are best reviewed by the evaluating physician. A herniated disk, which can be detected on MRI or CT scan in asymptomatic people, does not necessarily explain the origin of the back pain. An imaging result alone is insufficient to qualify for a DRE category. Electromyography (EMG) studies that are clearly positive support a diagnosis of radiculopathy and therefore qualify the individual for at least DRE category III. Note the strict definition of a positive EMG and the need for a well-trained and qualified electromyographer.

The following table summarizes some key clinical findings and their corresponding DRE category. Note that an individual with the given clinical finding will meet criteria for at least the corresponding DRE category, but may be classified into a higher DRE category if other findings are present.

Clinical Findings That Indicate Corresponding DRE Categories

Clinical Findings	DRE category	Impairment Rating (%)
No clinical findings, no documented neurologic impairment, no change in structural integrity or fractures, only symptoms	I	0
Muscle spasm alone	II	5%-8%
Muscle guarding alone	II	5%-8%
Asymmetry of spinal motion	II or higher	≥ 5%-8%
Nonverifiable radicular root pain alone	II	5%-8%
Reflex abnormalities or marked asymmetry between arms or legs	II or higher	≥ 5%-8%
Weakness or sensory loss in dermatomal distribution, caused by spinal pathology	III or higher	≥ 10%-13%
Atrophy, caused by spinal pathology	III or higher	≥ 10%-13%
Radiculopathy	III or higher	≥ 10%-13%
Electrodiagnostic verification of radiculopathy	III or higher	≥ 10%-13%
AOMSI	IV or higher	≥ 20%-23%
Cauda equina syndrome	Higher than V; see neurology assessment (Chapter 13)	> 28%
Urodynamic tests	Higher than V; see neurology assessment (Chapter 13)	> 28%

MEDICAL TIP

The physician may choose to validate SLR by using the following methods:
• Gentle ankle dorsiflexion and hip internal rotation increase pain.
• Ankle plantar flexion and hip external rotation decrease the sciatica.
• Symptomatic responses to supine and sitting SLR should be similar, although the angle at which pain is elicited may vary.

LEGAL TIP

Check to see that medical reports that use SLR signs include descriptions of testing in multiple positions, location of pain, and validation maneuvers, especially in cases where radiologic studies are unclear.

15.1b Description of Clinical Studies
Motion Segment Integrity and AOMSI

Alteration of motion segment integrity (AOMSI) remains a criteria for placing an individual within a DRE category. Motion segment integrity is defined as an expected or normal degree of motion at two adjacent vertebrae, the intervertebral disk, and the associated soft-tissue structures. In the Fifth Edition, new levels for normal motion were defined and the criteria for defining AOMSI were changed on the basis of work by White and Punjabi (*Guides 5th*, p 378). The following tables illustrate the newly defined normal levels of movement and changes in translation and angular motion criteria, as indicated in the fifth and fourth editions of the *Guides*.

Normal Levels of Spine Movement Newly Defined in the *Guides 5th*

Region	Flexion-Extension	Lateral Bending	Axial Rotation
Cervical	C2-C3 10° C5-C6 20° C6-C7 20°	Lower cervical 5°-6°	Upper cervical 30°-40° Lower cervical 5°-6°
Thoracic	Upper thoracic 4° Mid thoracic 6° Lower thoracic 12°	Upper thoracic 6°	Upper thoracic 5°-6°
Lumbar	L1-L2 12° L5-S1 20°	L3-L4 8°-9°	Minimal

Spine Vertebral Translation Criteria: Abnormal Motion

Level	5th Edition	4th Edition
Cervical	> 3.5-mm translation	> 3.5-mm translation
Thoracic	> 2.5-mm translation	> 5-mm translation
Lumbar	> 4.5-mm translation	> 5-mm translation

Spine Angular Motion Criteria: Abnormal Motion

Region	5th Edition	4th Edition
Cervical	> 11°	> 11°
Lumbar	L1-L2, L2-L3, and L3-L4 greater than 15° L4-L5 > 20° L5-S1 > 25°	L5-S1 motion 15° greater than L4-L5 level

Note that, if an individual had a fusion that would cause AOMSI, the individual would meet criteria for DRE level IV or higher. However, if the individual had more than one symptomatic condition within the same spinal region, the physician would use the ROM method instead. If an individual has AOMSI or the clinical findings listed below, with involvement at only one level or different spinal regions (eg, lumbar and cervical), the physician can more easily categorize the individual's permanent impairment into a particular DRE category, using the table on page 188.

15.2 Determining the Appropriate Method for Assessment

Both the DRE and ROM methods (previously referred to as models) are retained for the Fifth Edition. Both DRE and ROM methods provide ratings in whole person impairment (WPI). To convert from whole person to regional body part impairment, use the different conversion factors as listed in the Fifth Edition, Section 15-13.

The DRE and ROM methods provide some interesting differences. As mentioned, the DRE method has diagnostic categories that account for common neurologic and muscular changes associated with the condition. The ROM method accounts for diagnoses and directly measures neurologic and ROM changes.

This section of the *Guides 5th* discusses when to use each method for rating spine impairments. The algorithm is shown in Figure 15-4, with explanatory notes. Always use the DRE method if the individual can be classified by the DRE method and does not meet criteria for the ROM method, discussed below. *"The DRE method is the principal methodology used to evaluate an individual who has had a distinct injury.* When the cause of the impairment is not easily determined and if the impairment can be well characterized by the DRE method, the evaluator should use the DRE method" (*Guides 5th*, p 379). The ROM method is used only if criteria are met for its use.

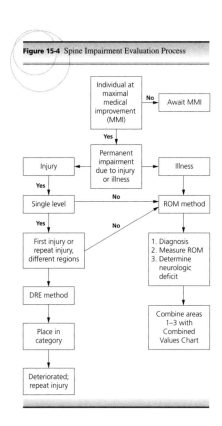

Figure 15-4 Spine Impairment Evaluation Process

Use of the DRE Method

EXAMPLE

While lifting at work, John develops low back pain (LBP) with radiation down his right thigh into his right foot. An SLR test is positive on the right side at 60°. Magnetic resonance imaging (MRI) indicates a herniated disk at L4-L5 with L5 nerve impingement, along with slight degenerative joint disease (DJD) at L4-L5 and L5-S1. John previously had intermittent LBP but no radiation of pain, and no prior radiologic studies were done. Despite physical therapy, he continues to have radiating pain and he is at MMI.

Rating: DRE III, 10%.

Discussion

John has a distinct injury, he is at MMI, and his condition of LBP with radiculopathy correlates with the findings on MRI. His permanent impairment is well characterized by DRE category III, 10%. Since his pain and function are as expected for this condition, he would receive the lower end of the rating scale. Even though John has DJD at two levels, the ROM would not be used here since it is his radiculopathy that is responsible for his pain, and the radiculopathy involves only one level.

EXAMPLE

Steve has had no previous medical treatment for back injury and suffers a work-related disk herniation from a lifting incident. The clinical history and exam are typical for a herniation. Imaging studies confirm the disk herniation and reveal spondylolisthesis and arthritic changes.

Discussion

Since the disk herniation is a new injury, use DRE, despite the radiographic evidence of preexisting pathology. Symptoms are consistent with the disk herniation based on the information given.

Use of the ROM Method

1. Use the ROM method when an impairment is not caused by an injury, the cause of the condition is uncertain, the DRE method does not apply, or an individual cannot be easily categorized by means of the DRE method.

EXAMPLE

John does manual labor and has chronic LBP, which he has reported over a 2-year period. His last episode was especially severe, with some radiation of pain down both thighs. He does not recall a specific incident at work but indicates that last week, with more lifting than usual, his back became very sore, with radiating pain, at the end of the week. An MRI indicates spinal stenosis at L4-L5. In this case, the ROM method would be used since spinal stenosis does not easily fit into a DRE category.

Discussion

Spinal stenosis is not the result of a specific injury, although it may become symptomatic as the result of an injury. Spinal stenosis does not easily fit into DRE categories I to V; therefore, the ROM method is appropriate. An individual may present with bilateral radiculopathy alone that cannot be determined to be related to spinal stenosis or a central disk herniation until an imaging study is performed. On the basis of results of the imaging study, correlated with symptoms and physical findings, the individual with stenosis-related symptoms will be rated by the ROM method, whereas the person with central disk herniation will be rated in a DRE category. Note also that if an individual with foraminal stenosis develops radiculopathy following trauma, the individual would be rated in a DRE category.

2. Use the ROM method when there are multilevel or multiple episodes of involvement in the same spinal region (eg, fractures at multiple levels, symptomatic disk herniations, recurrent injury, or stenosis with radiculopathy at multiple levels or bilaterally). Multilevel involvement indicates multiple levels of pathology with concurrent symptoms and clinical findings. Asymptomatic degenerative changes or asymptomatic disk herniations at multiple levels do not constitute multilevel involvement, according to the *Guides*.

EXAMPLE

Jeff has severe arthritis at C4-C5 and C5-C6 with a symptomatic herniated disk at C4-C5 documented on an MRI. Despite therapy, he still has radiculopathy on the left and an absent biceps tendon reflex.

Rating: DRE II, 5%.

Discussion

Although arthritic changes are noted at two levels, Jeff's symptoms are related only to C4-C5. Symptomatically, he does not have multilevel involvement, and he would be rated appropriately with the DRE method for radiculopathy and the herniated disk at C4-C5.

EXAMPLE

Three years later, Jeff's symptoms worsen, with decreased sensation along the left thumb and index finger and weakness of the left wrist extensors, consistent with C6 radiculopathy. A repeat MRI indicates a herniation at C5-C6. Since he now has symptoms and clinical and radiologic findings consistent with radiculopathy at both levels affecting both C5 and C6 roots, this would constitute multilevel involvement and the ROM method would be used.

Discussion

Radiculopathy and disk herniations at two levels constitute multilevel involvement in the same spinal region, cervical, and therefore require ROM assessment.

3. Use the ROM method where there is AOMSI (eg, fusions or instability) at multiple levels in the same spinal region.

EXAMPLE

Jane, who has chronic neck pain with spondylolisthesis, is in a motor vehicle accident and develops AOMSI. After physical therapy fails, she undergoes a fusion at C5-C6, with good results.

Rating: Cervical DRE IV, 25%.

Discussion

There was a specific injury, and findings meet the criteria for cervical DRE IV.

EXAMPLE

Five years later, Jane falls on ice at work and develops neck pain. She had been relatively asymptomatic after fusion and now has significant instability (AOMSI) at C4-C5, the level above the previous fusion. She undergoes a second fusion at C4-C5 and is rated by the ROM method.

Discussion

This individual had AOMSI that warranted a DRE rating (DRE IV), but then developed AOMSI at another level in the same region, so the ROM method applies.

4. Use the ROM method where there is recurrent radiculopathy caused by a new or recurrent disk herniation or where there is new radiculopathy caused by a recurrent injury in the same spinal region.

   "New injury" means an injury to a spine area that was essentially injury-free before the incident that necessitates medical evaluation, even though other aging or degenerative but asymptomatic changes may be present.

   A "recurrent injury" means an injury to a spine region that has a history of injury. *Recurrent* refers to the same condition, which is asymptomatic between episodes. An illness or condition is also considered to be recurrent if its symptoms worsen but are still considered to be due to or are a normal progression of the original condition.

EXAMPLE

Al has a medically documented 15-year history of intermittent LBP, without radiation or radiculopathy, that has remained stable with conservative treatment and a 0% WPI. Bulging disks at L5-S1 and L4-L5 have been noted on prior imaging. A lifting incident at work leads to more serious injury, with disk herniation and free fragments noted on imaging at L4-L5 and progression of clinical signs of radiating pain and L5 radiculopathy. This is a "new" injury, because the clinical signs and radiologic findings have changed and are now consistent with a measurable impairment.

Rating: DRE method, when at MMI.

Discussion

New injury, specific incident, with new radiculopathy.

EXAMPLE

Al's condition stabilizes after physical therapy and he becomes asymptomatic, except for an occasional flare of radicular leg pain with strenuous activity. Al is in a motor vehicle accident and develops severe worsening of his condition, without additional changes on MRI. This is a recurrence of his L5 radiculopathy, supported by the same radiologic findings, but with more severe symptoms.

Discussion

He would be evaluated with the ROM method since both clinical findings and imaging studies indicate this is a recurrence of his L5 radiculopathy.

EXAMPLE

Jim has a small herniated disk at L3-L4 with radiculopathy, which resolves after physical therapy. He is rated by the DRE method (DRE II). Three years later, he develops severe, radiating back pain and radiculopathy with a large herniation at L4-L5.

Discussion

This is a new disk herniation within the same spinal region (lumbar), and he would now be rated with the ROM method. His earlier rating could be subtracted from the current rating, if apportionment is requested.

5. Use the ROM method where there are multiple episodes of other pathology producing AOMSI and/or radiculopathy.

EXAMPLE

Joan has repeated episodes of neck pain, with spondylytic changes on x-ray at at C4-C5 and C5-C6, and radiculopathy requiring therapy every few years for symptomatic relief. She has never received an impairment rating, as there was no precipitating event. She is in a motor vehicle accident and sustains a whiplash injury. She develops AOMSI at C5-C6 and worsening radiculopathy that is unresponsive to physical therapy.

Discussion

She would be rated with the ROM method at MMI since she has had multiple episodes affecting the same region (cervical).

EXAMPLE

Joel has a lumbar disk herniation at L4-L5 that requires surgical intervention, a laminectomy and disk excision. Postoperatively he does well for 6 months and then has another injury, after which a recurrent disk herniation is identified at L4-L5. A laminectomy is performed to remove the recurrent disk. One year later, Joel complains of persistent LBP, and flexion-extension x-rays of the lumbar spine demonstrate instability at the previously operated-on level.

Discussion

Joel has had multiple episodes of a pathology—a primary disk herniation at L4-L5 and then a recurrence that, after surgical treatment, resulted in AOMSI at that level. ROM assessment is indicated.

EXAMPLE

Janet injures her lower back while putting wet towels into the dryer at work. She complains of LBP and bilateral posterior thigh pain. Plain x-rays of the lumbar spine show a degenerative spondylolisthesis at L4-L5 with 5 mm of translation. MRI of the lumbar spine shows spinal stenosis at L4-L5.

Rating: Lumbar DRE IV, 20%, or ROM.

Discussion

Degenerative spondylolisthesis and spinal stenosis often appear concurrently. However, often only the instability component (back pain) or the spinal stenosis component (neurogenic claudication) presents symptomatically. Degenerative spondylolisthesis with AOMSI falls into DRE Category IV, 20% to 23%. Even if another pathology is present at the same region (eg, spinal stenosis), unless this condition is symptomatic, the DRE rating is appropriate. If the predominant symptoms relate to spinal stenosis, this would require that the ROM method be used. The ROM method is used for symptomatic spinal stenosis, unless radiculopathy with disk herniation is present following the trauma.

Rating for ROM: Assume flexion is 30° (4% impairment), extension is 10° (3% impairment), and lateral side bends are 15° bilaterally (2% impairment each side, 4% total) = 11% for ROM impairment.

Determine rating for spinal stenosis: 7% impairment, Table 15-7 (IIIA, lumbar region). Neurogenic rating component 4%.

Total impairment: Combine 11% (ROM) with 7% (spinal stenosis) and 4% (neurogenic). Using the Combined Values Chart, the combined WPI rating = 20%.

6. Use the ROM method if statutorily mandated in a particular jurisdiction.

   Several states still use the Third Edition of the *Guides* or have their own rating system that includes the ROM method. Some states (eg, West Virginia) did not recognize the DRE method.

MEDICAL TIP

In the case of multiple injuries or conditions, determine whether the pathology affects different spinal regions, in which case the DRE method is applied to each region if possible. If the pathology, recurrent or repeat injury, affects the same spinal region, use the ROM method.

If uncertain whether the DRE or ROM method is most appropriate, assess the individual with both methods and use the method that provides the higher rating.

Discuss why the DRE or ROM method was selected, if there is potential for misunderstanding.

Use the state references listed in Chapter 2 of this book to identify which edition of the *Guides* your state uses and whether any changes have been adopted to apply the *Guides* in a different manner.

When asked to compare a current rating with a prior rating, determine how the prior rating was established and whether direct comparisons can be made when different editions of the *Guides* are used.

LEGAL TIP

"New" and "recurrent" as used here are not intended to supplant traditional notions of causation but are used only to determine whether the DRE or ROM method of evaluating spinal impairment should be used. Note that the Medical Tips here have as much legal as medical significance.

If there is no indication as to which method was used for a prior rating, determine whether the earlier injury was in the same region of the spine as the current injury. If the region is the same (eg, lumbar for both injuries), use the ROM method for the subsequent evaluation and apportion through subtraction or as statute dictates. If the region is different (eg, the prior injury is to the lumbar region and the current injury is to the cervical region), use the DRE for the cervical injury, assuming there is no indication for use of the ROM method.

As stated in the *Guides*, in the small number of instances in which the DRE and ROM methods can both be used, evaluate the individual with both methods and award the higher rating.

To apportion ratings, the percent impairment due to previous findings can simply be subtracted from the percent based on the current findings. Either the DRE or the ROM method may be used to apportion impairment caused by more than one condition or event. If the ROM was previously used, it must be used again. If the DRE method was used, either DRE or ROM can be used, if applicable, for the second rating.

EXAMPLE

Joel's prior lumbar disk herniation at L4-L5 required surgical intervention, a laminectomy, and disk excision. He is asymptomatic at MMI and receives a DRE III rating of 10%. Postoperatively he does well for 6 months, and then has another injury after which a recurrent disk herniation is identified at L4-L5. A laminectomy is performed to remove the recurrent disk.

Rating: ROM, assume 26%.

Rating due to repeat injury: 26% − 10% = 16%.

One year later, Joel complains of persistent LBP, and flexion-extension x-rays of the lumbar spine demonstrate instability at the previously operated-on level.

Rating: ROM method, 38%.

Apportionment: 38% − 26% = 12%.

Note: It would not be appropriate to subtract the 16%, since the 26% obtained from the ROM method accounts for the earlier impairment of 16%, with the individual at MMI.

The following table provides common examples regarding the application of the ROM and DRE methods.

Example	ROM	DRE	Reason
1st disk herniation, L4-L5		X	1st injury
2nd herniation, L5-S1	X		Same region—lumbar area
Spinal stenosis	X		No specific precipitating episode; often multiple levels affected
Spondylolisthesis, with AOMSI, and herniation, lumbar region	X		Multiple episodes of ratable pathology, same region
Spondylolisthesis and disk herniation L4-L5, evaluated by ROM initially, now disk herniation at L5-S1	X		ROM for two reasons: it was used previously and must be used again; also, repeat injury in same region
Fractures at L5 and S1		X	Two different regions (lumbar and sacral) determined independently

15.3 Diagnosis-Related Estimates Method

The DRE method has been revised to overcome two earlier concerns: inability to adjust for individual variation and changes in the condition resulting from treatment.

To address these concerns, the Fifth Edition DRE method has the following changes:

1. Rating occurs after MMI has been reached to account for individual responses to treatment and to more accurately reflect long-term prognosis and permanency.

2. Small ranges are provided within each DRE category (eg, DRE III, 10%-13%) to allow the physician to account for individual variation, depending on the severity of the condition, the impact of the condition on ADL, and the outcome of treatment for the condition.

3. Differential ratings are provided for those with back surgery, since surgery alters anatomy and produces a functionally different spine.

4. Corticospinal impairment is assessed with a functional approach, derived from the neurology, gastrointestinal, and urology chapters, using Section 15.7, to assess extremity, bowel, or bladder dysfunction caused by spinal cord injury.

The DRE method now has five diagnosis-related estimates (DRE I-V) for each of the three spinal regions (cervical, thoracic, and lumbar). In the Fifth Edition, DRE categories are discussed in relation to the lumbar, cervical, and (least common) thoracic impairments. When pathologies involve overlapping spinal regions, eg, cervical-thoracic, evaluate the condition on the basis of the more proximal involved region. Thus, an L5-S1 injury would be rated by the lumbar spine criteria, and C7-T1, by the cervical criteria (C8 root involvement).

DRE categories I through V are used when no corticospinal (spinal cord) injury is present. The DRE categories VI through VIII from the Fourth Edition were removed, since individuals with spinal cord damage are now evaluated on the basis of methods in the neurology chapter, which are listed in the spine chapter in Section 15.7. DRE VI through VIII are mistakenly referred to in Section 15.3 because of a typographical error. Apart from category I (0% WPI), each DRE category now includes a range to account for the resolution or continuation of symptoms and their impact on the ability to perform ADL.

To use the DRE method, obtain an individual's history, examine the individual, review the results of applicable diagnostic studies, and place the individual in the appropriate category. Although there are five categories for each spinal region, almost all individuals will fall into one of the first three DRE categories. Altered motion segment integrity (ie, increased motion or loss of motion) qualifies the individual for category IV or V. A fracture, dislocation, or both, with or without clinical symptoms, permits placement of the individual into a DRE category with no additional verification. If there are impairments in different spinal regions, rate each spinal region separately by the DRE method, then combine the ratings by means of the Combined Values Chart on *Guides 5th* pages 604 to 606.

As noted in Section 15.7, when spinal cord damage is present, assess bowel and bladder impairments separately. Combine any bowel or bladder dysfunction with assessment of extremity use and gait. This new system provides consistency with the neurology chapter and enables a range of severity to be accounted for in individuals with bladder or bowel dysfunction due to spinal cord involvement.

Symptoms and signs (eg, clinical findings in the Fifth Edition) and their corresponding minimum DRE category are listed below and compared with similar terms from the Fourth Edition.

5th Edition Clinical Findings	Corresponding Minimum DRE Category (5th Edition) for Abnormal Clinical Finding	4th Edition: Differentiators
Muscle spasm: sudden, involuntary contraction of muscle or group of muscles. Occasionally visible as a contracted paraspinal muscle, but more often diagnosed by palpation (a hard muscle); doesn't relax with weight bearing on one foot. Present standing and supine, frequently causing scoliosis. Seen more commonly after acute spinal injury, rare in chronic back pain.	II	Paravertebral guarding or spasm: nonuniform loss of ROM, dysmetria, present or documented by a physician. Seen with radiculopathy, following expected distribution but without neurologic findings.
Muscle guarding: contraction of muscle to minimize motion or agitation of the injured or diseased tissue. Not true muscle spasm because the contraction can be relaxed. In lumbar spine, contraction frequently results in loss of normal lumbar lordosis, and it may be associated with reproducible loss of spinal motion.	II	Paravertebral guarding or spasm: nonuniform loss of ROM, dysmetria, present or documented by a physician. Seen with radiculopathy, following expected distribution but without neurologic findings.
Asymmetry of spinal motion: in one of the 3 principal planes, is sometimes caused by muscle spasm or guarding. Finding must be reproducible and consistent, and examiner must be convinced that the individual is cooperative and giving full effort	II	Concept similar; not a differentiator.
Nonverifiable radicular root pain: pain in the distribution of a nerve root but has no identifiable origin; ie, there are no objective physical, imaging, or electromyographic findings.	II	Concept similar; not a differentiator.
Reflexes: reflexes may be normal, increased, reduced, or absent. To be valid, involved and normal limb(s) should show marked asymmetry with contralateral side on repeated testing. Lost reflexes rarely return.	III	Loss of reflexes: loss of arm or leg reflexes, verified by electrodiagnostic studies.

5th Edition Clinical Findings	Corresponding Minimum DRE Category (5th Edition) for Abnormal Clinical Finding	4th Edition: Differentiators
Loss of sensation and weakness: valid sensory findings must be in strict anatomic, dermatomal distribution. Weakness should be consistent with affected nerve structure(s). Significant, long-standing weakness is usually accompanied by atrophy.	III	Concept unchanged; not a differentiator.
Atrophy: measured with a tape measure at identical levels on both limbs. For reasons of reproducibility, the difference in circumference should be 2 cm or greater in the thigh and 1 cm or greater in the arm, forearm, or leg. The evaluator can address asymmetry due to extremity dominance in the report.	III	Decreased circumference or atrophy: atrophy is loss of girth of 2 cm or more above or below the elbow or knee. Atrophy cannot be explained by non–spine-related problems and can be verified by electrodiagnostic studies.
Radiculopathy: defined as significant alteration in the function of a nerve root or nerve roots and is usually caused by pressure on one or several nerve roots. The diagnosis requires a dermatomal distribution of pain, numbness, and/or paresthesias. A root tension sign is usually positive. The diagnosis of herniated disk must be substantiated by appropriate findings on imaging study. The presence of findings on imaging study alone does not make the diagnosis of radiculopathy. There must also be clinical evidence as described above.	III	Concept similar; not a differentiator.
Electrodiagnostic verification of radiculopathy: unequivocal electrodiagnostic evidence of acute nerve root pathology includes presence of multiple positive sharp waves or fibrillation potentials in muscles innervated by one nerve root. Electromyography should be performed only by a qualified, licensed physician.	III	Electrodiagnostic evidence of acute nerve root compromise, such as multiple positive sharp waves or fibrillation potentials; or H-wave absence or delay greater than 3 mm/s; or chronic changes such as polyphasic waves in peripheral muscles.

5th Edition Clinical Findings	Corresponding Minimum DRE Category (5th Edition) for Abnormal Clinical Finding	4th Edition: Differentiators
AOMSI: motion segment alteration can be either loss of motion segment integrity (increased translational or angular motion) or decreased motion secondary to developmental fusion, fracture healing, healed infection, or surgical arthrodesis. Evaluate with flexion and extension roentgenograms. See tables on p 189 for values of AOMSI.	IV	Loss of motion segment integrity: flexion and extension roentgenograms show significant injury-related anterior-to-posterior translation of two adjacent vertebrae as defined in table.
Cauda equina syndrome: manifested by bowel or bladder dysfunction, saddle anesthesia, and variable loss of motor and sensory function in lower extremities.	Neurology method, Section 15.7	Loss of bowel or bladder control: rectal exam indicates loss of sphincter tone or loss of bladder control, requiring use of an assistive device such as a catheter.
Urodynamic tests: cystometrograms are useful in individuals in whom a cauda equina syndrome is possible but not certain. Normal cystometrogram makes the presence of nerve-related bladder dysfunction unlikely.	Neurology method, Section 15.7	Bladder studies: cystometrograms showing unequivocal neurologic compromise of bladder with resulting incontinence.

In most cases, using the definitions provided in Box 15-1, the physician can assign an individual to DRE category I, II, or III. An individual in category I has only subjective findings. In category II, the individual has objective findings but no verifiable radiculopathy or alteration of structural integrity, while in category III, radiculopathy with objective findings must be present. Since an individual is evaluated after having reached MMI, a history of objective findings may not define the current, ratable condition but is important in determining the medical course and whether MMI has been reached. The impairment rating is based on the condition once MMI is reached, not on prior symptoms or signs.

If the individual had a radiculopathy caused by a herniated disk or lateral spinal stenosis that responded to conservative treatment and currently has no radicular symptoms or signs, he or she is placed in category II, since at MMI there is no radiculopathy. Category III is for individuals with a symptomatic, one-level radiculopathy, either preoperatively or postoperatively.

MEDICAL TIP

Use the DRE method as the method of choice.

When determining what end of the range to use, determine whether the condition and its impact on ADL is consistent with that condition, or if the impairment has led to worse functioning. If ADL are more severely impacted than expected for the condition, use the upper end of the scale.

Document impairments that may have predated the injury and may have been aggravated as a result of the injury, eg, spondylolysis, spondylolisthesis, and herniated disk without radiculopathy.

If pain is disproportionate for the condition, use the pain chapter for determining whether a qualitative and additional quantitative amount (1%-3%) should be combined with the DRE or ROM rating.

LEGAL TIP

Because the rating of the impairment under this method is when the individual reaches MMI, and criteria are more precise, some impairments will be rated higher than in the Fourth Edition and some lower, although disability awards based on them should not change significantly. All episodes of muscle spasm and radiculopathy that recover would be rated lower. See the examples in the discussions that follow concerning DRE use in lumbar, thoracic, and cervical spine cases.

15.4 DRE: Lumbar Spine

The differences between the lumbar spine DRE categories in the fourth and fifth editions are summarized in the following table, along with common conditions and their current rating.

	5th Edition		4th Edition		
DRE Category	Criteria	Rating	Criteria	Rating	Examples of Clinical Conditions and Ratings
I	No objective signs: no guarding, spasm, complaints, or symptoms	0%	No objective signs: no guarding, spasm, com-plaints, or symptoms	0%	Low back pain (LBP), no objective findings on clinical exam or radiologic studies 5th: 0% 4th: 0%

| DRE Category | 5th Edition | | 4th Edition | | Examples of Clinical Conditions and Ratings |
	Criteria	Rating	Criteria	Rating	
II	a. Injury, muscle guarding, or spasm, nonverifiable radicular complaints	5%-8%	a. Injury, muscle guarding, or spasm, nonverifiable radicular complaints	5%	LBP, muscle guarding resolved 5th: 0% 4th: 5%
	b. Resolved radiculopathy following nonsurgical treatment		d. No objective radiculopathy e. Fractures: <25% compression of 1 vertebral body, healed posterior element fracture without dislocation or AOMSI, spinous or transverse fracture with displacement. With no vertebral body fracture or canal disruption		LBP, herniated disk, radiculopathy resolved nonsurgically 5th: 5% 4th: 10%
	c. Fractures: <25% compression of 1 vertebral body, healed posterior element fracture without dislocation or AOMSI, spinous or transverse fracture with displacement. With no vertebral body fracture or canal disruption				
III	a. Current radiculopathy with objective signs, including herniation	10%-13%	a. Current radiculopathy with objective signs, including herniation	10%	LBP, radiculopathy resolved after surgery 5th:10% 4th:10%
	b. History of radiculopathy, treated successfully with surgery, asymptomatic		c. Fractures: 25%-50% compression of 1 vertebral body, healed posterior element fracture with displacement, disrupting spinal canal, no AOMSI		LBP, radiculopathy continues after surgery 5th:13% 4th:10%
	c. Fractures: 25%-50% compression of 1 vertebral body, healed posterior element fracture with displacement, disrupting spinal canal, no AOMSI				

DRE Category	5th Edition		4th Edition		Examples of Clinical Conditions and Ratings
	Criteria	Rating	Criteria	Rating	
IV	AOMSI, fracture AOMSI: 4.5-mm translation, angular motion >15° L1-L2, L2-L3, L3-L4; >20° L4-L5; >25° L5-S1; near-complete or complete loss of segment motion due to developmental fusion, successful or unsuccessful surgical arthrodesis Fractures: >50% compression without neurologic compromise	20%-23%	AOMSI or bilateral or multilevel radiculopathy AOMSI: 5-mm translation, angular motion >11° L1-L2, L2-L3, L3-L4, L4-L5; >15° L5-S1; near-complete or complete loss of segment motion due to developmental fusion, successful or unsuccessful surgical arthrodesis Fractures: >50% compression without neurologic compromise Multilevel spine segment structural compromise	20%	Bilateral radiculopathy due to spinal stenosis 5th: ROM 4th: 25% Multilevel radiculopathy: first L3-L4, then L4-L5 5th ROM method, apportionment for 1st injury (10% with DRE from 4th Edition) 4th: 25%, could apportion 10% from earlier injury Fracture L2 and L3, without neurologic compromise 5th: ROM 4th: DRE IV: 20%
V	Radiculopathy and AOMSI criteria for DRE III (radiculopathy) and IV (AOMSI), lower extremity impairment (either atrophy, loss of reflexes, dermatomal pain, or sensory changes), or EMG changes consistent with DRE III and IV Or fractures >50% of 1 vertebral body with unilateral neurologic compromise	25%-28%	Radiculopathy and AOMSI criteria for DRE III (radiculopathy) and IV (AOMSI), lower extremity impairment (either atrophy, loss of reflexes, dermatomal pain, or sensory changes), or EMG changes consistent with DRE III and IV Or fractures >50% of 1 vertebral body with unilateral neurologic compromise	25%	Radiculopathy L5 (lost reflex + EMG) and spondylolisthesis with 15° angular motion L4-L5 5th: DRE III: 10%-13% 4th: DRE V: 25% Radiculopathy S1 (lost reflex + EMG) and spondylolisthesis with 26° angular motion L5-S1 5th: DRE III: 25%-28% 4th: DRE V: 25%

	5th Edition		4th Edition		
DRE Category	Criteria	Rating	Criteria	Rating	Examples of Clinical Conditions and Ratings
VI	See Section 15.7, also neurology, urology, gastrointestinal chapters	Incorporates impairment from all body systems	Cauda equina–like without bowel or bladder	40%	
VII	See Section 15.7, also neurology, urology, gastrointestinal chapters	Incorporates impairment from all body systems	Cauda equina syndrome with bowel or bladder	60%	
VIII	See Section 15.7, also neurology, urology, gastrointestinal chapters	Incorporates impairment from all body systems	Paraplegia, neural compression l umbar spine region	75%	

The following examples taken from the Fifth Edition indicate similarities and differences in ratings and approach between the fourth and fifth editions.

EXAMPLES

Example 15-1: 0% Impairment Due to Lumbar Injury

Diagnosis: Minor lumbar strain; only pain, no significant clinical findings

5th Edition Impairment Rating: 0% impairment of the whole person

4th Edition Impairment Rating: 0% impairment of the whole person

Example 15-2: 5% to 8% Impairment Due to Lumbar Injury

Diagnosis: Left posterolateral disk herniation at L5-S1 with left S1 radiculopathy, resolved

5th Edition Impairment Rating: 5% impairment of the whole person (DRE II)

4th Edition Impairment Rating: 10% impairment of the whole person (DRE III)

Comment: This individual had a radiographically confirmed herniated disk, at the level and side expected from the physical examination. Most symptoms resolved with conservative treatment. At the time of evaluation, the individual was doing well, with no evidence of residual radiculopathy.

Example 15-3: 10% to 13% Impairment Due to Surgically Treated Herniated Disk

Diagnosis: Left posterolateral herniated disk at L5-S1 with left S1 radiculopathy, partially resolved status postdiskectomy

5th Edition Impairment Rating: 10% impairment of the whole person (DRE III)

4th Edition Impairment Rating: 10% impairment of the whole person (DRE III)

Example 15-4: 10% to 13% Impairment Due to Radiculopathy

Diagnosis: Chronic low back pain and radiculopathy, not resolved after surgery

5th Edition Impairment Rating: 13% impairment of the whole person (DRE III)

4th Edition Impairment Rating: 10% impairment of the whole person (DRE III)

Example 15-5: 20% to 23% Impairment Due to Fracture With Greater Than 50% Compression of Vertebrae

Diagnosis: Burst fracture L2 > 50%

5th Edition Impairment Rating: 20% impairment of the whole person (DRE IV)

4th Edition Impairment Rating: 20% impairment of the whole person (DRE IV)

Example 15-6: 25% to 28% Impairment Due to Radiculopathy and Alteration of Motion Segment Integrity

Diagnosis: Left posterolateral disk herniation at L5-S1 with S1 radiculopathy and severe disk degeneration, unresolved status postdiskectomy and L5-S1 fusion

5th Edition Impairment Rating: 28% impairment of the whole person (DRE V)

4th Edition Impairment Rating: 25% impairment of the whole person (DRE V)

15.5 DRE: Thoracic Spine

The new DRE section on the thoracic spine follows the rating system in the Fourth Edition as outlined for the thoracolumbar and not the cervicothoracic spine.

To evaluate thoracic spine problems:

1. If no corticospinal, bowel, or bladder dysfunction is present, use DRE I-V.

2. If corticospinal or bowel or bladder dysfunction is present, use Section 15.7, derived from the neurology, gastrointestinal, and urology chapters.

The thoracic spine impairment DRE categories are summarized in Table 15-4 of the *Guides*. The differences between the thoracic spine DRE categories in the fourth and fifth editions are summarized in the following table, along with common conditions and their current rating.

	5th Edition		4th Edition		
DRE Category	**Criteria**	**Rating**	**Criteria**	**Rating**	**Examples of Clinical Conditions and Ratings**
I	No objective signs: no guarding, spasm, complaints, or symptoms	0%	No objective signs: no guarding, spasm, complaints, or symptoms	0%	Upper back pain (UBP), no objective findings on clinical exam or radiologic studies 5th: 0% 4th: 0%
II	f. Injury, muscle guarding or spasm, nonverifiable radicular complaints g. Herniated disk, resolved radiculopathy after nonsurgical treatment h. Fractures: <25% compression of 1 vertebral body, healed posterior element fracture without dislocation or AOMSI, spinous or transverse fracture with displacement. With no vertebral body fracture or canal disruption	5%-8%	Minor impairment d. Injury, muscle guarding or spasm, nonverifiable radicular complaints i. No objective radiculopathy j. Fractures: <25% compression of 1 vertebral body, healed posterior element fracture without dislocation or AOMSI, spinous or transverse fracture with displacement. With no vertebral body fracture or canal disruption	5%	UBP, herniated disk, radiculopathy resolved nonsurgically 5th: 5% UBP, herniated disk, radiculopathy at diagnosis, later resolved with nonsurgical treatment 4th: 15% (DRE III)

Chapter 15

	5th Edition		4th Edition		
DRE Category	**Criteria**	**Rating**	**Criteria**	**Rating**	**Examples of Clinical Conditions and Ratings**
III	a. Current radiculopathy with objective signs, including herniation e. History of radiculopathy, treated successfully with surgery, asymptomatic f. Fractures: 25%-50% compression of 1 vertebral body, healed posterior element fracture with displacement, disrupting spinal canal, no AOMSI	15%-18%	a. Current radiculopathy with objective signs, including herniation c. Fractures: 25%-50% compression of 1 vertebral body, healed posterior element fracture with displacement, disrupting spinal canal, no AOMSI	15%	UBP, radiculopathy resolved after surgery 5th: 10% 4th: 10% UBP, radiculopathy continues after surgery 5th: 13% 4th: 10%
IV	AOMSI, fracture AOMSI: 4.5-mm translation, angular motion >15° L1-L2, L2-L3, L3-L4; >20° L4-L5; >25° L5-S1; near-complete or complete loss of segment motion due to developmental fusion, successful or unsuccessful surgical arthrodesis Fractures: >50% compression without neurologic compromise	20%-23%	AOMSI or bilateral or multilevel radiculopathy AOMSI: >2.5-mm translation Fractures: >50% compression without neurologic compromise; multilevel spine segment structural compromise	20%	AOMSI or bilateral or multilevel radiculopathy AOMSI: >5-mm translation Or angular motion 11° more than adjacent segment Fractures: >50% compression without neurologic compromise; multilevel spine segment structural compromise

| DRE Category | 5th Edition | | 4th Edition | | Examples of Clinical Conditions and Ratings |
	Criteria	Rating	Criteria	Rating	
V	Radiculopathy and AOMSI criteria for DRE III (radiculopathy) and IV (AOMSI), lower extremity impairment (either atrophy, loss of reflexes, dermatomal pain, or sensory changes), or EMG changes consistent with DRE III and IV Or fractures >50% of 1 vertebral body with unilateral neurologic compromise	25%-28%	Radiculopathy and AOMSI criteria for DRE III (radiculopathy) and IV (AOMSI), lower extremity impairment (either atrophy, loss of reflexes, dermatomal pain, or sensory changes), or EMG changes consistent with DRE III and IV Or fractures >50% of 1 vertebral body with unilateral neurologic compromise	25%	Radiculopathy L5 + EMG and spondylolisthesis with 26° angular motion L4-L-5 5th: DRE III: 25%-28% 4th: DRE V: 25%
VI	See neurology, urology, gastrointestinal chapters	Dependent upon impairment	Cauda equina–like without bowel or bladder	35%	
VII	See neurology, urology, gastrointestinal chapters	Dependent upon impairment	Cauda equina syndrome with bowel or bladder	55%	
VIII	See neurology, urology, gastrointestinal chapters	Dependent upon impairment	Paraplegia, neural compression of lumbar spine region	70%	

The following examples taken from the Fifth Edition indicate potential differences in ratings and approach between the fourth and fifth editions.

EXAMPLES

Example 15-7: 0% Impairment Due to Thoracic Injury

Diagnosis: Upper back pain

5th Edition Impairment Rating: 0% impairment of the whole person

4th Edition Impairment Rating: 0% impairment of the whole person

Example 15-8: 5% to 8% Impairment Due to Thoracic Injury

Diagnosis: Degenerative disk disease at T1 with tingling along the chest and underarm

5th Edition Impairment Rating: 5%-8% impairment of the whole person

4th Edition Impairment Rating: 5% impairment of the whole person

Example 15-9: 15% to 18% Impairment Due to Thoracic Injury

Diagnosis: Compression fracture at T8 with residual left lower extremity neurologic involvement

5th Edition Impairment Rating: 15% impairment of the whole person

4th Edition Impairment Rating: 15% impairment of the whole person

Example 15-10: 20% to 23% Impairment Due to Compression Fracture of T1

Diagnosis: Compression fracture of T1 with bilateral radiculopathy. New-onset seizure disorder

5th Edition Impairment Rating: 20% impairment due to musculoskeletal disorder; combine with appropriate rating due to the seizure disorder to determine whole person impairment (see Combined Values Chart, p 604)

4th Edition Impairment Rating: 20% impairment due to musculoskeletal disorder

Example 15-11: 25% to 28% Impairment Due to Radiculopathy and Alteration of Motion Segment Integrity

Diagnosis: Compression fracture of T8 treated surgically, with mild residual right lower extremity neurologic involvement

5th Edition Impairment Rating: 25% impairment of the whole person by DRE V category. If the symptoms and impact on ADL were more significant, increase the rating to 28%. In this case, impairment using the ROM method would need to be determined also, with the physician assigning the higher rating

4th Edition Impairment Rating: 25% impairment of the whole person

15.6 DRE: Cervical Spine

The cervical spine assessment follows the principles discussed for the lumbar and thoracic regions and uses the major criteria as listed in the Fourth Edition. The key differences in this edition are that values for translation and angular motion have been changed, different ratings are used for radiculopathy, and injury to the corticospinal tract is assessed on the basis of Section 15.7, and in the nervous system (Chapter 13), digestive tract (Chapter 6), and urinary and reproductive (Chapter 7) chapters, as previously discussed in this chapter.

The *Guides 5th* also notes that injuries may be distinguished from congenital and developmental conditions by examining preinjury roentgenograms or a bone scan performed after the onset of the condition. A bone scan will help determine whether bony changes are recent or from prior conditions.

The differences between the cervical spine DRE categories in the fourth and fifth editions are summarized in the following table, along with common conditions and their impairment ratings.

	5th Edition		4th Edition		
DRE Category	**Criteria**	**Rating**	**Criteria**	**Rating**	**Examples of Clinical Conditions and Ratings**
I	No objective signs: no guarding, spasm, complaints, or symptoms	0%	No objective signs: no guarding, spasm, complaints, or symptoms	0%	Upper back pain (UBP), no objective findings on clinical exam or radiologic studies 5th: 0% 4th: 0%
II	Injury, muscle guarding or spasm, nonverifiable radicular complaints Herniated disk, resolved radiculopathy after nonsurgical treatment Fractures: <25% compression of 1 vertebral body, healed posterior element fracture without dislocation or AOMSI, spinous or transverse fracture with displacement. With no vertebral body fracture or canal disruption	5%-8%	Minor impairment: injury, muscle guarding or spasm, nonverifiable radicular complaints; no objective radiculopathy Fractures: <25% compression of 1 vertebral body, healed posterior element fracture without dislocation or AOMSI, spinous or transverse fracture with displacement. With no vertebral body fracture or canal disruption	5%	UBP, herniated disk, radiculopathy resolved nonsurgically 5th: 5% UBP, herniated disk, radiculopathy at diagnosis, later resolved with nonsurgical treatment 4th: 15% (DRE III)

DRE Category	5th Edition Criteria	Rating	4th Edition Criteria	Rating	Examples of Clinical Conditions and Ratings
III	Current radiculopathy with objective signs, including herniation; history of radiculopathy, improved with surgery Fractures: 25%-50% compression of 1 vertebral body, healed posterior element fracture with displacement, disrupting spinal canal, no AOMSI	15%-18%	Current radiculopathy with signs of depressed reflex, loss of motor strength, or sensory alteration with imaging study demonstrating herniation Fractures: 25%-50% compression of 1 vertebral body, healed posterior element fracture with displacement, disrupting spinal canal, no AOMSI	15%	UBP, radiculopathy resolved after surgery 5th: 15% 4th: 15% UBP, radiculopathy continues after surgery 5th: 18% 4th: 15%
IV	AOMSI, fracture AOMSI: 3.5-mm translation, angular motion >11° at adjacent levels, near-complete or complete loss of segment motion due to developmental fusion, successful or unsuccessful surgical arthrodesis Fractures >50% compression without neurologic compromise	20%-23%	AOMSI or bilateral or multilevel radiculopathy AOMSI: >3.5-mm translation, angular motion >11° at adjacent segments; near-complete or complete loss of segment motion due to developmental fusion, successful or unsuccessful surgical arthrodesis Fractures: >50% compression without neurologic compromise Multilevel spine segment structural compromise	20%	Bilateral radiculopathy due to spinal stenosis 5th: ROM or DRE IV 4th: 20% Multilevel radiculopathy: first C5-C6, then C4-C5 5th: ROM method or DRE 20%-23%, apportionment for 1st injury (15% with DRE from 4th Edition) 4th: 20%, could apportion 15% from earlier injury Fracture of C6 without neurologic compromise 5th: DRE IV: 20%-23% 4th: DRE IV: 20%

	5th Edition		4th Edition		Examples of Clinical Conditions and Ratings
DRE Category	Criteria	Rating	Criteria	Rating	
V	Use of external adaptive device or total loss at single level or severe, multilevel neurologic dysfunction or fractures with severe upper extremity sensory and motor deficits, no lower extremity deficit	35%-38%	Use of external adaptive device or total loss at single level or severe, multilevel neurologic dysfunction or fractures with severe upper extremity sensory and motor deficits, no lower extremity deficit	35%	5th: DRE V: 35%-38% 4th: DRE III: 35%
VI	See gastrointestinal, urology, neurology chapters (6, 7, 13)	Dependent upon impairment	Cauda equina syndrome without bowel or bladder	40%	
VII	See gastrointestinal, urology, neurology, chapters (6, 7, 13)	Dependent upon impairment	Cauda equina syndrome with bowel or bladder	60%	
VIII	See gastrointestinal, urology, neurology, chapters (6, 7, 13)	Dependent upon impairment	Paraplegia, total loss of lower extremity function	75%	

EXAMPLES

Example 15-12: 0% Impairment Due to Cervical Injury

Diagnosis: Intermittent cervical neck strain

5th Edition Impairment Rating: 0% impairment of the whole person

4th Edition Impairment Rating: 0% impairment of the whole person

Example 15-13: 5% to 8% Impairment Due to Cervical Injury

Diagnosis: Herniated disk at C5-C6 with resolved right C6 radiculopathy

5th Edition Impairment Rating: 5% impairment of the whole person

4th Edition Impairment Rating: 15% impairment of the whole person

Example 15-14: 15% to 18% Impairment Due to Radiculopathy

Diagnosis: Radiculopathy due to disk herniation at C6

5th Edition Impairment Rating: 15%-18% impairment of the whole person

4th Edition Impairment Rating: 15% impairment of the whole person

Example 15-15: 25% to 28% Impairment Due to Alterations of Motion Segment Integrity

Diagnosis: Herniated disk at C6-C7 with C7 radiculopathy resolved after anterior cervical diskectomy and C6-C7 fusion

5th Edition Impairment Rating: 25% impairment of the whole person

4th Edition Impairment Rating: 25% impairment of the whole person

Example 15-16: 35% to 38% Impairment Due to Radiculopathy, AOMSI, and Fusion

Diagnosis: Herniated C5-C6 disk treated surgically with residual bilateral C6 radiculopathy compromising ADL, requiring adaptive devices

5th Edition Impairment Rating: 35%-38% impairment of the whole person

4th Edition Impairment Rating: 35% impairment of the whole person

15.7 Rating Corticospinal Tract Damage

Corticospinal tract injury refers to injury of the spinal cord or cauda equina. Corticospinal tract impairment is now rated on the basis of principles in the nervous system chapter. As previously discussed, the spine chapter no longer has corticospinal DRE rating categories V through VIII. Individuals with spinal cord injury are evaluated according to the procedure in the neurology chapter, Section 15.7 of the spine chapter, and Table 15-6. For rating spinal cord injury, identify the highest neurologic level of function and whether upper extremity, lower extremity, bowel, bladder, sexual, or respiratory dysfunction is present. Combine the ratings for impairments to these body systems by using the Combined Values Chart. The Fifth Edition adopts this approach not only for greater consistency, but to ensure that individuals with neurologically based disorders will be evaluated with that focus and by physicians with expertise in neurologic assessment.

EXAMPLES

Example 15-17: 69% Impairment Due to Compression Fracture With Corticospinal Tract Damage

Diagnosis: C6 compression fracture nearly 40%, with corticospinal tract damage. Difficulty with dexterity movements of both upper extremities; unable to walk without braces; no bowel or bladder dysfunction

5th Edition Impairment Rating: 69% impairment of the whole person, based on a 39% WPI for upper extremity impairment (Table 15-6b, class 2), combined with 39% WPI for lower extremity impairment (Table 15-6c, class 3), and 15% for the vertebral fracture (DRE III). Using the Combined Values Chart for 39%, 39%, and 15% yields a 69% WPI

4th Edition Impairment Rating: 69% impairment of the whole person, based on the neurology chapter, 61% based on the spine chapter (40% DRE cervicothoracic VI with 35% cervicothoracic DRE V, Combined Values Chart)

Example 15-18: 78% Impairment Due to Burst Fracture With Cauda Equina Syndrome

Diagnosis: Burst fracture of L2 with cauda equina syndrome

5th Edition Impairment Rating: 78% impairment of the whole person (39% in Table 15-6c, class 3, 40% in 15-6d, class 4, 20% in 15-6e, class 2, and 10% from DRE category III, combined under chart to 78% WPI)

4th Edition Impairment Rating: 60% impairment of the whole person (DRE VII)

15.8a-c Range-of-Motion Method

The new and important changes to the Fifth Edition pertain to when the ROM method is used and how to obtain ROM measurements with greater reproducibility and accuracy. The ROM method requires assessment of three components: (1) ROM, (2) neuropathic changes, if any, and (3) diagnosis of spine disorders, as listed in Table 15-7. The purpose of this method is to provide an impairment rating for complex spine disorders and conditions that are not directly related to an injury. As noted in the Fifth Edition, evaluate the individual only after the condition is stable, at MMI. Also, as noted in the Fourth Edition, the ROM method already includes pain in the impairment rating.

Use the ROM method only if (1) the DRE method is not applicable (no verifiable injury); (2) multilevel involvement has occurred in the same spinal region; (3) recurrent (episodes stemming from a known event or condition)

radiculopathy is present in the same spinal region; (4) there are multiple episodes of other pathology producing AOMSI and/or radiculopathy; or (5) statutorily mandated by the involved jurisdiction (often a reference to Colorado and Oregon, which still use the Third Edition, Revised).

The use of the ROM method will likely increase slightly with the implementation of this edition, since the ROM is now the method of choice for repeat and multiple injuries in the same spinal region. It is thought that the ROM more accurately characterizes function and the ability to perform ADL in a person with repeat injuries to a particular spinal region. Although some practitioners used the Fourth Edition DRE for repeat injuries and provided sequential impairment ratings, this approach was not advocated and did not account for the functional changes from an earlier and relevant spine injury. The Fourth Edition did not have a DRE category for recurrent, repeat, or multiple injuries.

All impairment estimates shown in the tables of this section are expressed as WPIs. Section 15.13 explains how to express a whole person spine impairment as a regional spine impairment. Tables 15-8 through 15-14 provide estimates for rating ankylosis and range of motion, while neurologic impairments are rated on the basis of Tables 15-15 through 15-18.

The Fifth Edition also includes a description of principles of inclinometry, including subtle differences in discussions of gravitational plane and stabilization. The examiner measures the three planes of motion: sagittal, frontal (coronal), and transverse (axial or rotation), and adds the reproducible and lowest impairment ratings (highest ROM measurements) from each plane of motion. Two inclinometers are used for most measurements.

The ROM method has been criticized mainly because it exhibits some variability, partly dependent on individual motivation and uncertain correlation with function. Variability can be reduced if physicians consistently use standardized measurement methods and note the time and circumstances when the measurements are made. A standardized measurement approach is discussed in greater detail in this edition. Individual motivation is partially assessed by ensuring reproducible measurements, indicating the individual is giving a consistent, full effort. ROM measurements correlate with some types of function. The other components of the method—the diagnosis and neurologic assessment—provide further information on function.

Another criticism has been the use of a single set of normal values for ROM measurements, which are not adjusted for gender and age differences. The contributors believed that the scientific data are too inconsistent to develop specific gender-normal values and stated that gender differences in normal

ROM decrease with advancing age. Lifestyle factors also have a major impact in ROM ability and are not easily adjusted. Changes in normative data are too small for age groups 20 to 59 years to warrant age adjustment.

An individual with ankylosis of the spine is given a separate ROM impairment rating, as indicated in Tables 15-9 through 15-14. The ankylosis values replace the ROM impairment ratings for that plane of motion. In the Fifth Edition, measure lateral bending (flexion) by means of two inclinometers. Use the validity checks and obtain at least three of six consecutive measurements, which must lie within 5° or 10% of the mean, whichever is greater. Use the impairment estimate based on the highest (least impairing) angle of a valid set.

EXAMPLE

Jim has a small herniated disk at L3-L4 with radiculopathy, which resolves after physical therapy. He is rated by the DRE method (DRE II). Three years later, after a motor vehicle accident without a seat belt, he developed severe, radiating back pain and radiculopathy with a large herniation at L4-L5, which became relatively asymptomatic after therapy. One year later, while lifting and twisting, his symptoms returned during a lifting accident. The herniation progressed, requiring surgery.

5th Edition Rating: DRE rating: first injury, DRE II, 5%; second injury, ROM, 22%; third injury, ROM, 26%

4th Edition Rating: DRE rating: first injury, DRE III, 10%; second injury, DRE III, 10%; third injury, DRE III, 10%

Discussion

The ROM method, when used for a single, multilevel event, may provide higher impairment ratings than a single DRE rating. However, when two or more injuries occur within the same spine region, as in this case, using the ROM method for the second and all subsequent ratings being done may give a lower rating than using the DRE method repeatedly.

15.8d Estimating Whole Person Impairment Using the ROM Method

This section outlines steps in estimating WPI by the ROM method. The first three steps refer to the use of Table 15-7 for rating specific spine disorders to be used as part of the ROM method.

Once the physician decides to use the ROM method, assess whether the underlying condition that resulted in the reduced ROM is listed in Table 15-7. The physician uses the most significant (impairing) spine disorder for a single region. The conditions represented in Table 15-7 include four major categories: (1) fractures; (2) intervertebral disks or other soft-tissue lesions; (3) spondylolysis and spondylolisthesis, not operated on; and (4) operated-on conditions including spinal stenosis, segmental instability, spondylolisthesis, fracture, or dislocation.

When multiple operations are performed or multiple levels are operated on, add 1% for involvement of multiple levels and 2% for the second operation, as indicated in Table 15-7. Once a final spine disorder impairment rating is obtained, this number is combined with the impairment rating from the ROM measurements and neurologic assessment, as discussed in the following steps.

MEDICAL TIP

If spinal stenosis is present but was not operated on, the physician may use IIB in Table 15-7 to provide a rating for the associated tissue damage, pain, and rigidity that can accompany spinal stenosis. Use Table 15-7 only when a ROM impairment is also assigned. If a diagnosis is not found in Table 15-7 that pertains to the specific spine disorder, then use only the ROM measurements, combined with any nerve deficits. Thus, Table 15-7, representing specific spine disorders, may be omitted or used in combination with ROM losses but may not be used alone. If Table 15-7 is omitted, a written rationale should be included in the report.

LEGAL TIP

For conditions covered by both the DRE and ROM methods (eg, intervertebral disk, spinal fusion), ensure that the physician uses the DRE method if only a single symptomatic pathology within a single region is involved. If multiple symptomatic pathologies are present within a single spinal region, the ROM method must be used.

The next steps in using the ROM method are summarized below. Summary points new to the Fifth Edition for ROM measurements:

1. Specify a warm-up protocol before ROM measurements (see Section 15.8a), eg, flexion and extension twice, left and right rotation twice, left and right lateral bending twice, and one additional flexion and extension.

2. Ensure that landmarks are accurate, the body part is stabilized, and the measurement device is properly stabilized on the spine (see Section 15.8b).

3. *Lateral flexion* is renamed *lateral bending* to keep these discrete movements separate.

4. A new appendix that outlines a numerical recording method (SFTR) could facilitate electronic communication of ROM measurements (see *Guides 5th* Appendix).

5. Use of one inclinometer for measuring lateral lumbar bending (Fourth Edition) has been replaced by use of two inclinometers for greater accuracy (Fifth Edition). Use of two inclinometers is now the standard method of measurement, except for thoracic and cervical rotation, in which one inclinometer may be used because adjacent spinal regions can be well stabilized.

Use only ROM measurements that are reproducible, indicating a consistent and true indicator of the ROM. To ensure reproducibility, obtain at least three consecutive measurements and calculate the mean (average) of the three. Measurements should not change substantially with repeated efforts. If substantial change is present, the effort in ROM may vary, indicating that the individual is not consistently giving his or her best effort.

If the average is less than or equal to 50°, three consecutive measurements must fall within 5° of the mean; if the average is greater than 50°, three consecutive measurements must fall within 10% of the mean. Motion testing may be repeated up to six times to obtain three consecutive measurements that meet these criteria. If, after six measurements, inconsistency persists, the spinal motions are considered invalid. Use the highest value (least impairing) measurement to determine the impairment rating. Record ROM measurements on the summary sheets (Figures 15-10, 15-15, and 15-18) or as detailed in the *Guides 5th* Appendix, using a standardized, numerical recording system.

When lumbosacral flexion and extension are less than normal, perform a validity assessment as discussed in the *Guides 5th* (p 406). The accessory validity test listed in the *Guides* is:

Tightest SLR − [sacral flexion + sacral extension] ≤ 15° for validity

Note: This accessory validity test is useful only when lumbosacral flexion plus extension is less than the average for normal individuals (ie, average lumbosacral flexion + extension is 65° for women and 55° for men). At these levels or above, the difference between sacral motion and supine SLR will usually exceed 15° because the hamstring and gluteal muscles are contracted in the standing flexed position and relaxed in the supine position. However, below the threshold of 65° for women and 55° for men, the tightest supine SLR angle should not be more than 15° greater than the combined sacral (hip) impairment due to limited lumbar spine flexion because individuals with limited hip flexion have increased impairment with limited lumbar flexion.

The examples given in the Fifth Edition in most cases do not discuss why the ROM method was chosen instead of the DRE method. Examples 15-19 to 15-22 only illustrate the proper use of ROM measurements in determining the ROM impairment. The ROM method is indicated by Examples 15-22 and 15-23. The ratings would be the same for the Fourth Edition.

M E D I C A L   T I P

ROM measurements need to be taken with two inclinometers, except when cervical and thoracic rotation are measured, in which one inclinometer will suffice, if the lower part of the body is stabilized.

If the first three measurements are inconsistent, tell the individual that the entire ROM evaluation may be discounted unless he or she gives his or her best effort for each measurement. Take three more measurements for a total of six meaurements to obtain a set of three measurements.

Obtain six measurements for each range of motion direction; use the highest value for the impairment rating calculation.

Add ROM impairment ratings at a single level; eg, impairment ratings for lumbar flexion, extension, and bending are added, not combined, with the Combined Values Chart.

L E G A L   T I P

Ensure that the physician notes indicate that at least three measurements were taken and that the best or highest value is used as the ROM value to determine the impairment rating.

The impairment ratings for loss of range of motion in the lumbar, thoracic, and cervical areas are unchanged from the Fourth Edition. The main difference is the use of two inclinometers for all measurements except thoracic and cervical rotation.

Impairment ratings based on the ROM method are subject to review and possible denial when:

1. there is no justification for the method in the examiner's report, or

2. the examiner fails to discuss why any portion of the ROM method is not included (eg, ROM measurements, Table 15.7, and any nerve or spinal cord impairment), or

3. measurements are considerably variable and not reproducible, or

4. appropriate tools, such as inclinometry, are not used.

15.9 ROM: Lumbar Spine

15.10 ROM: Thoracic Spine

15.11 ROM: Cervical Spine

Sections 15.9, 15.10, and 15.11 provide new and updated figures to assist the examiner in the proper measurement of ROM. The examiner should be familiar with the use of inclinometers and proper stabilization and measurement techniques, and understand how to interpret variability in measurements.

15.12 Nerve Root and/or Spinal Cord

The next step in the ROM method is determining neurologic deficits. This section has been expanded, with information from the neurology chapter (Chapter 13) inserted for easy reference.

The purpose of this section is to provide an impairment rating for upper or lower extremity dysfunction resulting from a spine disorder. Sensory loss and/or motor deficits caused by nerve root injury are rated and combined with ROM and spine disorder impairments. The nerve roots that are commonly affected when the spine is injured are weighted on the basis of their perceived importance. The Fifth Edition retains the same weights from the Fourth Edition (Table 15-18) and includes new weights for the cervical and T1 nerve roots. In the unlikely situation in which a lower thoracic nerve root is compressed (T2-T12), the physician may refer to the nervous system chapter and assess thoracic nerve root dysfunction on the basis of the effects on other body parts, eg, extremities. If long tract signs are present consistent with spinal cord dysfunction, use the assessment criteria in the nervous system chapter.

The impairment ranges assigned for sensory loss and motor deficits, as listed in Tables 15-15 and 15-16, enable the physician to account for differences in severity of the condition and the impact of the condition on the ability to perform ADL. For example, someone with greater sensory loss that impacts the ability to perform ADL will receive a higher sensory deficit rating.

M E D I C A L   T I P
Combine all components of the ROM method: ROM impairment, specific spine disorder impairment (Table 15-7), and nerve root dysfunction.
Ensure that nerve root involvement, leading to sensory or motor deficits, is documented by appropriate imaging studies.

L E G A L   T I P
An evaluator's impairment rating, based on ROM, is subject to attack in litigation if it fails to address all the factors that may be addressed in determining a ROM-based impairment (eg, failure to indicate why the rating from Table 15-7 is omitted may make the evaluator appear to have incompletely evaluated the claimant or plaintiff).

The reader may use the following table when using the ROM method. Record the ROM (I), any accompanying spine disorder (II), and sensory and/or motor deficit (IIIa and IIIb; see table). The impairment ratings for these three components are then combined as listed in the last column, to obtain a WPI rating by using the ROM method.

Template for Use of the ROM Method

Spine Region	Extension°, IR %	Flexion °, IR %	Left Rotation°, IR %	Right Rotation°, IR %	Left Lateral Bending °, IR %	
Cervical						
Thoracic						
Lumbar						

IR = impairment rating.

15.13 Criteria for Converting Whole Person Impairment to Regional Spine Impairment

The spine chapter provides WPI ratings. To obtain regional spine impairments, divide the WPI rating by the weight listed below. The weights, unchanged from the Fourth Edition, are as follows:

Region	DRE	ROM
Cervical	0.35	0.80
Thoracic	0.20	0.40
Lumbar	0.75	0.90

If regional impairments exceed 100%, they are rounded down to 100%.

For some states, it is important that spine impairment ratings be expressed as body regions, or only spine impairments. Only 10 states have a schedule for the spine (eg, the spine is worth 374 weeks out of 520), and only six of those use the *Guides*. The six states are Connecticut, Delaware (spine scheduled by court decision), Georgia, North Dakota, Oregon (which still uses the Third Edition Revised), South Carolina, and South Dakota.[2]

For example, in a state where the back is scheduled as a 374-week body part, if the spine were evaluated by region, a lumbar 10% WPI by the DRE method would be divided by 0.75, resulting in a 13.33% lumbar impairment

Right Lateral Bending °, IR %	I. Total IR % From ROM (Add Extension, Flexion, etc)	II. Spine Disorders IR %, Table 15-7	IIIa. Sensory Loss IR %, Table 15-15	IIIb. Motor Deficit IR %, Table 15-16	Final IR: Combine Region Row IR I, II, IIIa, IIIb

(rounded to 13%), or an impairment equal to 48.62 weeks (0.13 × 374), or 48 weeks and 4 days. Calculate the economic value of this spine injury at 48 weeks and 4 days times a weekly benefit amount; if the amount is $475.00, the disability award is $23,071.43.

Impairment percentages, as noted in Chapter 1, are rounded to the next whole number. It is common for states to recognize weeks and days of disability, so in this case, 0.62 weeks would equal 4 days. Some states also state the rating as a percentage of a week, eg, 48.62 weeks.

Using a state with a 374-week value for a back, a thoracic spine impairment rated at 25% WPI under the ROM method yields a 31.25% impairment of the thoracic spine, or a 116-week impairment. The calculations are as follows: (25%/0.80) = 31.25% (rounded to 31%), 31% × 374 weeks = 115.94 weeks (0.94 is rounded to 7 days, or 1 week).

Additional state peculiarities related to evaluation of spine impairments are discussed in the state-by-state section in Appendix B.

15.14 The Pelvis

The methods used and pelvic impairments evaluated in the Fifth Edition have not changed. Although initially there was interest in evaluating pelvic disorders with muscular and ligament dysfunction, a consensus was not reached regarding the manner of evaluation and listed impairment ratings.

15.15 Spine Evaluation Summary

Table 15-20 in the *Guides,* reprinted below, provides a format to record the impairment ratings. Note that the DRE method is not combined with impairment from nerve root assessment within the same spinal region. Nerve root assessment is accounted for in the DRE method. The DRE method can be combined with pelvic impairments (Table 15-19) or impairments from the DRE or ROM method affecting another spine region. It is recommended that readers use Table 15-20 or another similar table to report their findings, in addition to a qualitative report.

Table 15-20 Spine Evaluation Summary

Name _____ Soc. Sec. No. _____ Date _____

Impairment	Cervical	Thoracic	Lumbar
1. DRE Method (Tables 15-3 through 15-5)			
2. Range-of-Motion Method (and Table 15-8)			
3. Nerve root: Loss of sensation with or without pain / Loss of strength			
4. Other (From Section 15.14)			
5. Regional impairment total (combine impairments in each column using the Combined Values Chart, p. 604)			
6. Spine impairment total (combine all regional totals using the Combined Values Chart)			

7. Impairment(s) of other organ systems: for each impairment list condition, page number in *Guides,* and percentage of impairment.

Impaired System	% Impairment	*Guides* Page Number
a.		
b.		
c.		
d.		
e.		

8. Impairment of the whole person: Use Combined Values Chart to combine spine impairment with the impairment(s) listed in 7 above. If several impairments are listed, combine spine impairments with the larger or largest value, then combine the resulting percentage with any other value(s), until all the listed impairments have been accounted for.

Total whole person impairment: _____

References

1. Netter FH. *Atlas of Human Anatomy.* Summit, NJ: Ciba-Geigy; 1989: plates 150, 455, and 511.

2. Barth PS, Niss M. *Permanent Partial Disability Benefits: Interstate Differences.* Cambridge, Mass: Workers Compensation Research Institute; 1999: Table 3-6.

The Upper Extremities

Introduction

This chapter provides an overview of key points and changes (identified with an icon **G**) made in Chapter 16 of the AMA *Guides to the Evaluation of Permanent Impairment, Fifth Edition* (*Guides 5th*), illustrates these changes in a table comparison, and discusses the purpose and implications of the major changes, with illustrative examples. The numbered section titles within this chapter correspond to sections within *Guides 5th*. Only key principles or important changes are included in this chapter.

Key Points and Changes

Principles of Assessment

Loss of function due to impairment of a digit (finger) is compared with complete loss of function due to amputation.

Hand dominance is not accounted for in upper extremity impairment ratings (IRs), but the impact on function can be discussed qualitatively in the evaluation report.

The upper extremity is weighted at 60% whole person impairment (WPI).

Combine most upper extremity impairments, of the same unit or denominator, and convert the upper extremity to a WPI rating.

Amputations

IRs for amputations of different fingers are added, after conversion to the same unit (hand, upper extremity, or WPI), not combined.

Fingers are weighted differently on the basis of perceived importance (eg, the thumb is worth 40%, the index and middle fingers 20% each, and the ring and little fingers 10% each of the overall hand value).

IRs for amputation can be combined with other impairments, eg, skin disorders, peripheral nerve problems, phantom limb pain.

Sensory Impairment Due to Digital Nerve Lesions

Measure digital nerve sensory loss by using the classic Weber static two-point discrimination test.

Characterize digital nerve sensory loss as none, partial, or total, as well as transverse or longitudinal.

Evaluating Abnormal Motion

Add IRs for range of motion (ROM) measurements for a particular joint.

If the IR does not express the impairment, because the contralateral side is different than the population normals, the physician can adjust the IR.

For joints in ankylosis, the IR given for ankylosis in a nonfunctional position is included in the pie charts and is larger than the IR for ankylosis in the functional position.

G To detect limited motion due to lack of tendon excursion, flexion is measured in all joints of the finger while the finger is in maximum active flexion; then extension is measured in all joints while the finger is in a position of maximum active extension.

Calculate the IR for each finger joint and combine joint IR values to give the IR due to limited motion of the fingers.

Impairment of the Upper Extremities Due to Peripheral Nerve Disorders

G Sensory impairments, previously graded on a scale of 1 to 5, are now graded on a scale of 0 to 5.

Entrapment neuropathies can be evaluated by either the upper extremity or neurology chapter methods; use the method that provides the higher rating.

G Document the diagnosis of entrapment peripheral neuropathies with electromyography, or sensory and motor nerve conduction studies.

G If complex regional pain syndrome (CRPS) is not present, the rating for peripheral nerve disorder stands alone and is not combined with any loss of ROM due to the nerve deficit.

G If both peripheral nerve disorder and causalgia (CRPS II) are present, then
the condition is rated according to the new section on causalgia, by means
of the approach in either the upper extremity or the nervous system chapter.

G If surgery is performed for carpal tunnel syndrome (CTS), wait until the
individual has reached maximal medical improvement (MMI) before assigning a permanent impairment rating.

G After CTS surgery, if clinical signs have resolved but abnormal electrophysiologic changes persist, an impairment rating up to 5% may be assigned.

Repeat nerve conduction studies after surgery are not required.

G If sensibility (two-point discrimination), opposition strength, and nerve conduction studies are normal after CTS surgery, a 0% impairment rating
applies on the basis of the upper extremity chapter. The neurology chapter
(Table 13-23) can also be used to assess residual changes of sensory deficit
or pain from peripheral nerve disorders.

Impairment of the Upper Extremities Due to Vascular Disorders

G Assessment for Raynaud's syndrome is now consistent in both the upper
extremity and cardiovascular chapters.

G For classifying an individual with Raynaud's syndrome, class 2, obtain
objective vascular flow studies, measuring either the finger/brachial ratio
index or laser Doppler flowmetry.

Impairment of the Upper Extremities Due to Other Disorders

G When upper extremity impairments are not well characterized by ROM
deficit, peripheral nerve, or vascular disorders, categorize the impairment on
the basis of "other" methods, including bone and joint deformities, tendinitis, arthroplasty, and musculotendinous impairments.

Comparison of Tables Between the Fifth and Fourth *Guides* Editions

The following table summarizes the key points and changes in tables
between the fourth and fifth editions of the *Guides*.

Comparison of Tables Between the Fifth and Fourth *Guides* Editions

Table Topic	5th Edition Table Number	4th Edition Table Number	Summary of Changes in 5th Edition
Digit-to-hand % conversion	16-1	1	Stylistic
Hand to upper extremity impairment (UEI) % conversion	16-2	2	Stylistic
Upper extremity to whole person % conversion	16-3	3	Stylistic
Amputation UEI	16-4		New UEI table, consistent with 4th Edition Figures 2 and 3
Sensory quality impairment	16-5		New; sensory impairment classifications carried from text in 4th Edition
Thumb and little finger transverse and longitudinal sensory loss	16-6	4, 8	Incorporates transverse, longitudinal, and combined rating for both nerves
Index, middle, and ring finger transverse and longitudinal sensory loss	16-7	9	Incorporates transverse, longitudinal, and combined rating for both nerves
Thumb impairment, abduction and ankylosis	16-8a	6	Includes lack of radial adduction as cause of impairment
Thumb impairment, adduction and ankylosis	16-8b	5	None
Thumb ankylosis and lack of opposition impairment	16-9	7	None
Sensory deficit or pain from peripheral nerve disorder (PND)	16-10	11	Revised descriptors; reverses gradations and adds grade 0; see Table 15-15
Individual muscle rated motor and loss of power from PND	16-11	12	Slight terminology changes; also see Table 15-16

Comparison of Tables Between the Fifth and Fourth *Guides* Editions, *continued*

Table Topic	5th Edition Table Number	4th Edition Table Number	Summary of Changes in 5th Edition
Brachial plexus peripheral nerve origins and functions	16-12a	10	Changes in categories and anatomic terminology within primary and secondary branches; functions more detailed
Brachial plexus peripheral nerve origins and functions	16-12b (median and ulnar)	10 (median and ulnar)	Changes in terminology and anatomic descriptions within primary and secondary branches; functions more detailed
Individual spinal nerve unilateral motor or sensory or combined 100% deficits	16-13	13	None; also in Table15-17
Brachial plexus unilateral motor or sensory or combined 100% deficits	16-14	14	Stylistic
Major peripheral unilateral motor or sensory or combined 100% deficits	16-15	15	% increases in combined motor and sensory deficits and for median nerve (above and below midforearm)
Reflex sympathetic dystrophy (RSD)/ causalgia (CRPS) diagnostic criteria	16-16		New; CRPS/RSD/ causalgia
Entrapment neuropathy		16	Deleted; replaced by Sections 16.5d and 13.9c
Peripheral vascular disease impairment	16-17	17	Expanded discussion of Reynaud's syndrome; elastic support reference deleted
Digit, hand, wrist, elbow, or shoulder specific joint or unit disorder impairment value	16-18	18	Increased % for metacarpophalangeal (MP) thumb loss; decreased % for some partial finger losses
Joint crepitation		Table 19	Deleted
Synovial hypertrophy	16-19	20	None

Chapter 16

Comparison of Tables Between the Fifth and Fourth *Guides* Editions, *continued*

Table Topic	5th Edition Table Number	4th Edition Table Number	Summary of Changes in 5th Edition
Active ulnar or radial deviation	16-20	21	Stylistic
Digital deformity rotational impairment	16-21	22	Stylistic
Persistent subluxation or dislocation joint impairment	16-22	23	None
Excessive passive mediolateral joint instability	16-23	24	None
Excessive active mediolateral wrist and elbow joint deviation	16-24	25	Stylistic
Carpal instability pattern UEI	16-25	26	Significant revision; different measurement methods and criteria for impairment, and impairment percentage increases
Symptomatic shoulder instability pattern UEI	16-26		New; allows instability to be rated on its own
Specific bone or joint arthroplasty UEI	16-27	27	Significant revision; implant IR % reduced; resection IR % increased for shoulder, elbow, ulnar head, and thumb, but reduced for fingers
Intrinsic tightness digit impairment	16-28	28	None
Constrictive tenosynovitis digit impairment	16-29	29	None
MP joint extensor tendon subluxation	16-30	30	None
Occupational average grip strength	16-31	31	None
Grip strength by age	16-32	32	None
Occupational lateral pinch strength	16-33	33	None
Lost grip or pinch strength joint UEI	16-34	34	None

Comparison of Tables Between the Fifth and Fourth *Guides* Editions, *continued*			
Table Topic	5th Edition Table Number	4th Edition Table Number	Summary of Changes in 5th Edition
Individual motion unit manual muscle testing–based musculoskeletal disorder strength deficits UEI	16-35		New; numerical ratings based on shoulder and elbow manual muscle testing

Introduction

The upper extremity chapter contains some significant departures from the remainder of the *Guides*, based on the work of chapter chairs Frank E. Jones, MD, and Genevieve de Groot Swanson, MD, and their committees, with final approval of the upper extremity chapter by Gunnar Andersson, MD, PhD.

The upper extremity consists of the hand, wrist, elbow, and shoulder. The upper extremity chapter has been reorganized and uses primarily anatomic and ROM approaches to evaluate upper extremity disorders. The Fifth Edition discusses abnormal motion for the thumb, fingers, wrist, elbow, and shoulder in a single section, instead of in separate subparts as in the Fourth Edition.

Compared to Section 3.1 in the Fourth Edition, Chapter 16 in the Fifth Edition provides additional explanations and more examples to assist in its application. Only those sections with either changes or critical content are discussed in this book.

The major changes, which will be discussed in this chapter, include the following:

1. Clarification of impairment due to amputation

2. Adding a method to evaluate limited motion due to tendon impairments in the fingers

3. New criteria for the diagnosis of complex regional pain syndromes (reflex sympathetic dystrophy, causalgia, etc)

4. A revised approach to entrapment neuropathies, including CTS

5. Clarification of the use of weakness as a criterion for impairment

16.1 Principles of Assessment

16.1a Principles of Impairment Evaluation

This new section in the Fifth Edition incorporates material from the Fourth Edition and expands on the principles for use of the upper extremity chapter. Impairment determination in the upper extremity consists of a primarily anatomic approach, which for some conditions includes cosmetic and functional assessment. As emphasized throughout the *Guides*, when the physician can choose a range of values, it is important to consider the impact on the ability to perform activities of daily living (ADL) in determining the value within a range. In cases where a range is not provided but the rating does not reflect the impairment's impact on ADL, this should be noted in the report.

16.1b Impairment Evaluation: Documentation and Recording

The anatomic basis for upper extremity impairment ratings relies on a grouping of seven conditions into which particular diagnoses or impairments can be categorized. The physician begins with an examination of the most distal parts of the upper extremity, beginning with the thumb, fingers, wrist, elbow, and shoulder. Using a systematic approach, as with Figures 16-1a and 16-1b, ensure that all impairments are recorded and combined or added as appropriate. The physician may choose to use the impairment evaluation records for the upper extremity, Figures 16-1a and 16-1b, to ensure that all upper extremity changes are assessed and noted. Impairments within the following categories are noted and rated separately:

Amputation

Digital nerve lesions

Restriction of active motion/ankylosis

Peripheral nerve disorders

Peripheral vascular disease

Other musculoskeletal disorders

Strength evaluation

16.1c Combining Impairment Ratings

Impairments from each body part are weighted. The upper extremity is weighted at 60% whole person impairment. Thus, the maximum impairment rating one could obtain for complete loss of use or amputation of the upper extremity is 60%. Other weightings are represented as follows.

Body Part	Hand Value %	Upper Extremity %	Whole Person %
Thumb at MP joint	40	36	22
Index or middle finger at MP joint	20	18	11
Ring or little finger	10	9	5
Wrist		90-95	54-57
Below elbow		95	57
Shoulder		100	60

Thus, an upper extremity impairment affecting only one limb cannot exceed 60% WPI. A scapulothoracic amputation is rated to the body as a whole (70%), since the scapula is considered part of the trunk. In addition, the physician can either use the conversion tables provided in Tables 16-1, 16-2, and 16-3 or do the following multiplications.

Thumb impairment $\times$ 0.4 = hand impairment

Index or middle finger impairment $\times$ 0.2 = hand impairment

Ring or little finger impairment $\times$ 0.1 = hand impairment

Hand impairment $\times$ 0.9 = upper extremity impairment

Upper extremity impairment $\times$ 0.6 = whole person impairment

Impairment ratings are converted into impairments of the same type (eg, either upper extremity or whole person impairment). These like body part impairments are then combined for a single value of impairment, either upper extremity or whole person impairment, by means of Table 16-3.

16.1d Principles for Adding Impairment Values

Most upper extremity impairments are combined. Ensure that only the same body units are combined (eg, for wrist and elbow impairments, convert each impairment to an upper extremity impairment, then combine the upper extremity impairments). It would not be appropriate to combine a wrist and an elbow impairment.

Add impairments in three situations:

1. Add impairments in different directions of active ROM at a single joint (eg, add ROM impairment ratings for the shoulder at flexion and extension).

2. Add impairments of all thumb joint motions.

3. Add all finger impairment ratings after they have been converted into hand impairment ratings (eg, thumb, index, and little finger IR are converted into hand impairment, then added together).

MEDICAL TIP

Follow a systematic approach, using Figure 16-1a, Figure 16-1b, or another worksheet to record all ratings. Have the following equipment available: goniometers (large and small) or an inclinometer, two-point discrimination devices (Disk-criminator, DeMayo two-point discrimination), Jamar dynamometer, pinch gauge, and individual radiographs.

LEGAL TIP

Despite the trends to characterize impairments on the basis of a diagnosis, upper extremity impairment evaluation still is focused on anatomic changes or losses and is highly individualized.

16.2 Amputations

Values for amputation of a part of the upper extremity receive the highest impairment rating compared with the other six categories discussed in Section 16.1. Amputations are assessed on the basis of the remaining portion. The physician evaluates the most proximal section remaining. The measurements are made without a prosthesis in place, if it is removable. The evaluator uses Figure 16-2 to determine the upper extremity impairment for corresponding amputations. For amputations between the specified levels on Figure 16-2, the physician should extrapolate, using his or her clinical judgment, and assign the higher impairment rating if in doubt.

16.2b Amputation Impairment: Levels Proximal to Digits

16.2c Amputation Impairment: Digital Levels

Amputations of digits (fingers) or part of a digit are assessed on the basis of Figures 16-4 and 16-5, extrapolating to the closest and highest value. Each finger amputation IR is converted to a hand IR. As previously discussed, since the digits are involved, add the finger amputation IRs to obtain the total hand IR. The hand impairment rating is converted to an upper extremity and whole person IR by means of Tables 16-1 through 16-3 or by multiplying by the weighting or conversion factors, as indicated in Section 16.2.

16.2d Conditions Associated With Amputation

Use the Combined Values Chart to combine impairment ratings due to amputation with the following conditions, if present:

1. Some peripheral nerve disorders (RSD, neuromas): Evaluate in the nervous system or upper extremity chapter. Differences in approach will be discussed subsequently. In most cases, do not combine the amputation IR with a peripheral nerve IR for nerves that have been transected, since loss of peripheral nerve function was accounted for in the amputation IR. A separate IR for peripheral nerve transection may be combined if the nerve transection occurred at a level proximal to the amputation level).

2. Skin disorders (breakdown, scarring): Evaluate with the skin chapter (Chapter 8).

3. Phantom limb pain: See the pain chapter (Chapter 18), which provides an additional IR up to 3% and a qualitative assessment.

4. Mental and behavioral conditions, for a qualitative assessment of psychiatric sequelae.

5. Proximal loss of ROM for remaining joints.

6. Proximal peripheral vascular disorders.

EXAMPLE

A 35-year-old machinist with diabetes sustains an amputation at the MP joint of his thumb and at the proximal interphalangeal (PIP) joint of his index finger in his dominant right hand. He has continued pain in the thumb stump, with some skin breakdown, extending beyond the stump into the hand, requiring intermittent treatment. The intermittent skin breakdown further limits his ability to use his right hand. Despite a year of therapy, he is still depressed, as he can no longer work as a fine tool machinist or pursue his prior hobbies—woodworking, car repair, and designing and building model villages. He also is distraught about his appearance and has become more reclusive.

IR Calculation

Amputation of thumb: 40% of hand

Amputation of index finger: 16% of hand (80% of 20%) (Figure 16-3)

Total hand IR due to finger amputation: 40% + 16% = 56% hand IR

56% hand IR × 0.9 upper extremity = 50% of upper extremity

50% upper extremity IR × 0.6 whole person = 30% WPI due to amputation

Combine this 30% IR for amputation with the IR for the skin disorder and intermittent skin breakdown, a class 2, 10% to 24% WPI (Table 8-2). The individual could be assessed for up to an additional 3% IR if the pain is excessive and slightly increases the burden of the condition. If warranted, a moderate psychiatric impairment would be noted in the report.

MEDICAL TIP
Ensure impairments are of the same type, eg, hand, upper extremity, or whole person, before adding or combining.
When multiple digits are involved due to amputation, convert each digit IR to a hand IR and then *add* the hand IR to give the total hand IR.

LEGAL TIP
In states where loss of use is compared to amputation or where any anatomic loss may be grounds for a permanent impairment, combining may be considered inappropriate, especially where the *Guides* has not been formally adopted by statute or agency regulation. Multiple losses may be required to be added, instead of combined, in such legal environments.

There may be division of opinion about whether the skin problem in the preceding example should be rated separately from and then combined with the amputation impairment rating. Some argue that doing so exceeds an axiomatic limit of the amputation value, such that the amputation value cannot be exceeded for a host of cumulative problems affecting the same digit. Others may argue that two distinct body systems (skin and musculoskeletal) are affected by the procedure, which therefore may allow a combined rating for each system's condition.

16.3 Sensory Impairment Due to Digital Nerve Lesions

Sensory loss in the upper extremity is evaluated by one of two methods, depending on the cause of the loss. If the loss develops from dysfunction to a digital nerve, which is typically found with isolated hand injuries, it is evaluated within the hand section. If the sensory loss involves more than the digits of the hand because of a peripheral nerve lesion, it is assessed separately in Section 16.5 or in the nervous system chapter.

The section on assessment of sensory loss due to digital nerve impairment has been expanded to discuss other methods of sensory testing, such as the Semmes-Weinstein monofilament pressure anesthesiometer. However, to determine the impairment rating, the two-point Weber static discrimination test is retained from the Fourth Edition, and values from that test, as listed in Table 16-5, are the same and are used to determine the impairment rating.

The other additions in this section are columns added to Tables 16-6 and 16-7 indicating that if both digital nerves are impaired for any finger, the impairment ratings from each digital nerve are added. This practice was the same in the Fourth Edition but was not explicitly stated in the table.

The Fifth Edition adds an expanded description of rating neuromas, using the same method as the Fourth Edition. The severity grade for pain, as indicated in Table 16-10, is multiplied by the maximum value for total loss of the digital nerve, as listed in Tables 16-6 and 16-7, and converted to upper extremity and whole person impairment. If this is the only digit impairment, the severity grade for pain is multiplied by the sensory deficit or pain impairment value in Table 16-7, which has already been converted to the upper extremity impairment rating. As previously stated, different tables in this chapter present the information in multiple ways, to account for the multiple stages of conversion.

Sensory impairment due to digital nerve lesions can be longitudinal, in which one digital nerve is involved, or transverse, in which both digital nerves are impaired. After determining whether the loss is longitudinal or transverse, determine whether the degree of sensory loss is partial or total, measured by two-point discrimination.

Sensory Loss	2-Point Discrimination Value
None	≤ 6 mm
Partial	7-15 mm
Total	>15 mm

Using Table 16-6 or 16-7, determine the IR based on the length of nerve or digit involved. As is seen in this table, hand IRs due to loss of both nerves in a digit are added. If additional sensory loss is detected in the palm, due to impairment of the palmar or dorsal ulnar cutaneous nerve, up to 5% additional hand IR can be added to the digital sensory loss.

EXAMPLE

After a woodcrafting accident, an individual sustains a thumb laceration that heals well except for some lost sensation over the ulnar surface of the thumb, distal to the interphalangeal (IP) joint. Since only the ulnar surface is involved, this would be classified as a longitudinal loss. A loss up to the IP joint includes approximately half the thumb length. Two-point discrimination detected a 9-mm sensory discrimination, indicating a partial sensory loss. Thus, on the basis of Table 16-6, there is a 50% digit length involved in a partial ulnar digit loss for an 8% impairment of the digit. Using Table 16-1, 8% thumb = 3% of the hand. From Table 16-2, a 3% hand IR = 3% upper extremity IR. The 3% upper extremity IR is converted to 2% WPI by means of Table 16-3.

MEDICAL TIP
For conditions other than amputations, even in the fingers, IRs due to different disorders are combined, not added. For example, an IR due to decreased ROM of the thumb is combined with the IR due to a neuroma on the thumb.

LEGAL TIP
Traditional statutory schedules in workers' compensation may also rate each finger in a descending rate (eg, 22% WPI for the thumb, 14% WPI for a forefinger, 11% WPI for a middle finger, 5% WPI for a ring finger, and 3% WPI for a little finger). Again, jurisdictions that compare partial losses of use to amputations may also require a slightly different approach than that described in the *Guides*.

EXAMPLE

Example 16-8: A partial transverse loss distal to the PIP joint: 20% of the statute's index finger 14% WPI equals 2.8% WPI. Using the *Guides* and rounding to whole numbers, 20% index finger = 4% hand = 4% upper extremity = 2% WPI.

16.4 Evaluating Abnormal Motion

The method for evaluating abnormal ROM in the fingers has been expanded, but the technique, terminology, and rating remain unchanged from the Fourth Edition. The Fifth Edition still includes separate sections for assessment of thumb ROM and the remaining fingers, followed by wrist, elbow, and shoulder. Since ROM is covered in detail in Section 16.4, only highlights and key points will be discussed here, to avoid duplication. The pie charts were retained and remain the easiest method to assess motion impairment for each specific joint, once they are understood. Adduction, as indicated in Figure 16-18, is measured in centimeters.

This edition, however, does contain new and specific instructions for measuring ROM after tendon injuries, where the measurement of individual joints could be normal or near normal. To assess tendon injuries, measure flexion at each joint while all joints are held in a position of maximum active flexion. Measure extension of each joint while all three joints are held in maximum extension. In this way, the motion of the digit is measured. Use the joint measurement technique that best depicts the permanent impairment.

Also new in the Fifth Edition are instructions in Section 16.4c for correcting for individual normal values that differ from population norms. If the contralateral "normal" joint has less than normal ROM, the impairment value of the uninvolved joint can be subtracted from the more impaired joint. Similarly, if the uninvolved "normal" joint has a greater ROM than normal, the physician can correct for an IR that may reflect less than the actual impairment, correcting up to 2% of the maximum impairment rating and discussing this in detail in the chart.

Before making a correction for the normal values listed in the pie charts, recognize that individuals are asymmetric, and ensure that the injured joint had limited ROM at the same level or worse than the normal joint. It would be inappropriate to use a contralateral comparison as normal if there had been a prior injury to the contralateral, reportedly normal joint. As stated in the *Guides*, the individual should be taken at his or her word, unless there is medical documentation to support a prior condition indicating a preexisting limitation in range of motion.

EXAMPLE

Jean has moderately severe rheumatoid arthritis with decreased ROM in multiple joints, including both of her hands and wrists. After a fall, with a fracture to her right wrist, Jean has further loss of motion. She acknowledges and her medical reports support a preexisting loss of range of motion in both hands. Her exam indicates a right wrist extension of 10° (IR = 8%) and flexion of 10° (IR = 8%), using Figure 16-28. She has a 16% impairment of the upper extremity due to decreased wrist flexion and extension, or a 10% WPI.

MEDICAL TIP

If the physician is asked to apportion the individual's loss of ROM to the rheumatoid arthritis and crush injury in the prior example, there are two options. The physician can assign an impairment rating as indicated in the pie charts and discuss in the report any preexisting limitations in ROM in the rheumatoid, injured hand. Alternatively, if adequate documentation exists about her preinjury ROM, the physician can use the preinjury ROM measurements to calculate any impairment rating due to the rheumatoid arthritis and subtract that from the ROM impairment after injury.

LEGAL TIP

If an individual's contralateral side has greater ROM than expected because of hypermobility, and the injured side has reduced ROM but it falls within normal values, the physician should indicate this in the medical report. If a numerical rating is required as a guideline, the physician may indicate a value not greater than 2% of the regional unit's worth.

Figure 16-9 illustrates the different movements and their representation on the pie charts, such as Figure 16-12. Ankylosis refers to complete absence of motion at a joint. Full extension or the neutral position is considered to be 0°. Hyperextension, which is extension beyond 0°, is indicated on the pie charts by a plus sign. Extension lag, which is defined as incomplete extension or inability to reach the neutral position, is indicated by a minus sign. Only active ROM measurements are used. Within a given unit (eg, a single finger joint or a wrist), all ROM impairment ratings are added. For ROM measurements that lie between the values on the pie charts, extrapolate and use the higher value if in doubt. When a joint is in ankylosis or a fixed position, determine if it is in the functional position, which is the lowest IR under $I_A\%$ in the pie chart.

EXAMPLE

An elbow is ankylosed in 90° of flexion and 30° of supination. Neither of these ROMs is in the functional range. Ankylosis in 90° flexion is 25% upper extremity impairment (Figure 16-34). Ankylosis in 30° supination is 23% upper extremity impairment (Figure 16-37). These are added for total upper extremity impairment of 48%.

Normal ROM values for the upper extremity as listed in the *Guides 5th* are organized below for rapid reference.

Fingers	Flexion	Extension	Abduction (cm)	Adduction (cm)	Opposition (cm)
Thumb				8 to 0	0 to 8
CMC			8		
MP	60°	0°-40°			
IP	80°	10°-30°			
All other fingers					
MP	90°	20°			
PIP	100°	0°-30°			
Distal IP (DIP)	70°	0°-30°			

	Flexion	Extension	Abduction	Adduction	Internal Rotation	External Rotation
Wrist	60°	60°	Radial deviation 20°	Ulnar deviation 30°		
Elbow	140°	0°	Pronate 80°	Supinate 70°-80°		
Shoulder	180°	50°	170°-180°	40°-50°	80°-90°	60°-90°

16.5 Impairment of the Upper Extremities Due to Peripheral Nerve Disorders

The section on peripheral nerve disorders has been expanded. This section was designed to be used for peripheral nerve disorders with definite nerve injury. A new section has been added to address entrapment neuropathies, a subset of peripheral nerve disorders. Entrapment neuropathies include the common CTS. Differences exist between the rating of a peripheral nerve disorder in the new upper extremity section and the nervous system chapter. The rating of most peripheral nervous system disorders, with the exception of disorders leading to CRPS, have remained the same in the nervous system chapter from the Fourth Edition to the Fifth Edition.

16.5b Impairment Evaluation Methods
Grading Sensory Deficits or Pain

The major change to the sensory section involves Table 16-10, which replaces Table 11 in the Fourth Edition. A new six-level gradation classification (grade 0 for 100% sensory deficit impairment and grade 5 for 0%) was created with more detailed criteria on which to help classify an individual into grades 5 to 0, instead of 1 to 5. The ordinal scale has been inverted, with grade 5 now indicating 0% impairment, to be consistent with the motor scale of grade 5 (Table 16-11) being 0% motor impairment.

Although consistent with Table 16-11 (formerly Table 12), this contrasts with both the Fourth Edition scale and the peripheral nerve disorder scale in the nervous system chapter (Table 13-23). The rating for grade 1 has been changed to 81% to 99%, whereas in the Fourth Edition grade 5 was 81% to 100%.

The overall method of rating peripheral nerve disorder has remained the same in both the nervous system and upper extremity chapters. The degree of nerve impairment is identified on the basis of the symptoms, signs, and nerve conduction or electromyographic (EMG) tests. The severity of sensory or motor deficit is graded on a scale of 0 to 5, and the corresponding percent deficit is determined. This severity of sensory or motor deficit is then multiplied by the maximum value of this function of the nerve. The upper extremity impairment rating equals sensory or motor deficit times the maximum impairment rating of this function for the peripheral nerve. The sensory and motor upper extremity deficits due to the peripheral nerve disorder are combined. The total upper extremity IR is then multiplied by 0.6 to obtain a whole person impairment rating.

The evaluator may choose to use either the more detailed descriptors in the upper extremity section or those in the nervous system section, depending on what is most appropriate for the individual being rated. With both methods, the rating should be the same or very close, although expressed in a different format. If the two methods produce different results, the physician is advised to use the method that provides the higher rating.

The sections providing maximum upper extremity IR for spinal nerve disorders (Table 16-13) and brachial plexus disorders (Table 16-14) have remained unchanged.

16.5c Regional Impairment Determination

This section has remained the same for the assessment of impairments of spinal nerves, brachial plexus injuries, and major peripheral nerves.

16.5d Entrapment/Compression Neuropathy
Impairment Rating of Entrapment/Compression Neuropathies

The Fifth Edition brings a major change in the evaluation and rating of entrapment neuropathy. In the Fourth Edition, entrapment neuropathy, with the most common condition being CTS, was evaluated on the basis of Table 16, and a rating was based on whether the condition was deemed to be mild, moderate, or severe. No criteria were provided to indicate whether the mild, moderate, or severe rating was decided on the basis of symptoms, function, nerve conduction tests, or a combination of the above. To address these concerns and the variability in ratings that were assigned to entrapment neuropathies, several criteria are now stated explicitly in the Fifth Edition:

1. The diagnosis should be documented by electromyography and sensory and motor nerve conduction studies (*Guides 5th*, p 493). These findings are presumed to be present if the individual had surgery.

2. The individual needs to reach MMI before a rating is assigned. After surgery, maximal recovery can vary, depending on the level of injury, duration, and upper extremity function.

3. If objective physical findings of loss of nerve function are present, evaluate the condition on the basis of peripheral nerve assessment as outlined above or in the nervous system chapter (Section 13.9).

4. If CRPS is not present, the rating for peripheral nerve disorder stands alone and is not combined with loss of ROM that is due to the nerve palsy.

5. If both peripheral nerve disorder and causalgia (CRPS II) are present, then the condition is rated according to the new section on causalgia, using the approach in either the upper extremity or nervous system chapter.

When more than one approach can be well justified, as in the upper extremity or nervous system chapter, use the approach that provides the higher rating.

The upper extremity chapter discusses CTS primarily in cases in which surgery has been performed. If the individual's condition is not well characterized by the upper extremity chapter, the physician can evaluate CTS in the neurology chapter, under Section 13.9. The following interpretations apply in the upper extremity chapter:

- If surgery is not performed (or after surgery), and residual median nerve dysfunction is documented by clinical findings and electrophysiologic studies, use the rating for peripheral nerve disorder in either the upper extremity or the nervous system chapter.

- Since symptoms are subjective, they are insufficient to qualify an individual for an IR, even if they remain after surgery. However, if any clinical findings indicate peripheral nerve impairment, or any EMG/nerve conduction velocity (NCV) tests are abnormal in the presence of symptoms, this would meet criteria for an IR.

The following table lists some possible presentations of CTS and the *Guides 5th* interpretation, assuming the individual is at MMI.

Case No.	CTS Symptoms	Clinical Findings	Positive EMG or NCV Findings	Surgery	Chapter Discussed	IR
1	Yes	No	No	No	Upper extremity (UE)/nervous system	0%
2	Yes	Yes	No	No	Nervous system/UE	>0%
3	Yes	No	No	Yes	UE	0%
4	Yes	No	Yes	Yes	Nervous system/UE	>0%
5	No	No	Yes	No	Nervous system/UE	0%
6	No	No	Yes	Yes	UE	0%
7	Yes	No	No	Yes	Nervous system/UE	0%

EXAMPLE

Susan works as a meat cutter and develops right CTS (right hand dominant). She has documented thumb weakness (grade 4/5), numbness, tingling, and changes indicative of CTS on NCV studies and EMGs. One year after surgery, there is minimal improvement, partial sensory loss (8 mm two-point discimination) along the radial thumb, pain, and thenar weakness, and some slight slowing on her NCV tests. She uses her right hand when necessary for many common activities. Based on her residual pain, weakness, and electrophysiologic studies, she would be assessed under the section on peripheral nerve disorder in either this chapter or the nervous system chapter.

Impairment Rating

Using the procedure in this chapter, given that the thumb is the only affected digit, the sensory deficit described in this individual would meet criteria for a grade 3, or 60%, sensory deficit (Table 16-10). Use Table 16-15 to identify the maximum upper extremity impairment due to this median nerve, radial digit deficit, which corresponds to a 60% × 7% (maximum sensory deficit for the radial thumb) or a 4% upper extremity sensory impairment. Given a motor deficit of grade 4, or a 25% motor deficit (Table 16-11), use Table 16-15 to mutiply by the maximum motor deficit for the median nerve, or 10%, for a 3%

motor deficit. Combine the 4% upper extremity sensory deficit with the 3% upper extremity motor deficit, using the Combined Values Chart, for a 7% upper extremity impairment, which converts to 4% WPI. If Susan's sensory loss and strength were restored, but her neurologic tests indicated some residual damage, she would receive up to a 5% upper extemity or 3% whole person impairment rating.

Using the neurology chapter for the same individual, one could obtain the exact same rating.

EXAMPLE

Patrick is a rebar setter, laying, bending, and tying together steel reinforcing bars weighing up to 100 pounds for road and building construction. He develops CTS, with positive Tinel's sign and EMG findings, and is removed from work for 8 months. His symptoms abate, and EMG/NCV tests are negative, but his treating physician recommends a change in employment and restricts him from work that requires repetitive wrist movements and constant twisting of his wrists. On the basis of the lack of permanent, objective changes, he would not receive an impairment rating.

MEDICAL TIP

In evaluating CTS, ensure that the individual is at MMI. Document the sensory, motor, and electrophysiologic changes. If, after surgery or after rehabilitation or both, clinical sensory and motor findings have resolved but electrophysiologic findings persist, maximum impairment is 5%.

LEGAL TIP

Compare the case of Patrick and this approach with the mandate in some statutes to compensate for *any* anatomic loss. Although this may not constitute a hindrance in performing ADL, it nonetheless represents a permanent anatomic loss (and vocational opportunity loss) and may not qualify for a rating under the *Guides*. Patrick's condition may be ratable, especially in those states that use the *Guides* by custom or as evidence, rather than as a regulatory or statutory mandate.

16.5e Complex Regional Pain Syndromes (CRPS), Reflex Sympathetic Dystrophy (CRPS I), and Causalgia (CRPS II)

The section on causalgia and RSD in the Fourth Edition has been markedly revised. In the Fourth Edition, causalgia and RSD were evaluated on the basis of peripheral nerve changes, as previously described. This section has been changed, with two methods being available to evaluate CRPS. The upper extremity approach, outlined in method 1, distinguishes two types of CRPS, RSD (CRPS I) and causalgia (CRPS II), providing different approaches for each variant of CRPS. The nervous system method, as indicated in Section

13.8, uses only Table 13-22 and rates the impairment on the basis of the ability to perform ADL, with a differential rating for the dominant extremity.

The upper extremity chapter uses a complex anatomic assessment of ROM and sensory loss. CRPS I or RSD is rated differently from CRPS II or causalgia. The diagnosis of CRPS is made when at least eight criteria are met, as indicated in Table 16-16. These criteria, as indicated in the nervous system chapter, are not seen in all individuals with CRPS. These criteria were put forth by a *Guides* user and were thought to represent a valuable, but not the only, perspective. They are a guide and should not be construed as the definitive definition of CRPS.

On the basis of the upper extremity chapter:

1. Make a diagnosis of CRPS I or RSD on the basis of criteria in Table 16-16. If CRPS I or RSD is present, evaluate loss of ROM at each joint involved in the upper extremity. This could involve assessment of the shoulder, elbow, wrist, each finger, and each finger joint for ROM. Calculate total upper extremity IR for ROM deficits.

2. Determine an IR for sensory loss or pain from Table 16-10 and combine the value for sensory deficit for the upper extremity with the ROM value. No maximal nerve value multiplier is used. "No additional impairment is assigned for decreased pinch or grasp strength" (*Guides 5th*, p 496). The maximum attained with this method is 100% upper extremity or 60% whole person impairment.

3. If CRPS II is present, evaluate loss of ROM, then sensory deficits and motor deficits, by using the maximal nerve value multiplier, and combine them. The maximum attained with this method is 100% of the upper extremity or 60% whole person impairment.

On the basis of the nervous system chapter:

1. Establish the diagnosis of CRPS on the basis of clinical criteria given in Table 16-16. Radiologic studies, such as a bone scan or patchy demineralization on the radiograph, or altered blood flow on Doppler studies, are not always positive but, if present, support the diagnosis.

2. Determine whether the dominant or nondominant arm is affected.

3. Determine the extent of limitation of ADL.

4. Maximum for the dominant extremity is 60% whole person impairment, and maximum for the nondominant extremity is 45% whole person impairment.

MEDICAL TIP

Both the musculoskeletal and nervous system approaches to CRPS provide similar conclusions. The upper extremity chapter requires the physician to obtain detailed measurements of ROM of all the affected joints. The nervous system method focuses on ability to do ADL. Use whichever method best characterizes the individual impairment and provides the higher rating.

LEGAL TIP

Use of the higher rating may be required in jurisdictions where the *Guides* is accepted or mandated, but allow for an ambiguity, that is, two or more reasonable conclusions or interpretations. Note where the jurisdiction requires the law to be construed most favorably to the individual seeking benefits.

EXAMPLE

A 35-year-old woman has a wrist fracture from a fall at work and during the next year develops RSD. Despite attempts at therapy, the right arm still has decreased ROM, increasing, constant pain, and is not usable for ADL, especially when in contact with hard surfaces. It is mottled, cool, and edematous. A radiograph of the wrist shows bone demineralization.

IR Method

Upper extremity approach: Upper extremity loss of ROM; wrist flexion, 30° (5% IR, Figure 16-28), extension lag of −10° (13% IR, Figure 16-28). Adding, *not combining,* impairments from flexion and extension = 18% hand IR

Sensory/pain deficit: 65% (Table 16-10, grade 2, 61%-80%)

Combine 18% ROM with 65% sensory/pain IR = 71% upper extremity = 43% WPI

Nervous system approach: Class 4: individual cannot use the involved extremity for self-care or daily activities, nondominant extremity 30% to 45% WPI (if the 35-year-old woman is left-handed), dominant extremity 40% to 60% WPI (if she is right-handed).

16.6 Impairment of the Upper Extremities Due to Vascular Disorders

The criteria for evaluating a vascular disorder of the upper extremity were slightly amended and are now consistent with the criteria for these disorders in the cardiovascular system. Although the impairment ratings were retained, new criteria were added for the diagnosis of Raynaud's syndrome. To meet diagnostic criteria for Raynaud's syndrome, class 2, the individual needs to have obstructive physiology documented by measurements of finger/brachial indices (the arterial pressure ratio between affected digit[s] and brachial [arm] pressure) of less than 0.8, or measured low digital temperatures, that do not normalize with warming of the affected digits. For class 1, signs of vascular damage are required, but obstructive physiology measures are not needed. In class 1, these changes completely respond to lifestyle change and/or medication. For class 2, the response to therapy is incomplete.

LEGAL TIP

In Table 16-17, class 5 vascular damage from amputation of both extremities is only a 100% upper extremity impairment, 60% WPI, or, at most, with the Combined Values Chart, 84% WPI. But in many statutory disability schedules, this condition presumptively treats the individual as having 100% WPI and, consequently, as being totally disabled as well.

16.7 Impairment of the Upper Extremities Due to Other Disorders

This category of other disorders includes a series of conditions that are specific and do not meet impairment criteria for ROM deficit or peripheral nerve or vascular disorders. Use these categories only when other criteria are insufficient to characterize the impairment. These categories can be grouped as bone and joint deformities, tendinitis, arthroplasty, and musculo-tendinous impairments.

In both the fourth and fifth editions, these impairments are given an IR, then weighted on the basis of the maximum value of the structure. In the Fourth Edition, the maximum value of the structure was the maximum value attributed to the structure if there was an amputation. In the Fifth Edition, the values for finger joints in Table 16-18 were decreased, since their maximum value does not equal that of an amputated or missing part.

Changes to this section include a revised weighting system for finger joints and a new entry under the shoulder of sternoclavicular change. The text includes a description of which disorders can be combined. To simplify use, a table similar to that in the lower extremity chapter follows, indicating which disorders can be combined. An X indicates that the methods are not to be used together in evaluating an upper extremity impairment.

Guide to the Combination of "Other" Upper Extremity Impairments

Open boxes indicate impairment ratings derived from these methods can be combined.

	Synovial Hypertrophy	Digital Lateral Deviation	Rotational Deformity	Subluxation or Dislocation	Mediolateral Instability	Mediolateral Deviation	Carpal Instability	Decreased Joint Motion	Arthroplasty	Musculo-tendinous	Strength Evaluation	Shoulder Instability
Synovial Hypertrophy		X	X	X	X	X	X	X	X	X	X	
Digital Lateral Deviation	X		X	X					X		X	
Rotational Deformity	X	X		X					X		X	
Subluxation or Dislocation	X	X	X					X	X		X	
Mediolateral Instability	X						X		X		X	X
Mediolateral Deviation	X						X		X		X	X
Carpal Instability	X				X	X			X	X	X	X
Decreased Joint Motion	X			X						X	X	
Arthroplasty	X	X	X	X	X	X	X					X
Musculo-tendinous	X						X	X				X
Strength Evaluation	X	X	X	X	X	X	X	X				X
Shoulder Instability					X	X	X		X	X	X	

X = Do not use these methods together for evaluating a single impairment.

Chapter 16

16.7a Bone and Joint Deformities
Carpal Instability
The section on carpal instability has been totally revised in the Fifth Edition. There was sufficient evidence to indicate that previous impaired values are actually the lower limits of normal. On the basis of recommendations from hand surgeons, use the scapholunate angle for base measurement, instead of the angles listed in the Fourth Edition. An illustration (Figure 16-51) has been added to show how to measure wrist angles to assess the impairment values in new Table 16-25.

Shoulder Instability
The Fifth Edition contains a new section on shoulder instability. In the Fourth Edition, shoulder subluxation was evaluated on the basis of changes in strength, sensation, and ROM. The Fifth Edition simplifies the assessment, with a separate impairment rating given for shoulder subluxation, which is then combined with any loss of ROM.

EXAMPLE

While lifting, Harry sustains a subluxation of the right shoulder that is reduced to its anatomic position. He has had prior episodes of shoulder subluxation while playing basketball. There is decreased sensation over the lower two thirds of the deltoid, which does not significantly limit ADL. He could abduct the shoulder fully against gravity and some resistance, starting with the arm alongside the body. As listed in the Fourth Edition (p 3/49), the impairment of the axillary nerve is 25% × 5% = 1% for sensory loss and 25% × 35% or 9% due to motor deficit, which combined give a 10% upper extremity or 6% whole person impairment.

Impairment Rating

On the basis of the Fifth Edition, this individual would have a 12% upper extremity impairment, combined with the loss of ROM, which was not considered in the Fourth Edition.

16.7b Arthroplasty
The section on arthroplasty was also changed, with different impairment ratings assigned to cases of implant and resection arthroplasty. The following table outlines the differences in impairment ratings between the fifth and fourth editions. Based on the chapter chairs' clinical experience with improvement in implant devices, and editorial review, the Fifth Edition makes significant changes in arthroplasty rating. The result is that resection and implant ratings were usually reversed from the Fourth Edition, so that implants now obtain a lower rating, while resection rates are higher. Implants are improving and, in some cases, restore greater function than a resection.

	Implant Rating (%)		Resection Rating (%)	
Level of Arthroplasty	**5th Edition**	**4th Edition**	**5th Edition**	**4th Edition**
Shoulder	24	30	30	24
Distal clavicle			10	10
Proximal clavicle			3	
Total elbow	28	35	35	28
Radial head	8	10	10	8
Total wrist	24	30		
Radiocarpal	16			
Ulnar head	8		10	
Proximal row carpectomy			12	
Carpal bone	8		10	
Radial styloid			5	
Thumb				
CMC	9	13	11	11
MP	2	2	3	1
IP	4	3	5	2
Index or middle finger				
MP	4	9	5	7
PIP	2	7	3	6
DIP	1	4	2	3
Ring or little finger				
MP	2	4	2	3
PIP	1	3	1	3
DIP	1	2	1	2

Chapter 16

16.7c Musculotendinous Impairments

The section on musculoskeletal impairment due to intrinsic tightness has been retained, with the same impairment ratings provided, and more specific instruction not to combine decreased ROM with intrinsic tightness, constrictive tenosynovitis, or extensor tendon subluxation. Combining these types of impairment would be duplicating the rating, since all of these conditions are associated with decreased ROM.

16.7d Tendinitis

This new section discusses tendinitis, which is only given an impairment rating if another impairment (eg, ROM) is present. If tendinitis was treated surgically, or if it was caused by an underlying impairment such as tendon rupture, the individual can receive a rating for muscle weakness or decreased ROM that would account for the effect of the tendinitis. Although this section indicates that impairment rating for strength loss after surgery for tendinitis should not be determined less than a year after surgery, the physician needs to use his or her own judgment regarding when MMI has been reached. If MMI is reached before 1 year, then the impairment rating is done before the 1-year point.

EXAMPLE

While playing golf, John develops lateral epicondylitis. It persists for a year despite discontinuation of golf and institution of physical therapy and strengthening exercises. He continues to have pain and is developing some weakness because of lack of use. A magnetic resonance image shows considerable scarring and restriction of the extensor tendons at the lateral epicondyle. He has surgery to release the restricted tendons, with improvement of symptoms 1 year later but some weakness of grip, which has not resolved. On the basis of a 10% strength loss index, he is given a 10% upper extremity IR or 6% WPI.

The Fourth Edition also stated that, for other musculoskeletal conditions or individual conditions not adequately accounted for with the current rating, the physician had the discretion to adjust an impairment rating if the rating did not reflect either the clinical or objective findings of the condition. On the basis of principles of the *Guides*, this is still permissible, with the physician documenting why an increase is warranted. In cases when the impairment is increased because of unexpected, yet feasible, pain that impacts ADL, the pain chapter can be used to provide an additional rating up to 3%, which is combined with the upper extremity rating.

16.8 Strength Evaluation

The section on strength evaluation has retained the normal values and impairment ratings for measurement of grip and pinch strength in the hand. Strength is to be assessed separately and used as an impairment criterion only when other, more specific impairment criteria cannot be used. The discussion has been slightly expanded and discusses the importance of measuring strength when the individual reaches MMI. This section has several new and important points. Strength testing can be subjective and influenced by motivation, although some techniques can be used to assess consistency and motivation. Also, loss of strength may not correlate well with the performance of ADL. Therefore, a small loss of strength may not impact ADL and the impairment rating, but may have a significant impact on the ability to perform essential occupations and, hence, disability.

16.8a Principles

Strength is measured on the basis of the anatomic region. For loss of strength in the hand, wrist, or forearm, measure grip and pinch strength. For strength testing in the elbow and shoulder, use manual muscle testing, as is done in clinical practice. Strength is measured after MMI. The authors contend that MMI is *usually* not reached until a year or more after an injury or surgery, in their experience. Again, the physician needs to use his or her clinical judgment, based on the medical evaluation and ancillary records, as from physical therapy, integrated with guidance from the medical literature regarding the condition, to determine when MMI is reached for each individual.

MEDICAL TIP

Physicians are advised to consult the medical literature regarding recovery time and to review their knowledge of the individual patient when determining whether the individual's strength is at MMI and whether an impairment rating can be performed.

The physician can note in his or her report the contribution of any loss of strength to the ability to perform ADL and, if requested, work capability.

LEGAL TIP

The 1-year delay in evaluating strength loss in the Fifth Edition is not a prohibition on rating earlier than 1 year postoperatively, so long as the general MMI criteria discussed in Chapter 1 of the *Guides* are met. Strength loss is used in the "rare case," in the absence of any better way to rate.

In some jurisdictions, a typical consequence of protracted rating is perpetuation of temporary disability benefits and a secondary disability created simply by the individual's absence from the workforce.

16.8b Grip and Pinch Strength

Instructions are given in this section for determining grip and pinch meas-urements. Grip and pinch strength measurements are repeated at least three times, at different points throughout the exam, and should not vary by more than 20%. Strength measurements can also vary because of fatigue, pain, or motivation. To assess consistency of effort, the physician can use evaluation methods such as plotting out the grip strength measurements at the five han-dle settings, which should normally produce a bell-shaped curve, or the rapid exchange grip technique, which should indicate similar readings for each hand.

Normal values are listed for grip and pinch strength, adjusted for sex and age. These values were retained from the Fourth Edition. In cases where a single extremity is affected, the physician can use the unaffected or "nor-mal" hand. If bilateral impairment is present, the physician may use Tables 16-31 to 16-34. The physician would calculate a strength loss index and an upper extremity impairment rating, as indicated in Table 16-34.

As noted in this section, "wide variations exist in strength, even among per-sons doing the same kind of work" (p 509). The normal values listed here may differ from other published normal values. If the physician believes that the normal values listed here are not best suited for an individual, the physician can discuss this in his or her report, using other normal values that may be more appropriate for the individual.

The physician would calculate a strength loss index and an upper extremity impairment rating, as indicated in Table 16-34.

16.8c Manual Muscle Testing

This is a new section in the Fifth Edition. The authors have developed Table 16-35 to enable the physician to evaluate an individual with loss of strength due to weakness in the forearm or upper arm not caused by nerve injury. Use Table 16-35 for mild loss of strength, from grade 3/5 up to 5/5. For loss of strength of 3/5 or less, other, more specific signs such as atrophy are present, and the impairment rating would be based on the more specific criteria.

The physician would determine whether the loss of strength, given measure-ments in several planes, would correspond to either a 5% to 25% or a 30% to 50% level. On the basis of the severity of the strength loss and its impact on ADL, the physician would choose an impairment rating within the range listed and add the IR for different types of motion of the shoulder or elbow.

The relative values given for different regions (eg, shoulder abduction has a 12% relative value) were based on ROM relationships and not strength relationships. However, the ranges within IR enable the physician to adjust for changes in importance of strength loss for each individual.

EXAMPLE

John has a history of being a pitcher, with prior shoulder injuries during baseball in college, which resolved. He now pitches only in a softball league, with no overhand pitching. While lifting a heavy package over his head at work, he slips and tears his right rotator cuff. Despite physical therapy of 6 months' duration, he still has not regained full strength, compared to his left, nondominant right side. His ROM is normal and no significant atrophy is present. On physical examination, his strength measurements are as follows: shoulder abduction: grade 3/5 muscle strength: 40% deficit, 5% IR (Table 16-35); external shoulder rotation: grade 3/5 muscle strength: –20% deficit, 2% IR. He would receive an impairment rating of 7% of the upper extremity (5% abduction loss added to 2% external rotation loss).

16.9 Summary of Steps for Evaluating Impairments of the Upper Extremity

This section provides a systematic method for assessing upper extremity impairment, beginning with the more distal region (fingers) and working up toward the proximal area (shoulder). The physician can use Figures 16-1a and 16-1b to ensure that all regions of the upper extremity have been evaluated and accounted for in determining the final WPI rating.

Chapter 16

Figure 16-1a Upper Extremity Impairment Evaluation Record–**Part 1 (Hand)**   Side ☐R ☐L

Name _____ Age _____ Sex ☐M ☐F   Dominant hand ☐R ☐L   Date _____

Occupation _____ Diagnosis _____

	Abnormal Motion				Amputation	Sensory Loss	Other Disorders	Hand Impairment%
	Record motion or ankylosis angles and digit impairment %				Mark level & impairment %	Mark type, level, & impairment %	List type & impairment %	●Combine digit imp % ★Convert to hand imp %

Thumb — IP Angle°/Imp %, MP Angle°/Imp %; Motion, Ankylosis, Imp %; CMC: Radial abduction Angle°/Imp %, Adduction Cm/Imp %, Opposition Cm/Imp %

Abnormal motion [1]; Amputation [2]; Sensory loss [3]; Other disorders [4]; Total digit imp % ●Combine 1, 2, 3, 4

‡UE IMP % = [5]

Add digit impairment %   CMC + MP + IP =   [1] Digit [2] IMP % =, Digit [3] IMP % =, Digit [4] IMP % =   **Hand impairment % ★Convert above**

Index — DIP, PIP, MP Angle°/Imp %; ●Combine digit impairment % MP, PIP, DIP =
Abnormal motion [1]; Amputation [2]; Sensory loss [3]; Other disorders [4]; Total digit imp % ●Combine 1, 2, 3, 4

Middle — DIP, PIP, MP Angle°/Imp %; ●Combine digit impairment % MP, PIP, DIP =
Abnormal motion [1]; Amputation [2]; Sensory loss [3]; Other disorders [4]; Total digit imp % ●Combine 1, 2, 3, 4

Ring — DIP, PIP, MP Angle°/Imp %; ●Combine digit impairment % MP, PIP, DIP =
Abnormal motion [1]; Amputation [2]; Sensory loss [3]; Other disorders [4]; Total digit imp % ●Combine 1, 2, 3, 4

Little — DIP, PIP, MP Angle°/Imp %; ●Combine digit impairment % MP, PIP, DIP =
Abnormal motion [1]; Amputation [2]; Sensory loss [3]; Other disorders [4]; Total digit imp % ●Combine 1, 2, 3, 4

Each finger row: [1] Digit [2] IMP % =, Digit [3] IMP % =, Digit [4] IMP % =   **Hand impairment % ★Convert above**

Total hand impairment: Add hand impairment % for thumb + index + middle + ring + little finger = ____ %
Convert total hand impairment to upper extremity impairment† (if thumb metacarpal intact, enter on Part 2, line II) = ____ %
‡Add thumb ray upper extremity amputation imp [5] ____ % + hand upper extremity imp ____ % = ____ %
If hand region impairment is only impairment, convert upper extremity impairment to whole person impairment§ = ____ %

● Combined Values Chart (p. 604).   ★Use Table 16-1 (digits to hand).   †Use Table 16-2 (hand to upper extremity).   §Use Table 16-3.
Courtesy of G. de Groot Swanson, MD, Grand Rapids, Michigan.

Figure 16-1b Upper Extremity Impairment Evaluation Record–**Part 2 (Wrist, elbow, and shoulder)**   Side ☐R ☐L

Name _____   Age_____   Sex ☐ M ☐ F   Dominant hand ☐ R ☐ L   Date _____

Occupation _____   Diagnosis _____

		Abnormal Motion				Other Disorders	Regional Impairment %	Amputation
		Record motion or ankylosis angles and impairment %				List type & impairment %	•Combine [1] + [2]	Mark level & impairment %
Wrist		Flexion	Extension	Ankylosis	Imp %			
	Angle°							
	Imp %							
		RD	UD	Ankylosis	Imp %			
	Angle°							
	Imp %							
	Add Imp % Flex/Ext + RD/UD =				[1]	Imp % =	[2]	
Elbow		Flexion	Extension	Ankylosis	Imp %			
	Angle°							
	Imp %							
		Pronation	Supination	Ankylosis	Imp %			
	Angle°							
	Imp %							
	Add Imp % Flex/Ext + Pro/Sup =				[1]	Imp % =	[2]	
Shoulder		Flexion	Extension	Ankylosis	Imp %			
	Angle°							
	Imp %							
		Adduction	Abduction	Ankylosis	Imp %			
	Angle°							
	Imp %							
		Int Rot	Ext Rot	Ankylosis	Imp %			
	Angle°							
	Imp %							
	Add Imp % Flex/Ext + Add/Abd + Int Rot/Ext Rot =				[1]	Imp % =	[2]	Imp % =

I. Amputation impairment (other than digits)   =   %

II. Regional impairment of upper extremity
   •(Combine hand _____ % + wrist _____% + elbow _____% + shoulder _____%)   =   %

III. Peripheral nerve system impairment   =   %

IV. Peripheral vascular system impairment   =   %

V. Other disorders (not included in regional impairment)   =   %

Total upper extremity impairment (•Combine I, II, III, IV, and V)   =   %

Impairment of the whole person (Use Table 16-3)   =   %

• Combined Values Chart (p. 604).

If both limbs are involved, calculate the whole person impairment for each on a separate chart and *combine* the percents (Combined Values Chart).

Chapter 17

The Lower Extremities

Introduction

This chapter provides an overview of key points and changes (identified with an icon **G**) made in Chapter 17 of the AMA *Guides to the Evaluation of Permanent Impairment, Fifth Edition* (*Guides 5th*), illustrates these changes in a table comparison, and discusses the purpose and implications of the major changes, with illustrative examples. The numbered section titles within this chapter correspond to sections within Chapter 17 of the *Guides 5th*. Only key principles or important changes are included in this chapter.

Key Points and Changes

Principles of Assessment

Obtain a comprehensive, accurate medical history; a careful and thorough physical examination; and a review of all findings of relevant laboratory, radiologic (imaging), and ancillary tests.

Ensure that lower extremity impairment is not due to a spine disorder; if so, follow methods in the spine chapter.

Include a description of how the impairment rating was calculated.

The lower extremity is weighted at 0.40 or 40% of the whole person.

Methods of Assessment

Determine the diagnosis.

Ensure the individual is at maximal medical improvement (MMI).

Identify which evaluation methods are appropriate and most specific for a given diagnosis.

Calculate the impairment ratings, based on appropriate methods.

G Use Table 17-2 to indicate which evaluation methods can be combined.

Select the evaluation method that combines the most specific characterization of the impairment with the highest rating.

Combine IRs from all lower extremity methods for a specific limb, and then convert to whole person impairment.

Combine whole person impairment ratings for each extremity if both extremities are involved.

G Limb length discrepancies are best measured with teleroentgenography (scanograms/orthoroentgenograms).

G Gait derangement is used if no other method applies, and can serve as a measure of relative impairment rating compared to other methods.

G To use muscle atrophy, the contralateral leg must be normal. Record and indicate where leg circumference readings are taken. Do not combine atrophy with gait, weakness, or peripheral nerve injury.

Manual muscle testing results should be within the same grade among examiners (eg, 4+ and 4– are consistent recordings).

Add range of motion (ROM) losses within a given joint area.

G Add additional ankylosis impairment for joints not fixed at the most optimal ankylosis position.

G Patient position and taking of arthritis films must be standardized for accurate readings.

Diagnosis-based estimates (DBEs) assign ranges of impairment based on severity of the condition, ability to perform activities of daily living (ADL), and score on standardized assessment evaluation.

Skin loss can be used for osteomyelitis or other skin impairments of the lower extremity.

Peripheral nerve deficit assessment is very specific and a method of choice if peripheral nerve damage is present. Combine motor, sensory, and dysesthesia evaluation for peripheral nerve deficit into a total peripheral nerve impairment.

Vascular disorders are used for claudication and combined with amputation.

Comparison of Tables Between the Fifth and Fourth *Guides* Editions

The following table summarizes the key points and changes in tables between the fourth and fifth editions of the *Guides*.

Comparison of Tables Between the Fifth and Fourth *Guides* Editions

Table Topic	5th Edition Table Number	4th Edition Table Number	Summary of Changes in 5th Edition
Methods used to evaluate impairments of the lower extremities	17-1		New; groups evaluation methods discussed in the chapter into 3 categories
Guide to the appropriate combination of evaluation methods	17-2		New; indicates which evaluation methods can be combined
Whole person impairment values calculated from lower extremity impairment	17-3		New; provides conversion table for lower extremity to whole person impairment (WPI)
Impairment due to limb length discrepancy	17-4	35	None
Lower limb impairment due to gait derangement	17-5	36	Stylistic
Impairment due to unilateral leg muscle atrophy	17-6	37	None
Criteria for grades of muscle function of the lower extremity	17-7	38	None
Impairment due to lower extremity muscle weakness	17-8	39	None
Hip motion impairment	17-9	40	None
Knee impairment	17-10	41	None
Ankle motion impairment estimates	17-11	42	None
Hindfoot impairment estimates	17-12	43	None
Ankle or hindfoot deformity impairments	17-13	44	None
Toe impairments	17-14	45	None
Impairment due to ankylosis in hip flexion	17-15	46	None
Impairment due to ankylosis in hip internal rotation	17-16	47	None

Chapter 17

Comparison of Tables Between the Fifth and Fourth *Guides* Editions, *continued*

Table Topic	5th Edition Table Number	4th Edition Table Number	Summary of Changes in 5th Edition
Impairment due to ankylosis in hip external rotation	17-17	48	None
Impairment due to ankylosis in hip abduction	17-18	49	None
Impairment due to ankylosis in hip adduction	17-19	50	None
Impairment due to knee ankylosis in varus	17-20	51	None
Impairment due to knee ankylosis in valgus	17-21	52	None
Ankle impairment due to knee ankylosis in flexion	17-22	53	None
Ankle impairment due to knee ankylosis in internal or external malrotation	17-23	54	None
Ankle impairment due to ankylosis in plantar flexion or dorsiflexion	17-24	55	None
Ankle impairment due to ankylosis in varus position	17-25	56	None
Ankle impairment due to ankylosis in valgus position	17-26	57	None
Ankle impairment due to ankylosis in internal malrotation	17-27	58	None
Ankle impairment due to ankylosis in external malrotation	17-28	59	None
Impairment for loss of the tibia–os calcis angle	17-29	60	None
Impairment of the foot due to ankylosis of toes	17-30	61	None

Chapter 17

Comparison of Tables Between the Fifth and Fourth *Guides* Editions, *continued*

Table Topic	5th Edition Table Number	4th Edition Table Number	Summary of Changes in 5th Edition
Arthritis impairments based on roentgenographically determined cartilage intervals	17-31	62	None
Impairment estimates for amputations	17-32	63	None
Impairment estimates for certain lower extremity impairments	17-33	64	None
Rating hip replacement results	17-33, 17-34	65	None
Rating knee replacement results	17-33, 17-35	66	None
Impairments for skin loss	17-36	67	None
Impairments due to nerve deficits	17-37	68	None
Lower extremity impairment due to peripheral vascular disease	17-38	69	Stylistic

Chapter 17

Introduction

The lower extremity chapter in *Guides 5th* covers impairments of the feet, hindfeet, ankles, legs, knees, hips, and pelvis. This chapter has remained very similar to that in the Fourth Edition. Perhaps the most significant change with practical implications is the acknowledgment of a multifaceted approach to lower extremity disorders, considering how an impairment impacts anatomy, function, and diagnoses. A new method of rating causalgia, reflex sympathetic dystrophy (RSD), and complex regional pain syndrome (CRPS) illustrates the emphasis on function, in which the lower extremity chapter adopts the functional assessment used in the neurology chapter.

Although using multiple evaluation methods can lead to inconsistencies among examiners when not well understood, the ability to choose among several evaluation methods enables the examiner to customize the assessment for each individual. For example, a fractured femur can have residual shortening, rotation, and/or angulation, depending on individual characteristics. The physician would choose the method(s) of evaluation that is most specific and that, in combination, provides the highest rating.

Three major changes have been made to the lower extremity chapter: (1) the section on causalgia and CRPS has been revised to account more for functional loss, (2) a table and guidelines have been added to facilitate use of different methods, and (3) additional cases and a reorganization of the chapter have made it easier to use.

17.1 Principles of Assessment

The *Guides 5th* adds a section on a detailed assessment of key questions in the history and physical. Especially in the lower extremity, where multiple evaluation methods can be used, it is important for the evaluator to explain why, on the basis of the medical evaluation, a particular evaluation method was chosen. When more than one method can be used, use the method that provides the higher impairment rating. As in the Fourth Edition, complete loss of a lower extremity is rated at 40% WPI.

17.2 Methods of Assessment

In earlier editions, 17 characteristics and diagnoses were used to determine lower extremity impairment. To facilitate use and discussion, these characteristics were organized into three types of assessment: anatomic, functional, and diagnosis based, recognizing that these "types of assessment" and the dysfunction within each method overlap. Thus, only some methods can be combined, to avoid duplicate accounting for the same impairment with methods that overlap in characterizing impairment. For example, an amputation already accounts for the impairment seen with a limb length discrepancy, so these methods would not be combined. Table 17-2, the cross-usage chart, lists the impairment methods that can be combined. The Fifth Edition clearly lists the allowable combinations and expands the concepts of combination or exclusive use of a method more than prior editions did.

To facilitate use, the different methods have been grouped here into three categories: anatomic-, functional-, and diagnosis-based categories.

Anatomic methods include measures to assess anatomic changes and include ROM, limb length discrepancy, arthritis, skin changes, amputation, muscle atrophy, nerve impairment, and vascular derangement. Arthritis is evaluated on the basis of narrowing of the joint space as measured from x-rays. Causalgia, RSD, and CRPS are evaluated by means of a combination of ROM and peripheral neurologic evaluation techniques.

Use diagnosis-based estimates for conditions with well-defined diagnostic criteria, including fractures and deformities, ligamentous instability, bursitis, and various surgical procedures, including joint replacements and meniscectomies.

Functional impairments are chosen for conditions when anatomic changes are difficult to categorize or when functional implications have been documented. Functional impairments are assessed last.

Key features of these assessment methods are outlined below. Any changes from the Fourth Edition are identified with a **G**. All impairment ratings in the *Guides 5th* are unchanged from the Fourth Edition unless otherwise noted.

Method of Assessment	Key Features of Assessment	Considerations	When to Apply Method
Anatomic limb length discrepancy, 17.2b	Teleroentgenography is recommended over tape measure; separate criteria for length discrepancy due to malalignment or fracture deformities. **G** Slightly higher impairment rating for postfracture deformities associated with limb shortening.	Objective measurement.	Healed femur fracture with permanent shortening from bone loss or growth inhibition.
Muscle atrophy (unilateral), 17.2d	**G** Now specifies where to take measurements—for thigh, 10 cm above patella; for calf, widest circumference. Do not combine with any other method unless muscle dysfunction is present. If muscle dysfunction is present, use atrophy, gait derangement, muscle weakness, peripheral nerve injury.	Dependent on examiner; varies depending on condition; contralateral limb must be normal; edema, varicosities can give false impressions.	Healed tibia fracture, calf atrophy and weakness.

Method of Assessment	Key Features of Assessment	Considerations	When to Apply Method
Ankylosis, 17.2g	Continue to add additional impairment if ankylosis not in optimal functional position as defined in text. Rated on basis of optimal position of fusion or ankylosis; supplemental rating given if joint malaligned. Limb length shortening can be combined with this, but not atrophy. Hip joint: all movement malpositions are combined.	Severe malposition may be correctable with surgery.	Hip malrotation, lower extremity may be non-functional.
Amputation, 17.2i	Signifies maximum impairment of a region or limb.	Set schedule, unchanged.	Compare to statutory schedules in the appendices.
Arthritis, 17.2h	Roentgenographic grading system based on narrowed cartilage interval. Hip replacement results assessed on basis of function and anatomic change. Don't combine with atrophy, weakness, ROM.	Standardized x-ray—weight bearing, 90 cm (36 in) source to film distance; feet must be parallel to joint; otherwise interval may look narrower.	Posttraumatic knee, varus orientation, medial joint space to 1 mm, lateral joint space 6 mm. Rate based on medial compartment narrowing.
Skin loss, 17.2k	This method used for chronic osteomyelitis.	Skin loss can make function (kneeling, walking, sitting) difficult.	Osteomyelitis, chronic skin ulcers.
Peripheral nerve injury, 17.2l	Combine motor, sensory, and/or dysesthesia estimates of impairment. Consider ADL for determining impairment rating within the range. Do not combine with muscle weakness or atrophy.	Follows procedure in upper extremity chapter.	Sural nerve injury postlaceration.
Vascular, 17.2n	Use alone unless vascular disorder led to amputation; then combine with amputation.	Amputation IR accounts for vascular disorder within amputated region.	Claudication; amputation due to vascular disorder.
Causalgia, RSD, and CRPS, 17.2m	**G** New method; use neurology Table 13-8 or gait abnormality method in lower extremity. Previously rated according to peripheral nerve assessment method in upper extremity.	Higher rating now since impairment reflects function more than an anatomic change alone.	RSD.

Method of Assessment	Key Features of Assessment	Considerations	When to Apply Method
ROM, 17.2f	**G** Take 3 measurements, active ROM, valid if within the same class (mild, moderate, severe); use the highest value. Add ROM impairment ratings of a single joint (ankle) for each direction of movement; eg, limitations in *all* six directions of movement in hip are added. Combine impairments of multiple joints within the same region (eg, knee and ankle).	Monitor for consistency; dependent on individual.	Tibia, fibula fracture with loss of motion of ankle.
Gait derangement, 17.2c	Nonspecific; use if other methods are inappropriate. This method stands alone and should not be combined with any other lower extremity evaluation methodology.	Method of last resort; use only if no other method describes the condition. Typically provides higher rating than other methods.	Eg, hip pathology, Trendelenberg.
Muscle strength/manual muscle testing, 17.2e	Valid only if repeat measurements are within the same muscle grade (0-5); not to be used when strength is limited from pain or fear.	Check consistency among different evaluators; partially dependent on individual. Fatigue factor of muscle in normal life activities not considered. Grade 0-2, not functional. Differentiation between grade 4 and 5 difficult. Isokinetic testing can sometimes help determine inconsistencies.	Compartment syndrome with residual weakness.
Diagnosis-based estimates (DBE), 17.2j	Impairment rating broad classes. Hip and knee replacements evaluated on basis of replacement results scoring system.	Specific impairment rating based on clinical condition and impact of impairment on ADL.	Fractures, ligament injuries, meniscectomies, foot deformities, hip and pelvis, femur, knee, ankle, foot conditions.

Chapter 17

MEDICAL TIP

Determine the method of assessment that is most specific and provides the highest rating.

LEGAL TIP

Where two different evaluation methods are equally applicable, use the method that provides the higher rating. This is consistent with the examples that illustrate differences (such as 17-25) and are also consistent with most states' rules that ambiguity should be construed in favor of the injured worker. Where the rating for a preexisting condition is assigned more than one rating, the lowest rating should be used for the preexisting condition, again consistent with the general rule of construction favoring the injured individual.

Some states use schedules that may rate amputation of a lower extremity greater or less than 40% WPI and may also require that partial losses or losses of use be compared to loss through amputation. Statutory schedules for those states and the District of Columbia are included in Appendix B. If both the statutory schedules and the AMA *Guides* may be used, or if a loss not listed in a law-mandated schedule is considered an "unscheduled" loss, use the higher rating.

17.3 Lower Extremity Impairment Evaluation Procedure Summary and Examples

Key steps to assessment:

1. Establish the diagnoses.

2. Verify MMI.

3. Record, for each anatomic region, the diagnoses and potential methods of impairment.

4. Calculate the impairment ratings for each anatomic region and each applicable method (Table 17-1).

5. Record any peripheral nervous system (PNS) impairment.

6. Record any peripheral vascular system impairment.

7. Record any RSD/CRPS impairment.

8. Use gait derangement method as a check and if no other methods apply.

9. Select the most appropriate method(s) (greatest specificity and highest rating). Use the cross-usage table (Table 17-2) to combine appropriate methods.

10. Convert lower extremity impairment rating to WPI. Combine WPIs for each leg injury/illness (p 604).

11. If both extremities are affected, combine both lower extremity WPI ratings for a single WPI rating.

EXAMPLE

Jack sustained the following injuries during a skiing accident:

Right leg: Right anterior cruciate ligament (ACL) reconstruction with scarring, patellar tendon graft, posterior horn of lateral meniscus removed, occasional sport brace, ADL slightly decreased in repeat squatting activities, no effusion, 1-cm atrophy in quads and calf, 4/5 evertor strength, 130° flexion, + Lachman, loss of sensation in right superficial peroneal distal foot.

Left leg, great toe interphalangeal (IP) joint: Fracture, dislocation

Chapter 17

	Right	**Left**
1. Establish the diagnoses	ACL tear, lateral meniscus tear, common peroneal nerve neuropraxis	Fracture, dislocation, great toe IP joint
2. Verify MMI	Yes	Yes
3. Record, for each anatomic region, the diagnoses and potential methods of impairment	Thigh: atrophy Knee: DBE lateral meniscectomy, ACL laxity Calf: Atrophy	Great toe: ROM deficit
4. Calculate the impairment ratings for each anatomic region and each applicable method (Table 17-1)	Lower extremity impairment rating (IR): thigh atrophy, 3%; calf atrophy, 3%; mild ACL laxity, 7%; partial lateral meniscectomy, 2%; DBE, 9% (combined 7% and 2%)	Great toe loss of ROM, 2%
5. Record any PNS impairment	Partial common peroneal nerve: 4% motor, 2% sensory, combined = 6% lower extremity IR	None
6. Record any peripheral vascular system impairment	None	None
7. Record any RSD/CRPS impairment	None	None

	Right	**Left**
8. Use gait derangement method as a check and if no other methods apply	N/A	N/A
9. Select the most appropriate method(s) (specificity, highest rating); use the cross-usage table (Table 17-2) to combine appropriate methods	Cross-usage table combinations: A. Atrophy alone (6%) B. DBE and PNS (9%, 6% = 14%) Most appropriate method: DBE and PNS	ROM only (2%)
10. Convert lower extremity IR to WPI. Combine WPIs for each leg injury/illness (p 604)	14% × 0.4 = 6% WPI right leg	2% × 0.4 = 1% WPI left leg
11. If both extremities are affected, combine both lower extremity WPI ratings for a single WPI rating	Combining 6% (right) and 1% (left) = 7% total WPI	

The physician may record the findings in a form such as Figure 17-10, reprinted on page 275, or a similar form.

Figure 17-10 Lower Extremity Impairment Evaluation Record and Worksheet

Name _____ Age _____ Sex _____ Side ☐R ☐L Date _____

Diagnosis _____

Potential Impairments							Final Impairment Utilized	
		Regional			Amputation			
Region	Abnormal Motion	Impairments	Table #	Percent	Location	Percent	Methodology	Percent
Pelvis		DBE	17-33	%			DBE	%
		DJD	17-31	%			DJD	%
		Skin	17-36	%			Skin	%
		Leg Length	17-4	%			Leg Length	%
		Amp	17-32	%			Amputation	%
Hip	Tables 17-9 and 17-15 to 17-19	DBE	17-33/34	%			DBE	%
	[Flexion/Extension/Ankylosis/Impairment %; Abduction/Adduction/Ankylosis/Impairment %; Internal Rot/External Rot/Ankylosis/Impairment %] Angle Impairment. Add impairment % ROM or use largest ankylosis = ____ %	DJD	17-31	%			DJD	%
		Skin	17-36	%			Skin	%
		Leg Length	17-4	%			Leg Length	%
		Weakness	17-8	%			Weakness	%
		Amp	17-32	%			ROM	%
							Amputation	%
Thigh	(Consider related pathology at hip and knee)	Atrophy	17-6	%			Atrophy	%
		DJD	17-31	%			DJD	%
		Skin	17-36	%			Skin	%
		Leg Length	17-4	%			Leg Length	%
		Amp	17-32	%			Amputation	%
Knee	Tables 17-10 and 17-20 to 17-23	DBE	17-33/35	%			DBE	%
	[Flexion/Extension/Ankylosis/Impairment %] Angle Impairment. Add impairment % ROM or use largest ankylosis = ____ %	DJD	17-31	%			DJD	%
		Skin	17-36	%			Skin	%
		Weakness	17-8	%			Weakness	%
		Amp	17-32	%			Amputation	%
Calf	(Consider related pathology at knee and ankle)	Atrophy	17-6	%			Atrophy	%
		DBE	17-33	%			DBE	%
		Skin	17-36	%			Skin	%
		Leg Length	17-4	%			Leg Length	%
		Amp	17-32	%			Amputation	%
Ankle/Foot	Tables 17-11 to 17-13 and 17-24 to 17-28	DBE	17-29/33	%			DBE	%
	[Dorsiflex/Plantarflex/Ankylosis/Impairment %; Inversion/Eversion/Ankylosis/Impairment %] Angle Impairment. Add impairment % ROM or use largest ankylosis = ____ %	DJD	17-31	%			DJD	%
		Skin	17-36	%			Skin	%
		Weakness	17-8/9	%			Weakness	%
		Amp	17-32	%			ROM	%
							Amputation	%
Toe	Tables 17-14 and 17-30	DBE	17-33	%			DBE	%
	[Great Toe: MP Dorsiflex/IP Plantarflex/Ankylosis/Impairment %; Lesser Toes: MP Dorsiflex/Ankylosis/Impairment %] Angle Impairment. Add impairment % ROM or use largest ankylosis = ____ %	DJD	17-31	%			DJD	%
		Skin	17-36	%			Skin	%
		Weakness	17-8/14	%			Weakness	%
		Amp	17-32	%			ROM	%
							Amputation	%

Peripheral Nervous System Impairment	Grade %	Nerve %	Total %	Nerve	Maximum Motor %	Maximum Sensory %	Maximum Dysesthesia %	
Motor Grade (Table 16-14)	_____	_____ ×	_____ = _____					
Sensory Grade (Table 16-15)	_____	_____ ×	_____ = _____					
Dysesthesia Grade	_____	_____ ×	_____ = _____		Combine all neurologic components		%	

Peripheral Vascular System Impairment (Table 17-38)		
Grade	_____	Total vascular system impairment	%

Gait Derangement (This is a *stand-alone* impairment and may *not* be combined) (Table 17-5) | %

Final Combined Impairment (An explanation should be provided if more than one methodology is used, justifying the rationale for each methodology used) | %

DBE = diagnosis-based estimates; DJD = degenerative joint disease (arthritis).

Chapter 17

Pain

Introduction

This chapter provides an overview of key points and changes (identified with an icon **G**) made in Chapter 18 of the AMA *Guides to the Evaluation of Permanent Impairment, Fifth Edition* (*Guides 5th*) and discusses the purpose and implications of the major changes, with illustrative examples. The numbered section titles within this chapter correspond to sections within Chapter 18 of the *Guides 5th*. Only key principles or important changes are included in this chapter.

Since the publication of the *Guides 5th*, three of the authors of Chapter 18 have field-tested and taught the pain evaluation methodology discussed in the pain chapter. Based on this experience, the authors have modified Figure 18-1 (*Guides 5th,* p 574), primarily to indicate a more efficient sequence for examiners to follow when evaluating impairment associated with pain that *is not accounted for by the conventional impairment rating (CIR) in the Guides 5th.* This modified figure now provides a systematic method, consistent with the text of the Fifth Edition, to assign PRI for individuals whose pain condition slightly increases the burden of illness and clarifies that up to a 3% rating may be awarded only if the pain condition meets ratable criteria. The modified version of this figure is shown on page 292. Also, the authors have developed a detailed Pain-Related Impairment Worksheet (see Form C, pp 322-325) to facilitate and standardize use of the *Guides* pain chapter. *This chapter provides multiple examples using the Pain-Related Impairment Worksheet.*

Key Points and Changes

G The pain chapter in the *Guides 5th* is completely revised from the Fourth Edition.

G *The Guides 5th* uses the International Association for the Study of Pain definition: "Pain is an unpleasant sensory and emotional experience associated with actual or potential tissue damage or described in terms of such damage."

G Pain is subjective and cannot be readily validated or objectively measured.

G In the pain chapter, impairment ratings based on measurable losses of function are termed *conventional impairment ratings (CIRs)*.

G CIR accounts for pain that can normally accompany a permanent impairment.

G Chapter 18 now designates a *pain-related impairment (PRI) rating* to account for pain in excess of pain-related limitations that most people experience with the same permanent impairment.

G The pain chapter provides a rating for individuals with pain who fall into one of three groups: (1) excess pain, not rated with the CIR, (2) well-established pain syndrome not rated in the *Guides,* or (3) excess pain not rated with the CIR, since only some individuals with the impairment have the condition (eg, only some amputees have phantom limb pain).

G Determine PRI using a systematic methodology to evaluate individuals' subjective reports regarding excess pain and the burden of their illnesses.

G For PRI, the evaluator may combine up to an additional 3% whole person impairment (WPI) for pain with the existing permanent impairment rating if (1) the individual's pain is not accounted for by the CIR and (2) the PRI increases the burden of the individual's condition, slightly or substantially.

G An individual without any CIR can receive up to a 3% PRI only if their pain condition is a well-established pain syndrome as indicated in Table 18-1 of the *Guides 5th* or under step 8, Form C, Pain-Related Impairment Worksheet.

G Besides a quantitative pain rating, the individual may receive a qualitative (categorical) rating of mild, moderate, moderately severe, or severe.

G Since the *Guides* already factors pain into impairment ratings, most individuals with permanent impairments will not meet criteria for a PRI.

G Consider subjective, self-report data in the assessment of PRI.

G The methodology to evaluate PRI incorporates evaluators' opinions on the individual's credibility and *pain behaviors* (observable expressions of pain, distress, and suffering).

G The evaluator needs to balance individual self-reports with clinical judgment based on his or her experience and observation of the individual throughout the evaluation process.

G Chronic pain is sometimes independent of any well-established medical condition. An examiner should characterize an individual's chronic pain as *unratable* if it cannot be related to a *well-established* medical condition.

G The judgment that a condition is unratable should not be taken to indicate that the report of pain is suspect.

G Individuals qualify for a PRI if one of three conditions is met: (1) excess pain, with more pain-related limitations than most individuals with the same permanent impairment; (2) a well-established pain syndrome, not easily rated by the *Guides* (eg, migraine headache); or (3) excess pain not included in the CIR, since only a subset of the individuals have the pain (eg, phantom limb pain in amputees).

G Do not use the pain chapter for a PRI if the pain is adequately rated with the CIR, the individual has low credibility, or the pain syndrome is ambiguous or controversial (eg, whiplash, fibromyalgia).

G A new Pain-Related Impairment Worksheet (Form C) will facilitate and standardize use of the *Guides 5th* pain chapter.

Introduction

This section of the *Guides 5th* provides a summary of features of the new pain chapter. The new pain chapter provides an overview of pain and a systematic protocol, using the Pain-Related Impairment Worksheet (Form C) to evaluate pain not accounted for by the CIR. Pain is assessed using a combination of subjective self-report data and the examiner's assessment of the individual's credibility and pain behaviors.

18.1 Principles of Assessment

Chronic pain is more difficult to assess than acute pain or objectively measurable loss of function of an organ. Chronic pain states may persist, despite the lack of objective evidence of an ongoing disease process.

18.2 Overview of Pain

The definition of pain used in the *Guides* is that described by the International Association for the Study of Pain, "an unpleasant sensory and emotional experience associated with actual or potential tissue damage or described in terms of such damage" (*Guides 5th*, p 566). This section acknowledges that "pain is subjective [and] cannot be readily validated or objectively measured. . . . [P]ain can exist without tissue damage, and tissue damage can exist without pain" (p 566).

This section of the *Guides 5th* provides a review of the current understanding of pain. Chronic pain can become independent of the initial injury or illness that precipitated its development (*Guides 5th*, p 566). This independence produces a dissociation between an individual's reports of chronic pain and any measurable evidence of an ongoing biological abnormality that might reasonably account for the pain. At least two conceptual models have been developed to account for the dissociation. Chronic pain syndrome was elaborated during the 1970s. It is viewed as a behavioral syndrome characterized by abnormal illness behavior, sleep disturbance, emotional distress, and abnormal social behavior in the context of chronic pain. Conceptually, chronic pain syndrome can be thought of as an abnormal adaptation to ongoing pain. Just as an individual may adapt poorly to a variety of medical conditions (eg, diabetes mellitus), he or she might adapt poorly to a chronically painful condition. Central sensitization (or neural plasticity) in response to a nociceptive barrage was demonstrated in animal research during the 1980s. Many studies have shown that central processing of sensory information changes after injury. Central sensitization is a neurophysiologic concept; it has nothing to do with abnormal illness behavior, but it can lead to dissociation between an initial injurious stimulus and the pain behavior that emerges over time.

18.3 Integrating Pain-Related Impairment Into the Conventional Impairment Rating System

The focus of the pain chapter is to provide a limited quantitative and mainly qualitative system for rating PRI among individuals who fall into one of three groups:

1. Excess pain in the context of verifiable medical conditions that cause pain. Their condition typically is associated with both pain and objectively ratable impairment, but the individual appears to have excess pain (ie, more pain-related limitations than most people with the same condition).

2. A well-established pain syndrome without significant, identifiable organ dysfunction to explain the pain (eg, migraine headache).

3. Other associated pain syndromes with the following characteristics: *(a)* occurs as a component of a condition (such as spinal cord injury) that is ratable according to the conventional rating system; *(b)* only some of the individuals with the underlying condition have the pain syndrome; and *(c)* the CIR does not capture the added burden of illness borne by individuals who have the associated pain syndrome. (See p 571 and Table 18-2.) Examples include postparaplegic pain, phantom limb pain, and brachial plexus avulsion pain.

PRI is difficult to integrate with impairments rated according to other chapters of the *Guides* (here referred to as CIRs) for several reasons. One of the major barriers is that the *Guides* attempts to factor pain into CIRs. As stated in Chapter 1, "Physicians recognize the local and distant pain that commonly accompanies many disorders. Impairment ratings in the *Guides* already have accounted for commonly associated pain, including that which may be experienced in areas distant to the specific site of pathology" (*Guides 5th*, p 10). Thus, an examining physician must decide whether the individual's PRI increases the burden of illness and is not accounted for by the CIR due to an excess of what is usually seen or expected for the permanent impairment or whether it is a well-established pain syndrome, not rated in the *Guides.*

As indicated in steps 2, 3, 8, and 9 of the Pain-Related Impairment (PRI) Worksheet (see p 321), if an examining physician believes that *(a)* an individual's PRI increases the burden of illness slightly and *(b)* the PRI is ratable, the physician can award a discretionary 1%, 2%, or 3% WPI to reflect this. If the examining physician's judgment is that even the full 3% discretionary allowance does not adequately capture the individual's burden of illness, he or she can perform a formal PRI assessment on the individual and place the individual in an impairment category or class (mild, moderate, moderately severe, or severe). After the PRI assessment is completed, the physician is asked (in step 9 of the PRI Worksheet, Form C) to state the magnitude of the impairment and again to consider the question of whether the impairment has been adequately captured by the individual's CIR.

The discretionary, quantitative assessment was capped at 3% for consistency with other features of the *Guides*, in which up to 3% was historically given for effects that are difficult to quantify, such as treatment effects. Note that the 3% is a WPI rating and is combined with the other CIR to form the final WPI rating. Also, note that if an individual is given a discretionary impairment award based on concepts in another chapter of the *Guides* (eg, Chapter 15 on impairment of the spine), the examiner should not give a second discretionary award based on the individual's pain. For example, Chapter 15, Example 15-4 (p 386), describes diagnosis-related estimate (DRE) lumbar category III with a range of 10% to 13% WPI. If an individual is rated category III and a CIR of 13% WPI is assigned on the basis of pain and difficulty in performing ADL, then an additional discretionary 3% should not be assigned because of the individual's PRI.

Use the pain chapter to render a rating under the following circumstances:

1. When an individual has a condition typically associated with both pain and objectively ratable impairment, but appears to have excess pain (ie, more pain-related limitations than most people with the same condition).

   Examples: An individual with an unusually painful orthopedic condition, or one with a disorder of the peripheral nervous system, might fit within this group. The key question for the examiner would be: Does this individual convincingly report symptoms and activity limitations that exceed the norm for the diagnosed condition?

2. When an individual has a well-established pain syndrome that ordinarily does not produce measurable organ dysfunction and, therefore, is not ratable on the basis of other chapters of the *Guides*.

   Examples: Headaches (most, not all), tic douloureux, erythromelalgia (see Table 18-1).

   Note: Although Table 18-1 includes "any injury to the nervous system," this is meant to convey any well-established pain syndrome that develops because of nervous system injury and is not ratable on the basis of concepts elaborated in Chapter 13 of the *Guides*. An example would be postherpetic neuralgia, if not already addressed in the nervous system chapter. Chapter 13 rates postherpetic neuralgia involving cranial nerve V.

3. When an individual has a pain syndrome with the following characteristics: *(a)* it occurs as a component of a condition (such as spinal cord injury) that is ratable according to another chapter of the *Guides*; *(b)* only some of the individuals with the underlying condition have the pain syndrome; and *(c)* the conventional impairment rating provided in another chapter of the *Guides* does not capture the added burden of illness borne by individuals who have the associated pain syndrome. See *Guides* page 571 and Table 18-2. Examples include postparaplegic pain, phantom limb pain, and brachial plexus avulsion pain.

EXAMPLE

A 43-year-old man suffers a traumatic below-elbow amputation of the right upper extremity in a sawmill accident. Subsequently, he reports a variety of painful sensations in his (now absent) right hand.

The rationale for awarding PRI to an individual like this is that the conventional rating system does not permit a basis for distinguishing between individuals who do and those who do not have phantom limb pain after an amputation. The conventional system would dictate that the individual in the above example receive a 54% WPI rating (based on Tables 16.2 and 16.3, p 435).

Since the individual would receive this rating even if he had no phantom limb pain, the conventional system does not appear to capture the added burden of illness and impact on ADL for an individual with phantom limb pain in addition to his upper extremity amputation (see example of PRI class 3 on p 308).

In determining whether to award additional PRI to individuals with conditions such as spinal cord injuries or amputations, the examiner should consider two questions: (1) Does the conventional impairment rating system permit different ratings to be given to individuals who have a well-established pain syndrome associated with their conditions vs those who do not have the syndrome? and (2) Does the individual report activity limitations using the second section (Activity Limitation or Interference) of the self-report questionnaire included in Table 18-4 (pp 576-577, Impairment Impact Inventory [I³], Form A) that are plausible consequences of the established pain syndrome, but are *not* inevitable consequences of the loss of mechanical function associated with the diagnosed condition? For example, if the individual in the above example reported that his pain limited his ability to walk or to concentrate, these limitations could not plausibly be construed as direct consequences of his amputation.

Chapter 18

MEDICAL TIP
Well-established pain syndromes are those that are accepted and well received by the medical community, without significant controversy.

LEGAL TIP
Medical reports should contain references to medical literature that establishes the well-established pain syndrome.

18.3b When *Not* to Use the Pain Chapter to Evaluate Pain-Related Impairment

In order to use the pain-related impairment assessment system described in Chapter 18, an examiner must determine (1) that it is necessary to do such an assessment in order to capture the burden of illness borne by an individual; (2) that a pain-related impairment assessment can be validly performed; and (3) that the pain-related impairment identified during an assessment is a consequence of a well-recognized medical condition. If any of the above conditions does not apply, the system described in Chapter 18 cannot be used in toto, although portions of it can be used when condition 3 does not apply. Thus, Chapter 18 should not be used to rate PRI under the following circumstances:

1. When conditions are adequately rated in other chapters of the *Guides*, ie, the evaluation for PRI is *unnecessary*.

2. When rating individuals with low credibility, ie, the evaluation for PRI is *invalid*.

3. When there are ambiguous or controversial pain syndromes, ie, PRI is considered *unratable*.

PRI Is Unnecessary

It is unnecessary to award a PRI when an individual's CIR adequately encompasses the burden of illness imposed by his or her condition. It is expected that this will be the typical situation. That is, the CIR described in chapters of the *Guides* other than Chapter 18 take into account the pain that is typically experienced in various medical conditions. Thus, an examiner should award impairment for pain only if he or she concludes that the burden of illness and impact on ADL for a particular individual is not captured by the individual's CIR.

EXAMPLE

An independent medical examination is performed on a 41-year-old male who underwent an L5-S1 diskectomy for left lower extremity (LLE) sciatica. He had short-term resolution of his pain but a recurrence of his preoperative symptoms 5 weeks after surgery. A repeat MRI scan demonstrated epidural scarring involving the left S1 root but no evidence of a recurrent disk herniation. Conservative therapy, including three epidurals, did not produce significant relief. Currently, he reports pain in the lumbosacral region with radiation into the LLE in an S1 pattern. Pain is aggravated by bending and "moving."

Exam

No myofascial pain in the lumbosacral region. Lumbar flexion = 30°; extension = 10°; lateral bending = 20° bilaterally. Individual reported radicular symptoms in the LLE with flexion and lateral bending to either side. Straight leg raising (SLR) was negative on the right; it was positive on the left with reproduction of radicular symptoms at 50° of hip flexion. Neurologic exam revealed an absent left Achilles tendon jerk. Individual reported diminished pinprick sensation throughout the left lower extremity and demonstrated pain-inhibited weakness in all LLE muscles tested.

Step 1 of PRI Worksheet (see Form C)
Diagnosis = lumbar postlaminectomy syndrome with persistent left S1 radiculopathy.

Step 2 of PRI Worksheet
Conventional impairment rating (CIR) = 13% whole person impairment (WPI). (Individual warrants DRE category III, from Table 15-3.)

Step 7 of PRI Worksheet
Pain-Related Impairment Data:

a. Pain intensity (Section I, Form A) = 14.

b. Activity interference (Section 2, Form A) = 12.

c. Emotional distress (Section III, Form A) = 2.

d. Credibility (see *Guides 5th* p 581 and methodology below): The individual appeared sincere, and there are no obvious systems factors that might provide incentives for him to exaggerate his presentation. Credibility score = +5.

e. Pain behavior (see *Guides 5th* pp 579-580 and methodology below): Some of the individual's behaviors during the exam were congruent with a diagnosis of S1 radiculopathy, but he has some nonorganic findings (eg, diffuse LLE weakness). Pain behavior score = +3.

f. Pain-related impairment class (Step 7 of the PRI assessment methodology summarized below) = moderate.

Chapter 18

Step 8 of PRI Worksheet

PRI is considered ratable. Individual has pain associated with a medical condition that typically produces both pain and objectively measurable impairment.

Step 9 of PRI Worksheet

Final impairment rating:

a. Conventional impairment = 13%

b. Discretionary PRI allowance = 0%

c. Pain-related impairment (PRI) class = moderate

d. Final rating: It is decided that the individual's pain-related impairment is adequately encompassed in his CIR. The final impairment rating is 13%.

Comment

1. This individual has clear-cut evidence of a persistent S1 radiculopathy. DRE category III (Table 15-3) is specifically designated to capture the burden of illness of this condition. Although the individual has reported significant pain-related impairment, he has not reported incapacitation that is beyond what one would expect for an individual with a persistent S1 radiculopathy (ie, he has not demonstrated evidence of excess pain).

2. Note that lumbar spine impairment DRE category III is associated with a range of WPI from 10% to 13%. The text of the spine impairment chapter (Chapter 15) indicates that adjustments of up to 3% can be made when impairment is rated on the basis of the DRE system. In this instance, 3% was added for the *scarring and persistent pain* which, in effect, substitutes for the 3% allowance that can be made on the basis of the pain chapter.

3. In this case history, the examiner went through a formal PRI assessment and then concluded that the individual's CIR adequately captured the full burden of his condition. Thus, it might appear that the formal PRI assessment was unnecessary. However, it is important to note that the examiner has a better basis for reaching a conclusion about an individual's PRI if the examiner has carefully assessed it. Thus, regardless of whether or not an examiner decides to award additional impairment based on an individual's pain, his or her decision will have more credibility if it is based on a careful assessment of the individual's PRI.

PRI Is Invalid

The assessment of PRI is invalid if an individual demonstrates such poor credibility that the examiner cannot rely on his or her subjective reports. This limitation is necessary, since an assessment of PRI relies heavily on self-reports. If an examiner determines that an individual will not or cannot provide accurate information about the burden of the medical condition that is being rated, the examiner should abort an assessment of PRI and indicate in his or her report that the individual's credibility was too compromised to permit a valid PRI assessment to be completed.

EXAMPLE

A 45-year-old man undergoes an independent medical examination for low back pain related to a work injury 3 years ago. He has consistently had axial back pain only. Advanced imaging studies have demonstrated degenerative changes in the L4-L5 and L5-S1 disks but no frank herniation and no compromise of neural elements. He has been treated conservatively. When the examining physician attempts to elicit a history, the individual is belligerent. He answers questions with tirades against the workers' compensation system and the examiner. In doing so, he provides very little factual information for the examiner to use in forming opinions about his medical condition. The examiner aborts his pain-related assessment, indicating in his report that he was able to perform a CIR of the individual's spine based on concepts in Chapter 15 but was unable to elicit enough cooperation to perform a pain-related assessment.

Chapter 18

PRI Is Unratable

In some instances, a PRI assessment appears to be necessary and can be performed validly, but the PRI identified during the assessment is considered unratable. PRI is considered unratable when it occurs in the context of a vague or controversial medical syndrome. Unratable impairments do not receive any quantitative rating, but the evaluator may go through the pain evaluation process to better characterize the individual's pain and its impact on ADL and to provide a qualitative rating of the individual's PRI.

It is important to note that the term *unratable* refers to the relation between (1) an individual's symptoms and reported activity restrictions and (2) the medical condition thought to underlie them. Physicians will sometimes have difficulty distinguishing between well-established medical conditions that are ratable and ambiguous or controversial syndromes that are unratable. The examining physician should ask the following three questions: (1) Do the medical findings match any known medical condition? (2) Is the presentation typical of the condition? (3) Is the diagnosed condition widely accepted by physicians as having a well-defined pathophysiologic basis?

If the answer to any of the above questions is no, then the PRI associated with the condition should be considered unratable. In this situation, a PRI assessment can be performed to determine the qualitative class that best describes the burden of illness borne by an individual because of pain, but a quantitative impairment rating cannot be given.

Of note is that an examiner generally makes a decision about whether an individual's PRI is ratable on the basis of the relationship between the individual's symptoms and the medical condition thought to explain these symptoms, rather than on the basis of the diagnosed condition in the abstract. A few conditions are considered unratable in Chapter 18 because they are inherently controversial or vague. The best example is fibromyalgia. The more common and more subtle setting for unratable pain is one with the following features: (1) an individual's symptoms have been attributed to a condition that is well accepted and can have well-defined objective markers; and (2) the individual does not have the objective markers that are typically found in the diagnosed condition and does not have symptoms that represent a textbook case of the condition. An example is a diagnosis of thoracic outlet syndrome in an individual who has an ill-defined chronic pain syndrome affecting an upper extremity, and whose vascular and electrophysiologic studies are negative for arterial, venous, or neurogenic thoracic outlet syndrome. The problem in this example is that the diagnosis of thoracic outlet syndrome is not based on any objective indices and may well be misleading, since it implies that the individual's symptoms are attributable to a specific, ongoing biologic abnormality. The more likely explanation of the individual's symptoms is that they reflect pain that is independent of an ongoing, specifically definable biologic abnormality, because of either central sensitization or the development of a chronic pain syndrome. An examiner should consider the PRI for an individual like this to be unratable.

The difficulty of distinguishing between ratable and unratable PRI is aggravated by the fact that the medical nomenclature sometimes provides numerous labels for essentially the same condition. For example, an individual with nonradicular low back pain could be designated as having several different ICD-9 diagnoses, including lumbar strain (847.2), lumbar disk degeneration (722.52), or "low back pain" (724.2). Some diagnoses have general credibility in the medical community, whereas others come from a variety of sources and have less credibility.

A condition designated under one label may be amenable to rating (either by the conventional system or by the concepts in Chapter 18), but the same condition with a different designation may be intractable from a rating standpoint. An example of this problem is whiplash. The origin of the term *whiplash* is obscure. It is not an ICD-9 diagnosis. It may well have come from the legal community. Whiplash identifies a medical syndrome on the basis of the inciting event, rather than on the basis of some presumed pathophysiology. This is akin to creating a diagnosis of lifting a heavy object injury. Just as a person who lifts a heavy object could sustain a variety of injuries, so whiplash does not describe a distinct medical condition.

What should be the approach to rating impairment for an individual with a whiplash injury? The most typical problem among these individuals is neck pain. An examiner has to rule out major syndromes, such as a cervical radiculopathy or fracture. The remaining individuals (ie, ones with local neck pain only) could be construed as having sustained cervical strains. They should receive a CIR in the same manner as any individual with a cervical strain. Many individuals with whiplash injuries also report headaches. These should be rated in an evaluation of an individual with whiplash. Thus, an individual with a whiplash disorder might receive (1) CIR based on a diagnosis of cervical strain, if DRE or ROM criteria are met; and (2) additional PRI, based on both the individual's neck pain and his or her headaches. (As always, an examiner would award additional PRI only if he or she concluded that the individual's burden of illness was not adequately encompassed in the CIR award.)

As indicated on page 572 of the *Guides 5th*, the determination that PRI is unratable does not mean that the pain is fabricated or unreal. PRI is considered unratable when, in the judgment of the examiner, either the condition thought to produce the PRI is a vague or controversial one, or the individual's symptoms and reported behavioral limitations are so nonspecific that it is difficult to relate them to any well-defined medical disorder.

Thus, an examiner's decision that PRI is unratable should be construed as a statement about "the limits that exist in the science and practice of impairment evaluation" (p 572), rather than a statement about the authenticity of the individual's pain reports.

> ### M E D I C A L   T I P
> The physician needs to document in his or her report the basis for indicating that a condition is unratable.

Chapter 18

LEGAL TIP

An examiner has the responsibility of assessing conventional impairment, assessing PRI when this seems appropriate, and judging whether pain-related impairment is ratable vs unratable. The response to this information by agencies that administer benefit programs is difficult to predict and will probably vary from one agency to another. In essence, the decision whether to "count 'conventional' impairment ratings and pain-related impairment ratings on an equal footing, to discount pain-related impairment ratings, or to disregard them entirely" (Section 18.3c, p 572) reflects policy decisions over which physicians and the AMA have no control. The policy decision to use PRI as a basis for an economic award should be made by the appropriate legislative, administrative, or other organization.

18.3d How to Rate Pain-Related Impairment: Overview

18.3e Classes of Pain-Related Impairment

18.3f How to Rate Pain-Related Impairment: Practical Steps

Sections 18-3d through 18.3f provide further detail on the use of the pain chapter. Table 18-4, now included in this chapter under Form A, is used to assess the self-reported impact of pain; and Table 18-5, now included, is used to assess pain behavior.

18.4 Behavioral Confounders

This section provides information on the interpretation of pain behaviors and how these are incorporated into impairment ratings. Assess pain behaviors based on (1) congruence with established conditions, (2) consistency over time and situation, (3) consistency with known anatomy and physiology, (4) agreement among different observers, and (5) their incorporation with other behavioral confounders.

18.5 How to Rate Pain-Related Impairment: A Sample Protocol

This chapter follows the algorithm shown in the figure on page 292. The algorithm is similar to the one given as Figure 18-1 in Chapter 18, but the following changes have been made: (1) Examiners are asked to make a determination about whether PRI is ratable in step VI, rather than in step VII; (2) examiners may give a discretionary allowance of 1%, 2%, or 3% only if PRI is judged to be ratable; and (3) examiners are given the option of awarding impairment for pain even when an individual's PRI is determined to be only mild.

To facilitate use of the algorithm, a detailed PRI Worksheet has been developed (see Form C) and included in this chapter. This worksheet incorporates the information provided in Figure 18-1 (Revised) but makes the application of the information easier. The present discussion will be centered around this worksheet. The purpose of the discussion is to provide the reader with a step-by-step description of how to perform PRI assessments. The discussion below covers material presented in Sections 18.3d through 18.5 in Chapter 18.

Preliminary Steps

In some instances, a formal PRI assessment will be requested by the agency that has referred an individual for evaluation. In this setting, the examiner should simply perform the assessment as part of his or her overall evaluation of the individual.

In other instances, an examiner will not know whether or not to perform a formal PRI assessment when he or she first sees an individual. The examiner takes a thorough history and performs a careful physical examination, just as he or she would do for any individual undergoing an impairment evaluation. As in any impairment evaluation, the examiner addresses the following questions: (1) What are the individual's diagnoses? Which of the diagnosed conditions are to be rated? (2) Is the individual at maximal medical improvement (MMI) with respect to the conditions to be rated? (3) How credible is the individual's presentation? (4) What is the examiner's impression of the pain behaviors demonstrated by the individual during the evaluation?

At the end of the evaluation, the examiner should decide whether to proceed to a formal PRI assessment based on whether the PRI appears to increase the burden of the individual's condition substantially (Figure 18-1) beyond the impairment awarded on the basis of his or her CIR.

The process of determining PRI requires approximately 10 minutes of physician time, 15 minutes of the individual's time, and 5 minutes of an assistant's time. In addition, a physician who performs a formal PRI assessment will need approximately 10 extra minutes to describe the results of the assessment in a report.

Figure 18-1, with modifications, is reprinted below.

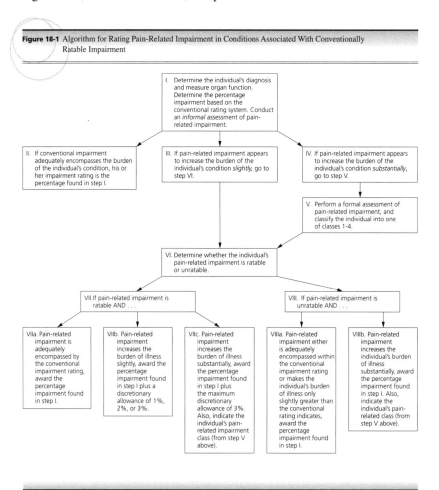

Figure 18-1 Algorithm for Rating Pain-Related Impairment in Conditions Associated With Conventionally Ratable Impairment

I. Determine the individual's diagnosis and measure organ function. Determine the percentage impairment based on the conventional rating system. Conduct an *informal* assessment of pain-related impairment.

II. If conventional impairment adequately encompasses the burden of the individual's condition, his or her impairment rating is the percentage found in step I.

III. If pain-related impairment appears to increase the burden of the individual's condition *slightly*, go to step VI.

IV. If pain-related impairment appears to increase the burden of the individual's condition *substantially*, go to step V.

V. Perform a formal assessment of pain-related impairment, and classify the individual into one of classes 1-4.

VI. Determine whether the individual's pain-related impairment is ratable or unratable.

VII. If pain-related impairment is ratable AND . . .

VIII. If pain-related impairment is unratable AND . . .

VIIa. Pain-related impairment is adequately encompassed by the conventional impairment rating, award the percentage impairment found in step I.

VIIb. Pain-related impairment increases the burden of illness slightly, award the percentage impairment found in step I plus a discretionary allowance of 1%, 2%, or 3%.

VIIc. Pain-related impairment increases the burden of illness substantially, award the percentage impairment found in step I plus the maximum discretionary allowance of 3%. Also, indicate the individual's pain-related impairment class (from step V above).

VIIIa. Pain-related impairment either is adequately encompassed within the conventional impairment rating or makes the individual's burden of illness only slightly greater than the conventional rating indicates, award the percentage impairment found in step I.

VIIIb. Pain-related impairment increases the individual's burden of illness substantially, award the percentage impairment found in step I. Also, indicate the individual's pain-related class (from step V above).

Chapter 18

If a formal pain assessment is performed, the following method applies:

1. Reproduce and use the PRI Worksheet (Form C) to facilitate performance of PRI assessments.

2. Table 18-4 in the *Guides 5th* has now been reformatted and renamed the Impairment Impact Inventory (I^3). The inventory is reproduced as Form A at the end of this chapter. Have the individuals undergoing formal PRI assessments complete the I^3. (This takes less than 15 minutes.) The examiner should specify which conditions the individual should consider when filling out the I^3. The I^3 should be filled out only in reference to conditions being rated.

3. The examiner (or an assistant) scores the I^3 (Form A) according to instructions given (Form B). The same information is given in Table 18-6 (p 584) of the *Guides 5th*; however, there is a minor error in these instructions. The sum of the scores of items dealing with emotional distress should be divided by 5, not by 4 as listed in the *Guides 5th*. The goal is to obtain the average of five items, A through E. They are designated 22 through 26 in Form A.

4. The examiner should then complete the PRI Worksheet (Form C). This will permit him or her to determine the extent of an individual's PRI and to determine whether this impairment is adequately incorporated into the individual's CIR.

The PRI Methodology Step-by-Step Worksheet
Step 1. Record the diagnoses.

Step 2. Provide CIR for conditions being rated.

Step 3. Make a clinical judgment about whether an individual's apparent PRI (1) is adequately encompassed by his or her CIR, (2) makes the burden of the individual's condition slightly greater than the conventional impairment awarded, or (3) makes the burden of the individual's condition substantially greater than the conventional impairment awarded.

If the examiner chooses option 1, the evaluation is terminated and the individual is awarded the impairment ascertained in step 2 above. If the examiner chooses option 2, he or she needs to proceed to step 8 of the worksheet to determine whether the individual's PRI is ratable or unratable. If the examiner chooses option 3, he or she should proceed to the formal PRI assessment algorithm described in steps 4 to 7 of the worksheet.

Step 4. Have the individual complete the Impairment Impact Inventory (I^3, Form A). The examiner needs to designate the condition(s) that the individual should consider when filling out the I^3 (Form A). To avoid confusion, the examiner or an assistant should write the conditions being considered at the top of the I^3 before the individual fills it out.

Step 5. Assess credibility, both qualitatively and quantitatively. The qualitative question is: Does the individual demonstrate enough credibility for a pain-related impairment assessment to be performed?

Since the examiner must rely on the individual's self-reports in order to assess PRI, the examiner needs to consider the PRI invalid if an individual's self-reports are not credible. There are many reasons why an individual's credibility might be judged to be so low that a valid PRI assessment cannot be performed. Some individuals deliberately misrepresent their situations. Some demonstrate severe cognitive deficits that make it impossible for the examiner to elicit accurate information. Some are hostile and overtly uncooperative. The examiner should declare a PRI assessment invalid only under extreme circumstances. If an individual's credibility is somewhat suspect, the examiner should complete the PRI assessment but give the individual a low score for credibility.

If an individual is judged to have enough credibility for a valid PRI assessment to be done, the examiner must provide a quantitative score from -10 to $+10$ to indicate how much credibility the individual has. Chapter 18, pages 581 to 583 and pages 585 to 586, discuss issues to consider in rating credibility. Note that the factors that go into decisions about the credibility of individuals are complex and that there is no evidence about the reliability or validity of the credibility judgments that physicians make about individuals.

Examiners should consider the following when providing quantitative credibility ratings for an individual: (1) Does the individual seem sincere in his or her presentation? (2) Does the individual provide historical information that is detailed, coherent, and apparently complete? (3) Is there any information from collateral sources? Does it tend to validate or invalidate reports by the individual? (4) Is there any evidence that the individual is trying to impress the examiner regarding the severity of his or her suffering? (5) Are there any systems issues that might provide incentives for the individual to exaggerate the severity of his or her suffering?

It is recommended that if an individual appears to have high credibility on the basis of criteria 1 through 5 above, but is undergoing an impairment rating in an adversarial setting (such as an independent medical examination), the examiner rate the individual's credibility cautiously (ie, close to the midpoint, zero). This recommendation reflects the fact that evidence to date suggests that physicians are not particularly adept at interpreting the presentations of individuals in such settings.

Step 6. Evaluate pain behavior. Pages 579 to 583 of Chapter 18 discuss factors an examiner should consider when rating an individual's pain behavior. The range for ratings is –10 to +10. The examiner may assign any of 21 whole-number values between and including –10 and +10 to rate an individual's pain behavior, as is made clear in Table 18-5, notwithstanding the contrary remark in Table 18-6. Give a negative rating (less than zero) when an individual demonstrates exaggerated or nonphysiologic pain behaviors. Give positive pain behavior ratings (ie, ratings > 0) on the basis of two considerations:

1. Up to +5 if an individual does not demonstrate any exaggerated or non-physiologic pain behaviors and gives a good effort throughout the examination.

2. Up to +5 additional if an individual demonstrates a combination of:

   a. Specific findings that are pathognomonic for the condition being rated (eg, sensory and motor loss in an L5 pattern for an individual with an L5 radiculopathy)

   b. Normal findings outside the affected area (eg, normal sensory and motor function in dermatomes and myotomes other than L5)

Note that an individual can receive a score close to +10 only if he or she scores high on both 1 and 2. Also, note that some medical conditions have pathognomonic findings, while others do not. For example, there are specific physical findings that are classically associated with an L5 radiculopathy. In contrast, there are no well-accepted, specific physical findings associated with most axial lumbar spine pain syndromes (eg, pain thought to be secondary to facet joint arthropathy or internal derangement of a disk).

EXAMPLE

A 30-year-old woman with a persistent right-sided L5 radiculopathy after an L4-L5 diskectomy is examined. She demonstrates a mild "steppage" gait and a slight list to the left when standing and deviates slightly more to the left during active flexion of the lumbar spine from a standing position. She reports reproduction of her typical radicular symptoms during flexion. Extension and lateral bending of the lumbar spine are normal. There is no myofascial pain. She demonstrates positive straight leg raising on the right and also positive crossed straight leg raising. In both instances she calmly reports a gradually worsening combination of pain and tingling in an L5 pattern as her hip is flexed. She demonstrates moderate atrophy of right calf muscles. Neurologic examination reveals 2+ and symmetric knee and ankle jerks. She demonstrates moderate weakness in right ankle eversion, inversion, and dorsiflexion, and also moderate weakness in extensor hallucis longus function. She gives excellent effort during manual muscle testing and demonstrates good function in all other muscle groups in the right lower extremity, as well as all groups in the left lower extremity. Pinprick examination shows diminished sensation in an L5 pattern in the right lower extremity. Throughout the examination, the individual remains calm and consistently gives excellent effort (pain behavior score = +10).

EXAMPLE

A 45-year-old man has undergone L5 to sacrum fusion for refractory axial low back pain attributed to a posterior L5-S1 disk herniation. Postoperative diagnostic studies have not shown evidence of a lumbar radiculopathy or recurrent disk herniation, and the individual's pain is primarily limited to the lumbosacral junction region. Gait is normal. Posture is noteworthy in that there is some reduction of the lumbar lordosis. There is no myofascial pain. He displays a mild to moderate reduction in active flexion and extension of the spine and reports increased lumbosacral pain with these maneuvers. Lateral bending to either side is normal in extent and pain free. Straight leg raising is normal bilaterally. Neurologic exam in the lower extremities is normal. He gives good effort throughout the examination (pain behavior score = +5).

The examiner needs to avoid confounding an assessment of an individual's pain behavior with an assessment of the individual's overall credibility. Credibility refers primarily to what an individual says (ie, it refers to the ability and willingness of an individual to provide detailed, accurate information about his or her condition). Pain behavior is rated largely on the basis of an individual's nonverbal behavior, primarily during a physical examination and secondarily during an interview.

Step 7. Calculate the PRI class on the basis of the following data: (1) the individual's responses to the I^3 (Form A), (2) the individual's pain behavior rating (step 6), and (3) adjustment for the individual's credibility rating (step 5).

An individual's PRI class is determined by the total score he or she receives in step 7a (Form C).

Step 8. Indicate whether PRI is ratable or unratable.

For ratable PRI, the examiner needs to indicate whether it is ratable on the basis of (1) excess pain associated with a medical condition that typically produces both pain and objectively measurable impairment; (2) pain associated with a well-recognized condition that normally does not produce objectively measurable impairment; or (3) pain with the following characteristics: (*a*) it is a characteristic pain syndrome that occurs as a component of a condition (such as spinal cord injury) that is ratable according to the conventional rating system, (*b*) only some of the individuals with the underlying condition have the pain syndrome, and (*c*) the CIR does not capture the added burden of illness borne by individuals who have the associated pain syndrome.

Note: If the examiner concludes that the individual's PRI does not match any of the above three categories, he or she should indicate that it is unratable.

The examiner should proceed to step 9 if he or she determines that an individual's PRI is ratable, or to step 10 if he or she determines that the individual's PRI is unratable.

Step 9. Determine the final impairment rating (for ratable PRI).

In part a, the examiner should copy the CIR calculated in step 2.

In part b, the examiner determines whether the individual should be awarded any discretionary impairment because of pain. In effect, this step requires the examiner to reconsider the clinical judgment made in step 3, taking into account the results of the formal PRI assessment. If the examiner concludes that the burden of illness borne by the individual is *slightly* greater than the CIR indicates, he or she should give a discretionary award of 1%, 2%, or 3%. If the examiner concludes that the burden of illness borne by the individual is *substantially* greater than the CIR indicates, he or she should always give the full discretionary award of 3%.

In part c, the examiner should copy the individual's PRI class that was determined in step 7b.

In part d, the examiner combines information from parts 9a, 9b, and 9c, and gives a final impairment rating. Note that if the examiner awards discretionary impairment, he or she should *combine* this with the individual's CIR in order to quantify the total impairment.

1. If the examiner concludes that the individual's PRI is adequately encompassed within the CIR that has been awarded, the individual's total impairment is the conventional impairment calculated in step 2 of the worksheet.

2. If the examiner concludes that the individual's PRI makes his or her burden of illness slightly greater than the CIR indicates, the examiner awards the CIR plus a discretionary allowance of 1%, 2%, or 3%.

Chapter 18

3. If the examiner concludes that the individual's PRI makes his or her burden of illness substantially greater than the CIR indicates, the examiner awards the CIR plus the maximum discretionary allowance of 3%. Also, the examiner indicates the patient's PRI class.

In parts 9b and 9d, the examiner must judge whether an individual's PRI is adequately encompassed within the CIR identified in step 2. The fact that an individual has a PRI does not automatically mean that his or her total impairment award should exceed the CIR identified in step 2 of the worksheet. For such an individual, the examiner must address the more subtle issue of whether the patient's PRI (1) has been adequately encompassed by the CIR that he or she has been awarded or (2) increases the burden of illness beyond what is reflected in the CIR. The analysis of this issue varies, depending on the relationship that the examiner hypothesizes between the individual's pain and a well-accepted medical condition.

1. For conditions such as a lumbar radiculopathy or a painful arthritic joint, the individual's PRI would be judged to be encompassed by the CIR, unless he or she demonstrated a burden of illness that seemed significantly higher than the one borne by most people with the diagnosed condition.

2. For a condition such as migraine headache, an examiner would almost always conclude that an individual's PRI is not adequately encompassed in his or her CIR.

3. For a condition such as phantom limb pain in an amputee, the examiner needs to make a decision about whether or not the conventional rating adequately encompasses the individual's pain on the basis of the two questions mentioned previously (ie, Does the conventional rating system distinguish between individuals with the condition [amputation] who do have chronic pain vs ones who do not? Does the individual report activity restrictions that are *not* inevitable consequences of his or her amputation but appear, rather, to reflect limits imposed by pain?)

Step 10. Determine the final impairment rating (for unratable PRI).

In part a, the examiner should copy the CIR calculated in step 2.

Part b indicates that if the examiner did not perform a formal PRI assessment, the total impairment awarded to the individual being evaluated should be the CIR. In essence, this means that if an examiner judges in step 3 that an individual's PRI increases the burden of illness slightly, and determines in step 8 that the individual's PRI is unratable, the individual receives no award for his or her PRI.

In part c1, the examiner should copy the individual's PRI class that was determined in step 7b.

In part c2, the examiner uses the information obtained from the formal PRI assessment to reconsider the options that he or she considered informally in step 3 of the worksheet and to choose the one that best fits the individual undergoing evaluation. Note that the examiner must choose between only two options: the individual's PRI is judged either to be adequately encompassed within his or her CIR or to be substantially greater than the CIR indicates.

1. If the examiner concludes that the individual's PRI is adequately encompassed within the CIR that has been awarded, or that it increases the burden of illness only slightly, the individual's total impairment is the conventional impairment calculated in step 2 of the worksheet.

2. If the examiner concludes that the individual's PRI makes his or her burden of illness substantially greater than the CIR indicates, the examiner awards the CIR and indicates the patient's PRI class.

The fact that an individual has PRI does not automatically mean that the PRI makes the burden of his or her illness greater than what is reflected in the individual's CIR. For such an individual, the examiner must address the more subtle issue of whether the person's PRI (1) has been adequately encompassed by the CIR that he or she has been awarded or (2) increases the burden of illness substantially beyond what is reflected in the CIR.

The Final Report

The examiner's final report for an impairment evaluation should include the rationale underlying his or her decisions regarding PRI in the individual who has been evaluated. In particular, the report should include a discussion of the basis for the examiner's choice to perform (or choice not to perform) a formal PRI assessment, the basis for his or her judgments regarding the individual's credibility and pain behavior, and the basis for his or her responses in step 9 of the worksheet.

LEGAL TIP

As a matter of legal sufficiency, or to sustain a challenge to the foundation for a rating for pain based on Chapter 18 in excess of or combined with any rating given from another chapter, a report that rates pain, even on a discretionary basis, must:

1. Discuss which of the three categories (or combination of them) under Section 18.3a constitutes the starting point for the evaluation, and include a narrative explaining the physician's initiation of the PRI using the format specified under Section 18.3d.

2. Rule out any medically probable condition stated in Section 18.3b that negates use of Chapter 18 as a basis for PRI, stated in explanatory, not conclusory, terms. The report should also affirmatively and in explanatory, not conclusory, terms answer all three questions on page 572 as part of ruling out the preclusion of Chapter 18 because the pain syndrome is ambiguous or controversial.

3. Contain a narrative or outline-form discussion of the six steps noted in Section 18.3f, to determine (1) MMI, (2) severity of pain, (3) activity restrictions, (4) presence of emotional distress, (5) presence of authentic or exaggerated pain behavior, and (6) credibility, and include written results of any tests or screens administered as part of these steps.

4. Include a copy of the completed I³ (Table 18-4, Form A), with a written note as to whether it was completed by self-report or interview.

5. Include an explanation by the physician describing steps taken to avoid iatrogenic origin of the pain rating (Section 18.4c).

6. Discuss in detail all subcategories under Section 18.4a: (1) Congruence With Established Conditions, (2) Consistency With Anatomy and Physiology, (3) Observer Agreement, and (4) Other Inappropriate Illness Behavior, and the effect each category has on both pain behaviors and credibility (Section 18.4b).

7. Utilize the reporting format contained in Table 18-6 and the methodology provided above and in the attached form.

8. Describe the ratable pain in medically probable terms consistent with the definition of pain, using association with actual or potential tissue damage or description in terms of such damage.

18.6 Psychogenic Pain

This section discusses psychogenic pain disorders and how to determine if a pain condition is psychologically based. If the psychological factors played a major role in the initiation of the pain syndrome or are playing a major role in its continuation, then the pain disorder is assessed in the mental and behavioral disorders chapter (Chapter 14).

18.7 Malingering

Malingering, or conscious deception for the purpose of gain, is not a disease but a volitional deception (*Guides 5th*, p 587).

> ### MEDICAL TIP
>
> If the physician suspects malingering, document behaviors that are discordant with the clinical condition.

> ### LEGAL TIP
>
> Since a physician cannot determine which individuals may be malingering, his or her report needs to address any discrepancies in behavior with the clinical condition and leave the conclusion of malingering to the workers' compensation system to settle. Workers' compensation judges and administrators may view with skepticism "discretionary ratings" that omit references to reductions in ADL that would otherwise justify heightened ratings.

18.8 Conclusion

This chapter provides physicians with a method to integrate pain reports and behaviors and determine a limited quantitative and qualitative assessment of pain and its impact on the ability to perform ADL.

> ### MEDICAL TIP
>
> Determine how pain is addressed in the state where you practice, and incorporate the information required by your state into the medical report.

> ### LEGAL TIP
>
> Chapter 18 provides a system for placing individuals into pain-related impairment classes, but it does not provide a method for determining whole person impairment from these classes or for quantitatively combining PRI ratings with CIRs. At the present time, there is uncertainty about how administrative agencies will use information provided by examiners about PRI. The authors of Chapter 18 recognize this uncertainty in Section 18.3c:
>
>> The system described here distinguishes between an impairment rating using the organ system approach and impairment awarded on the basis of pain. This distinction permits administrative agencies to count "'conventional" impairment ratings and pain-related impairment ratings on an equal footing, to discount pain-related impairment ratings, or to disregard them entirely. Similarly, the present system identifies individuals with unratable pain-related impairment so that administrative agencies can make informed decisions about whether or not to compensate these individuals (p 572).
>
> Even the 14 states that require, by statute, use of the "latest" or "most recent" edition of the *Guides* may not be required, under the *Guides*' terms, to award an impairment rating (or a disability rating in those states where disability is a formulaic result of an impairment rating) based on the qualitative method if the foundation or evidence for a PRI rating is considered not to constitute reliable evidence. Regardless of the legal status one imparts to the *Guides*, a report that rates pain but does so without fastidious foundational detail should not be considered as a basis for an economic award based on impairment.

18.9 Case Examples

The case examples listed in the *Guides 5th* were not assigned numerical PRI ratings, although the scores and information to provide a PRI are included. In summary, the quantitative ratings are as follows.

The individual in Example 18-1 would not receive any CIR. She would be awarded a discretionary PRI of 2%. The individual in Example 18-2 is not given any discretionary PRI, because his conventional rating adequately encompasses the burden of his condition. The pain-related classes for the individuals in Examples 18-3 and 18-4 are appropriate, and these individuals should be awarded the discretionary 3% PRI.

How to Rate PRI: Practical Steps

To assess PRI, an informed physician's judgment must contain information from several domains. Both medical and legal judgments about PRI must integrate medical data, psychological data, and other evidence about an individual's litigation and compensation status. The following cases include information necessary to make a determination of PRI. The information is in six domains: (1) medical history; (2) symptoms; (3) systems issues, including the individual's involvement in litigation or a workers' compensation claim (this tells an examiner whether an individual might have an incentive to present himself or herself in a certain light); (4) past medical history; (5) physical examination, including (where appropriate) information about mental status and pain behaviors, as well as findings that support a particular medical diagnosis; and (6) pain-related impairment data, including the individual's responses to the I^3 (Table 18-4), in order to reach an informed judgment about the individual's PRI. Similar judgments are required about the individual's credibility and pain behaviors.

EXAMPLE: MILD PRI—CLASS 1

Medical History

An independent medical examination is performed on a 45-year-old woman. Two years ago, she slipped and fell backward at work, hitting her head against a concrete floor. There was no definite loss of consciousness. Coworkers, who found her approximately 2 minutes after the fall, reported that she was alert and oriented but complained of nausea and a severe headache. She was taken to an emergency department. Her neurologic exam was normal, and a computed tomographic scan showed no evidence of a skull fracture, subdural/epidural hematoma, or intracerebral bleeding.

The woman has continued to report headaches since her fall. Numerous neurologic exams have been normal. Extensive workups, including MRI of the brain, electroencephalograms, and cervical MRI, have all been negative. The individual has tried a wide range of pharmacologic regimens, with only modest benefit, and also failed to benefit from a 3-month medication-free trial to evaluate the possibility of rebound headaches. Nonpharmacologic therapies including physical therapy and biofeedback have been ineffective.

Symptoms

The individual reports daily headaches that last most of the day. They start in the occipital region and spread to involve her head diffusely. About once per month, she gets more severe headaches in the same region lasting about 2 days, and they are associated with photophobia, nausea, and vomiting. She reports that she typically has to rest in a dark room during these headaches.

Systems Issues

The individual has filed a third-party legal action regarding her fall. She is currently working full-time.

Past Medical History

There is no history of significant headaches and no general medical problems.

Physical Exam

The physical exam, performed at a time when the individual reports a typical daily headache, is completely normal.

Step 1 of PRI Worksheet
Diagnosis = Posttraumatic headache with migrainous features.

Step 2 of PRI Worksheet
Conventional impairment rating = 0.

Step 7 of PRI Worksheet
Pain-Related Impairment (PRI) data. (Note that, to save space, we are printing the information that would usually appear in the PRI Worksheet for this individual. To see how the PRI Worksheet [Form C] might look when completed, see Example Class 3 below).

a. Pain intensity = 10.

b. Activity interference = 4.

c. Emotional distress = 5.

d. Credibility: Individual appeared sincere; during the evaluation she did not appear to engage in any obvious attempts to exaggerate the severity of her suffering but has significant systems issues (see above). Credibility score = +2.

e. Pain behavior: Individual did not demonstrate dramatic pain behaviors; there are no pathognomonic pain behaviors associated with her problem. Pain behavior score = 0.

f. Pain-related impairment (PRI) class = mild.

Step 8 of PRI Worksheet
Pain-related impairment is considered ratable. She has a well-established pain syndrome that is normally not associated with measurable organ dysfunction *but that does impact ADL.*

Step 9 of PRI Worksheet
Final impairment rating:

a. Conventional impairment = 0%.

b. Discretionary PRI allowance = 3%.

c. Pain-related impairment (PRI) class = mild.

d. Final rating: It is decided that pain-related impairment makes the individual's burden of illness slightly greater than the conventional rating indicates. The final impairment rating is 0% (her conventional impairment) + 3% (discretionary allowance) = 3% WPI.

Comment

This individual has a condition that is inherently not ratable via the conventional rating system. Thus, if she is to be awarded any impairment, it will be via the rating of pain-related impairment.

MEDICAL TIP

An additional assessment for pain, with the use of the pain chapter, is provided only when pain is plausible and greater than expected for a particular impairment.

LEGAL TIP

This example illustrates the narrow ground on which a PRI of up to 3% may be awarded absent any other impairment rating.

EXAMPLE: MODERATE PRI—CLASS 2

Medical History

An independent medical examination is performed on a 49-year-old right-handed man who experienced the gradual onset of pain around the medial epicondyle bilaterally 7 years ago. There was no definite injury, but the individual performed vigorous repetitive activities with his upper extremities in the course of his work as a mechanic. He underwent bilateral cubital tunnel releases 4 to 6 months after onset of his symptoms. He has had no significant postoperative problems with his left upper extremity (LUE). His right upper extremity (RUE) also did reasonably well for about 2 years after surgery, but he then experienced a return of pain in his RUE similar to the discomfort he had had before surgery. There was no definite injury. He underwent a right ulnar transposition 3 years ago, with no improvement. He then had a series of conservative therapies, including steroid injections to the right elbow and several pharmacologic trials. One year ago he underwent an exploration of the right ulnar nerve at the elbow, with extensive neurolysis. He obtained modest benefit from the surgery. A postoperative electrodiagnostic evaluation demonstrated slowing of ulnar conduction in the elbow region but no evidence of ongoing denervation. He is not felt to be a candidate for further ulnar nerve surgery.

Symptoms

The individual says his worst pain is a "toothache" pain in a 4-inch circle around the right medial epicondyle. He also experiences lancinating pain into the distal RUE in an ulnar distribution. This can be provoked by pressure in the region of the medial epicondyle and by a variety of innocuous activities, such as stroking the medial aspect of his forearm. He also reports aching pain in the metacarpophalangeal joints of the fourth and fifth digits of his right hand. He reports numbness in the hypothenar aspect of his hand and in the fifth digit. He experiences weakness in the right hand and diffusely in the entire RUE. He denies phenomena associated with complex regional pain syndrome (ie, he denies swelling in the RUE and reports no difference between LUE and RUE in color, temperature, or perspiration pattern). He says pain in the epicondylar region is present virtually all the time. It is aggravated by pressure over the ulnar nerve and by forceful or repetitive use of his right hand.

Systems Issues

The individual has a workers' compensation claim. He currently works full-time in a lead position for a group of mechanics for an aircraft company. However, he has been off work several times during the past 5 years and reports difficulty keeping up with the physical demands of his job.

Past Medical History

Past medical history is noteworthy for intermittent depression during the past 5 years.

Physical Exam

The individual appears moderately depressed and very anxious about his RUE. Inspection of the elbow reveals multiple surgical scars and atrophy of soft tissues around the medial epicondyle. There are no stigmata of complex regional pain syndrome. Range of motion of the elbow, wrist, and fingers is normal. Gentle tapping in the region of the ulnar nerve causes severe local pain and some lancinating pain into the distal RUE. Tactile stimulation of the medial forearm and hand does not cause any pain. On manual muscle testing, the individual demonstrates mild weakness in all muscle groups tested in the RUE and reports significant pain. There is more pronounced weakness affecting finger abduction and flexor digitorum profundus function to the fourth and fifth digits. Grip strength is 49 pounds on the right vs 72 pounds on the left. Two-point discrimination is 8 mm in the fourth and fifth digits of his right hand vs 3 mm in the other digits.

Step 1 of PRI Worksheet
Diagnosis = right ulnar neuropathy at the elbow.

Step 2 of PRI Worksheet
Conventional impairment rating = 7% WPI.

a. Individual is judged to have 60% loss of ulnar nerve sensory function, based on increased two-point discrimination plus pain (Table 13-23). Upper extremity (UE) impairment due to sensory loss = .60 × 7% = 4% of UE (Table 16-15).

b. Individual is judged to have 15% loss of ulnar nerve motor function (Table 13-24). UE impairment due to motor loss is .15 × 46% = 7% (Table 16-15).

c. a and b are combined (p 604) to yield total UE impairment of 11%.

d. 11% UE impairment converts to 7% whole person impairment (Table 16-3).

Step 7 of PRI Worksheet
Pain-Related Impairment data. (Note that, to save space, we are printing the information that would usually appear in the PRI Worksheet for this individual. To see how the PRI Worksheet [Form C] might look when completed, see Example Class 3 below).

a. Pain intensity = 12.

b. Activity interference = 15.

c. Emotional distress = 4.

d. Credibility: Individual seems sincere, but it appears that his emotional distress leads him to describe his problem in somewhat exaggerated terms. Systems issues are described above. Credibility score = +1.

e. Pain behaviors: Individual does not demonstrate grossly exaggerated pain behaviors during exam. He demonstrates sensory and (to some extent) motor loss in an anatomic pattern. However, he also demonstrates pain-limited weakness affecting the entire RUE. Pain behavior score = +2.

f. Pain-related impairment class = moderate.

Step 8 of PRI Worksheet
PRI is considered ratable. Individual has pain associated with a medical condition that typically produces both pain and objectively measurable impairment.

Step 9 of PRI Worksheet
Final impairment rating:

a. Conventional impairment = 7%.

b. Discretionary PRI allowance = 3%.

c. Pain-related impairment (PRI) class = moderate.

d. Final rating: It is decided that pain-related impairment makes the individual's burden of illness slightly greater than the conventional rating indicates. Conventional impairment (7%) combined with discretionary allowance for pain 3% = 10% WPI.

Comment

The AMA *Guides* chapter on disorders of the nervous system (Chapter 13) permits pain to be considered in awarding impairment for a peripheral nerve injury. However, the extent of these awards is limited by the extent to which sensory dysfunction of an individual nerve is judged to limit function in an extremity. In the case of an ulnar neuropathy, a complete loss of sensory function (or a combination of pain and sensory dysfunction that is judged to be equivalent to a 100% loss of sensory function) receives a 7% impairment of the upper extremity. By Table 16-3, this translates to 4% whole person impairment. Thus, although this individual had both sensory and motor loss in the ulnar nerve and was awarded sensory dysfunction in the ulnar nerve partly on the basis of his pain, his total whole person impairment based on the conventional system did not fully account for his pain and decreased ADL. Given his moderate pain rating, he was given an additional 3% whole person impairment to more adequately account for his pain.

EXAMPLE: MODERATELY SEVERE PRI— CLASS 3

Medical History

An independent medical examination is performed on a 38-year-old, right-handed man who was involved in a motorcycle accident 2 years ago, with myonecrosis of the left arm. He was hospitalized for 7 weeks, and after multiple surgical attempts to save the left arm, it was amputated at the gleno-humeral joint.

Symptoms

The man's main problem is phantom limb pain in the LUE, described as generalized stiffness with shooting pain into the fifth digit and a sense that his fingernails are digging into the flesh of his palm.

Systems Issues

The individual is currently taking college courses, majoring in computer science. No litigation is in progress, and he is not receiving workers' compensation.

Past Medical History

History is significant for alcoholism (blood alcohol level at the time of his motorcycle accident was 235 mg/dL). The individual reports sobriety since his accident.

Physical Exam

No exaggerated pain behaviors were apparent. Range of motion of the neck and right shoulder were normal. Palpation of soft tissues around the left shoulder girdle did not reveal cutaneous hypersensitivity or myofascial pain. Tapping over the stump of the left arm produced a report of tingling in the left hand.

Step 1 of PRI Worksheet
Diagnosis = (1) traumatic amputation of LUE; (2) phantom limb pain.

Step 2 of PRI Worksheet
Conventional impairment rating (based on Table 16-3) = 60% WPI.

Step 7 of PRI Worksheet
Pain-Related Impairment (PRI) data. (Note that for purposes of clarity, the PRI Worksheet for this individual is printed below.)

a. Pain intensity = 18.

b. Activity interference = 19.

c. Emotional distress = 7.

d. Credibility: Individual seems genuine; there were no obvious sources of sec-ondary gain detected. Credibility score = +5.

e. Pain behaviors: Individual described classic symptoms of phantom limb pain in response to mild tapping over his amputation stump and did not demonstrate any obvious nonphysiologic findings on exam. Pain behavior score = +5.

f. Pain-related impairment (PRI) class (Step 7) = moderately severe.

Step 8 of PRI Worksheet
The PRI is judged to be ratable. It represents a well-defined pain syndrome that sometimes occurs as a component of a condition that is independently associ-ated with significant impairment according to the conventional rating system.

Step 9 of PRI Worksheet
Final impairment rating:

a. Conventional impairment = 60%.

b. Discretionary PRI allowance = 3%.

c. Pain-related impairment (PRI) class = moderately severe.

d. Final rating: It is decided that pain-related impairment makes the individual's burden of illness substantially greater than conventional rating indicates. Conventional impairment (60%) combined with discretionary PRI (3%) = 61% WPI. In addition, the individual has moderately severe PRI.

Comment

This individual has very substantial impairment based on the conventional rating system. Thus, the question arises whether he should be awarded additional impairment based on his reports of phantom limb pain. It is important to note that the conventional system apparently relies primarily on loss of function (rather than on pain) when it awards 60% whole person impairment for an amputation at the shoulder. Also of note is that careful review of the individual's self-report questionnaire (I³; see Table 18-4) reveals that he reports ADL limita-tions that can be caused by pain and that he attributes to pain, but that cannot be the direct results of an amputation at the shoulder. Examples include his reported difficulties in walking and sexual functioning. Thus, it appears that the individual has PRI that is not included in his conventional rating.

The PRI Worksheet for this individual is shown below.

Chapter 18

Pain-Related Impairment Worksheet©
A Training Tool Based on the AMA *Guides*, 5th Edition

STEP 1	Condition(s) being rated on this worksheet: <u>amputated left arm</u>
STEP 2	The conventional impairment rating (CIR) is: <u>60</u>% of whole person
STEP 3	Check ONE of the following:

    ☐ The conventional impairment rating (CIR) above appears to encompass the burden of this condition(s) <u>adequately</u>.

    STOP HERE. The total rating for this condition is the number in STEP 2 above.

    ☐ The pain-related impairment (PRI) appears to make the burden of the condition(s) <u>slightly</u> greater than the conventional impairment rating (CIR) in STEP 2 above.

    SKIP TO STEP 8.

    ☒ The pain-related impairment (PRI) appears to make the burden of the condition(s) <u>substantially</u> greater than the conventional impairment rating (CIR) in STEP 2 above.

    PROCEED TO THE FORMAL PRI ASSESSMENT (Steps 4-7)

FORMAL PAIN-RELATED IMPAIRMENT (PRI) ASSESSMENT

STEP 4	**The I³:** After the history and physical, ask the individual to fill out the Impairment Impact Inventory (I³) given in Table 18-4, pages 576-577. Instruct the individual to answer questions only in relation to the condition(s) being rated.
STEP 5	**Credibility:** Is the individual's presentation credible enough to warrant a formal pain-related impairment (PRI) assessment? (If needed, refer to Behavioral Confounders in Section 18.4, pages 581-583, as well as Section 18.3b, pages 571-572.)

    ☐ No.

    SKIP TO STEP 8. Formal PRI assessment cannot be completed.

    ☒ Yes.

    Circle the number below that best represents the individual's credibility. Enter the number in Step 7.

    -10 -9 -8 -7 -6 -5 -4 -3 -2 -1 0 1 2 3 4 ⑤ 6 7 8 9 10

    Very low credibility   Very high credibility

STEP 6	**Pain Behavior:** Circle the number that best represents the individual's pain behavior. (If needed, refer to pages 579-580 and Table 18-5.) Enter the number in Step 7.

    -10 -9 -8 -7 -6 -5 -4 -3 -2 -1 0 1 2 3 4 ⑤ 6 7 8 9 10

    Pain behaviors   Pain behaviors are
    are exaggerated,   appropriate and tend to
    nonphysiologic.   confirm other clinical findings.

Pain-Related Impairment Worksheet©
A Training Tool Based on the AMA *Guides*, 5th Edition, *continued*

STEP 7

a. Pain-Related Impairment Score (PRI): Copy scores into Table 18-6 to the right:

Section I is from the I³* (Pain Intensity).

Section II is from the I³ (ADL).

Section III is from the I³ (Emotional Distress).

Pain Behavior rating is from Step 6 on page 1 of this worksheet.

Adjust for credibility using the number copied from Step 5 on page 1 of this worksheet.

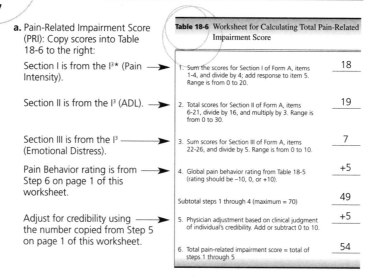

Table 18-6 Worksheet for Calculating Total Pain-Related Impairment Score

1. Sum the scores for Section I of Form A, items 1-4, and divide by 4; add response to item 5. Range is from 0 to 20.	18
2. Total scores for Section II of Form A, items 6-21, divide by 16, and multiply by 3. Range is from 0 to 30.	19
3. Sum scores for Section III of Form A, items 22-26, and divide by 5. Range is from 0 to 10.	7
4. Global pain behavior rating from Table 18-5 (rating should be –10, 0, or +10).	+5
Subtotal steps 1 through 4 (maximum = 70)	49
5. Physician adjustment based on clinical judgment of individual's credibility. Add or subtract 0 to 10.	+5
6. Total pain-related impairment score = total of steps 1 through 5	54

*I³ = Impairment Impact Inventory given in Table 18-4, pages 576-577.

b. The pain-related impairment (PRI) class is (circle one class using total score from Step 7a):

Class:	1 (mild)	2 (moderate)	3 (moderately severe)	4 (severe)
Score	7-24*	25-42	43-60	61-80

Please note: As stated in the AMA *Guides*, 5th Edition, in Table 18-7 on page 584, neither this class nor the corresponding score should be construed to be an impairment rating. That is, they do not represent percentages of whole person impairment.

*A score of 0-6 = no significant pain-related impairment (no class designation)

Chapter 18

Pain-Related Impairment Worksheet©
A Training Tool Based on the AMA *Guides,* 5th Edition, *continued*

STEP 8   **Indicate whether pain-related impairment (PRI) is ratable or unratable.**

☐ RATABLE. (Check one of the boxes below to indicate the reason why PRI is ratable. Then go to Step 9.)

☐ Individual has pain associated with a medical condition that typically produces both pain and objectively measurable impairment. (See page 570. An example is persistent lumbar radiculopathy following lumbar diskectomy.)

☐ Individual has a well-established pain syndrome that is typically not associated with objectively measurable impairment. (See pages 570-571 and Table 18-1. Examples include headache, postherpetic neuralgia, tic douloureux, erythromelalgia, and CRPS type 1 [RSD].)

☒ Individual has a pain syndrome with the following characteristics: (1) occurs as a component of a condition (such as spinal cord injury) that is ratable according to the conventional rating system; (2) only some of the individuals with the underlying condition have the pain syndrome; and (3) the conventional impairment rating does not capture the added burden of illness borne by individuals who have the associated pain syndrome. (See page 571 and Table 18-2. Examples include postparaplegic pain, phantom limb pain, and brachial plexus avulsion pain.)

☐ UNRATABLE. (Check this option if the individual's PRI does not fit into any of the three groups above. Then go to Step 10.)

STEP 9   **Final Impairment Rating:** (For Ratable Pain-Related Impairment)

a. Conventional Impairment Rating (CIR) (Copy from Step 2) = <u>60% whole person</u>

b. Discretionary PRI allowance: 0%   1%   2%   (3%)

1) Award 0% if you conclude that the individual's CIR adequately encompasses the burden of his or her condition).

2) Award a discretionary 1%, 2%, or 3% whole person impairment if you conclude the burden of illness borne by the individual is slightly greater than the CIR indicates. Award the maximum discretionary allowance of 3% if you conclude that the individual's burden of illness is substantially greater than the CIR indicates.

c. Pain-related impairment (PRI) class (check one—See Step 7b):

☐ Mild   ☐ Moderate   ☒ Moderately Severe   ☐ Severe

d. Check one of the boxes below to indicate which of the following options applies and calculate total impairment.

☐ Conventional impairment rating encompasses the burden of illness adequately

a) CIR = _____ total impairment

☐ Pain-related impairment makes the individual's burden of illness slightly greater than conventional rating indicates

a) CIR = _____
b) Discretionary allowance =
   1%   2%   3%   (circle one)
c) Total impairment = a + b =
   _____%

Pain-Related Impairment Worksheet©
A Training Tool Based on the AMA *Guides,* 5th Edition, *continued*

☒ Pain-related impairment makes the individual's burden of illness substantially greater than conventional rating indicates	a) CIR = <u>60</u>%
	b) Maximum discretionary allowance = 3%
	c) PRI class (from Step 7b) is <u>Moderately Severe</u>
	d) Total impairment = ("a" combined with "b") AND "c"
	  (1) "a" combined with "b" = <u>61%</u> whole person impairment
	  (2) AND individual has (indicate class) <u>moderately severe</u> pain-related impairment

STEP 10   Final Impairment Rating: (For UNRATABLE Pain-Related Impairment)

  a. Conventional Impairment Rating (CIR) (Copy from Step 2) = ___% whole person

  b. If formal pain-related impairment assessment (Steps 4-7 above) was NOT done, STOP. The patient's total impairment is the CIR given in "a" above.

  c. If formal pain-related impairment assessment WAS done,

   1) Indicate the individual's pain-related impairment (PRI) class (check one—See Step 7b):

   ☐ Mild   ☐ Moderate   ☐ Moderately Severe   ☐ Severe

   2) Check one of the boxes below to indicate which of the following options applies and calculate total impairment

☐ Conventional impairment rating encompasses the burden of illness adequately	a) CIR = _____ total impairment

☐ Pain-related impairment makes the individual's burden of illness substantially greater than conventional rating indicates	a) CIR = _____% = total ratable impairment
	b) Also, the individual has unratable PRI. The individual's PRI class is (circle one):
	  Mild
	  Moderate
	  Moderately Severe
	  Severe

Chapter 18

EXAMPLE: SEVERE PRI—CLASS 4

Medical History

A physician performs an impairment evaluation on a 43-year-old woman whom he has treated for several months for chronic neck pain. The woman was involved in a rear-end motor vehicle accident in 1989, leading to persistent neck pain. No clear-cut radiculopathy was present. Anterior C5-C6 and C6-C7 diskectomy and fusion were performed in 1991. The woman did well for a year, then neck pain returned. A C4-C5 anterior diskectomy and fusion were performed in 1993. She did well for 4 years, then had another rear-end motor vehicle accident, with return of neck pain. Anterior diskectomy and fusion at C3-C4 were performed 6 months later. The individual reports persistent pain after the last surgery.

Symptoms

The individual reports midline pain starting at about the C3 level and extending down to the T8 level. Pain is described as spreading from the midline to involve the upper back diffusely on both sides. There is no upper extremity pain, but she describes a symmetric pattern of numbness involving posterior and lateral arms, dorsal forearms, and all five fingers of both hands. No focal weakness, lower extremity symptoms, or problems with bowel or bladder control are reported or detected. Pain is aggravated by almost any neck motion and by UE activities overhead. Also, gentle tactile stimulation of the lower neck and posterior shoulder girdle produces burning pain.

Systems Issues

The individual is out of the work force, except for babysitting for her daughter's children. She receives financial support from her daughter. She does not have a workers' compensation claim, is not engaged in litigation, and is receiving no disability benefits.

Physical Exam

Myofascial pain is reported over the upper trapezius and posterior shoulder girdle bilaterally. Active range of motion of neck was as follows: flexion = 30°, extension = 40°, rotation (right/left) = 60°/50°, lateral bending (right/left) = 30°/25°. Neurologic exam revealed diminished right triceps tendon jerk; diffuse, nonsegmental diminution of pinprick sensation in both upper extremities; and mild weakness in elbow flexion, elbow extension, and shoulder abduction on the left side. No long tract signs were detected.

Diagnostic Testing

Recent electromyography showed no acute denervation in the upper extremities. Recent MRI demonstrated multilevel cervical fusions and mild kyphotic deformity at C3-C4. No compromise of neural elements was found. A bone scan showed increased uptake anteriorly at C4-C7, thought to be consistent with her history of surgery at these levels.

Step 1 of PRI Worksheet
Diagnosis = cervical postlaminectomy syndrome.

Step 2 of PRI Worksheet
Conventional impairment rating (using the Range of Motion model, pp 398ff) = 23% WPI

a. Diagnosis-related impairment (Table 15-7)
   1) 9% for surgically treated disk lesion
   2) 3% for multiple levels
   3) 3% for multiple surgeries
   4) Total = 15% WPI

b. Impairment based on loss of range of motion (pp 417-422)
   1) Loss of flexion/extension = 4%
   2) Loss of lateral bending = 2%
   3) Loss of rotation = 3%
   4) Total = 9%

c. Total conventional impairment (CIR) = combination of 15% and 9% = 23% WPI

Step 7 of PRI Worksheet
Pain-related impairment data. (Note that, to save space, we are printing the information that would usually appear in the PRI Worksheet for this individual. To see how the PRI Worksheet [Form C] might look when completed, see Example Class 3 above.)

a. Pain intensity = 19.

b. Activity interference = 28.

c. Emotional distress = 9.

d. Credibility: Individual seemed genuine. She is not receiving disability benefits, nor is there any pending litigation or disability claim. Credibility score = +9.

Chapter 18

e. Pain behavior: Individual's pain behaviors are difficult to interpret. The overall complexity of her presentation, particularly the fact that she has undergone fusions at four different levels, makes it difficult for an examiner to differentiate between "physiologic" and "nonphysiologic" pain behaviors. Pain behaviors score = 0.

f. Pain-related impairment (PRI) class (Step 7) = severe.

Step 8 of PRI Worksheet
PRI is considered ratable. Individual has pain associated with a medical condition that typically produces both pain and objectively measurable impairment.

Step 9 of PRI Worksheet
Final impairment rating:

a. Conventional impairment rating (23%) combined with discretionary PRI allowance (3%) = 25% WPI.

b. AND individual has severe PRI.

Comment

This individual has significant impairment based on the conventional rating system. In this setting, it is difficult for an examiner to determine whether she should be awarded additional impairment on the basis of her reported pain and pain-related limitations. As a practical matter, there are no normative data that indicate how much pain and pain-related ADL limitations usually occur in individuals who have undergone cervical spine fusions at four levels. Thus, it is difficult to determine whether this individual has "excess pain" or pain that is anticipated and already incorporated into her CIR. In this example, the individual was awarded additional PRI because there was evidence that she was experiencing a severe disruption of almost all of her activities.

Form A Impairment Impact Inventory (I³)©

Name/ID #:_____ **Date:**_____

INSTRUCTIONS: An important part of our evaluation includes examination of pain from YOUR perspective. You know your pain better than anyone, so the information you give will be very helpful.

Please read each question below carefully and then do your best to answer each one. Do not skip any questions. After you have completed the questionnaire, check your responses to make sure that you have answered each question.

Please answer each question below regarding your pain. Circle a number from 0 to 10 (0 = No pain/No aggravation of pain/Rarely), 10 = Most severe can imagine/All of the time).

1. Rate how severe your pain is right now, at this **MOMENT:**

   0   1   2   3   4   5   6   7   8   9   10

   No pain   Most severe can imagine

2. Rate how severe your pain is at its **WORST:**

   0   1   2   3   4   5   6   7   8   9   10

   No pain   Most severe can imagine

3. Rate how severe your pain is on **AVERAGE:**

   0   1   2   3   4   5   6   7   8   9   10

   No pain   Most severe can imagine

4. Rate how much your pain is aggravated (increased, made worse) by **ACTIVITY:**

   0   1   2   3   4   5   6   7   8   9   10

   Activity does not   Most severe can
   make pain worse   imagine after any activity

5. Rate how often/frequently you experience **PAIN:**

   0   1   2   3   4   5   6   7   8   9   10

   Rarely   All the time

Please answer each question regarding your ability to perform each of the activities listed. Circle a number from 0 to 10 (0 = No restrictions/Interference, 10 = Complete/Total restriction/Interference/Inability to perform activity) indicating the impact of your pain on the activity indicated in each question.

6. How much does your pain interfere with your ability to **WALK 1 BLOCK?**

   0   1   2   3   4   5   6   7   8   9   10

   Does not restrict   Pain makes it impossible
   ability to walk 1 block   for me to walk 1 block

7. How much does your pain interfere with your ability to **LIFT 10 POUNDS?**

   0   1   2   3   4   5   6   7   8   9   10

   Does not prevent me   Pain makes it impossible
   from lifting 10 pounds   for me to lift 10 pounds

Chapter 18

Form A Impairment Impact Inventory (I³)©, *continued*

---

8. How much does your pain interfere with your ability to **SIT FOR 1/2 HOUR?**

0   1   2   3   4   5   6   7   8   9   10

Does not restrict my   Pain makes it impossible
ability to sit for 1/2 hour   for me to sit for 1/2 hour

9. How much does your pain interfere with your ability to **STAND FOR 1/2 HOUR?**

0   1   2   3   4   5   6   7   8   9   10

Does not interfere   Pain makes it impossible
with ability to stand for   for me to stand for 1/2 hour
1/2 hour

10. How much does your pain interfere with your ability to **SLEEP?**

0   1   2   3   4   5   6   7   8   9   10

Does not prevent me   Pain makes it
from sleeping   impossible to sleep

11. How much does your pain interfere with your ability to participate in **SOCIAL ACTIVITIES?**

0   1   2   3   4   5   6   7   8   9   10

Does not interfere   Pain completely interferes
with social activities   with social activities

12. How much does your pain interfere with your ability to **TRAVEL UP TO 1 HOUR** by car or bus?

0   1   2   3   4   5   6   7   8   9   10

Does not interfere   Pain makes it impossible
with my ability to travel 1 hour   for me to travel 1 hour

13. In general, how much does your pain interfere with your **DAILY ACTIVITIES?**

0   1   2   3   4   5   6   7   8   9   10

Does not interfere   Pain completely interferes
with daily activities   with daily activities

14. How much do you **LIMIT YOUR ACTIVITIES** to avoid or to prevent your pain from getting worse?

0   1   2   3   4   5   6   7   8   9   10

I do not have to   I have to completely
limit activities at all   limit my activities

15. How much does your pain interfere with your **RELATIONSHIP WITH FAMILY/ PARTNER/SIGNIFICANT OTHERS?**

0   1   2   3   4   5   6   7   8   9   10

Does not interfere   Pain completely interferes
with relationships   with relationships

Please continue on to the next page   2

Form A Impairment Impact Inventory (I³)©, *continued*

16. How much does your pain interfere with your ability to do **ROUTINE OR ORDINARY JOBS/CHORES AROUND YOUR HOME?**

    0   1   2   3   4   5   6   7   8   9   10

    Does not interfere   Pain makes me unable
    with ability to do jobs   to do any jobs around home
    around home

17. How much does your pain interfere with your ability to shower or **BATHE WITHOUT HELP FROM SOMEONE?**

    0   1   2   3   4   5   6   7   8   9   10

    Does not interfere   Pain makes it impossible
    with ability to shower/   for me to shower/bathe
    bathe myself   without help

18. How much does your pain interfere with your ability to **WRITE OR TYPE?**

    0   1   2   3   4   5   6   7   8   9   10

    Does not interfere   Pain makes it impossible
    with my ability to write/type   for me to write/type

19. How much does your pain interfere with your ability to **DRESS YOURSELF?**

    0   1   2   3   4   5   6   7   8   9   10

    Does not interfere   Pain makes it impossible
    with ability to dress myself   for me to dress myself

20. How much does your pain interfere with your ability to **ENGAGE IN SEXUAL ACTIVITIES?**

    0   1   2   3   4   5   6   7   8   9   10

    Does not interfere   Pain makes it impossible
    with sexual activities   to engage in any sexual activity

21. How much does your pain interfere with your ability to **CONCENTRATE** on tasks?

    0   1   2   3   4   5   6   7   8   9   10

    Does not interfere   Pain makes it impossible
    with my ability to concentrate   for me to concentrate

Chapter 18

Form A Impairment Impact Inventory (I³)©, *continued*

For each of the questions in this section, please rate the effect of pain on your mood, how you feel (0 = Good/Not upset, 10 = Bad/Extremely upset)

22. Rate your **OVERALL MOOD** during the past week:

| 0 | 1 | 2 | 3 | 4 | 5 | 6 | 7 | 8 | 9 | 10 |

Extremely high/   Extremely low/
Good   Bad

23. During the past week, how **ANXIOUS OR WORRIED** have you been because of your pain?

| 0 | 1 | 2 | 3 | 4 | 5 | 6 | 7 | 8 | 9 | 10 |

Not at all anxious/   Extremely anxious/
Worried   Worried

24. During the past week, how **DEPRESSED** have you been because of your pain?

| 0 | 1 | 2 | 3 | 4 | 5 | 6 | 7 | 8 | 9 | 10 |

Not at all depressed   Extremely depressed

25. During the past week, how **IRRITABLE** have you been because of your pain?

| 0 | 1 | 2 | 3 | 4 | 5 | 6 | 7 | 8 | 9 | 10 |

Not at all   Extremely
irritable   irritable

26. In general, how **ANXIOUS/WORRIED** are you about **PERFORMING ACTIVITIES BECAUSE THEY MIGHT MAKE YOUR PAIN WORSE?**

| 0 | 1 | 2 | 3 | 4 | 5 | 6 | 7 | 8 | 9 | 10 |

Not at anxious/   Extremely anxious/
Worried   Worried

Form B Instructions for Scoring Form A©

Instructions for Scoring the Impairment Impact Inventory (I³)

I. Basic Instructions

   A. Pain Intensity Section

     1. Add the scores of items 1 through 4

     2. Divide by 4 (to get the average)

     3. Add the score on item 5 to the result in "b"

   B. Interference With Daily Activities Section

     1. Add the scores on items 6 through 21

     2. Divide by 16 (to get the average)

     3. Multiply the result in "b" by 3

   C. Emotional Distress Section

     1. Add the scores on items 22 through 26

     2. Divide by 5 (to get the average)

II. Special Scoring Issues

   A. An individual should be asked to fill out the I³ questionnaire (Form A) on the basis of the pain problems that are the subject of the impairment evaluation.

     1. An individual may have pain problems that are irrelevant to the conditions that are being rated. In that instance, the individual should be instructed to fill out the I³ on the basis of the conditions that are being rated.

     2. An examiner should typically wait until he or she has finished the history and physical examination before asking an individual to fill out the I³. At that time, the examiner should tell the individual what pain problem(s) to consider when filling out the I³.

     3. Example: A 42-year-old man with a history of a motorcycle accident in 1981, with a brachial plexus lesion and a fused right shoulder. Since then, he has had chronic neuropathic pain in his RUE and has been on maintenance opiates. Had auto accident at work in May 2000, with injuries to thoracolumbar spine and right knee. Now has a workers' compensation claim for back and right knee.

       a. The issue here is that the individual has a claim that covers his back and his right knee. However, he had a chronic pain problem before his work injury.

       b. The individual should be instructed to fill out the I³ *solely on the basis of pain in his back and his right knee.*

   B. If an individual circles more than one number when answering an item on the I³ (typically to indicate a range of score), the examiner should compute the mean of the items circled and use this as the score for that item.

     1. If an individual omits items on the I³, prorate his or her scores.

       a. Example: An individual fills out only 14 of the 16 items that compose the ADL interference section of the I³. The examiner should add the individual's total score on these 14 items, divide by <u>14</u>, and then multiply by 3.

       b. If an individual omits more than 25% of the items on any section of the I³, the examiner will need to make a clinical judgment about whether the questionnaire (and, therefore, the entire pain-related assessment procedure) is valid.

©Dennis C. Turk, James P. Robinson, John D. Loeser, 2001.

Form C Pain-Related Impairment Worksheet©
A Training Tool Based on the AMA *Guides,* 5th Edition

STEP 1	Condition(s) being rated on this worksheet:
STEP 2	The Conventional Impairment Rating (CIR) is:___% of whole person
STEP 3	Check ONE of the following:

☐ The Conventional Impairment Rating (CIR) above appears to encompass the burden of this condition(s) <u>adequately.</u>

STOP HERE. The total rating for this condition is the number in STEP 2 above.

☐ The pain-related impairment (PRI) appears to make the burden of the condition(s) <u>slightly</u> greater than the conventional impairment rating (CIR) in STEP 2 above.

SKIP TO STEP 8.

☐ The pain-related impairment (PRI) appears to make the burden of the condition(s) <u>substantially</u> greater than the conventional impairment rating (CIR) in STEP 2 above.

PROCEED TO THE FORMAL PRI ASSESSMENT (Steps 4-7)

FORMAL PAIN-RELATED IMPAIRMENT (PRI) ASSESSMENT

STEP 4	**The I³:** After the history and physical, ask the individual to fill out the Impairment Impact Inventory (I³) given in Table 18-4, pages 576-577. Instruct the individual to answer questions only in relation to the condition(s) being rated.
STEP 5	**Credibility:** Is the individual's presentation credible enough to warrant a formal pain-related impairment (PRI) assessment? (If needed, refer to Behavioral Confounders in Section 18.4, pages 581-583, as well as Section 18.3b, pages 571-572.)

☐ No.

SKIP TO STEP 8. Formal PRI assessment cannot be completed.

☐ Yes.

Circle the number below that best represents the individual's credibility. Enter the number in Step 7.

-10 -9 -8 -7 -6 -5 -4 -3 -2 -1 0 1 2 3 4 5 6 7 8 9 10

Very low credibility	Very high credibility

STEP 6	**Pain Behavior:** Circle the number that best represents the individual's pain behavior. (If needed, refer to pages 579-580 and Table 18-5.) Enter the number in Step 7.

-10 -9 -8 -7 -6 -5 -4 -3 -2 -1 0 1 2 3 4 5 6 7 8 9 10

Pain behaviors are exaggerated, nonphysiologic.	Pain behaviors are appropriate and tend to confirm other clinical findings.

Form C Pain-Related Impairment Worksheet©

A Training Tool Based on the AMA *Guides,* 5th Edition, *continued*

STEP 7

a. Pain-Related Impairment Score (PRI): Copy scores into Table 18-6 to the right:

Section I is from the I^3* (Pain Intensity). ⟶

Section II is from the I^3 (ADL). ⟶

Section III is from the I^3 (Emotional Distress). ⟶

Pain Behavior rating is from Step 6 on page 1 of this worksheet. ⟶

Adjust for credibility using the number copied from Step 5 on page 1 of this worksheet. ⟶

Table 18-6 Worksheet for Calculating Total Pain-Related Impairment Score

1. Sum the scores for Section I of Form A, items 1-4, and divide by 4; add response to item 5. Range is from 0 to 20.	_____
2. Total scores for Section II of Form A, items 6-21, divide by 16, and multiply by 3. Range is from 0 to 30.	_____
3. Sum scores for Section III of Form A, items 22-26, and divide by 5. Range is from 0 to 10.	_____
4. Global pain behavior rating from Table 18-5 (rating should be –10, 0, or +10).	_____
Subtotal steps 1 through 4 (maximum = 70)	_____
5. Physician adjustment based on clinical judgment of individual's credibility. Add or subtract 0 to 10.	_____
6. Total pain-related impairment score = total of steps 1 through 5	_____

*I^3 = Impairment Impact Inventory given in Table 18-4, pages 576-577.

b. The pain-related impairment (PRI) class is (circle one class using total score from Step 7a):

Class:	1 (mild)	2 (moderate)	3 (moderately severe)	4 (severe)
Score	7-24*	25-42	43-60	61-80

Please note: As stated in the AMA *Guides*, 5th Edition, in Table 18-7 on page 584, neither this class nor the corresponding score should be construed to be an impairment rating. That is, they do not represent percentages of whole person impairment.

*A score of 0-6 = no significant pain-related impairment (no class designation)

Chapter 18

Form C Pain-Related Impairment Worksheet©
A Training Tool Based on the AMA *Guides*, 5th Edition, *continued*

STEP 8	**Indicate whether pain-related impairment (PRI) is ratable or unratable.**

☐ RATABLE. (Check one of the boxes below to indicate the reason why PRI is ratable. Then go to Step 9.)

    ☐ Individual has pain associated with a medical condition that typically produces both pain and objectively measurable impairment. (See page 570. An example is persistent lumbar radiculopathy following lumbar diskectomy.)

    ☐ Individual has a well-established pain syndrome that is typically not associated with objectively measurable impairment. (See pages 570-571 and Table 18-1. Examples include headache, postherpetic neuralgia, tic douloureux, erythromelalgia, and CRPS type 1 [RSD].)

    ☐ Individual has a pain syndrome with the following characteristics: (1) occurs as a component of a condition (such as spinal cord injury) that is ratable according to the conventional rating system; (2) only some of the individuals with the underlying condition have the pain syndrome; and (3) the conventional impairment rating does not capture the added burden of illness borne by individuals who have the associated pain syndrome. (See page 571 and Table 18-2. Examples include postparaplegic pain, phantom limb pain, and brachial plexus avulsion pain.)

☐ UNRATABLE. (Check this option if the individual's PRI does not fit into any of the three groups above. Then go to Step 10.)

STEP 9   **Final Impairment Rating:** (For Ratable Pain-Related Impairment)

a. Conventional Impairment Rating (CIR) (Copy from Step 2) = __% whole person

b. Discretionary PRI allowance: 0%   1%   2%   3%

    1) Award 0% if you conclude that the individual's CIR adequately encompasses the burden of his or her condition).

    2) Award a discretionary 1%, 2%, or 3% whole person impairment if you conclude the burden of illness borne by the individual is slightly greater than the CIR indicates. Award the maximum discretionary allowance of 3% if you conclude that the individual's burden of illness is substantially greater than the CIR indicates.

c. Pain-related impairment (PRI) class (check one—See Step 7b):

    ☐ Mild   ☐ Moderate   ☐ Moderately Severe   ☐ Severe

d. Check one of the boxes below to indicate which of the following options applies and calculate total impairment.

☐ Conventional impairment rating encompasses the burden of illness adequately	a) CIR = _____ total impairment
☐ Pain-related impairment makes the individual's burden of illness slightly greater than conventional rating indicates	a) CIR = _____ b) Discretionary allowance = 1% 2% 3% (circle one) c) Total impairment = a + b = ___%

Form C Pain-Related Impairment Worksheet©

A Training Tool Based on the AMA *Guides,* 5th Edition, *continued*

☐ Pain-related impairment makes the individual's burden of illness substantially greater than conventional rating indicates	a) CIR = ___% b) Maximum discretionary allowance = 3% c) PRI class (from Step 7b) is _____ d) Total impairment = ("a"combined with "b") AND "c" (1) "a" combined with "b" = ___% whole person impairment (2) AND individual has (indicate class) _____ pain-related impairment

STEP 10 Final Impairment Rating: (For UNRATABLE Pain-Related Impairment)

a. Conventional Impairment Rating (CIR) (Copy from Step 2) = ___% whole person

b. If formal pain-related impairment assessment (Steps 4-7 above) was NOT done, STOP. The patient's total impairment is the CIR given in "a" above.

c. If formal pain-related impairment assessment WAS done,

1) Indicate the individual's pain-related impairment (PRI) class (check one—See Step 7b):

☐ Mild   ☐ Moderate   ☐ Moderately Severe   ☐ Severe

2) Check one of the boxes below to indicate which of the following options applies and calculate total impairment

☐ Conventional impairment rating encompasses the burden of illness adequately

a) CIR = _____ total impairment

☐ Pain-related impairment makes the individual's burden of illness substantially greater than conventional rating indicates

a) CIR = _____% = total ratable impairment

b) Also, the individual has unratable PRI. The individual's PRI class is (circle one):

Mild

Moderate

Moderately Severe

Severe

Chapter 18

Appendix A

Judging Causation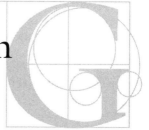

Causation, as defined in the *Guides to the Evaluation of Permanent Impairment, Fifth Edition* (*Guides 5th*), is an identifiable factor that results in a medically identifiable condition. Causes referred to in the *Guides 5th,* and used in workers' compensation settings, include constitutional, exciting, immediate, local precipitating, predisposing, primary, proximate, remote, secondary, specific, and ultimate (*Guides 5th,* p 11).

The determination of causation, along with the diagnosis and permanent impairment rating, are key elements used in disability assessment to assign responsibility and, ultimately, financial liability. Understanding causation is also important from the standpoint of treatment and prevention, on both an individual and a population basis. If the cause of a condition is identified and removed, then prevention of the condition (primary prevention) or of its complications (secondary prevention) is more likely.

Determining causation in complex cases is difficult, because of the multi-factorial nature of injuries and illnesses and our ignorance regarding the spectrum of contributing factors and their relative contributions. We estimate the unknowns and apply relative weights based on a blend of medical evidence, clinical judgment, and legal judgment. Physician evaluators have a responsibility to evaluate the clinical and epidemiologic evidence, interpret the level of certainty of the medical information, and provide this information to interested parties in an understandable format. Ajudicators need to weigh this information, along with their state regulations, to determine the degree of association they can accept as causative.

This appendix is not a comprehensive discussion of the determination of causation. It is a discussion of approaches used by some epidemiologists, physicians, and adjudicators to judge causation, highlighting the complexity of this seemingly simple question: Did this work-related event cause this individual's condition?

Medical and Legal Perspectives on Causation

The approaches to the assessment of causation overlap within the medical and legal arenas: both disciplines rely on deductive reasoning to prove that a particular hypothesis is false and that an alternative hypothesis correctly explains the events. The major differences between the legal and medical arenas are in the extent or burden of proof required to label events as causally related and, in the legal arena, emphasis on the outcome of an individual case.

Medical interpretations of causation rely on clinical experience as well as scientific evidence and medical reports. Medically related research considers an association to indicate a high level of certainty when the association is statistically significant, meaning it is not due to chance more than 95% of the time. In most legal applications, for an event to be causally related, the degree of likelihood must be more likely than not, or >50% burden of proof. Legal statutes focus on different aspects of the causal association—such as predominant cause, proximate cause, and contributing cause—often depending on the degree of uncertainty and association they have financially decided to compensate.

Physician evaluators asked to provide medical input on causation need to focus their assessment on interpreting, weighing, and presenting the medical evidence. Physicians need to understand their state's interpretation of causation and ensure their language is consistent with their state's use of such terms. The legal and adjudicative bodies also need to weigh the medical opinion in light of their regulations and case precedent.

The legal origin of causation is not complex, although its application often is. As noted in Appendix B, Analysis of US Workers' Compensation Statutes, causation can sometimes be as simple as a "but for" test, in which a condition would not have existed "but for" the occurrence of a certain event. In workers' compensation, the legal perspective of causation is the economically and politically acceptable relatedness of workplace events to identifiable medical conditions. Accordingly, since workers' compensation varies in its political and economic reach from state to state, what constitutes the cause of a disease or injury varies, depending on the liberality or parsimony of the legislation that creates workers' compensation.

An interesting recent legislative reform approach has been to narrow the range of causes attributable to workplace events as part of making workers' compensation more affordable to employers. Oregon enacted such restrictions in 1995, requiring that "The worker must prove that employment conditions were the major contributing cause of the disease."[1] The major contributing cause standard means a cause, or combination of causes, that contributes more to the injury for which the worker seeks compensation than all other causes combined, or most of the cause.

In *Smothers v Gresham Transfer*,[2] a recent Oregon Supreme Court case finding that restriction on causation is unconstitutional, the Court noted that Oregon's statutory scheme prior to the 1995 legislation did "not weigh the relative importance of the several causes that bring about the injury—it [was] sufficient if the accident occurring through employment is a contributing cause of the result." The Oregon Supreme Court decided that the "major contributing cause" restriction, combined with the exclusive remedy clause, violated Oregon's constitutional "remedy clause." Oregon's remedy clause, in turn, was traced to the common law provision that for every wrong there is a common law right of redress, or remedy. The Oregon Supreme Court suggests that even contributory causes may be constitutionally protected in Oregon. By eliminating causes that might be contributory, the law impermissibly eliminated any redress for Smothers' alleged workplace exposure.

Hundreds of cases are brought for legal review each year on the grounds that an employer has improperly denied compensation, alleging that the employee has not shown the requisite work-related cause. Almost all the Web sites mentioned in Appendix B contain links to cases adjudicated in the 50 states, and those who wish to read a particular state's approach are invited to start the process through those portals.

Cause in a legal sense also is one adjudicated not by experts in the field of medicine, but usually by nonphysicians, often attorneys. Adjudicators determine if there are sufficient connections as to time, place, probability, and likelihood of association of the result with the alleged causative events that the exposure or accident or other described events arising out of and in the course of the employment "caused" the injury or disease. As noted below, this inquiry generally is not too far afield from the approaches taken by a more scientifically rigorous approach to causation.

From a historical perspective, questions regarding the cause of specific phenomena have been asked since antiquity. Aristotle, for one, noted formal, material, final, and efficient causes in attempting to explain how things come to be.[3] Aristotle criticized Plato and others for maintaining confined and restricted views about the nature and types of causes. The discussions that follow summarize the breadth and depth of contemporary scientific approaches to this inquiry.

Appendix A

Scientific Approach to Causation

Leading philosophers and scientists, including Einstein, have struggled with the approach and evidence required to establish causation. Rothman provides an excellent summary of these debates.[4] According to the philosopher Karl Popper, hypotheses about the world cannot be proved, as with mathematics, but they can be falsified. Hence, the testing of hypotheses occurs in science by virtue of trying to falsify them.[4] Post-Popperian philosophers assert that the process of falsification or refutation is really only a choice between refuting the infrastructure within which the hypotheses emerged or the hypotheses themselves. Brown and others believe that acceptance or rejection of a scientific hypothesis comes through a consensus of the scientific community and that the prevailing scientific viewpoint ("normal science") occasionally undergoes major shifts.[5]

Falsification of a premise, followed by acceptance of its alternative, underlies the acceptance of both experimental and observational studies. When testing a new treatment, the underlying hypothesis is that the new treatment is not significantly better than the standard alternative. The hypothesis is disproved, and the alternative achieves acceptance on the basis of either a significant clinical effect (eg, beta blockers after a myocardial infarction increase longevity) or a smaller clinical effect with significant public health implications (eg, a 30% increase in the risk of breast cancer from alcohol consumption).[5]

In the assessment of causation, the underlying premise is that a particular factor, such as smoking cigarettes, does not lead to the development of a health outcome, such as lung cancer. Once a hypothesis is disproved, its alternative gains support. Multiple, complementary studies within different areas of science are conducted before scientific and popular consensus considers the evidence to be sufficiently compelling to support a causal association. The medical and social consensus that cigarette smoking leads to lung cancer required many studies from the observational and experimental arena. Observational epidemiologic studies initially linking tobacco to chronic obstructive pulmonary disease (COPD) were done in the 1950s, providing early clues to the wide spectrum of health effects of tobacco.[6] Findings from these studies were explored in greater detail through subsequent epidemiologic, toxicologic, and biochemical studies to identify the detrimental and carcinogenic constituents of tobacco, test their effects on cellular components and different species, and understand mechanisms of action.

Epidemiologic Perspective on Causation

Within the medical field, determining causation within populations has probably been most studied by practitioners in the field of epidemiology. A relatively new science that grew after WWII, epidemiology is based on the work of physicians seeking to understand the occurrence of diseases and all factors that contribute to their occurrence, with the goal of facilitating their prevention. The advantage of epidemiology is that it can document causation without concern about dose extrapolation or species variability and can account for potential modifiers.[7] Causation, in epidemiologic terms, is "an event, condition, or characteristic that plays an essential role in producing an occurrence of the disease."[4]

Epidemiologic studies are observational or experimental. Observational studies are classified as cross-sectional, case control (retrospective), or prospective. Cross-sectional and case control studies typically require fewer resources to perform than prospective or experimental studies (eg, clinical trials), but their results are more prone to interpretive errors of causation because of systematic errors, known as bias and confounders. These biases can lead to false conclusions that certain practices are causally related to a health outcome. Trichopoulos, a well-known epidemiologist, conducted a highly publicized study, which has not been replicated, linking coffee drinking and pancreatic cancer.[8] Although he accounted for (controlled for) the effects of smoking 5 years prior to the diagnosis of pancreatic cancer, he did not control for earlier smoking histories that may have been responsible for the perceived differences among coffee drinkers and non–coffee drinkers, leading to a false association.[5] The difficulties in anticipating, identifying, and controlling for systematic errors have led epidemiologists to devise methods for evaluating the strength of medical evidence. Given the multifactorial nature of human disease, some scientists question whether epidemiology has faced a limit in its ability to sort out the complex relationships and interactions among associated risk practices.[5]

Although further understanding of the human genome will provide many answers, the complex interactions between genetic predisposition, the environment, and development of injury or illness are better understood by incorporating epidemiologic evidence.

Models to Assess Causation

Historically, epidemiologists have used different models to assess causation, trying to explain the mutlifactorial nature of conditions using distinct yet complementary methods of analysis. Models to assess causation in epidemiology are receiving greater study.[9,10] Many authors are in agreement that no cause acts alone but rather is conditioned upon contextual circumstances.[10] However, when determining causation—especially to attribute responsibility—evaluators seek to understand the unique contribution of a single risk factor or practice. Models are used to separate and examine these interacting factors. Some epidemiologists recommend that these different models be used less as "rules" and more as "values" that change depending on the study and circumstances. These models have found their way into decision making regarding causation in medical, legal, and potentially regulatory applications.[11] For example, the National Institutes of Health, in their summary *Musculoskeletal Disorders and Workplace Factors,* used widely referenced criteria to assess potential relationships among workplace practices and musculoskeletal disorders.[12]

Hill's criteria, developed by Hill and members of the US Public Health Service, are listed below, grouped, and discussed in the order of importance when assessing causality.[13,14] Due to their limitations with assessment of complex associations, these criteria, often used as rules, are probably best considered as values, which are critically scrutinized and do not require conformity for causal criteria to be met.[11]

1. strength of the association

2. temporality

3. consistency among studies

4. biologic gradient

5. experimental evidence

6. plausibility of a biologic mechanism

7. coherence of evidence

8. analogy to a similar effect produced by a similar agent

9. specificity of outcome

1. **Strength of the association** pertains to the statistical magnitude of the ratio of incidence rates of those with both the condition and the risk factor compared with those with the condition and without the risk factor. The type of ratio and its strength depend on the type of epidemiologic study. Prospective studies generate odds ratios (ORs); case control or retrospective studies generate relative risks (RRs). Both ORs and RRs provide estimates of the risk of a particular health outcome, given a particular practice or exposure.

   The strength of the association is one of the most important parameters used by epidemiologists to identify whether or not an association is causal.[10,15] Many epidemiologists will not strongly consider a factor as causally related unless the OR or RR is 3 or greater.[5,15] Potent risk factors, such as smoking, can overshadow and potentiate other less strong environmental or occupational factors. Single occupational risk factors commonly have RRs or ORs under 4.0. For musculoskeletal disorders and work relatedness, the higher risks occur when multiple risk factors are combined (eg, heavy and repeat lifting with forceful movements is more strongly associated with the development of back disorders than lifting alone).[12] Lower RRs or ORs may be due to a systematic bias, such as confounding; or, as Rothman states, the strength of an association can also simply reflect its prevalence relative to another cause, appearing artificially low or high.[4,9,12]

The epidemiologic literature debates the importance attributed to small studies that show an OR or RR with a confidence interval that includes 1, indicating the results are likely to be due to chance more than 5% of the time.[5] From a medical standpoint, these studies may have important clues for subsequent investigations, but they have not yet met the statistical standards of significance for scientific studies. Consider these possibilities when interpreting either low or high OR or RR.

2. **Temporality** indicates that the cause predated the development of the condition. The necessity of temporality is accepted; discerning this relationship is often problematic. Establishing temporality for a specific factor is most easily recognized in prospective epidemiologic studies, where individuals are initially categorized as participants with or without the purported risk factor. In case control or retrospective studies, identifying a temporal sequence of cause followed by effect is problematic when the exposure is chronic and the initiation is unclear. Furthermore, the clinical condition, such as cancer, may be present but not yet clinically manifest. Although the cancer was detected after exposure to workplace carcinogens, did it develop prior to work due to environmental factors, such as an earlier history of smoking? Recall of exposure can be subject to multiple biases. The effects of multiple biases become less influential when appropriate, multiple comparisons are made using well-designed control groups.

3. **Consistency among studies,** especially by different techniques, refers to the repeated observation in independent studies of an association of different populations and different circumstances. Many interpret consistency across different populations to lend support to an underlying mechanism that operates in different settings.[11] For example, the causal association between asbestos exposure leading to mesothelioma was observed in multiple studies and in different working populations, such as insulators, brake liners, and shipbuilders, all of whom regularly worked with asbestos. Although there is no set number of consistent studies needed to satisfy all evaluators, one study of epidemiologists found that the effect of the number of supportive studies reached saturation after it exceeded 12 studies.[15]

Appendix A

4. **Biologic gradient,** or a dose-response relationship, is commonly cited as an important consideration when present. In many circumstances, a threshold effect is seen. At a low enough level of exposure or activity, the body can compensate, repair, and recover. For some exposures and outcomes, such as cancer, a single exposure may permanently damage critical DNA, preventing normal repair and function and leading to malignant tumor growth. Many biologic effects simply do not exhibit a linear dose-response relationship. For example, the association between some biologic variables, such as cholesterol, weight, and longevity, is U-shaped, with both very low and very high biologic levels associated with adverse health. The need for a biologic gradient needs to be interpreted in the context of the condition or disease, exposure, and individual.

5. **Experimental evidence** to assess etiology directly is less common in humans. Experimental studies from animal models require cautious interpretation due to the limitations of extrapolation. Experimental evidence may provide clarity on the importance of a biologic gradient. Intervention studies may give clues to underlying mechanisms. Randomized trials of preventive strategies, such as ergonomic interventions (eg, shielding vibrating tools), can decrease the development of some conditions (eg, hand-arm vibration syndrome) and provide clues regarding etiology.

6. **Plausibility of a biologic mechanism** is an important consideration when it can be assessed. A biologically plausible association is one for which a reasonable mechanism can be developed, but for which no biologic evidence may exist.[16] For determining whether an agent causes cancer, the International Agency for Research on Cancer (IARC) emphasizes biologic evidence, such as animal studies or biomarkers, discussing the strengths and weaknesses of different types of evidence.[16]

7. **Coherence of evidence** signifies that the association is consistent with the natural history and biology of the disease. The distinction between coherence and plausibility may be blurred. The lack of coherence does not negate an association; however, conflicting information on coherence does raise doubts about the association.

8. **Analogy to a similar effect produced by a similar agent** can enhance the likelihood of associations. Consider, though, that this may increase the likelihood of understanding but still not be transferable to a different situation.

9. **Specificity of outcome** refers to a cause leading to a single effect. This is probably the least helpful value. Given the interdependence of our organ and body systems, it is unlikely that a single exposure or cause leads to a single effect, unless the body's homeostatic mechanisms can sufficiently compensate for the other effects that are not clinically manifest. Whether cigarette smoking produces lung cancer, another smoking-associated cancer, or respiratory changes, such as COPD, depends on the individual's susceptibility and other environmental influences.

A major limitation of Hill's criteria is that they do not provide a framework in which to analyze the multifactorial nature of injury and disease and the relative contributions of multiple causes that commonly interact, producing additive or synergistic effects.

Rothman's model addresses a conceptual framework to consider these inter-relationships.[4] Rothman originated a widely used concept in epidemiology regarding the role of "sufficient and component causes."[4] A "sufficient cause" is a set of minimal conditions and events that inevitably produces disease; "minimal" implies that none of the conditions or events is superfluous. The completion of a sufficient cause may be considered equivalent to the onset of a disease. Although problematic for purposes of determining causation and compensation, Rothman appropriately notes that "for biological effects, most and sometimes all of the consequences of a sufficient cause are unknown."[4]

Each sufficient cause is made up of a constellation of component causes. The sufficient cause can represent the underlying mechanism of the condition. There may be more than one sufficient cause, and component causes can be present in more than one sufficient cause. Component causes interact with each other to produce disease.[4]

For example, consider the controversial case of an assembly line worker with high-repetition but low-force work, and carpal tunnel syndrome (CTS) that she alleges is work related. Her relevant medical history is diabetes under moderate control. Her hobbies included knitting, which she states she discontinued when she developed the pain at work.

Based on Rothman's model and an understanding of the pathophysiology of CTS, consider two possible sufficient and component causes, diagrammed below.

Appendix A

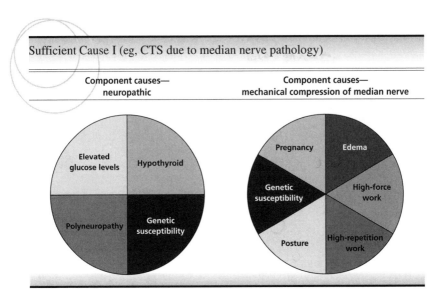

Sufficient Cause I (eg, CTS due to median nerve pathology)

Component causes—
neuropathic

Component causes—
mechanical compression of median nerve

Although carpal tunnel syndrome is most strongly associated with work that is high repetition and high force, the risk for developing CTS is increased with high-repetition work, even if high-force activities are absent.[12] The worker's high-repetition work can be interpreted as a component cause but insufficient by itself in the development of CTS. Other potential component causes would be her diabetes and knitting, due to repeated wrist flexion.

Suppose this individual had bilateral CTS of similar severity and did not use her left hand significantly at work. Under these circumstances, one could postulate that the CTS may be due primarily to her diabetes and non–work-related median nerve changes, as in Sufficient Cause I.

Rothman's model raises some interesting interpretation concerns for medical evaluators and legal adjudicators. In Rothman's model, the effects of a causal agent cannot occur unless the other complementary causes are present to create the conditions of a sufficient cause. For example, an individual may not acquire CTS, even with forceful, repetitive work, because he or she has an anatomically large tunnel that can accommodate additional swelling or changes without compressing the median nerve. Another individual may acquire CTS with less workplace force and repetition because of an underlying predisposition due to diabetes, thyroid disease, or pregnancy. Women are known to be at higher risk for CTS compared to men, possibly due to either hormonal or anatomic differences. Although being female is a risk factor for CTS, it does not cause CTS. A central question, then, is how, in Rothman's model, are component yet insufficient "causes" to be addressed in the medical and legal determination?

Given the complexity of the issues, the physician needs to integrate information from both epidemiologic and clinical assessments and weigh the contribution of the relative risk factors.

Medical Determination—Epidemiologist's Perspective

In one study, when epidemiologists were asked to attribute causality to 12 summaries of evidence concerning a disease and exposure, several characteristics were most important in their decision:

1. statistical significance

2. if alternative explanations could be refuted

3. strength of the association and adjunct information concerning biologic, factual, and theoretical coherence.[15]

Some leading epidemiologists indicate that they consider the strength of the association, with a 3 or greater increased risk, and a highly plausible biologic mechanism to be essential before considering a relationship to be causal.[5,11] Even among epidemiologists, agreement on causal judgments occurred only 12% more often than expected by chance.[11,15]

Clinical Practice

Physicians who integrate medical care delivery and prevention make assessments regarding causation as a standard part of medical assessment. A common medical evaluation includes an assessment of the importance of blood pressure, exercise, and cholesterol levels on the risk of developing cardiovascular disease. These assessments reflect an integration of both the underlying science that supports the use of these risk factors and their assessment within each individual.

An accelerating trend in medicine has been toward the use of evidence-based medicine (EBM) in clinical practice and medical decision making. Evidence-based medicine is the conscientious, explicit, and judicious use of current best evidence in making decisions about the care of individual patients. The practice of EBM means integrating individual clinical expertise with the best available external clinical evidence from systematic research.[17]

Limitations in EBM are an insufficient number of high-quality studies on which to base the majority of clinical decisions and difficulty in extrapolating from population findings to individual management. When adequate research is available though, which can be extrapolated and appropriately integrated into health care decisions, the level of accuracy will increase as decisions are made based on population experience instead of limited individual perspectives. Numerous free medical databases and resources are now available on the Internet, with MEDLINE being a primary source for accessing medical research.[18]

Practical Applications for Determining Causation

When the medical evaluator is asked to assess causation, the following steps may be of assistance:

1. Identify the diagnosis and permanent impairment.

2. Research the medical literature to identify all factors and social practices that may be component causes in producing the condition.

3. Investigate uncertain risk factors with the criteria listed above, concentrating on the strength of the association, temporality, consistency among studies, and biologic plausiblity.

4. Identify known or associated risk factors for the individual, using the medical records, history, and thorough clinical evaluation.

5. Determine the temporal relationship between the risk factors and development of the condition for the individual being evaluated.

6. Identify probable component and sufficient causes.

7. Identify temporal relationships among component and sufficient causes.

8. Identify a level of certainty or probability, as more likely than not, whether the component cause was a proximal or major contributor based on the above considerations.

9. Determine apportionment among multiple risk factors if asked and feasible.

10. Discuss how in the chain of events the "risk factor" has contributed or led to the outcome.

As an example of assessment of causation, consider an actual case, *Smothers v Gresham*,[2] discussed in the context listed above.

In the *Smothers* case, the employee worked as a truck lube technician for a trucking, transfer, and storage company. He worked in a pit 4 feet deep, so as to access vehicle chassis lubrication points. Nearby, trucks were washed by other employees using a spray mix of diluted sulfuric acid and small amounts of hydrochloric and hydrofluoric acids. When the doors to the shop were open, acid mist and fumes from the truck washing area drifted into the shop and down into the pit where Mr Smothers worked. For several months, Smothers experienced headaches, as well as itching, burning, and watering eyes.

In January 1993, Smothers developed an upper respiratory infection that progressed to pneumonia, requiring a 5-day hospitalization. He returned to work but sustained another episode of pneumonia in February 1993. In November 1993, his physician diagnosed him with bronchitis. In December 1993, his coworkers found him lying on the lunch room floor, coughing and in distress.

During December, he was off work with a repeated diagnosis of bacterial bronchitis. He called in sick several times and eventually quit because his illness prevented him from working there. He filed a workers' compensation claim, which was denied because he was not able to prove that his respiratory problems had their origins in workplace conditions that were "the major contributing cause" of his respiratory ailment. Smothers then filed suit, alleging that Gresham was negligent for exposing him to the fumes that led to his lung problems, as well as skin blisters; pain and swelling in the joints of his hands, elbows, and knees; degeneration of his toenails, fingernails, and teeth; and other physical ailments. The negligence suit was allowed to proceed because a predominant cause standard left him without a remedy under Oregon's workers' compensation standard.

Given these limited facts, the causal relation between Smothers' workplace exposures and his resulting maladies can be examined using the above-described 10-step process. Although the information presented is insufficient to fully analyze this case, the process described below is systematic and can direct the evaluator to obtain the additional information needed to assess probability and causation.

1. Diagnoses and permanent impairments: Sort out the diagnoses here. Possibilities include chronic bronchitis, bronchiectasis, asthma, dermatitis, rheumatologic disorders. Determine any permanent impairment based on the *Guides.*

2. Medical literature review: What medical impairments are associated with the described workplace exposures, eg, acids (hydrofluoric, hydrochloric, sulfuric) and lubricating oils? What nonworkplace and workplace exposures are suspected to cause the above conditions?

3. Characterize the associations between acid exposure and, for instance, chronic bronchitis or pneumonia. Is the association strong, temporally consistent, and of sufficient duration? Was there any prior exposure that may have led to the pneumonia? Is it biologically plausible, based on the degree of exposure, other health factors, and concerns?

4. What are Smothers' own risk factors? Is he or was he a smoker or exposed to chronic smoking? Is he diabetic, or does he have a history of asthma or other conditions?

Appendix A

5. Is there a temporal relationship between Smothers' exposure to the identified acids and the appearance of his various symptoms? Were there less serious episodes of respiratory problems prior to his work with Gresham Transfer?

6. What are the component and sufficient cause(s), on a more probable than not basis? Can a unified explanation account for his multiple body system complaints?

7. Determine whether a true temporal association exists between the diagnoses and the likely sufficient and component causes, eg, bronchitis, pneumonia, and acid mist and fume exposure, and other component causes such as smoking and infections. If temporality is not met, causation cannot be demonstrated.

8. Assess the level of probability and whether the "cause," if any, was a proximal or major contributor.

9. If feasible, consider apportionment of risk. Is the workplace exposure accountable for only a proportionate share?

10. Discuss in a narrative how the "risk factor," eg, the acid exposure, either contributed or led to the outcome.

References

1. ORS 656.802(2)(a).

2. *Smothers v Gresham Transfer,* __ OR. __, __P3d __, slip opinion SC S44512, May 10, 2001 (http://www.publications.ojd.state.or.us/S44512.htm).

3. On generation and corruption. In: McKeon, ed. *Basic Works of Aristotle.* Book II. New York, NY: Random House; 1941:chap 9; and Physics. In: McKeon, ed. *Basic Works of Aristotle.* Book II. New York, NY: Random House; 1941: chaps 3-9.

4. Rothman KJ. *Modern Epidemiology.* New York, NY: Little, Brown and Co; 1986:7-21.

5. Taubes G. Epidemiology faces its limits. *Science.* 1995;269:164-169.

6. US Public Health Service. *The Health Consequences of Smoking: Cancer.* Washington, DC: Office of the Surgeon General, US Dept of Health and Human Services; 1982.

7. Trichopoulos D. Letters—the discipline of epidemiology. *Science.* 1995;269:1326.

8. MacMahon B, Yen S, Trichopoulos D, Warren K, Nardi G. Coffee and cancer of the pancreas. *N Engl J Med.* 1981;304:630-633.

9. Kaufman JS, Poole C. Looking back on "causal thinking in the health sciences." *Annu Rev Public Health.* 2000;21:101-119.

10. Weed DL, Hursting SD. Biologic plausibility in causal inference: current method and practice. *Am J Epidemiol.* 1998;147:415-425.

11. Poole C. Causal values. *Epidemiol.* 2001;12:139-141.

12. *Musculoskeletal Disorders and Workplace Factors. A Critical Review of Epidemiologic Evidence for Work-Related Musculoskeletal Disorders of the Neck, Upper Extremity and Low Back.* US Dept of Health and Human Services. July 7, 1997.

13. Hill AB. The environment and disease: association or causation? *Proc R Soc Med.* 1965;58:295-300.

14. US Public Health Service. Smoking and health: report of the Advisory Committee to the Surgeon General of the Public Health Service. Washington, DC: US Department of Health, Education and Welfare; 1964. PHS publication 1103.

15. Holman CDJ, Arnold-Reed DE, de Klerk N, McComb C, English D. A psychometric experiment in causal inference to estimate evidential weights used by epidemiologists. *Epidemiol.* 2001;12:246-254.

16. Tomatis L, ed. Cancer: causes, occurrence and control. Lyon, France: International Agency for Research on Cancer; 1990:97-125. IARC scientific publication 100.

17. Sackett DL, Rosenberg WM, Gray JA, Haynes RB, Richardson WS. Evidence-based medicine: what it is and what it isn't. *BMJ.* 1996;312:71-72.

18. National Library of Medicine and Medline: www.nlm.nih.gov.

Appendix A

Appendix B

Analysis of US Workers' Compensation Statutes

This appendix discusses the history and philosophy of workers' compensation laws in the United States. It provides a state-by-state overview that includes contact names, Web sites where workers' compensation information can be obtained, and a brief discussion of the *Guides'* use in each state.

Many states use a statutory schedule to rate disability for amputations, hearing and sight losses, hernias, and disfigurement. These schedules frequently vary from the *Guides* ratings for amputation. In states that have a schedule and that also use the *Guides,* the *Guides* is usually used only in cases where the schedule does not address a body part or system, eg, internal organs, skin disease (nondisfiguring), and hematopoietic disorders.

History and Summary of Workers' Compensation Statutes

History

Workers' compensation is a historical product of 19th-century European industrialization. Some authors attribute its creation as a legislative system to Chancellor Bismarck in Germany. It was adopted in England in the 1800s and was first adopted in the United States in New York shortly after 1900. A constitutional challenge briefly postponed widespread adoption of workers' compensation laws in the United States, but nearly all states had a workers' compensation law in one form or another by 1920. In most states, workers' compensation is mandatory for most employers. Texas is the most populous exception.

Prior to the enactment of these laws, an employee injured in an accident arising out of and in the course of employment had the right to bring suit against his employer, usually based on the employer's negligence. Three types of employer defenses made it unlikely that the employee could win these lawsuits. The defenses, known as the "unholy trinity," were the employee's assumption of the risk created by the employer's negligence, the employee's contributory or comparative negligence, and the defense that the accident resulting in the injury was caused by a coworker rather than the employer.

As with other populist causes of the early 20th century, newspaper accounts of outlandish verdicts in the few successful cases and reports of widows and orphans receiving nothing after the death or complete incapacitation of the family wage earner led to broad public awareness of the injustice of workplace injury. A common political rallying cry was often published that the blood of the workman is a part of the cost of the product and ought to be passed on to the purchaser no differently than the depreciation or amortization of other means of production. Thus, enactment of workers' compensation, along with antitrust, food and drug, and similar laws, was part of the early 20th century's political and social landscape. A noticeable difference in the United States is that workers' compensation is not nationally uniform, and benefits and coverages differ from state to state.

Workers' compensation is a compulsory insurance system in which nearly all risks related to workplace injury and disease are covered. The insurance, often classed as a form of casualty insurance rather than life or health insurance, is offered either by a state-chartered insurance fund or through private sureties or carriers or, in the case of some employers, self-insurance. Some states allow insurance only through the state fund or self-insurance, some allow competition among the state fund and private carriers, and some have no state fund. In a few states, the state fund is administered by the same agency that adjudicates benefits, although the pattern in most states is for the fund to be operated independently of the adjudicatory court, board, or commission.

Since their adoption, most workers' compensation laws have precluded any form of legal action by a covered worker against his or her employer other than the remedies specified in the workers' compensation law. This is known as the "exclusive remedy." Accordingly, most fault-based legal claims against an employer are barred, on the premise that the injured worker's claims for common law damages, including general damages and damages for pain and suffering, are abrogated in return for "sure and certain relief." "Sure and certain relief" consists of medical benefits and income benefits for functional or anatomic loss and income benefits for any lost earning capacity that occurs as a consequence of the functional or anatomic loss, all without any traditional defenses from the "unholy trinity." Exceptions to the exclusive remedy vary from state to state.

Sure and certain relief is also assumed to mean that the injury or disease that results from exposure or accident arising out of and in the course of employment is expeditiously treated by an insurance adjuster or claims administrator. If, after reasonable inquiry, facts exist to suggest that the condition did not arise out of and in the course of employment, the adjuster may, usually within a prescribed time limit, deny liability for benefits. Benefit denials may also arise when facts, especially medical evidence and reports, fail to identify a workplace cause for the condition.

Another premise of these laws is that the injured worker should be restored to preinjury health as promptly as possible by the employer's provision of reasonable and thorough medical and hospital care. Workers' compensation benefits are generally characterized as medical or income benefits. Medical benefits include payment to doctors, hospitals, physical therapists, pharmacists, home health nurses, nursing homes, and other allied health care providers. Each jurisdiction's law varies as to what constitutes a medical expense payable under its workers' compensation law.

Medical Implication

Physicians play a key role in the disbursement of benefits, starting immediately on a worker's first postaccident or postexposure medical encounter. The physician's opinion about the injured worker's work ability is usually addressed in one of three ways: able to return to work with no restrictions (commonly called a "medical-only" claim); able to return to work with some restrictions (often called a "light duty release"); or unable to return to any work. In the latter two instances, some type of income benefit will be made available during the period of recovery or healing. This income benefit is known as "temporary disability." (For an injured/diseased worker unable to perform any work, the benefit rate is set as either a percentage of the injured worker's preinjury wage or a percentage of the average weekly wage of all workers in the jurisdiction.) *Failure of a treating physician immediately after the first postincident medical encounter to describe the limitation of the worker's ability may preclude the injured worker from receiving this temporary income benefit.*

In situations where the worker may return to work but with a physician's restrictions, the injured worker may be required to return to work if work within the medically prescribed restrictions is available. In some states, the work must be with the same employer. The worker's failure or neglect to return to "suitable" employment may bar him or her from any temporary disability benefit. If no work is available within the limitations or restrictions imposed by the physician, the employee is usually entitled to the total amount of disability allowed for workers who are totally precluded from work during the period of recovery. Sometimes work is available but at a lower rate of pay than the worker's preinjury wage. When lower-paying work is offered, the employer may be required to make up the "differential" between the rate for total disability and the actual wage paid. This is called "partial temporary disability" (PTD).

In situations where the worker is unable to return to any work, the physician's notes of this diagnosis or finding are critical. A worker whose work-related injury precludes any work during the period of recovery is usually entitled to "total temporary disability" (TTD) benefits. These benefits are a percentage, from 55% to 75%, and most commonly 66⅔%, of either the worker's pretax wage at the time of injury or a similar percentage of a state average for all or some group of workers.

EXAMPLE

Raphael, a farmworker, is struck by a bull while cleaning livestock pens, and his upper femur is fractured. He is transported to a rural community hospital and placed in a cast. The emergency room doctor's notes reveal no information about whether the cast prevents any return to work. Therefore, the claims adjuster denies Raphael's receipt of total temporary disability benefits. His recovery is uneventful and the bone achieves a near perfect union. To obtain his benefits, Raphael hires an attorney and receives his temporary disability benefits 20 weeks after the accident. The attorney takes the physician's deposition to demonstrate that the casting of the injury is a totally, though temporary, disabling treatment. While Raphael's total, temporary incapacitation from work may seem obvious, the physician's initial failure to make it explicitly known delayed Raphael's benefit and required him to inccur an attorney's fee.

Temporary disability benefits continue only until a worker achieves maximal medical improvement (MMI).

Calculation of Benefits

In most workers' compensation cases, the injured worker recovers with little or no permanent loss and has received coverage for medical benefits and an amount for lost wages.

Permanent partial disability is frequently developed on a 500-week or 300-week whole person model of compensation. Some workers' compensation laws hypothesize a "whole person" whose economic value is established at 500 weeks. For permanent impairments less than that total, and any disability less than a total that exceeds the impairment, the award equals the percentage of impairment or disability inclusive of impairment multiplied by 500 weeks. The resulting percentage of weeks is then multiplied by a weekly dollar amount to determine the dollar value of the permanent disability income benefit.

EXAMPLE

Marcia receives a 21% whole person impairment (WPI) for a work-related brachial plexus injury. The impairment also reduces her wage-earning capacity by 35%. Permanent disability benefits in Marcia's state are $325 per week, and the whole person is a 500-week model. Her disability, including the impairment, is deemed to be 175 weeks (0.35 x 500). Marcia's income benefit is 175 weeks at $325/week, or $56,875.

Statutory Standards for Scheduled Permanent Disabilities

Many states utilize a "schedule" for amputations, loss of vision, and loss of hearing. Some states also provide for loss of teeth, a loss that would, under the *Guides,* result in a 0% impairment.

A typical schedule using a 500-week whole person is as follows. This schedule's equivalent percentage of the whole person is indicated in brackets; the Fifth Edition's rating is in parentheses.

> Idaho Code §72-428. SCHEDULED INCOME BENEFITS FOR LOSS OR LOSSES OF USE OF BODILY MEMBERS. An employee who suffers a permanent disability less than total and permanent shall, in addition to the income benefits payable during the period of recovery, be paid income benefits for such permanent disability in an amount equal to fifty-five percent (55%) of the average weekly state wage stated against the following scheduled permanent impairments respectively:

	Weeks	[WPI%]	(Guides 5th %)
(1) Amputations of Upper Extremities			
Forequarter amputation	350	[70%]	(70%)
Disarticulation at shoulder joint	300	[60%]	(60%)
Amputation of arm above deltoid insertion	300	[60%]	(60%)
Amputation of arm between deltoid insertion and elbow joint	285	[58%]	(60%)
Disarticulation at elbow joint	285	[58%]	(57%)
Amputation of forearm below elbow joint proximal to insertion of biceps tendon	285	[58%]	(54%-56%)
Amputation of forearm below elbow joint distal to insertion of biceps tendon	270	[54%]	(54%-56%)
Disarticulation at wrist joint	270	[54%]	—
Midcarpal or midmetacarpal amputation of hand	270	[54%]	(54%)

	Weeks	[WPI%]	(Guides 5th %)
Amputation of all fingers except thumb at metacarpophalangeal joints	160	[32%]	(32%)
Amputation of thumb At metacarpophalangeal joint or with resection of carpometacarpal bone	110	[22%]	(22%)
At interphalangeal joint	80	[16%]	(11%)
Amputation of index finger At metacarpophalangeal joint or with resection of metacarpal bone	70	[14%]	(11%)
At proximal interphalangeal joint	55	[11%]	(8%)
At distal interphalangeal joint	30	[6%]	(5%)
Amputation of middle finger At metacarpophalangeal joint or with resection of metacarpal bone	55	[11%]	(11%)
At proximal interphalangeal joint	45	[9%]	(8%)
At distal interphalangeal joint	25	[5%]	(5%)
Amputation of ring finger At metacarpophalangeal joint or with resection of metacarpal bone	25	[5%]	(5%)
At proximal interphalangeal joint	20	[4%]	(4%)
At distal interphalangeal joint	12	[2.4%]	(3%)
Amputation of little finger At metacarpophalangeal joint or with resection of metacarpal bone	15	[3%]	(5%)
At proximal interphalangeal joint	10	[2%]	(4%)
At distal interphalangeal joint	5	[1%]	(3%)
(2) Amputations of Lower Extremities			
Hemipelvectomy	250	[50%]	(50%)
Disarticulation at hip joint	200	[40%]	(40%)
Amputation above knee joint with short thigh stump (3" or less below tuberosity of ischium)	200	[40%]	(40%)
Amputation above knee joint with functional stump	180	[36%]	(32%)
Disarticulation at knee joint	180	[36%]	(32%)
Gritt[i]-Stokes amputation	180	[36%]	—
Amputation below knee joint with short stump (3" or less below intercondylar notch)	180	[36%]	(32%)
Amputation below knee joint with functional stump	140	[28%]	(28%)
Amputation at ankle (Syme)	140	[28%]	(25%)

	Weeks	[WPI%]	(Guides 5th %)
Partial amputation of foot (Chopart's)	105	[21%]	(18%)
Midmetatarsal amputation	70	[14%]	(16%)
Amputation of all toes At metatarsophalangeal joints	42	[8.4%]	(9%)
Amputation of great toe With resection of metatarsal bone	42	[8.4%]	
At metatarsophalangeal joint	25	[5%]	(5%)
At interphalangeal joint	25	[5%]	(2%)
Amputation of lesser toe (2nd-5th) With resection of metatarsal bone	7	[1.4%]	(2%)
At metatarsophalangeal joint	4	[0.8%]	(1%)
At proximal interphalangeal joint	3	[0.6%]	(0%)
At distal interphalangeal joint	1	[0.2%]	(0%)
(3) Loss of Vision and Hearing			
Total loss of vision of one eye	150	[30%]	
Loss of one eye by enucleation	175	[35%]	
Total loss of binaural hearing	175	[35%]	

(4) Total loss of use. Income benefits payable for permanent disability attributable to permanent total loss of use or comparable total loss of use of a member shall not be less than as for the loss of the member.

(5) Partial loss or partial loss of use. Income benefits payable for permanent partial disability attributable to permanent partial loss or loss of use of a member shall be not less than for a period as the permanent impairment attributable to the partial loss or loss of use of the member bears to total loss of the member.

This example is based on a 500-week whole person, so each 5 weeks equals 1% of the whole person.

Note that the schedule is similar to the *Guides 5th* impairment estimates for many upper extremity and lower extremity amputations. But the schedule's traditional ranking of the digits of the hand has relatively more value from index to small finger, rather than the *Guides 5th*'s treatment of the middle and index amputation as the same, or similar treatment of the ring and small finger. There are also some discrepancies in the toes between this schedule and the *Guides 5th*.

In addition, some injuries are deemed total and permanent. In some states, total, permanent disability often requires the employer to provide lifetime income and medical benefits. Some purely anatomic conditions may create a presumption of total, permanent disability.

Appendix B

Statutes that create these presumptions may look like the following:

Idaho Code §72-407. CERTAIN INJURIES DEEMED TOTAL AND PERMANENT.

In case of the following injuries, if the employer disputes that the claimant is totally and permanently disabled, the burden of proof shall be on the employer to prove by clear and convincing evidence that the claimant is not permanently and totally disabled.

(1) The total and permanent loss of sight in both eyes.

(2) The loss of both feet at or above the ankle.

(3) The loss of both hands at or above the wrist.

(4) The loss of one (1) hand and one (1) foot.

(5) An injury to the spine resulting in permanent and complete paralysis of both legs or arms or of one (1) leg and one (1) arm.

(6) An injury to the skull resulting in incurable imbecility or insanity.

The above enumeration is not to be taken as exclusive.

An interesting aspect of these traditional "presumptive total permanent disabilities" is that they allow the sum to be greater than the parts, typically the opposite of the approach taken in the Combined Values Charts of the Fifth and prior editions of the *Guides.*

Impairments that are not included in a schedule like the one above are often adjudicated or evaluated based on the *Guides.*

State-by-State Summary

Alabama

Alabama uses a traditional amputation schedule and the AMA *Guides*. The whole person is valued at 300 weeks, so a 10% WPI would equal 30 weeks of benefits. Alabama's use of the *Guides* is not mandatory. Alabama Administrative Code states that the "fourth edition shall be the recommended guide." 480-5-5-35. Alabama also rates hernias according to statute. Code of Alabama 25-5-57(a)(6).

Alabama Department of Industrial Relations
Workers' Compensation Division
Scottie Spates, Administrative Chief
649 Monroe St, Montgomery, AL 36131
334 242-2868 or 800 528-5166
Fax: 334 242-8843
Web site: www.dir.state.al.us
E-mail: webmaster@dir.state.al.us

Regulations, including fee schedules, may be found at:
www.alabamaadministrativecode.state.al.us/docs/inrel/index.html

Alaska

According to Alaska Statutes Sec. 23.30.190, Alaska adopts the most recent version of the *Guides* within 90 days after the month of publication. The percentage of impairment is multiplied by $177,000 to determine the indemnity or income benefit award. Alaska does not have its own schedule for amputations, but it does consider loss of hands, feet, arms, legs, eyes, or any two of them to constitute total, permanent disability.

Workers' Compensation Division
Paul L. Grossi, Director
PO Box 25512, Juneau, AK 99802-5512
907 465-2790
Fax: 907 465-2797
Web site: www.labor.state.ak.us/wc/wc.htm
E-mail address for general information: Bruce_Dalrymple@labor.state.ak.us

Appendix B

Arizona

Arizona's use of the *Guides* is based on the *Guides* as evidence to support a medical opinion. The *Guides* is not formally adopted by regulation or statute, although it clearly is helpful in supplementing Arizona's statutory disability schedule, found in §23-1044, Arizona Revised Statutes. Arizona considers a combination of multiple amputations and binocular blindness to be total, permanent disability. §23-1045, Arizona Revised Statutes. Disability compensation for disfigurement, including loss of teeth, is limited to 18 months. Disability generally is calculated based on the difference between pre- and postinjury wages, multiplied by a certain number of months.

Arizona Industrial Commission
Larry Etchechury, Director
Phoenix Office
800 W Washington St, Phoenix AZ 85007

Claims Division
602 542-4661
Fax: 602 542-3373
Web site: www.ica.state.az.us/
E-mail: webmaster@ica.state.az.us

Arkansas

Arkansas uses a traditional amputation schedule for rating disability, which also refers to loss of hearing and vision and loss of testes. Nonscheduled impairment is addressed by rule, and the rule refers to the Fourth Edition of the *Guides,* but excluding straight leg raising (SLR) tests and range-of-motion (ROM) tests in assessing spine impairment. ROM, SLR, and pain complaints are not considered objective findings and may not be considered by physicians or workers' compensation judges in determining impairment. AWCC Rule 34. Also, the laws that mention both scheduled and nonscheduled awards state, "the guide shall not include pain as a basis for impairment." Arkansas has specific laws for rating hernia. Mental injury and injury to heart and lungs have special rules for proof of causation.

State of Arkansas Workers' Compensation Commission
4th and Spring Streets
PO Box 950, Little Rock, AK 72203-0950
501 682-3930 or 800 622-4472
Legal Advisor Direct: 800 250-2511
Arkansas Relay System TDD: 800 285-1131
Web site: www.awcc.state.ar.us/
E-mail: rlacy@awcc.state.ar.us

California

California uses a guide of its own. The schedule accounts for not only anatomic loss but also age and occupation. Although comprehensive, it contains guidelines for rating nonscheduled disabilities by analogy to scheduled ones. California's schedule may be downloaded from the Web site www.dir.ca.gov/DWC/PDR.pdf.

California treats loss of both hands, both eyes, "practically total paralysis," and severe brain injuries as total, permanent disability. *Total permanent disability awards are paid for life. California does not use the AMA* Guides.

Headquarters
Del Gaines, Northern Area Supervisor
455 Golden Gate Ave, 2nd Fl
PO Box 420603, San Francisco, CA 94142
415 703-5030

Dennis Ehrhardt, Central Area Supervisor
6150 Van Nuys Blvd, Rm 105, Van Nuys, CA 91401-3373
818 901-5376

Tess Snaer, Southern Area Supervisor
7575 Metropolitan Dr, Ste 202, San Diego, CA 92108
619 767-2170
Web site: www.dir.ca.gov/DWC/dwc_home_page.htm

Colorado

This state has developed its own guidelines based largely on the revised Third Edition of the *Guides.* Colorado also has a schedule established by statute. Nonscheduled impairments result in medical impairment benefits and require multiplication of the rating by an age factor times 400 weeks times a weekly benefit rate. Disfigurement for parts of the body normally exposed to view is limited to $2,000. Colorado utilizes treatment guidelines in a number of areas for occupational medicine.

Colorado Division of Workers' Compensation
1515 Arapahoe, Denver, CO 80202-2117
Customer Service: 303 318-8700
Toll-free: 888 390-7936
Spanish-speaking callers: 800 685-0891
Fax: 303 575-8882
Web site: workerscomp.cdle.state.co.us/default.htm
E-mail: workers.comp@state.co.us

Connecticut

Compensation for anatomic loss is limited to scheduled disabilities. However, when certain body systems are affected by less than total loss or loss of use, the *Guides* may still be used for medical evidence of the partial impairment. Connecticut also schedules certain presumptive total permanent disabilities for paraplegia, double amputations, blindness, and severe head injury. Connecticut treats the back as a scheduled body part to a maximum of 374 weeks. The cervical spine is scheduled at 117 weeks. A whole person is considered to equal 520 weeks of disability payments.

State of Connecticut Workers' Compensation Commission
Office of the Chairman
Capitol Place, 21 Oak St, Hartford, CT 06106
860 493-1500
Fax: 860 247-1361
Web site:wcc.state.ct.us/index2.htm
E-mail: wcc.chairmansoffice@po.state.ct.us

District of Columbia

The District uses the *Guides* and a disability schedule.

Office of Workers' Compensation
Office of Labor Standards
DC Department of Employment Services
1200 Upshur St NW, 3rd Fl, Washington, DC 20011
202 576-6265
Web site: does.dc.gov/services/wkr_comp.shtm

Delaware

Delaware provides a schedule for disabilities. The schedule includes a maximum award for disfigurement. Delaware accepts the *Guides* as evidence in cases of nonscheduled disabilities but does not mandate its use by either statute or regulation.

Delaware Office of Workers' Compensation
John Kirk, Administrator
4425 N Market St, Wilmington, DE 19802
Wilmington: 302 761-8200
Milford: 302 422-1392
Web site: www.delawareworks.com/divisions/industaffairs/workers.comp.htm
E-mail: dlabor@state.de.us

Florida

Florida has created its own guide, which uses an amalgam of sources, but primarily the Fourth Edition of the *Guides* (Florida Statutes Title XXXI §440.15(3)). Florida adopted this guide in 1996. Florida's guide may be accessed at:

www2.myflorida.com/les/wc/dwc/impairmentratingschedule/introduction.html

Section 14 of the Florida Uniform Permanent Impairment Rating Schedule (FUPIRS) contains illustrative examples of the difference between the Fourth Edition of the *Guides* and FUPIRS. If a category applicable to the impairing condition cannot be found in FUPIRS, then the category most closely resembling the impairment or the degree of impairment based on analogy should be chosen.

Florida Workers' Compensation
Director's Office
310 Hartman Bldg, 2012 Capital Cir SE, Tallahassee, FL 32399
Web site: www2.myflorida.com/les/wc/
E-mail: wilhelj@wcpost.fdles.state.fl.us

Georgia

In 2001, Georgia Code §34-9-263(d) was amended by House bill 497 to require that effective July 1, 2001, permanent partial impairment ratings shall be based on the American Medical Association's *Guides to the Evaluation of Permanent Impairment, Fifth Edition*. Hearing and hernia impairments have special statutory ratings. Georgia follows a traditional amputation schedule that also includes hearing and vision. The whole person is 400 weeks. Georgia allows employers to limit employee medical care to a posted list of approved physicians or to contract with a managed care organization approved by the Board of Workers' Compensation. One change within a posted panel or MCO is permitted without prior employer approval.

Georgia's workers' compensation medical report form may be obtained online at: www.ganet.org/sbwc/about/forms/wc-020a.pdf. It contains a reference to "percentage based on the AMA *Guides*."

Judge Julie John, Executive Director
270 Peachtree St NW, Atlanta, GA 30303-1299
404 656-2048

Claims Assistance: Pamela Culver and Angela Mitchell
404 656-3818; 800-533-0682 outside the Atlanta area
Web site: www.ganet.org/sbwc/
E-mail: RamseyR@sbwc.state.ga.us

Appendix B

Hawaii

Regulations DLIR §12-10-21(a) refer to the AMA *Guides*. The Fifth Edition has been adopted for contested case hearings. Disfigurement is subject to a $30,000 cap. Hawaii Revised Statutes §386-32 contains a schedule and rules for rating nonscheduled disability. The whole person for nonscheduled disability is 312 weeks.

Disability Compensation Division
830 Punchbowl St, Rm 209, Honolulu, HI 96813
Complaints/noncoverage: 808 586-9200
Workers' comp information: 808 586-9174
Medical fee schedule: 808 586-9181
Rehabilitation: 808 586-9171
Temporary disability: 808 586-9188
Prepaid health: 808 586-9188
Fax for all above numbers: 808 586-9219
Web site: http://www.state.hi.us/dlir/rs/loihi/
E-mail: jwright@dlir.state.hi.us

(The Workers' Compensation Division does not appear to have its own Web page, although much workers' compensation information is available from these Department of Labor and Industrial Relations' Web pages.)

Idaho

Idaho incorporates the *Guides* through the testimony or written evidence of a physician, although neither regulation nor statute requires it. Since publication, the Fifth Edition has found wide acceptance. Idaho schedules teeth by regulation at 0.1% of the whole person, excluding wisdom teeth. Since Idaho uses a 500-week whole person, a tooth equals one-half week. Idaho law may require compensation for any anatomic loss, notwithstanding its impact on activities of daily living (ADL).

Industrial Commission Main Office
James Kile, Chairman
317 Main St, PO Box 83720, Boise, ID 83720-0041
208 334-6000
Toll-free (outside Boise): 800 950-2110
Fax: 208 334-2321
Web site: www2.state.id.us/iic/
E-mail: kday@iic.state.id.us

Illinois

Illinois adopts a schedule (820 Illinois Compiled Statutes §350/8) that covers amputation; loss of sight and hearing; loss of testes; skull, facial bone, and vertebral fracture; and loss or loss of use of a kidney, spleen, or lung. Nothing in Illinois law or regulation mentions the *Guides*. Ratings are the result of medical opinion, not legal mandate based on a guide. Nonscheduled disabilities are rated as a percentage of a 500-week whole person. Disfigurement of the hand, head, face, neck, arm, leg below the knee, or chest above the axillary line may be compensated up to 150 weeks. State law also establishes rules for rating hearing loss. According to the Commission's handbook, pain, among other factors, may be considered in evaluating and rating disability.

Illinois Industrial Commission
John W. Hallock, Jr, Chairman

(Each Commission office can explain Commission procedures and provide forms, handbooks, etc.)

100 W Randolph St, #8-200, Chicago, IL 60601
312 814-6611

202 NE Madison Ave, #201, Peoria, IL 61602
309 671-3019

200 S Wyman, Rockford, IL 61101
815 987-7292

Main office for most filings:
701 S Second St, Springfield, IL 62704
217 785-7087
Telecommunication Device for the Deaf (TDD): 312 814-2959
Web site: www.state.il.us/agency/iic
E-mail: operations@mail.state.il.us

Indiana

Indiana uses a statutory disability schedule that includes ratings for amputations, vision loss (calculated both with and without glasses), and hearing loss. The *Guides'* use is not mandatory in Indiana, but the latest edition is normally used to evaluate nonscheduled impairment. Indiana does not use weeks or months, instead using degrees of impairment and multiplying those degrees by a sliding dollar value. For injuries occurring on and after July 1, 2001, each degree between 1 and 10 is worth $1,300. Between 11 and 35 degrees, each degree is worth $1,500. From 36 degrees to 50 degrees, each degree is worth $2,400, and each degree over 50 is worth $3,000. The award payable is expressed in dollars multiplied by degrees of impairment, not weeks. Certain amputations are valued at double the award for loss of use. For injuries that occurred between July 1, 2000, and before July 1, 2001, the maximum is $254,000. On and after July 1, 2001, the amount rises to $274,000, and on and after July 1, 2002, the amount goes to $294,000. Indiana Code 22-3-3-10. A handbook contains useful illustrations for calculating disability using the degrees-of-impairment approach. It can be downloaded from: www.state.in.us/wkcomp/handbook/HANDBK2001.html.

Workers' Compensation Board of Indiana
G. Terrence Coriden, Chairman
402 W Washington St, Rm W-196, Indianapolis, IN 46204

Office of the Executive Secretary
Sandy Fralich
317 232-3811
E-mail: sfralich@wcb.state.in.us

Administrative Division
Karrissa Longere
317 232-3809
E-mail: klongere2@wcb.state.in.us
Toll-free: 800 824-COMP
Web site: www.IN.gov/wkcomp/

Iowa

Iowa's statutory schedule rates a foot amputation at 150 weeks, or 30% WPI, and amputation between the hip and knee at the same rate as the loss of a leg, or 220 weeks, equal to 44% WPI, slightly higher than in the Fifth Edition. The whole person is 500 weeks in Iowa. Disfigurement awards appear to be limited to the head and face and are capped at 150 weeks. Iowa Code §85.34. Iowa's regulations refer to the *Guides* and indicate that an employer's payment in accordance with the *Guides* is prima facie evidence of compliance with the law. The regulations do not preclude use of other guides or evidence of impairment or disability and do not refer to a specific edition. Regulations §876-2.4(85).

Iowa Division of Workers' Compensation
Iris J. Post, Workers' Compensation Commissioner
1000 E Grand Ave, Des Moines, IA 50319
515 281-5387 or 800 JOB-IOWA
TTD: 515 281-4748 or 800 831-1399
Fax: 515 281-6501
Web site: www.state.ia.us/iwd/wc/index.html
E-mail: iwd.dwc@iwd.state.ia.us

Kansas

A statutory schedule lists impairments for amputation and loss of use of extremities, and loss of sight and hearing. Special rules limit awards for traumatic hernia. Kansas Statute No. 44-510d. The Fourth Edition of the *Guides* controls rating in all other cases. Kansas Statute No. 44-510e. Competent medical testimony may be allowed in cases not covered by the Fourth Edition or the statutory schedule.

General Information
Kansas Workers' Compensation
Department of Human Resources
800 SW Jackson, Ste 600, Topeka, KS 66612-1227
785 296-3441 or 800 332-0353

Medical Services and Fee Schedule Issues
Kansas Workers' Compensation
Department of Human Resources
800 SW Jackson, Ste 600, Topeka, KS 66612-1227
785 296-0846 or 800 332-0353

Philip Harness, Director
Web site: www.hr.state.ks.us/wc/html/wc.htm
E-mail Dick Thomas at rthomas2@hr.state.ks.us

Kentucky

Among a handful of states, Kentucky relies solely on the most recent edition of the AMA *Guides* to determine disability. To determine the disability award, the AMA percentage rating is multiplied by the following factors:

0% to 5%	0.65
6% to 10%	0.85
11% to 15%	1.00
16% to 20%	1.00
21% to 25%	1.15
26% to 30%	1.35
31% to 35%	1.50
36% and above	1.70

The product is multiplied by a weekly dollar value. KRS 342.730.(1)(b). Not rounding to the nearest 5% may be important in Kentucky. As in many other coal-producing states, Kentucky uses special statutory rules for compensating pneumoconiosis resulting from exposure to coal dust. KRS 342.732. Occupational hearing loss is subject to special statutes and regulations. KRS 342.7305. The Fifth Edition of the *Guides* was officially adopted effective March 1, 2001.

Ched Jennings, Commissioner
502 564-5550, X439
Fax: 502 564-5934

Cathy Costelle, Director, Division of Workers' Compensation Specialists and Ombudsmen
502 564-5550, X449
Fax: 502 564-9533

Department of Workers' Claims
Research and Information
Perimeter Park West, Bldg C
1270 Louisville Rd, Frankfort, KY 40601
Fax: 502 564-5741
Web site: dwc.state.ky.us/
E-mail: dawn.sullivan@mail.state.ky.us

Louisiana

State law provides both a schedule and a reference to the mandatory use of the most recent edition of the *Guides* for nonscheduled impairments (and apparently partial losses of scheduled impairments). LRS 23:1121. Hernias have special rating rules. Louisiana uses a formula based on a minimum 25% loss of a scheduled body part, together with an extended benefit for lost earnings where postinjury wages are less than 90% of preinjury wages. Benefits for nonscheduled losses are measured on lost wages and may extend to 520 weeks. Purely anatomic loss appears to be compensable, so long as it is ratable under the *Guides*. Special benefits are awarded for double amputation, binocular blindness, paraplegia, quadriplegia, and severe burns.

Office of Workers' Compensation Administration
PO Box 94040, Baton Rouge, LA 70804-9040
225 342-7555
Fax: 225 342-5665
Web site: www.ldol.state.la.us/sec2owca.asp
E-mail: OWCA@ldol.state.la.us

Maine

By statute, Maine schedules disability for amputations and loss of an eye. Total loss of sight in both eyes and double amputations, and "industrial loss of use" of hands and feet are total permanent disabilities. 39A MRS §212. Pursuant to rule 7.6, the Maine Workers' Compensation Board requires impairment to be determined by use of the Fourth Edition of the *Guides*. 90-351 CMR CH.7.§6.2. Maine has adopted treatment guides for acute low back pain, carpal tunnel syndrome, and pain management. 90-351 CMR CH.7.§2. Awards for disability are usually limited to 5 years (260 weeks) but may be extended under compelling circumstances. These extended benefits may be given after an unsuccessful attempt to return to work and are known as "section 213 benefits." 39A MRS §213.

Maine Workers' Compensation Board
27 State House Station, Augusta, ME 04333-0027
207 287-3751
TTY: 207 287-6119
Fax: 207 287-7198
Web site: www.state.me.us/wcb/
E-mail: paul.dionne.@state.me.us

Maryland

By statutory schedule, an arm in Maryland is a 60% whole person equivalent (300 weeks compared to a 500-week whole person), as is loss of a leg. Maryland Statutes §9-627. Double amputations of feet, hands, legs, and arms and loss of their use constitute total, permanent disability. §9-636. The *Guides* is not specifically mentioned in statutes that deal with partial, permanent disability, but it appears to be admitted as evidence in conjunction with medical testimony and reports.

Maryland Workers' Compensation Commission
Thomas Patrick O'Reilly, Chair
Joan Y. Case, Executive Director, Administration
10 East Baltimore St, 4th Fl, Baltimore, MD 21202-1641
410 864-5100
Toll-free, Maryland: 800 492-0479
Fax: 410 864-5101
Web site: www.charm.net/~wcc/
E-mail: wcc@charm.net

Massachusetts

Massachusetts incorporates the *Guides* by statute, requiring its use where statutory schedules for amputation do not provide a disability rating. Major (dominant) and minor hand and arm differences are recognized by law. An award for disfigurement is limited to $15,000. MGL Chapter 152: Section 36. The whole person is a 520-week value. MGL Chapter 152: Section 35.

Boston
Department of Industrial Accidents
600 Washington St, 7th Fl, Boston, MA 02111
617 727-4900 or 800 323-3249
Fax (7th floor): 617 727-6477
Fax (6th floor): 617 727-7122
Fax (Finance and Accounting): 617 727-8764
Fax (Impartial Medical Unit): 617 727-6974

Worcester
Department of Industrial Accidents
8 Austin St, Worcester, MA 01609
508 753-2072
Fax (Conciliation and Judges' Offices): 508 753-4780
Fax (OEVR): 508 798-7822

Springfield
Department of Industrial Accidents
436 Dwight St, Rm 105, Springfield, MA 01103
413 784-1133
Fax: 413 784-1138

Fall River
Department of Industrial Accidents
30 Third St, Fall River, MA 02720
508 676-3406
Fax: 508 677-0655
Web site: www.state.ma.us/dia/
E-mail: InfoDesk@dia.state.ma.us.
Code of Massachusetts Regulations (Workers' Compensation):
www.state.ma.us/dia/cmr/cmr.htm

Michigan

Both scheduled amputation and total permanent disabilities, including double extremity amputations (hand, foot) and eyes loss or a combination of them, or "insanity or imbecility," are listed in Michigan's law. Michigan is a pure "wage loss" state for nonscheduled partial permanent disability determinations and, thus, does not rely on a schedule to determine impairment as a predicate for disability. Wage loss is paid at 80% of the difference between pre- and postinjury wages. Special "heart-lung" presumptions apply for police and firefighters.

Workers' Compensation Appellate Commission
Jürgen Skoppek, Chairperson
Michigan State Government
Department of Consumer and Industry Services
1375 South Washington, PO Box 30468, Lansing, MI 48909-7968
517 334-9719
Fax: 517 334-9750

Bureau of Workers' Disability Compensation
Craig R. Petersen, Director
Michigan State Government
Department of Consumer and Industry Services
PO Box 30016, Lansing, MI 48909
517 322-1296
Fax: 517 322-1808
TDD in Lansing: 517 322-5987
Web site: www.cis.state.mi.us/wkrcomp/

Minnesota

In preparing its own schedule of permanent partial disability, Minnesota refers to the Third Edition of the *Guides* for some definitional purposes. Some charts and tables from the Third Edition are also adopted in Minnesota's guide. Definitions incorporated by reference also include *inter alia,* those found in *Dorland's Illustrated Medical Dictionary*; *Textbook on Anatomy* (Hollinshead WH. New York, NY: Harper & Row; 1985); and "The Estimation of Areas of Burns," in *Surgery, Gynecology and Obstetrics* (Lund, Browder. Vol 79. Chicago, IL: Surgical Publishing Company of Chicago; 1944:352-358). However, most spine conditions are rated by diagnosis and objective findings, not range of motion. Pain "not substantiated by persistent objective clinical findings" often results in a rating of zero. Minnesota Regulations 5223.0380 (thoracic spine) and 5223.0390 (lumbar spine). Categories of conditions not found in Minnesota's guide's categories may not be used to determine disability, but if "a category applicable to the impairing condition cannot be found in [the regulatory schedule], then the category most closely resembling the impairment or the percentage of permanent partial disability based on analogy shall be chosen." Minnesota Regulations 5223.0300.3.A and H. Minnesota also rates double amputations at the hip and shoulder, blindness in both eyes, complete paralysis, and total and permanent loss of mental faculties as total, permanent disabilities. The combining rules use the same formula as the *Guides* $(A + B[1 - A])$.

Minnesota Department of Labor and Industry
443 Lafayette Road N, St Paul, MN 55155
Metro area: 651 297-4377
Duluth area: 218 723-4670
Greater Minnesota: 800 DIAL-DLI (800 342-5354)
TDD: 651 297-4198
Web site: www.doli.state.mn.us/workcomp.html
Web site for Minnesota Schedules of Disability:
www.revisor.leg.state.mn.us/arule/5223/
E-mail: DLI.Communications@state.mn.us

Minnesota Workers' Compensation Court of Appeals
405 Judicial Ctr, 25 Constitution Ave, St Paul, MN 55155
Information: 651 296-6526
Fax: 651 297-2520
TTY/TDD: Contact through the Minnesota Relay Service at 800 627-3529
Web site: www.workerscomp.state.mn.us/

Mississippi

State law adopts a traditional amputation schedule for partial disability and states that "Loss of both hands, or both arms, or both feet, or both legs, or both eyes, or of any two (2) thereof shall constitute permanent total disability." Nonscheduled disability is based on a 450-week whole person, and the percentage of the whole person is based on impairment plus age, education, and other nonmedical factors. Disability (impairment) for more than one body part may be payable separately, not combined. Disfigurement is limited to $2,000. Mississippi Statutes §73-3-17. Special law applies to hernias. Mississippi Statutes §73-3-23. By regulation, Mississippi requires use of the Fourth Edition of the *Guides*. Mississippi Workers' Compensation Fee Schedule (2d Edition 1997), Medical Cost Containment Rules part VII.

The Mississippi Workers' Compensation Commission
1428 Lakeland Dr, PO Box 5300, Jackson, MS 39296-5300
601 987-4200

Ben Barrett Smith, Chairman
Barney Schoby, Commissioner
Lydia Quarles, Commissioner
Jo Ann McDonald, Commission Secretary: 601 987-4252
Scott Clark, Senior Attorney: 601 987-4266.
Web site: www.mwcc.state.ms.us/
E-mail: sclark@mwcc.state.ms.us.

Missouri

Missouri applies its own statutes to the evaluation of hernia and hearing loss. Missouri Revised Statutes §§287.195, 287.197. Total permanent disabilities are decided on their facts (§287.200), and a schedule exists for loss of an eye, total deafness, and most extremity losses. If the loss is by amputation, 10% is added to the scheduled loss. Nonscheduled losses are based on a 400-week whole person. Missouri Revised Statutes §287.190. No guide for nonscheduled losses is officially adopted, but impairment ratings from the *Guides* may be used, in conjunction with other nonmedical factors, in determining disability.

Missouri Division of Workers' Compensation
Director's Office
Lawrence D. Leip, Director
3315 W Truman Blvd, Rm 131, PO Box 58, Jefferson City, MO 65102-0058
573 751-4231
Fax: 573 751-2012
Web site: www.dolir.state.mo.us/wc/index.htm
E-mail: Workerscomp@central.dolir.state.mo.us

Montana

Although Montana's law requires use of the "current edition of the *Guides to Evaluation of Permanent Impairment* published by the American [M]edical [A]ssociation" for rating impairment, the law also states that impairment must be established by objective medical findings, casting the Fifth Edition's pain-related methodology for subjective complaints of pain into some doubt. Montana Code Annotated §39-71-711. Disfigurement at or above the neck is limited to a $2,500 award. MCA §39-71-708. Disability awards are a combination of impairment and loss in ability to earn wages, in turn based on age, education, and lost access to manual labor opportunities. The whole person for disability awards, and impairment in the absence of a lost wage earning capacity, is a 350-week disability.

Montana Department of Labor and Industry
Mike Foster, Commissioner
406 444-9091

Workers' Compensation Regulations Bureau
Keith Messmer
1805 Prospect Ave, PO Box 8011, Helena, MT 59624-8011
406 444-6541
Fax: 406 444-3465

Workers' Compensation Claims Assistance Bureau
John Weida
1805 Prospect Ave, PO Box 8011, Helena, MT 59604-8011
406 444-4661

Workers' Compensation Court
Judge Mike McCarter
1625 11th Ave, PO Box 537, Helena, MT 59624-0537
406 444-7794

Medical Provider Billing Information System
E-mail whenever possible at: medpro@state.mt.us.
Fax: 406 444-4140

Letters to:
Medical Provider Billing Information System
Claim Assistance Bureau, ERD
PO Box 8011
Helena, MT 59604-8011
Web site: wcc.dli.state.mt.us

Appendix B

Nebraska

Nebraska has implemented a schedule for amputations and losses of extremities and the nose, an eye, and an ear. Loss of hearing is a different disability than loss of an ear. Nebraska Statutes §48-121. Law allows the establishment of a special panel of physicians to conduct independent medical evaluations. §48-134.01. Although the *Guides* is not specifically mentioned, it appears to be commonly used in rating impairment as a predicate for disability evaluation.

Nebraska Workers' Compensation Court
PO Box 98908, Lincoln, NE 68509-8908
Street address: 129 North 10th St, Ste 300, Lincoln, NE, 68508
Toll-free in Nebraska: 800 599-5155
Lincoln and out of state: 402 471-6468
Fax: 402 471-8231
Web site: www.nol.org/workcomp/
E-mail: newcc@wcc.state.ne.us

Glenn W. Morton, Administrator
402 471-3602
Fax: 402 471-2700
E-mail: gmorton@wcc.state.ne.us

Nebraska Workers' Compensation Court
Su Perk Davis, Public Information Manager
PO Box 98908, Lincoln, NE 68509-8908
402 471-6455
Fax: 402 471-2700
E-mail: sdavis@wcc.state.ne.us

Nevada

Physicians are required to file first reports of injury, instead of employers or employees. Nevada Revised Statutes 617.352. Nevada adopts the Fourth Edition by administrative regulation. Nevada Administrative Code 616C.002. State law admonishes the agency to consider the latest edition. Only the factor of impairment may be considered in evaluating disability, and *disability* and *impairment* are considered equivalent terms. NRS 616C.490. Nevada law addresses cancer as a special risk to firefighters. NRS 617.453. Nevada also has a heart-lung law covering police and firefighters. NRS 617.455. Certain amputations and loss of sight in both eyes are considered a nonexclusive list of total, permanent disabilities. NRS 616C.435.

Industrial Insurance Regulation Section
400 W King St, Ste 400, Carson City, NV 89703
775 687-3033
Fax: 775 687-6305
1301 N Green Valley Pkwy, Ste 200, Henderson, NV 89014
702 486-9080
Fax: 702 990-0364

Medical Unit
Bob Loritz
702 486-9101

Web site: dirweb.state.nv.us/iirs.htm
E-mail: cverre@govmail.state.nv.us

New Hampshire
State law requires adoption of the most recent edition of the *Guides*. New
Hampshire also has a list of disabilities for extremities, eyes, and hearing.
New Hampshire Revised Statutes Annotated §281-A: 32. Regulations
require an affirmation from the evaluating physician that the assessment of
permanent bodily loss is determined from the most recent edition of the
Guides. Labor Rules 508.01(d)

New Hampshire Department of Labor
Workers' Compensation Division
Kathryn J. Barger, Director
95 Pleasant St, Concord, NH 03301
603 271-3176 or 800 272-4353
Coverage: 603 271-2042
Claims: 603 271-3174
Vocational Rehabilitation: 603 271-3328
Self-insurance: 603 271-6172
Web site: www.state.nh.us/dol/dol-wc/index.html
E-mail from site link

New Jersey

Losses for extremities, eyes lost through enucleation, and hearing are determined in a schedule. Nonscheduled losses are determined by a workers' compensation judge, based on competent medical evidence. If a loss is by amputation, a 30% increase in the award may be made. Four weeks of disability are awarded for each lost tooth. New Jersey Statutes Annotated 34:15-12. In New Jersey, a medical expert is one who performs a minimum of 25 workers' compensation examinations per year. No impairment guide is used in this process. Occupational hearing loss is handled under special provisions of New Jersey law. NJSA 34:15-35.10 through 34:15-35.22.

Cardiovascular or cerebrovascular injury to certain categories of firefighters, police, and volunteer rescue squads are presumed compensable if they occur during response to an emergency. NJSA 34:15-7.3.

NJ Department of Labor
Division of Workers' Compensation
Paul Kapalko, Chief Judge/Director
John Fitch Plaza, PO Box 381, Trenton, NJ 08625-0381
609 292-2515
Fax: 609 984-2515
Web site: www.state.nj.us/labor/wc/Default.htm
E-mail: dwc@dol.state.nj.us

New Mexico

New Mexico's workers' compensation law defines impairment as an anatomical or functional abnormality based on the most recent edition of the *Guides*. §52-1-24 New Mexico Statutes Annotated 1978. Impairment is the base value for disability and is modified by age, education, and physical capacity to determine disability. §§56-1-26 through 56-1-26-4 NMSA 1978. New Mexico provides a schedule for extremity, eye, and hearing losses, which may be extended if the consequence on wage earning is greater than the time allowed in the schedule. The schedule recognizes different values for dominant (dexterous) and nondominant (nondexterous) hand and arm losses. §52-1-43 NMSA 1978. Facial disfigurement is limited to an award of $2,500. §52-1-44 NMSA 1978. Special rules dictate compensability of hernias. §52-1-45 NMSA 1978.

State of New Mexico
Workers' Compensation Administration
2410 Centre Ave SE, PO Box 27198, Albuquerque, NM 87125-7198
505 841-6000
In state toll-free: 800 255-7965
Web site: www.state.nm.us/wca/
E-mail Office of the Director: Sarada.Gutierrez@state.nm.us
General information: Merilee.Danemann@state.nm.us

New York

By custom, New York uses its own guide, although it is not recognized by
either statute or regulation. New York's labor and workers' compensation
law section 49hh refers to the *Guides'* adoption of certain ophthalmology
standards but otherwise omits reference to any other guides of general application. New York uses a typical schedule for extremity, eye, and hearing loss
and adds disability for amputations over other losses of the same extremity.

New York Workers' Compensation Board District Offices
Albany
100 Broadway, Menands, Albany NY 12241
518 474-6674
For all accidents in following counties: Albany, Clinton, Columbia,
Dutchess, Essex, Franklin, Fulton, Greene, Hamilton, Montgomery, Orange,
Rensselaer, Saratoga, Schenectady, Schoharie, Ulster, Warren, Washington

Binghamton
State Office Building, 44 Hawley St, Binghamton, NY 13901
607 721-8356
For all accidents in following counties: Broome, Chemung, Chenango,
Cortland, Delaware, Otsego, Schuyler, Sullivan, Tioga, Tompkins

Buffalo
Statler Towers, 107 Delaware Ave, Buffalo, NY 14202
716 842-2166
For all accidents in following counties: Cattaraugus, Chautauqua, Erie,
Niagara

Rochester
130 Main St West, Rochester, NY 14614
716 238-8300
For all accidents in following counties: Allegany, Genesee, Livingston,
Monroe, Ontario, Orleans, Seneca, Steuben, Wayne, Wyoming, Yates

Appendix B

Syracuse
935 James St, Syracuse, NY 13203
315 423-2932
For all accidents in following counties: Cayuga, Herkimer, Jefferson, Lewis, Madison, Oneida, Onondaga, Oswego, St Lawrence

Downstate Centralized Mailing (for New York City, Hempstead, Hauppauge,and Peekskill district offices)

PO Box 29017, Brooklyn, NY 11202-9017
NYC: 800 877-1373
Hempstead: 516 560-7700
Hauppage: 631 952-6000
Peekskill: 914 788-5775
For all accidents in following counties: Bronx, Kings, Nassau, New York, Putnam, Queens, Richmond, Rockland, Suffolk, Westchester

David M. Donohue, Director of Operations
Web site: www.wcb.state.ny.us/index.htm

North Carolina

North Carolina requires the use of its own extensive guide. Its Web address is provided below. North Carolina also has a statutory schedule that covers the usual extremity losses. It also provides dollar amounts for loss to unscheduled internal organs, a limit of $2,000 on facial disfigurement, and a limit of $10,000 for other bodily disfigurement not covered in other scheduled losses. The loss of both hands, both arms, both feet, both legs, both eyes, or any two thereof constitutes total and permanent disability. North Carolina General Statutes §97-31.

North Carolina Industrial Commission
4319 Mail Service Ctr, Raleigh, NC 27699-4319
919 733-4820
Fax: 919 715-0282
Web site: www.comp.state.nc.us/

Buck Lattimore, Chairman
919 807-2525
E-mail: lattimob@ind.commerce.state.nc.us

Stephen Gheen, Agency Legal Counsel
919 807-2540
E-mail: gheen@ind.commerce.state.nc.us

North Carolina's rating guide may be found at the following Web site:
www.comp.state.nc.us/ncic/pages/ratinggd.htm

North Dakota

North Dakota adopted the Fifth Edition of the *Guides* effective July 31,
2001, in House Bill 1161, 2001 session. The bill amends North Dakota
century code §65-05-12.2.6, which previously adopted the Fourth Edition.
The *Guides* is used to address areas not covered in other subsections of that
statute (as amended in 2001). North Dakota's statutory schedule lists a narrow range of extremity losses to finger, toe, leg, and eye. The maximum
award is a 1,500-week income benefit. HB 1161, 2001 leg. session.

North Dakota Workers' Compensation
500 E Front Ave, Bismarck, ND 58504-5685
701 328-3800 or 800 777-5033
Hearing Impaired: 701 328-3786

Paul R. Kramer, Executive Director/CEO
Art Thompson, Public Relations

Provider assistance line: 800 701-5177
Web site: www.ndworkerscomp.com/
E-mail: ndworkerscomp@web.state.nd.us

Ohio

Ohio provides benefits for certain workers who suffer from occupationally caused respiratory ailments in the form of transitional income to remove them from the workplace that caused the ailment. The same law also lists a traditional extremity loss disability schedule, including losses for an eye and for hearing. Ohio Revised Code §4123.57. Wage loss is added to nonscheduled impairments to determine disability. Ohio uses the Fourth Edition of the *Guides* by custom. Total permanent disability occurs on the "loss or loss of use of both hands or both arms, or both feet or both legs, or both eyes, or of any two thereof," and benefits are payable for life. ORC §4123.58. Ohio Administrative Rule 4123-5-18 requires objective medical evidence as the basis for a physician's evaluation of impairment.

Ohio Bureau of Workers' Compensation
30 W Spring St, Columbus, OH 43215-2256
800 OHIOBWC (800 644-6292)
Fax: 1 877 520-OHIO (6446)
Web site: www.ohiobwc.com

Oklahoma

Oklahoma defines permanent impairment with reference to the latest edition of the *Guides.* However, the definition mandates that "the examining physician shall not follow the guides based on race or ethnic origin." 85 Oklahoma Statutes §3.14. Oklahoma also modifies the fourth and fifth editions by prohibiting use of the DRE method for rating spine impairments. The Fifth Edition, modified as to DRE and race and excluding those disabilities listed in Oklahoma's statutory schedule, became effective for evaluations performed after the effective date in Oklahoma on June 28, 2001. Workers' Compensation Court Rule 21 amendments, adopted by the Oklahoma Supreme Court May 30, 2001. As with numerous other states, total permanent disability is presumed from "loss of both hands, or both feet, or both legs, or both eyes, or any two thereof." 85 Oklahoma Statutes §3.15. Workers Compensation Court Rules 32 and 33 also mention that there are special methods for evaluation of eye and hearing impairment.

Oklahoma Workers' Compensation Court
Marcia Davis, Administrator
Denver N. Davison Court Bldg, 1915 N Stiles Ave, Oklahoma City, OK 73105
405 522-8600

Rules of the Oklahoma Workers' Compensation Court are accessible through the Oklahoma State Court Network Web site: www.oscn.net/ or directly at the Oklahoma Courts' rules Web site: www.oscn.net/applications/oscn/index.asp?ftdb=STOKRUWC&level=1.

Oregon

Oregon uses its own guide, based largely on the Third Edition of the AMA *Guides*. This guide may be found at arcweb.sos.state.or.us/rules/OARS_400/ OAR_436/436_035.html, although the tables, charts, and figures apparently are not available online. Oregon also employs a statutory schedule. Oregon Revised Statutes §656.214. Nonscheduled impairment must be supported by objective medical findings. OAR 4336-035-0320(1). Oregon's Workers' Compensation Division addresses by regulatory ruling any condition not listed in its regulatory guide; these rulings are most often made by analogy to listed conditions.

Workers' Compensation Division (WCD)
350 Winter St NE, Rm 27, Salem, OR 97301-3879
Division Reception: 503 947-7810
TTY* only: 503 947-7993
Workers' Compensation Infoline (toll-free in Oregon): 800 452-0288
Administrator's Office: 503 947-7500
Communications Unit: 503 947-7723
Benefits Consultation Unit: 503 947-7840 or toll-free 800 452-0288
(V/TTY)
Web site: www.cbs.state.or.us/external/wcd/index.html

E-mail: workcomp.questions@state.or.us for attending physician questions, general medical and vocational/retraining questions, insurer medical exams

Policy Consultation Unit: 503 947-7504 for administrative rules, bulletins, and forms, policy research and legal issue coordination

Pennsylvania

Pursuant to law that requires independent rating evaluations (IREs) to be conducted under the AMA's most recent *Guides*, the Fifth Edition shall become effective for all ratings performed on and after August 1, 2001. Purdon's Statutes Title 77 §306, Vol 6 No 2 News and Notes, winter 2001. Pennsylvania also schedules extremity, vision, and hearing losses but only full losses under the schedule. Partial losses to the scheduled members are rated under the *Guides.*

Bureau of Workers' Compensation
Richard H. Thompson, Bureau Director
1171 S Cameron St, Rm 324, Harrisburg, PA 17104-2501
Local calls and calls from outside the state: 717 772-4447
Toll-free inside Pennsylvania: 800 482-2383

Training information regarding the Fifth Edition of the *Guides* is available from the Pennsylvania Bureau by contacting Eileen Wunsch at 717 772-1912.
Web site: www.li.state.pa.us/bwc/
E-mail: cmills@pawcnote.state.pa.us

Rhode Island

By law, functional impairment is based on the most recent edition of the American Medical Association's *Guides to the Evaluation of Permanent Impairment* or comparable publications of the American Medical Association. RIGL §28-29-2. Functional impairment is the base on which disability may be measured for nonscheduled injuries. Scheduled injury benefits are payable in addition to other benefits. RIGL §28-33-19. Total and irrecoverable loss of sight in both eyes or the reduction to one-tenth (1/10) or less of normal vision with glasses; loss of both feet at or above the ankle; loss of both hands at or above the wrist; loss of one hand and one foot; injury to the spine resulting in permanent and complete paralysis of the legs or arms; and injury to the skull resulting in incurable imbecility or insanity are conclusively presumed total permanent disability. Rhode Island also applies special tests established in law for evaluating loss of hearing.

Rhode Island Department of Labor & Training's Workers'
Compensation Unit
E. Jean Severance, Associate Director
Matthew P. Carey, Assistant Director
PO Box 20190, Cranston, RI 02920-0942
401 462-8100
Education Unit: 401 462-8125.
Fax: 401 462-8105
Web site: www.det.state.ri.us/wc/wcsite/
E-mail: APilozzi@DLT.state.ri.us

Rhode Island Workers' Compensation Court
Chief Judge Robert F. Arrigan
John Goodman, Director of Public Affairs
J. Joseph Garrahy Judicial Complex
1 Dorrance Plaza, Providence, RI 02903
401 458-5000
Fax: 401 222-3269

South Carolina

South Carolina Workers' Compensation Commission Regulations do not refer to a specific edition of the *Guides*. However both statutory and regulatory schedules cover most body parts and body systems; the value of any system or part not provided for in these schedules "may be determined in accordance with the American Medical Association's 'Guides to the Evaluation of Permanent Impairment'." South Carolina's list rates a tooth as 2 out of 500 weeks. Total loss of the tongue is 500 out of 500 weeks. South Carolina Regulations section 67-1101. Hearing loss is evaluated according to the Second Edition of the *Guides*. Regulations section 67-1102. Vision loss may be determined from the Snellen Notation as modified in the regulation, or the physician may rely on the *Guides*. Regulations section 67-1105. Paraplegia, quadriplegia, and brain damage allow extension of permanent total disability benefits beyond 500 weeks. SC Code §42-9-10.

South Carolina Workers' Compensation Commission
Holly Saleeby Atkins, Chairman
1612 Marion St, PO Box 1715, Columbia, SC 29202-1715
803 737-5663
Fax: 803 737-5768

Legal Division
Janet Godfrey Griggs, General Counsel
Marion Buraczynski, Paralegal
803 737-5749
E-mail: legal@wcc.state.sc.us

Regulations may be found at: www.wcc.state.sc.us/67.htm

Insurance and Medical Services Division
Glenn Simpson, Director
803 737-5743
Web site: www.wcc.state.sc.us/
E-mail: Medical@wcc.state.sc.us

Appendix B

South Dakota

By statute, South Dakota requires that impairment shall be determined using the Fourth Edition of the *Guides to the Evaluation of Permanent Impairment*. SD Code §62-1-1.2. Evidence concerning injury is given greater weight if it is supported by objective findings. A traditional schedule lists extremity losses, along with vision and hearing loss.

Labor and Management
James Marsh, Division Director
Kneip Bldg, 700 Governors Dr, Pierre, SD 57501-2291
605 773-3681
Fax: 605 773-4211
Web site: www.state.sd.us/dol/dlm/dlm-home.htm
E-Mail: labor@dol-pr.state.sd.us

Tennessee

Although either the AMA *Guides* or the *Manual for Orthopedic Surgeons in Evaluating Permanent Physical Impairment* (American Academy of Orthopedic Surgeons) is allowed, the most recent edition must be used. TCA §50-6-204(d). Tennessee allows a greater disability award for employees who are not rehired by their preinjury employers (up to six times the WPI rating) as compared with employees who are returned to work with their preinjury employers (2½ times the WPI rating). Disability is based on impairment plus other nonmedical factors such as age, education, skill, training, labor market, and work capacity. TCA §50-6-241. Serious disfigurement to the head, face, or hands may allow up to 200 weeks of additional benefits. A traditional schedule lists extremities and loss of hearing and vision. The whole person for nonscheduled benefits is 400 weeks. TCA §50-6-207(A)-(F).

Division of Workers' Compensation
Sue Ann Head, Administrator
Tennessee Department of Labor & Workforce Development
Andrew Johnson Tower, 2nd Fl, 710 James Robertson Pkwy, Nashville, TN 37243-0661
Within Tennessee: 800 332-2667
615 741-2395
Division Representatives: 615 532-4812
Web site: www.state.tn.us/labor-wfd/wcomp.html
E-mail: dcarvermcd@mail.state.tn.us

Texas

A set of presumptions comparable to other states determines lifetime benefits for total permanent disability. Texas Labor Code §408.161. Texas does
not use a statutory schedule for extremities. Texas law mandates the use of
the Third Edition of the *Guides* but allows the Texas Workers' Compensation
Commission to adopt the Fourth Edition by agency rulemaking. Texas
Labor Code §408.124. Texas recently moved from the third to the fourth
edition, effective for evaluations ("certifying examinations") performed on
or after October 15, 2001. TWCC extended the effective date of use of the
Fourth Edition to October 2001 so that legislation could be considered to
allow implementation of the Fifth Edition. No such legislation passed the
2001 session of the Texas legislature. Rule 130.1 (June 7, 2000). The
preamble to the rule that adopted the Fourth Edition mentions the difficulty
of obtaining the Third Edition because it is no longer in print and that the
Fourth Edition had found acceptance in nearly 80% of states that use a
rating guide and represented the most up-to-date medical consensus for a
host of impairments. Those same concerns may suggest adoption of the
Fifth Edition, even though a legislative act is required. Texas examines its
workers' compensation practices through a far-reaching oversight and
research committee, whose reports are valuable beyond Texas.

Virginia A. May, Acting Executive Director
Texas Workers' Compensation Commission
Southfield Bldg, MS-3, 4000 S IH-35, Austin, TX 78704-7491
512 804-4400
Injured Worker Hotline: 800 252-7031

TWCC Central Office
Office Switchboard Main Number: 512 804-4000
Fax: 512 804-4001

General Counsel
512 804-4420
Fax: 512 804-4421

Spinal Surgery/Spinal Surgery Second Opinion
512 804-4870
Fax: 512 804-4871

Medical Review Division
4000 S IH-35, MS-45, Austin, TX 78704-7491
512 804-4800
Fax: 512 804-4801
Web site: www.twcc.state.tx.us/
E-mail: customer.relations@twcc.state.tx.us

Appendix B

Utah

Utah has adopted its own rating guide based on the Fourth Edition of the AMA *Guides* and defers to the Fourth Edition for impairments not covered by its own guide. Rule 612-7-3. The impairment guides are apparently not available online but are sold by the Utah Division of Industrial Accidents for $25. Extremity, eye enucleation, and hearing loss are determined in a statutory schedule. Utah Code §34A-2-412. Utah rates hearing loss by statute. See Utah Code §§34A-2-503 through 34A-2-506. Utah has a staff medical director who is a licensed physician.

Utah Labor Commission
Mailing Address:
Division of Industrial Accidents
PO Box 146610, Salt Lake City, UT 84114-6610

Street Address:
160 E 300 South, 3rd Fl, Salt Lake City, UT 84111
801 530-6800
Toll-free (in state only): 800 530-5090
Fax: 801 530-6804
TDD: 801 530-7685

Administration
Joyce A. Sewell, Director
801 530-6988

Alan Colledge, Medical Director
801 530-7611

Web site: www.labor.state.ut.us/indacc/indacc.htm
E-mail: icmain.sjenson@email.state.ut.us

Vermont

By memorandum dated December 12, 2000, Vermont's Workers' Compensation Director advised that effective April 1, 2001, only ratings based on the Fifth Edition of the AMA Guides would be accepted by the Vermont Department of Workers' Compensation. Vermont Statutes §648 requires use of the most recent AMA Guides. Vermont workers' compensation Rule 11.a provides additional rules for determining the value of an impairment rating and rates impairment of the spine against a 550-week disability, whereas other impairments are rated against a 430-week disability. Total permanent disability is presumed for typical conditions of double amputation or loss at or above the foot or hand, severe head injury and blindness in both eyes, and paraplegia, although it may be proved for conditions not listed, and entitles the injured worker to lifetime benefits. Vermont Statutes §644.

Laura Collins, Workers' Compensation Director
Department of Labor and Industry
National Life Bldg, Drawer 20, Montpelier, VT 05620-3401
802 828-2286
Fax: 802 828-2195
Web site: www.state.vt.us/labind/wcindex.htm
E-mail: wcomp@labind.state.vt.us

Virginia

Virginia relies on impairment rating as the principle source of income or indemnity benefit awards. A statutory schedule also refers to loss of extremities that creates partial permanent disability and total permanent disability through the presumptions based on loss and amputation conditions common in many states. §65.2-503. Although no particular guide is mentioned in statute or regulation, the AMA *Guides* is the most frequently cited source of impairment. Hearing and vision losses and pneumoconiosis are rated by regulation; see Regulations 11,12, and 13 at: www.vwc.state.va.us/_rules.htm.

Virginia Workers' Compensation Commission
Central Office
1000 DMV Dr, Richmond, VA 23220
All correspondence to the Commission, including claim forms, should be directed to this address.
804 367-8600
Toll-free in Virginia: 877 664-2566
Fax: 804 367-9740
Web site: www.vwc.state.va.us/
E-mail: webmaster@vwc.state.va.us

Appendix B

Washington

The Washington Administrative Code refers to the *Guides* specifically only in reference to respiratory impairments (WAC 296-20-370) and range of motion measurement for total joint replacement (WAC 296-20-220(q)), largely because Washington's own "rules and categories" are extremely thorough in addressing impairment. Physicians who perform evaluations are asked not to give a percentage rating; the workers' compensation division of the Department of Labor and Industry apparently performs that step. WAC 296-20-220 (e).

Mailing Address:
Gary Moore, Director
PO Box 44400, Olympia, WA 98504-4400

Physical Address:
7273 Linderson Way SW, Tumwater, WA 98501-5414
Office of Information and Assistance: 800 LISTENS (547-8367)

Claims Administration
PO Box 44200
Georgia C. Moran, Program Manager
360 902-4300
Fax: 360 902-5035

Office of the Medical Director
PO Box 44321
Dr Gary Franklin, Medical Director
360 902-5020

Web sites: www.wa.gov/lni/insurance/
www.wa.gov/lni/pa/about.htm#INSURANCE
E-mail: mcgs235@lni.wa.gov

West Virginia

West Virginia's agency regulations adopt the Fourth Edition of the *Guides* but allow the use of specialty group rating guides if the physician believes that the AMA *Guides* is inappropriate or that another guide more appropriately addresses the condition being rated. 85 Virginia Code of State Regulations §16-4. Five statutory exceptions override the use of the *Guides*. They are cases of total permanent disability, respiratory impairment due to pneumoconiosis, mental and behavioral impairments, statutory schedule disabilities, and hearing losses. 85 CSR §16-6. West Virginia employs a traditional extremity schedule. Loss or loss of use of both eyes, both hands, both feet, or a hand and a foot are conclusively presumed to be total permanent disability. WVaCode §23-4-6(f) and (m). Separate laws and regulations address mental and behavioral impairments (85 CSR 22) and pneumoconiosis and hearing loss (85 CSR 13). Pneumoconiosis is rated by a separate rating board.

West Virginia Bureau of Employment Programs
Robert J. Smith, Commissioner
Workers' Compensation Division
4100 MacCorkle Ave SE, Charleston, WV 25304-1964
304 558-2630
Fax: 304 558-2992
Web site: www.state.wv.us/bep/wc/default.HTM
E-mail: RSMITH@WVBEP.ORG

West Virginia Workers' Compensation Appeal Board
104 Dee Dr, Charleston, WV 25301

Mailing Address:
PO Box 2628, Charleston, WV 25329-2628
304 558-5230
Fax: 304 558-1322
Web site: www.state.wv.us/bep/AppBd/default.htm

Appendix B

Wisconsin

Wisconsin Statute §102.44 allows for disability compensation for nonscheduled impairments. Wisconsin schedules most extremities but does not explain where ratings for nonscheduled disabilities should come from. Department of Workforce Development (DWD) Regs at 80.25 and 80.26 cover hearing loss and vision loss, largely using earlier versions of the AMA *Guides* (reading card and Snellen chart) or information developed by the AMA in conjunction with earlier editions. DWD regulations 80.32 and 80.33 rate lost motion in extremities, loss of a single kidney, and loss of sense of smell. DWD reg. 80.34 follows common procedure in suggesting factors of age, education, training, previous work experience, present occupation and earnings, participation in rehabilitation, willingness to make reasonable change in residence to obtain suitable employment, and other pertinent evidence.

Wisconsin Workers' Compensation Division
201 E Washington Ave, Rm C100, Madison, WI 53703

Mailing Address:
PO Box 7901, Madison, WI 53707-7901
608 266-1340
Fax: 608 267-0394

Judy Norman-Nunnery, Division Administrator: 608 266-6841
Jim O'Malley, Chief ALJ: 608 266-0331

Web site: www.dwd.state.wi.us/wc/
E-mail: dwddwc@dwd.state.wi.us

State's Schedules (pages and guide [pp 113-117]) may be downloaded from www.dwd.state.wi.us/notespub/WCWebDo/38a.htm. Click on any of the references to LIRC Administrative Rules, Wisconsin Workers'Compensation Chapter 102–1998, or Workers' Compensation Administrative Rules for a complete pdf version of the statute and agency regulations (181 pages).

Wyoming

By statute, an injured employee's impairment shall be rated by a licensed physician using the most recent edition of the American Medical Association's *Guides to the Evaluation of Permanent Impairment.* Wyoming Statutes §27-14-405(g). Wyoming does not use a traditional extremity schedule, and cases of total permanent disabilities are certified by a medical professional, without reference to traditional double amputation and total blindness standards. Wyoming Statutes §§27-14-406, 27-14-102(a)(xvi).

Wyoming Workers' Safety and Compensation Division
122 West 25th St, Cheyenne, WY 82002
Kathleen McKinna, Administrator
307 777-7159
Fax: 307 777-5946
Web site: wydoe.state.wy.us/doe.asp?ID=9
E-mail: atruji@state.wy.us

Epilogue

Use of the AMA *Guides* falls into the following general categories:

A. Twelve states and the District of Columbia use the most recent edition of the *Guides* either by legislative or agency mandate:

Alaska
District of Columbia
Kentucky
Louisiana
Montana
New Hampshire
New Mexico
Oklahoma
Pennsylvania (implementation delayed until October 2001 to allow physician training)
Rhode Island
Tennessee
Vermont
Wyoming

B. Two states' legislatures have recently enacted laws requiring the Fifth Edition's use:

Georgia
North Dakota

C. Four states refer to the AMA *Guides* but do not mention a preference for a particular edition. The Fifth Edition should be used in these states, as the AMA takes the position that the latest edition is the most authoritative.

Hawaii (Fifth Edition in use by compensation judges)
Iowa
Massachusetts
South Carolina

D. One state, Washington, uses the *Guides* to rate joint replacement, upper extremity, lower extremity, and hearing impairment, either by reference to the AMA *Guides* (no edition specified) or by statutory reference to "nationally recognized guides." Most other conditions are rated under the state's "rules and categories."

E. Eleven states do not mandate but permit use of the *Guides,* usually in conjunction with testimony or reports of an evaluating physician. If reliability is a basis for "expertise," the Fifth Edition should be used in these states:

Alabama (Fourth Edition is recommended but not mandated by state regulation)
Arizona
Connecticut
Delaware
Idaho
Indiana
Maryland
Missouri
Nebraska
Ohio
Virginia

F. Ten states, by law, regulation, or both, require the use of the Fourth Edition. For reasons mentioned above and in conjunction with the discussion of Texas' adoption of the Fourth Edition, they should consider adoption of the Fifth Edition.

Arkansas (uses the Fourth Edition, with modifications)
Florida (supplemented by its own guides and percentage ratings)
Kansas (by statute)
Maine (by regulation)
Mississippi (by regulation)
Nevada (by regulation, although state law recommends the most recent edition)
South Dakota (by statute)
Texas (the Fourth Edition is the most recent edition permitted by Texas law, effective as of October 2001)
Utah (by regulation with modifications)
West Virginia (by regulation, but other guides may be used if more appropriate; may also be said to fall into category E)

G. Four states use the Third Edition, Revised, usually with modifications:

Colorado (modified and required by regulation)
Minnesota (heavily modified; might be considered as its own guide)
Oregon (modified by regulations)
Texas (until October 2001; modified to replace goniometer with
inclinometer for ROM evaluation of the spine)

H. Four states use guides largely of their own design:

California
North Carolina
New York
Wisconsin

I. Three states profess to use no guide at all, relying instead on the expertise of the examining physician and the experience and precedent established by their workers' compensation judges:

Illinois
Michigan
New Jersey

Index

Index

Index